THE VILLE

THE VILLE

COPS AND KIDS IN URBAN AMERICA

UPDATED EDITION

GREG DONALDSON

EMPIRE
STATE
EDITIONS

Fordham University Press has no responsibility for the persistence or accuracy of URLs for external or third-party Internet websites referred to in this publication and does not guarantee that any content on such websites is, or will remain, accurate or appropriate.

Fordham University Press also publishes its books in a variety of electronic formats. Some content that appears in print may not be available in electronic books.

Visit us online at www.fordhampress.com.

Library of Congress Control Number: 2014952821

Printed in the United States of America

17 16 15   5 4 3 2 1

Updated edition

For John and Constance Donaldson

CONTENTS

FOREWORD

The re-publication of Greg Donaldson's *The Ville* by Fordham University Press is a great event for anyone interested in New York City history or the politics of drug enforcement. *The Ville* is, without question, the best book ever written about inner-city New York during the years of the crack epidemic. *The Ville* presents this tragedy from so many vantage points—those of the dealers, the police and prosecutors, the teachers and school principals, the families trying to raise children amidst the carnage, and the young people who, despite living in a danger zone, try to stay clear of a drug business that promised unprecedented rewards and even graver risks.

I can think of no other book that penetrates an inner-city neighborhood in New York in this era with such insight, such eloquence, and such respect and compassion for different groups of people trying to make a life in a world of limited opportunity rent by deadly violence. To put *The Ville* in perspective, I have to turn to media other than books. The only places I can find youth narratives of equal eloquence from the crack years in New York are in the hip-hop storytelling of JZ, Nas, Biggie Smalls, and Wu Tang Clan. *The Ville* is the perfect companion volume to three of the greatest hip-hop albums of all time, set in the housing projects of Brooklyn, Queens, and Staten Island: Nas's "Illmatic," JZ's "Reasonable Doubt," and Wu Tang Clan's "36 Chambers." Donaldson captures the worldview of young people in a world shaped by crack almost as well as these amazing artists—while also providing an equally compelling portrait of their major adversary, the police.

And here, to put *The Ville* in perspective, you have to turn to what many think is the greatest TV series ever made, "The Wire." *The Ville* is "The Wire" in print form, ten years earlier, set in Brownsville, Brooklyn, rather than Baltimore, Maryland. Donaldson brings to life what it means to be a police officer in the drug war without either demonizing or romanticizing the police. You see the heroism, the cynicism, the racism, the careerism, the price officers pay in health and family life for being in such a high-risk profession. Humanizing both the police and the sellers at the peak of the drug war is extremely challenging, but Donaldson manages to do it. This makes *The Ville* a unique contribution to urban ethnography and investigative journalism the way "The Wire" was groundbreaking television drama.

To understand what Greg Donaldson was able to do in *The Ville,* as well as the risks he took in writing it, you have to know something about the neighborhood he portrayed, as well as the period in which he did the bulk of his research. Brownsville, Brooklyn, was the most dangerous single neighborhood in New York City at a time—the late 1980s to the early 1990s—when the annual homicide rate in New York City approached 2,000. The streets Donaldson walked, the housing projects he visited regularly, even the high school (Thomas Jefferson) he spent time in were free-fire zones where bullets could begin flying at any time. I worked with community groups in East New York during those years and would not take my Fordham students with me because I could not expose them to the risks. One group I worked with, United Community Centers of New York, started a campaign called "Shield the Children" after a drug dealer in the Cypress Houses pulled a three-year-old out of a stroller to use as a human shield during a gun battle. The group was also up in arms about an incident in a library on New Lots Avenue in which the entire staff was taken hostage by armed intruders, and about five murders that took place in a single year inside Thomas Jefferson High School.

This was the challenge Greg Donaldson faced when he decided to spend two years in Brownsville accompanying police on buy-and-bust operations, visiting families in the local projects, working with the theater program and basketball team at Thomas Jefferson High School, and spending hours and hours talking to young people one-on-one in their apartments, in school, on the subway, and on project benches. And the way he won their confidence was by exposing himself to the same risks they faced every day and night. And because he was willing to face those risks, because he was literally willing to die to write this book, he won the respect of people who almost *never* trust outsiders.

"Willing to die" may seem to some who have never spent time in Brownsville or a community like it to be a tired cliché, but it was a powerful existential reality for those living amidst crack and poverty's overpowering influence. It is no accident that Biggie Smalls, one of the greatest hip-hop narrators of the crack years, entitled his best-known album "Ready to Die" or that the two great educators whom Donaldson portrays in his book, teacher and theater director Sharon King and principal Carol Beck, both indicate that they are willing to put their lives on the line to protect their students and command the respect necessary to do their jobs. In Brownsville, as Donaldson shows, risking one's life was a daily occurrence, and no one working in that community, whether teacher, police officer, or, in Donaldson's case, investigative journalist, is going to get the time of day from residents unless they show they are willing to do that.

Donaldson passed that test with everyone. And so he could present Brownsville from the inside in a wide variety of settings, from picnics and barbecues to plays and basketball games, to shootouts and beefs, to bitter conflicts in stationhouses between racist police officers and those who respected the neighborhood and its people. And also because he was able to help folks out. As a former college basketball player with a background in theater, Donaldson was a valuable resource for teachers, coaches, and young people and was involved with mentoring and opening up opportunities for the young people he was writing about. Given this, *The Ville* does not claim to be an objective work of social science. It is written from the perspective of a participant in the life of the community, motivated by a deep compassion for its residents and a profound understanding of how they were scarred by racism and poverty. Never does Donaldson let us forget that the Brownsville story is intimately connected to the history of racism and race-based economic inequality in the United States, and that the suffering of its residents, and the suffering its residents impose on one another, is something for which we all bear responsibility.

When you read this book, you will come away deeply saddened that life could be this grim and dangerous for so many people in the richest country in the world. But you will also come away with respect for the people who live amidst the violence, who take risks most people wouldn't, and, when they rise above the pain, display incredible courage and resilience. And you will also come away with respect for the much-maligned civil servants who work in those communities, the police and the teachers, some of whom have given up, but others who go well beyond their official job descriptions to give Brownsville residents opportunities to live a decent life

This beautifully written, courageous, insightful book is something that all who love New York and its people will cherish. I am so proud that the Press of the university where I teach is bringing it back into circulation for both a general audience and for college classes.

Mark D. Naison

PREFACE

This book about Brownsville and East New York, isolated and troubled neighborhoods in Brooklyn, New York, is an attempt to bring the people behind the cardboard images of cops and inner-city African American teenagers to life. It is an effort to fill a gap in understanding that troubles this country deeply.

There are people in Brownsville, thousands of them living in city housing projects, who overcome the conditions there and continue to prevail. The private and public struggles go on. The East Brooklyn Congregations has built large numbers of affordable private homes that are pockets of stability. It plans to erect thirty square blocks more of housing. Activists such as Reggie Bowman, who founded the Community Coalition to Save Brownsville, continue to fight a system that is content to allow levels of joblessness, despair, and violence to persist in Brownsville (and communities like it) that are destroying a generation of African Americans. Bowman has spent the better part of the past decade battling to make New York City deliver on its promise to construct East Kings High School on an empty lot on Bristol Avenue. Symbolically, the city recently broke ground for a $35 million high-tech juvenile detention facility on the site.

The story of the political struggle for the future of Brownsville and the many lost battles is one that should be heard. Instead, I have chosen to write of day-to-day life in Brownsville through the eyes of police officers and teenagers who live there now. On that excruciating line between officers of the law and young men of the streets I hope to catch the soul of a community.

To write *The Ville*, I spent more than two years in Brownsville and East New York. I accompanied the Housing police on every kind of call, from domestic disputes to shootings. Sometimes I followed officers and suspects from the initial radio call through pursuit, arrest, and court case. I visited Thomas Jefferson High School regularly, sat in the classrooms, and traveled with the basketball team. I walked the streets of Brownsville, was a guest in people's homes, attended community and church events. Whenever and wherever I could, I followed the central characters, officer Gary Lemite and young Sharron Corley. The events in the book are real, based on my own observations or interviews. Nonetheless, I saw fit to change the names and identities of some of the characters portrayed and to disguise some locations. In some instances, I have shifted the time frame of an event to suit the narrative.

I chose to follow Gary Lemite, a Housing police officer, instead of a New York City policeman because of the close and constant contact Housing police have with the people in the public housing projects they patrol. The officers I depict in the book are the ones I met; it is incorrect to assume that they are representative of all police in inner-city neighborhoods. In fact, I observed distinct differences between the performance of Housing police and NYPD officers from precincts serving Brownsville and East New York.

Likewise, the young men I have focused on are not representative of all black teenagers, even those in Brownsville itself. There are a number of two-parent households in the neighborhood that manage through herculean effort to guide their children past the dangers and on to productive lives.

I could have concentrated on one of those priceless victories, but instead I chose to tell the story of a young man from Brownsville who lives on the edge between success and disaster. Sharron Corley, who is the centerpiece of this book, does not have an impenetrable parental buffer. He is young and intelligent, sensitive and ambitious, and he is a living record of the relentless economic and social forces in his community and his country. To the extent that his travails reinforce negative stereotypes of black teenagers, the book has failed. To the measure that the story humanizes the struggle of inner-city black teenagers to make sense of their lives, not only to survive but to make something special of themselves, it will have succeeded.

ACKNOWLEDGMENTS

The Ville could not have been written without the complete cooperation of Sharron Corley and Gary Lemite. Above all, it is their book. I would like to thank them and their families.

I am indebted to the people of Brownsville and East New York, who treated my project with an open mind and in many cases welcomed me with real hospitality under extremely difficult circumstances, asking only that I "tell it the way it is."

I would also like to express my appreciation to Chief Joseph Keeney of the Housing police for allowing me to follow the activities of his officers at PSA 2, and the policemen there for letting me watch them work. I am grateful to the principal of Thomas Jefferson High School, Carol Beck, who trusted me enough to give me access to her teachers and students.

Acknowledgment is due to Alter F. Landesman and Gerald Sorin for their books on the history of Brownsville.

Special thanks goes to Ingrid Griffith for living with this project for three years, and my deep appreciation to Michael Fahey and Dave Young for their friendship and perspective.

Mercer Sullivan of the New School gave advice, and Sharon Zukin of Brooklyn College offered background on the history of Brownsville and criticism of segments of the manuscript. John Garvey and John Mogulescu of the City University supported me with optimism, ideas, and analysis throughout the process. Demographer Frank Vardi was a vital source of information. Thanks also to Alan Dichter, principal of the Satellite Academy High School, and Nathan Jackson for his fact checking.

The Ville also owes much to the photographs of Charlena

Berksteiner, Mitch Zykofsky, and Bruce Gilbert. I would like to thank Eli Reed, whose photos have added so much.

Dave Herndon and John Capouya, editors at *New York Newsday*, were early sources of advice and enthusiasm for my features on Brooklyn youth. Thanks to Rick Landan for his unstinting support.

Finally, credit goes to Matt Bialer, my agent, for suggesting the idea of approaching the story of Brownsville through its police officers and teenagers, and to Jane von Mehren, my editor at Ticknor & Fields. Only she and I know how mightily she labored to produce this book.

I shall not listen.
I shall not listen
When they tell me
Life is sad and brief.

— Anonymous graffiti on a memorial wall in Brownsville, Brooklyn

PROLOGUE: LIKELY

The salty breeze that lifts off Jamaica Bay and drifts past the towering high-rises of Starret City, over the roofs of the one-family houses in Canarsie, makes it only as far as Flatlands Avenue. From Linden Boulevard north, the air is dead still. This is Brownsville.

In their blue and orange patrol car, rolling through the midnight streets, the two Housing cops could be two buddies in that time between school and family — a bit too old to cruise for girls, too young for the burden of kids, two regular guys. But outside the windows of their sector car are the streets of Brownsville and East New York, where there have been 185 murders in the past twelve months. Where it is so dangerous the bars have been shut down for years, there are no movie theaters, and some newly renovated city-subsidized apartments on New Lots Avenue go unclaimed because of fear. Where the only establishment sure to be open is a narrow storefront on Rockaway Avenue flashing a neon sign, 24 HOURS, WE BUY GOLD. Outside the window of the patrol car is a red tide of rancor. The radio crackles. The radio tells that story.

Through a blizzard of static, the dispatcher jolts across with a message about a shooting. The words are laced with numbers, codes for conditions and offenses. One phrase is clear; it will be repeated again and again throughout the night, the season, and the year, words that are the mantra of Brownsville: "Shots fired." "Numerous calls," Central says. "One male shot at that location. K."

The Housing police of the PSA 2 do not customarily answer

OP (off-project) calls, but this is a shooting and car 9712 is close. The driver stomps on the gas pedal and rockets to the site, a schoolyard on Hopkinson and Pacific, near Saratoga. Across the darkened yard, a cluster of people consider a fallen human being.

The late spring night is thick and bright. A round of stars sits high above the rooftops. As is almost always the case in Brownsville, the body is that of a young black man. The cops kneel down next to the figure and fumble for a few moments. They have no medical supplies, will not give mouth-to-mouth unless a child is dying. Nor will they decide to carry the man to their patrol car and whisk him to Brookdale Hospital, the way they would if this were a 10-13, an officer shot. The crowd leans; a boy edges his bicycle forward and gapes. One officer reports over his radio that the young man is "likely," police jargon for either dead or soon likely to be.

The call for a bus (ambulance) was made several minutes ago, when somebody from a window high above made a 911 call. Somebody saw the youth fall, because no one in Brownsville would call an ambulance just because they heard shots fired. The cops crouch a moment longer, then straighten up. No sense pretending. In another half-minute, the orange and white EMS vehicle storms across the blacktop to the foot of the steps near the cornerstone of the school. An EMS technician in a green uniform hustles out and verifies the "likely" report. The boy is already dead. The medics prepare to load the body into the bus. The folks on hand exchange whispered information. "You know, the guy with the dreads. Nooo, dark skin, guy who *just got* the dreads."

The crowd swells. Here, murder is a curse laid on a people who have carried too many burdens, an unspeakable place where a segment of the African American population has found itself after a desperate journey.

In the first half of the century, Brownsville was a thriving Jewish enclave. But as viable a community as it was then, it was never a destination for the Jews who filled its roiling streets, looked out over its clothesline-crossed yards and ramshackle homes. It was, in Alfred Kazin's words, "a place that measured all success by our skill in getting away from it." The war provided the prosperity; the freeways and the automobile, the means.

Most of the buildings in Brownsville were tenements built before 1919, structures with commercial space on the first floor and apartments for often as many as five families above, or wood-frame two-family rental dwellings. As the old housing stock deteriorated, the vacant apartments became catch basins for the poor, because they were the only housing people could find. Community activists campaigned hard. "Brownsville must have public housing" was their clarion cry. The makeshift tenements were readily demolished. Between 1941 and 1955, four major public housing units were built, including the Brownsville Houses in 1948, which the *New York Times* called "terrifying new slums."

Between 1940 and 1950, the black population of Brownsville doubled. The synagogue on Riverdale Avenue near Hertzl Street became the People's Baptist Church. Integration in the projects, crime, and fear of crime spurred the departure of the remaining low-income Jews to nearby East Flatbush or Canarsie. Fires devoured the frame houses that were still standing. Weed-wild lots dotted the landscape. Some brick dwellings were constructed on side streets, but mostly the deterioration continued unabated. The 1960s brought the scourge of heroin, the living dead who scratched like chickens through the torched and abandoned private buildings around the projects. By 1970, in a community of 1.9 square miles, there were seven hundred completely deserted buildings. The city took the opportunity to load the area with clinics, halfway houses, and rehabilitation centers for the dysfunctional and the troubled.

At first the projects seemed an improvement over rural poverty and tenement life. But the new black residents of Brownsville, many of them migrants from the South, ran into an old brick wall. The March on Washington of 1963 and the Civil Rights Act of 1964 raised hopes, but governmental policy, gerrymandering, redlining by banks, and deindustrialization mocked ambitions. The winners were the property speculators, the demolition companies. Breadwinners lost their jobs. More poor people poured in. The Latino population swelled. The projects grew like mushrooms. There were uprisings, tumult in the streets. In 1968, residents of Brownsville and nearby Ocean Hill fought for community control of local schools, setting off a citywide teachers' strike. The National Welfare Rights Organization took the city to court to make the Housing Authority stop

3

banning welfare recipients. Over thirty years, the city lost six hundred thousand industrial jobs. Designed for the working poor, the projects filled up with the unemployed. Then, in the late 1980s, crack cocaine materialized and guns poured into the neighborhood by the trunkload. Soon the poverty of Brownsville's past seemed a golden age.

Places like the Cypress Hills Houses, a vast housing project at the eastern border of East New York, and, on the other side of the stark pillars of the elevated subway tracks in Brownsville, the Unity and Brownsville Houses, are now some of the most dangerous spots on earth to live. Last year eight people were murdered in the Unity Houses alone; one building is so deadly the Housing police call it the slaughterhouse.

Murder is horror, but it is also entertainment. The first people on the scene this night look and mutter, ask stupid questions. "Is he all right?" These are just the folks who happened to be nearby when someone chased this young man from the front of the school to the back and shot him in the chest, the people out and about when he staggered down the four cement steps and collapsed, when he went from the living to the "likely."

News of the deed begins to seep through the neighborhood as the Housing cops perform the first real function of their shift, looping a yellow and black crime scene tape around the area. They complain. Housing police officers in Brownsville are often patient, sometimes valiant, but they almost always complain. This time they grumble about the size of the area designated as a crime scene. They complain about guarding the scene of a homicide so obviously off-project.

When there is a crowd, EMS removes the body with some dispatch. So it is this spring night. But not before news of the shooting spreads beyond the curious to the boy's acquaintances, and from them to his family. A girl straddles a pink bicycle thirty yards off, at the entrance to the schoolyard. She holds four spread fingers to her open mouth. "Not my brother," she whispers.

Her big brother is dead in the schoolyard, the place where fifteen years before he arrived cleaned up and crisply dressed for school, where he stood, hand in mother's hand, waiting for kindergarten to start. Maybe the schoolyard wasn't such a strange place to die. This was where hope foundered, where the child came face to face with the country that didn't need him. Perhaps the school was the right spot for this, the place where the promise was made and where it was broken.

The words reach home, words that should have been swept away by the wind. A fifty-five-year-old woman in a housedress and bare feet sprints down the sidewalk beside the twenty-foot Cyclone fence that borders the blacktop. Arms pumping and knees high, she comes in undignified haste, followed by a man with a ghastly gray face. Eyes bulging with bad health, belly swollen, he runs but a step behind his wife. The parents charge across the yard, straight at the two cops, who halfheartedly block their approach to the bus just as the body of their son is loaded up.

Electronic derision now: the belch and shriek of sirens float up, a background for the human lamentations. The mother pounds on the Irish Housing cop's chest. "I know who did it. I know who did it!" she screams.

At first there were dreams, a trip from the South to New York, better schools, escape from poverty, segregation, and that deep dust of hatred. Some grabbed the frayed rope of opportunity and hoisted themselves up and out of the neighborhood. Others snatched up city-subsidized mortgages and carved out a homestead. But for many the hope flickered. The dream faded to simple daily pleasures, pocket money, girlfriends. Youths like the one who fell tonight found fast friends, squeezed thick nuts of bills in their pockets. Trouble. The parents watched and worried. Soon the worry wasn't a sharp twinge but a dull presence, and every time this young man left home there was the possibility he would not come back. He was so alive and so close to death. He was a son of Brownsville. Then, murder most predictable.

SUMMER

DON'T GIVE UP ON YOUR DREAMS

Seventeen-year-old Sharron Corley slides center stage. It is a glove-soft evening in early summer, downtown Brooklyn. Sharron is glowing with perspiration and conviction. Danny, the character he is playing in the opening night performance of the Thomas Jefferson High School play, *Don't Give Up on Your Dreams*, has had a revelation.

In the play, Danny is a singer who lives with his single mother and sister in a barren apartment in the ghetto. He is tortured by temptation, the conflict between the street and the straight, between selling drugs and suffering until he gets his break. Through the opening scenes, he wanders on the wide stage in a trance, wrestling with his moral dilemma like Hamlet. Then his singing group, Danny and the Dream Team, is cheated out of $50,000 in prize money for a talent show they deserve to win, and Danny decides to turn to the beckoning arms of Rufus, a jewelry-bedecked drug entrepreneur. "I know what I'm gonna do," Danny says. "I'm gonna make some real money for a change. That's right. Danny is gonna get paid." Rufus is upstage, coiled like a snake, chanting, "I've got what you want. I've got what you need. I've got what you're lookin' for and more."

The play is being performed at the Paul Robeson Theater, miles away from Pennsylvania Avenue in the Brownsville/East New York neighborhood where Jefferson is located. This is the first performance in a scheduled week-long run of shows, and already the production is tight. The audience is filled with beaming parents and girlfriends, wide-eyed younger brothers and sisters. The star is Sharron. He acts. He sings. He "profiles." At five-foot-nine, he is broad-shouldered, saluki-trim, and wickedly muscled. His split-level fade stands three inches straight up, a crisp headdress, autumnal gold on the top inch and deep walnut the rest of the way down.

All his short life, Sharron has wanted to be admired. But that is not what always happened. He was a quiet, shy child. "We used to think there might be something wrong with him," his sister, Shawanda, says. When he was fourteen years old, it came together. He grew, his shoulders stretched like wings; a modest regimen of pushups and his pectorals looked like burnished plates of armor. To his utter delight, girls started calling him "pretty boy." He could not believe his good fortune, checked himself in the mirror a score of times on the day he first heard the term. Nearly four years later, he holds still at the sight of his own reflection, unless he is in a great hurry.

Tonight Sharron does not need a mirror. At the end of the first act, as he approaches the footlights, he bursts into song. Then he strips off his jacket and casts his voice to the dusty rafters. The teenage girls in the packed house go mad. Their hands fly to their faces. They shriek and rise from their seats. How has it happened that the very sight and sound they conjured in the secret places of their hearts has come to life? Sharron sinks to the wooden floor. From a pushup position, he thrusts his hips down; his muscled stomach, chest, neck, and head follow. Undulation after undulation, faster and faster, until the rippling effect is lost in a series of rapid thrusts.

Throughout most of the second act, though, Sharron, as Danny, is depressed and worried. He is supposed to begin working for Rufus soon. In one scene he sits slumped over the kitchen table listening to the cautionary words of his mother. Then he leaps to his feet, turns his back on her, and broods in guilty silence. He fingers the flimsy curtains his mother is so proud of, and sneers. Danny craves legitimate success, wants to make his mother proud. But the path is just too difficult. Everything he sees around him is hollow and cheap. The goal of Hollywood, success in the world beyond the neighborhood, beckons, but the road? Where? How? Rufus and his ways are at hand, close at hand.

Danny steps out of the apartment onto the painted Brownsville street set, lifts his eyes to the rafters, and with a great racking shudder thunders, "Hell, no!" In a feat of rectitude, he reverses his decision to work for the drug dealer. Rufus is not pleased. He materializes on the apron of the stage, chuckling darkly, and allows his body to sag a bit to the left. With the move, Rufus's jacket swings away from his body. He glances sharply under the garment and back at Danny. Throughout the play, Rufus has habitually moved with this list, again and again looking under his coat. The body language is a reference to the weight of a big gun, the drag of a "burner." The maneuver is not wasted on Danny, who braces himself for the worst.

Rufus is lurking, scheming for just the right time and place to send a message through the neighborhood that "nobody plays me." Danny's girlfriend, Gloria, played by Nareida Torres, approaches Rufus to plead for her lover's life, but the pitiless gangster yanks his gun. *Bam bam bam;* three shots ring out, and she crumples to the stage, mortally wounded. From the fourth row of the audience, Torres's seven-year-old brother screams in horror, bolts from his seat, and runs to his fallen sister. He tries to vault onto the stage. "The black man shot her," he howls. The boy is led away, struggling. No amount of explanation will console him until after the show, when he sits in the first row of the lit theater and holds his sister's hand.

Indeed, this is just a play, adapted by the faculty director, social studies teacher Sharon King. As much as she stressed authenticity in the dialogue and realism in the professionally designed set pieces, to show the world of Brownsville, King allowed for a happy ending.

In the final scene, Sharron Corley, dressed in a tuxedo, approaches the microphone and wraps up the loose ends of the plot: "Danny and the Dream Team received the fifty-thousand-dollar prize money, and a few days later Rufus was slaughtered by his own men. Don't give up on your dreams."

As Sharron turns his profile to the audience in the rising houselights, a livid scar is visible, running like an arching fault line from an inch beyond his hairline next to his left ear to the dimple near the corner of his mouth. Far from being a tour de force by a professional makeup artist, the scar comes compliments of the Brownsville streets, delivered by a razor in a street fight on the day before last Valentine's Day.

Sharron drops his hands to his sides and bows his head to the audience. On cue, the full thirty-member cast floods the aisles of the old theater and belts out a medley of inspirational songs.

There is a flush of accomplishment on the faces of the performers as they filter from the cramped dressing quarters into the empty hall minutes later. The glow will last for hours, at least as long as it takes to ride the subway back to the neighborhood. These are just kids now. They are neither frightening nor afraid. Tonight, diminutive Sheryl, Sharron's new girlfriend in the cast, does not feel or look like one of the Gucci Girls from the Linden Houses when they eye a white girl's earrings on the A train. Sharron does not feel like a member of the LoLifes when they slip through the Fulton Mall, watching for the slow, the weak, the turned head, the unguarded rack of clothes. These are just children now, centers of attention, sources of hope.

The energy in the musty hall is mountain fresh as King assembles her cast to discuss what went right and what went wrong with the performance. They settle to immediate attention. There are no artificial constraints on speech. No threats, no pleading for silence. There are things King knows that the kids want to learn. The young teacher wears black leggings and an oversize white T-shirt; her tawny skin is damp. Her huge amber eyes scan a pad with notes about the performance — the missed entrances, the speeches that did not quite work. One girl gave a monologue during the talent show segment of the play, portraying a woman waking her sleepy young son for school. But the girl's diction was so bad the performance collapsed.

"If you don't start to enunciate the way Ms. Oldham taught you to do, we are going to have to take your speech out of the play," King warns. "It's as simple as that. You studied this voice thing for four months, and tonight you sounded like you hadn't had a voice lesson in your life." There are no tears, no tantrums. The girl takes King's words as truth.

"What do *you* say about tonight?" King asks the group. Willowy Kenya springs to her feet. Her portrayal of Rufus's atonal singer girlfriend brought the house down.

"There are some boys who are hanging around the area where we're supposed to change costumes for our song. That shit is hard enough without some peeping Toms."

Before the titters die out, a six-foot-three, squeaky-voiced bit player apologizes. "I think she's talking about me. I had no place to stand. It won't happen again."

"What happened to the breathing we taught you?" King asks. "You've *got* to breathe. All I'm hearing are lines. Remember, the script is your gun and the words are your bullets." A moment later she offers a gratuitous observation. "I have so much respect for you guys. It takes more courage to get up here on the stage than it does to pull the trigger of a nine." She is talking about a nine-millimeter semiautomatic gun, a popular weapon in Brownsville. Though King is from the Caribbean, not from the American urban or southern background of most of her students, when necessary she can switch from standard English to the most convincing black American slang.

There is a murmur of dissent from the actors. "It does," King insists, "it takes more courage to perform."

These teenagers have seen too much for such glibness. They have heard the hollow hump of the nine-millimeter and the boom of the .357, and they have watched the deadly series of moves that track to the instant of gunfire. They know all about these things, and they are not about to truck with a cliché, even from their beloved Ms. King.

It was sometime in late February when King decided that Sharron, a cinnamon-skinned ladies' man recently anointed homecoming king of Jefferson, would be the lead in the play. King invited him to the after-school drama program and auditioned him for the role of Danny. "Sharron was the only one who could sing, and that helped him. But he was also the best actor. He wrote his own monologue." When King posted the cast list and the unacademic Sharron won the lead, he snapped to attention.

The funding for *Don't Give Up on Your Dreams* came from a foundation called the Jackie Robinson Center for Physical Culture, which provides Brooklyn schools with a range of after-school enrichment activities. The foundation spent $20,000 on the production, and spent it wisely. Besides King, an actor with professional aspirations, they hired scene painters, an acting coach, and a voice teacher. The production staff held weekly meetings on Sunday at King's apartment. "We did everything right," King says.

13

The kids in the cast had seen the spacious old auditorium at Thomas Jefferson High School, and the ancient swimming pool, of course. But they knew that those grand features had been built for someone else, for the immigrants who had passed through Brownsville decades before. This school play was lavish and it was just for them. From the very outset, the program was a success. Sharron showed up at school every day and never missed an after-school rehearsal. For one hour after regular school ended at three o'clock, the cast attended academic classes and counseling sessions. The rest of the time, sometimes late into the night, they worked on acting technique and rehearsal. There were drills and improvisations. The young actors wrote and performed skits in which they imagined their characters in various situations. They practiced singing and dancing, and they helped King rewrite the dialogue. The superlative of the hour was not "awesome" or even "cool" but "mad," as in "mad house party." Dope dealers were "slingers." And the most important term of all, the word that explained much of the apparently irrational behavior in their world, was "props," probably derived from southern slang, "propers," meaning proper respect.

Sharron treated the play as if it were the chance of a lifetime. He bound his script elaborately to protect it from the elements, folded the pages in a way that gave him quick access to his scenes. He taped his lines on an audio cassette and lay for hours on his bed with his Walkman, listening to the words. He learned his lines before anyone else, even though he had five times as much dialogue as any other actor. In rehearsal he was all business, as if he had been an actor all his life. He set the standard for the others.

"He's a professional, for God's sake," King said. "You can ask him to do a scene a thousand different times, in a thousand different ways, and he'll do it happily. I couldn't get him out of the place at night. I couldn't get the rest of them out either."

The only problem King had with Sharron was his trademark whisper. When he came into his own with the girls, he developed a tone of voice that was too soft to be heard by anyone but a young girl who was somehow tuned to his soundwaves. Teachers, parents, even male friends, shook their heads and leaned ever closer to hear. But like a dog whistle, young Sharron's speech was meant for certain ears. "I got him to lift his voice,"

King says, "but there were still parts where he would whisper." The tough-guy segment of his performance had been fashioned in the neighborhood, where the reviews could be brutal. Sharron had always been convincing on the street — cold and heartless for the eyes of the little gangsters, sweet and wounded for the young ladies, reflective and earnest for the adults.

At the closing night party, the principal of Jefferson, Carol Beck, a brown-skinned woman in her mid-fifties with a spray of tiny moles beside her wary eyes, mingles with the guests and chats with the administrator of the Jackie Robinson Center. Nationally recognized as the savior of the high school, Beck has almost singlehandedly brought this troubled high school, rated the most dangerous in New York City just a couple of years ago, into an era when moments like this are possible. Now she stands in one spot and says little. Her presence stalks the room. When Kenya, the young actress, slips over to the tape player and switches off the bluesy voice of Sade, the conversation in the room stops. Beck lifts her eyebrows ever so slightly at Kenya, who offers a broad smile, injects her own tape, punches the play button, and puts her fingers in her ears to ward off the protests of her elders as a booming hip-hop beat fills the space. Beck's nod of acquiescence is imperceptible to all but Kenya, who charges off to recruit dancers. In a moment Ms. Sharon King, surrounded by her charges, hip-hops to the beat. "Go *Sha*ron. Go *Sha*ron." The dance is on.

In a corner, Sharron Corley's pretty thirty-five-year-old mother, Gloria, stands by, proud but shaky, not sure what to say or do. She doesn't know anyone. Wine is served, but Gloria is careful not to drink tonight. She drifts slowly into a back room, wipes her red hair out of her face with the back of her hand, and leans over a large sink to wash the dishes.

The actors who are not dancing assemble and reassemble, gossip, and nibble the hors d'oeuvres. They stand in clusters like spring flowers, drenched in promise. There is not a hint of disrespect or rowdy behavior from the kids in the room, and there are no sirens or gunshots in the night air outside the wide open windows. This is downtown, out of Brownsville. For one night, for one week, this is the way other kids grow up.

15

GUN COLLAR

Housing cop Eddie Hammil leans back in the driver's seat of 9717, the RMP (radio mobile patrol car) that stalls every few minutes, and handles the steering wheel with two thick fingers. Beside him is Del Migliore. The two are nearing the end of their eight-to-four shift on a sunny day in Brownsville. Both have been cops for three years. They are not regular partners, and they haven't been getting along well all day. When Hammil wants to eat, Migliore says ride. At the corner, Migliore nods to the right; Hammil makes a lazy left off Sutter Avenue onto Pennsylvania Avenue. Hammil, short and soft with an oval face, is a wise guy.

"I got passed over for the sweep team 'cause the other guy's black and I'm white," Migliore moans — the same complaint he has made all day.

Hammil slows the cruiser almost to a stop in front of Thomas Jefferson High School and peers at the square-jawed, handsome Migliore. "You're white?" he says.

The high school stands unceremoniously flush on Pennsylvania Avenue — no front walkway, no shrubbery, just two stone steps off the sidewalk to a mud-brown bank of double-locked metal doors flanked by Doric columns. The six-story red-brick and limestone building was built to last a long time.

The school is mute. It's 3:30, and the kids are gone for the day. But directly across the street is the corner of Dumont and Pennsylvania, home of the quick and the dead. Beneath a blue and red Puerto Rican flag, high and slack on a traffic light stanchion, a dozen men stand and shuffle, confer with arrivals, and duck inside a building. Mickey Mundell, a thirty-two-year-old "stem," as crackheads are known, fidgets in front of the corner bodega, studying the faces of people in the distance, looking for someone he knows so he can borrow three dollars for a vial of crack. The sand-colored brick wall of the corner building, 666 Dumont Avenue, is decorated with a crimson R.I.P. in memory of Lyty, a girl recently assassinated on the sidewalk there. Another memorial is painted close by, for Na Na, and above there is a humble benediction in black spray paint, "R.I.P. Cano."

Hammil makes another left turn, pulls up to the gaping maw of 666. Everything about the building is worn and grimy but the gleaming, newly installed inside security door, replaced and reinforced regularly by the crack dealers to slow the cops on their charges upstairs to the drug stash apartments. Hammil surveys the congregation of jumpy young men in their late teens and early twenties. Teenagers are rarely crack users in Brownsville; heroin addiction among teens of this generation is unheard of. Instead, kids are found in the center of the action as lookouts and street dealers, as gun bearers, and as they grow older, as shooters. There are almost no older adults hanging around today. Wary customers head quickly in and out the front door.

A twenty-two-year-old Hispanic in baggy shorts and bright white tube socks stretched to his knees limps over to the patrol car, using a cane to support a damaged right hip. "Wha's up?"

"I saw your brother," Hammil tells the youth.

The kid's eyebrows knit. "Where at?"

"Over at Brookdale. But he's O.K. I don't know what was wrong with him, but the doctors were treating him like shit."

"He wasn't shot or nothin'?"

"No, I don't know what it was. They were dissin' him big-time, though. He was pissed." As Hammil talks, his gaze floats to the front door, where traffic has slowed for a moment with the arrival of the police car, then resumed. The kid crouches slightly, using his cane for balance, and looks inside the RMP at Migliore.

"O.K., be safe now," Hammil says. "You haven't seen anybody selling any drugs around here, have you?"

The kid swivels his head. "Nah. Not lately."

Hammil rolls ever so slowly away from the spot up to the light. He turns to Migliore, who is staring straight ahead. Right now, Migliore is thinking about how great it is to be a cop, remembering last Saturday, when he was driving on the New Jersey Turnpike to Atlantic City and his girlfriend got nauseous. When he pulled over under a NO STOPPING sign, a Jersey state trooper drove up and asked for identification. Migliore was fishing for his badge when the girl threw up on the trooper's shoes. The trooper took a look at Migliore's badge, walked over to the tall grass, wiped his shiny black shoes off, and drove away. Respect. Migliore is smiling to himself when Hammil snickers.

"The mope doesn't even have a fucking brother."

Second-year Housing cop Gary Lemite has two, an older one who was a cop in Florida and a hell-raiser of a kid brother on Long Island. All three have creamy skin that turns dusky at the first kiss of sun, a wan mustache, and gleaming black crinkled hair. After being rejected for high blood pressure on his first ten department screening physical exams, Gary finally got on a police force himself. He sailed through the academy and spent the next eight months as a probationary officer. Though his uniform cap is a bit too large for his head, his chin vague, and his smile wide and gentle, Gary has the peace of mind of a man who has found his place in the world. He was born to be a cop.

At Police Service Area (PSA) 2, the Housing police station over on Sutter Avenue, near the border of Brownsville and East New York, just two blocks from Thomas Jefferson High School, Gary Lemite is downstairs at his locker getting dressed for his four-to-midnight shift. He scoops a bag of sunflower seeds from the vending machine and settles on a metal chair in the roll call room across the hall. In a few minutes the sergeant is calling the roll, giving out the posts. He's taking care of the guys he likes, putting the heavy hitters, the cops who like to make arrests, in the cars and the lazy guys on hospital duty, where they can sleep, and sending the PCOs, the footposts, out to their places in the projects. The Housing police are a separate entity from the New York City police, responsible for public housing. In Brownsville and East New York, that includes some scatter-site housing, but mostly it means the projects — the Howard Houses, Pink, Brownsville, Unity, and Tilden, Cypress, Linden, Van Dyke, and Langston Hughes, which the cops call Langston Blues. Fifty thousand people live in these buildings.

"Lemite. Exterior security."

Gary frowns. Exterior security is a no-action, no-arrest detail. The assignment is to walk around the PSA and guard officers' cars against vandalism.

"And yeah," the sergeant adds. "Pay attention to this. You get in an accident, rack up the RMP, and you lose three days' pay, no matter whose fault the accident was. So watch where you're driving and check the sector car before you take it out so you don't suffer for somebody else's mistake. And don't bitch, 'cause you've been told. It comes from the top."

Upstairs, Gary waits in line to check out his radio from the radio room. The devices are worth $1,500 and have to be signed for. If an officer loses his radio, he forfeits about five days' pay. When Lemite checks the device, it fails to operate.

"Drop it on the street. It'll work," a veteran advises him. "Really. Drop it on the sidewalk." Gary exchanges the radio.

He makes a lap around the building, back to the schoolyard, and a trip across the street to the parking lot on Sutter. Now he is just standing, rocking back and forth, thinking. His family — his wife, Lisa, and two young children, Erica, three, and Zachary, two — has been living in the basement apartment of his mother's house in Elmont for three years, and that cannot go on. Too much pressure. The wife has been threatening for over a year to move to her sister's house and take the kids. Her married sister is childless and would like nothing better than to have Erica and Zach around the house for a while, maybe forever. What Gary needs is a house, one like the house he grew up in. That would cut down on the arguments, the tension. The kids would have the yard; Gary could cook his special buffalo chicken wings in the spacious kitchen. But it is going to take time, overtime, and that comes from arrests.

Gary is thinking that he is not going to get any overtime standing in front of the PSA when along comes this big kid. Gary watches as fifteen-year-old Michael T., all six-foot-one, 230 pounds of him, walks past. Michael is wearing an oversize white sweatshirt with blue stripes and carrying something heavy. Lemite is new on the job, but he has ten years' experience as a store detective in department stores all over Long Island and Queens. He knows when someone is carrying something under his clothes.

He falls into step about twenty feet behind as the kid makes the turn off Alabama onto busy Sutter Avenue. You cannot miss Michael T., because he is about the biggest young guy on the block. He lives nearby, at 280 Georgia Avenue, in the Unity Houses, and hangs on the corner in front of the bodega, sometimes with his boys but mostly alone. Fact is, Michael has to do something crazy once in a while to keep his reputation intact. He believes the only thing worse than being a pussy is being a big pussy. Michael is huge, but he will never succeed as a real bad guy, a stickup kid, because the left side of his face is covered by a seared slab of skin, as if someone applied a red-hot iron to his cheek while he slept. Michael will never be able to get away with anything.

Michael T. has smoked marijuana lots of times, felt the slow dance of the reefer and the sour dry pop of a gulp from a forty-ounce bottle of Power Master when he is high. But that rush is weak stuff compared to the sensation of having a pistol in his hand or tucked in his waistband, feeling its hard advantage against his skin. The gun is the thing. With it, he no longer feels as if he's just wandering along Sutter Avenue with nothing to do. He feels as if he's in a movie.

Gary Lemite has a sixth sense about these things. Not only does Michael have a faint bulge under his sweatshirt, he holds the inside of his arm unnaturally tight to his side to pin whatever it is he's carrying, to make sure it does not fall to the sidewalk. Like a horse trainer moving around a stall, watching the thoroughbred's opposite flank for the flex that means the horse is about to shift its weight and deliver a kick, Lemite knows the subtle signs. "Hey," he shouts at Michael's back.

Michael T. may be in a conflict about letting people know he is carrying a "four-fifth" (.45) Ruger Red Hawk single-action hunting pistol, but he is not ambivalent about getting caught and spending time in the Spofford Juvenile Center in the Bronx, or upstate. Besides, he is still watching the movie with him in the starring role. What does the gangster do when a soft-looking, light-skinned Housing cop, probably some punk rookie, orders him to stop? Michael T. reaches for his four-fifth wheels, and points it straight at Lemite.

"What the *fuck* do you want?" he hisses.

Gary freezes at the sight of the gun leveled straight at him from killing distance. A moment, a long moment.

This is the first of many times he will face a gun in the year to come. He will see jolting flames from muzzles, he will dive from bullets, and he will fire back. This time he spins out of the line of fire and flattens himself against an abutment in the rough gray stone of the outer wall of the PSA.

The kid's play is bold and stupid. If Lemite had asked his question with his own gun drawn, things would have been different. "Looking back, I would draw and ask him to stop," he says. "In which case, if he turned and reached like that, I would've shot him. Send me in front of a grand jury. I'd rather be tried by twelve than carried by six."

Michael T. is not a "mad agent," Brownsville slang for a psychotic. He's not about to shoot a cop. He's buying time with the draw, and he uses the moment when Lemite dodges to turn and sprint to the corner of Williams and Sutter. Lemite is in pursuit now, yelling a breathless "10-13" (officer in trouble) into his radio. Maritza, the narrow-hipped, black-eyed proprietor of the bodega on Williams, watches the chase from the front of her store. Dave, the guy who cleans up the PSA, is sitting with a couple of his cronies across the street in front of the cops' parking lot. "Big kid. Big gun," he observes.

The PSA 2 crouches beside a six-story public housing building on Sutter. Behind the building is a narrow parking lot for patrol cars fronted by a Cyclone fence. Beyond the fence lies the wide asphalt playground of an elementary school. By the time Lemite gets to the corner, Michael T. has crashed through a pile of garbage on the sidewalk and made another turn, pushing his 230 pounds of muscle and baby fat across the schoolyard, back toward Alabama Avenue, where he hopes to dive into a building, disappear into an apartment.

Lemite has his gun drawn now, but there are kids on the sidewalk. There are kids in the schoolyard and there are kids on the street. The 10-13 has brought four cops out the back door of the PSA just ahead of Gary, only yards behind Michael T. as he rumbles down the street and heads into 580 Blake, a building near the corner. Sector cars from the nearby 75th and 73rd NYPD precincts stream to the scene. Two police cars collide with a glass-shattering crash and a whoosh of steam on the corner of Sutter and Williams. Radio in one hand and gun in the other, heaving with exhaustion, Lemite falls behind as Michael T. and the four officers trailing him plunge into the Blake Avenue address in the Unity Houses. The kid scrambles up a stairway, but the cops are right there to grab him. Captain Charles Kammerdener, the commanding officer of the PSA, is even on hand by the time Lemite comes deep-breathing to the spot where the kid is held, next to the second-floor garbage chute. Lemite nods vigorously at Michael T. and Kammerdener orders the young cop to cuff him up.

The rookie officer's hands are shaking as he does the honors on Michael. Three clicks and the silver cuffs are on. The NYPD Emergency Service Unit (ESU) arrives in moments to open the basement, where they find the six-shot hunting revolver sitting on top of the trash inside the garbage compactor. Then Lemite folds the big kid into an RMP for the short ride to the PSA.

A large American flag flaps over the front door of the PSA. Lemite opens the glass door for the handcuffed Michael T. Inside lies a wide bright room. On the right side of the room is an attached row of blue plastic chairs; beyond the chairs, the entrance to the detective squad room. Across the tiled floor to the left, a four-foot-high steel crossbar mounted on two poles keeps prisoners and complainants from approaching a high-countered partition. Lemite and his prisoner stand behind the bar as a lieutenant holds the huge pistol, turns it over in his hand, whistles, and passes the weapon over his shoulder to a cop who is a gun buff. Behind the partition two steel desks sit flush against one wall. Opposite the desks stands a huge radio receiver bedecked with flashing red lights. High behind the desks is an arrangement of framed photographs of Housing police brass and a duty chart for PSA personnel.

Lemite walks Michael T. down a short hallway to the lockup behind the desk area and guides him into the first of four holding cells. An old-timer sprawled on a chair beside another gray metal desk nods at Lemite and cocks his head at Michael T. "That's the same cell we used to lock Mike Tyson in. He used to stand on his hands with his feet against the bars and do push-ups. Nice guy, Tyson," the cop remembers, "robbery recidivist."

Michael T. is a "juvy," a juvenile, which complicates matters. He stands silently for two hours as Gary fills out the endless papers and snaps the required Polaroid of the exotic weapon. It is eight o'clock before Lemite can arrange a ride for Michael to the Spofford Juvenile Center in the Bronx.

Two months later, at his trial, Michael T., a.k.a. Miz, will plead guilty and burst out crying in front of the judge, while his lawyer importunes for a sentence that will keep the hulking fifteen-year-old out of hard-core Spofford. When he gets a sentence that sends him to an easy juvenile facility upstate, the tears stop. "You know I'm a gunman," Michael will say to the people in the hallway. "You know that, right?"

When Michael T. is gone, Lieutenant Jack Lenti, second in command to Kammerdener, joker to Charlie the K-Master's straight act, calls Lemite into his office.

"Why didn't you fire your weapon when the kid drew down on you?" he wants to know. Lemite doesn't answer. He understands that he is not here to talk, he is here to listen.

The black-haired, narrow-faced Lenti pushes himself back from his desk, puts both hands behind his head, and leans against the wall in his tiny square room. He removes his wire-rim glasses, opens his eyes wide, and squeezes them shut. He has been reading arrest reports all day. When he opens his eyes again, he studies the eager mocha-skinned cop in front of him.

"There were four rounds in the kid's gun, the . . . Ruger, whatever that big fucking thing was. Could be the kid pulled the trigger but there was no bullet in the cylinder." Lemite remains quiet. Lenti wants to make sure that he is not afraid to use his weapon. In the academy, the emphasis is on restraint. This is the street.

"Next time somebody pulls a gun on you, shoot him," Lenti says simply, and points to the door of his office.

On his way back downstairs, Gary passes a large bronze plaque on the wall of the front room, which memorializes Anthony O. McLean, a Housing cop shot dead by a drug dealer in the stairway of the Tilden Houses in 1988. An inscription beneath McLean's silver shield and bas-relief likeness reads, "Blessed are the peacemakers, for they shall be called the children of God."

ONE MALE BLACK

It is the heat that wakes Sharron, not the light. Though it is after nine on the abundantly sunny morning of the first Monday of his summer vacation, it is gloomy in his cluttered room. The view out the curtainless window is blocked by a gray cement wall ten feet away.

School is out. Usually that means there is not much for Sharron to do but stay out of trouble. But this summer it's going to be different. The man who painted the sets for *Don't Give Up on Your Dreams* has arranged a job for Sharron with Summer Youth Employment at Brooklyn Youth Outreach in downtown Brooklyn.

Sharron has no alarm clock. By the time he sits up on his dusty, sheetless day bed, it is almost nine-fifteen. Ms. King told him to be downtown by nine o'clock. No problem. There will be plenty of time to be just an hour late.

Sharron nudges the door of his room open with his foot. Sounds from the apartment drift in — the thud of a closing refrigerator, the rush of water from a flushed toilet. Sharron comes alive slowly. He stretches, rocks to his feet, and slouches to his dresser for his toothbrush and hair pick. The walls of his room are covered with curious artifacts, including no fewer than four signs that say POLO and a picture of Sharron with the caption "Sexy." On his small wooden dresser sits a trophy with a gold-painted figurine of indistinct reference. On the wall closest to the door is a two-foot-long sign that trumpets POLO in stenciled letters spaced widely apart, with the word "LoLifes" beneath. Nearby is another photo like the ones taken for a fee in front of garish dropcloths on Forty-second Street in Times Square. In the Polaroid, Sharron is dressed in a billowing outfit of matching yellow and green jeans and jacket that makes him look for all the world like a circus clown. There is a picture next to the closet door of Sharron in a crouch, eyeing the camera; above this photo is the nickname Shalo. On the outside of the door of the room is a sign that reads, "What are your suggestions? We'd like to know," above a photograph of Sharron stooped over with laughter.

Beside the bed is a red folder with the numbers 2010 stenciled on the cover. It is Sharron's imagined life story, which he wrote as part of a school assignment early in the year. A reflection back on his life, it is told from his perspective as if he were thirty-seven years old.

It often gets boring, explaining to people, mostly TV talk show hosts, my story. For those who don't know I'm a professional rhythm and blues recording artist. I was a late bloomer. I can't say I always looked as I do now. In high school I was blooming pretty fast and to add to that I had a smooth sensitive voice. I confess right now I have a strong sense of nostalgia. I graduated from Thomas Jefferson High School and went on to Howard University for a degree in business. During my college years I signed with Epic records. I have had twenty one albums. My albums hit gold sixteen times. My personal life isn't that special. Basically, due to my image, I keep my personal file as confidential as possible. I give to charity as much as I can, I also try to be a positive role model for the youth. I would like to say thanks to all my fans for their support and interest in me and my music throughout my career.

Sharron crosses the hall and pads to the bathroom. Before he turns on the water, he opens the mirrored door of the medicine cabinet so he can watch himself shower.

Sharron Corley's building, 830 Saratoga Avenue, sits on a small rise half a block from the bustle of Pitkin Avenue, a commercial street which, like Belmont Avenue a block away, trails sneaker outlets and record stores down the spine of Brownsville into East New York. When the Jews lived in this neighborhood, Pitkin was called the Fifth Avenue of Brownsville. It stood in regal contrast to Belmont Avenue, where fishmongers and egg sellers hawked their wares from pushcarts. Now, just a few feet from the public phone that Sharron considers his personal headquarters, an old movie theater houses a three-story furniture store selling gaudy bedroom sets on layaway. Both sides of Pitkin Avenue are lined with cheap yellow-and-red signs that advertise such appliances as refrigerators and washer-driers. Shops run by swarthy men with suspicious eyes sell clothing, jewelry, and sneakers. One store sells huge earrings shaped like Nefertiti's head for $39.99. In the window is a small old sign hawking "back-to-school gold."

This morning Sharron is delighted to be heading out of the neighborhood for the day. "It has been more than obvious for some time that there are just too many trigger fingers in the neighborhood," he wrote in another assignment for school this spring. Sharron has been in trouble himself lots of times, picked up for shoplifting and petty crime like jumping the turnstiles in the subway, and he believes he will be less likely to have such problems if he is keeping busy in another part of the city. But he is happy that he will be spending much of the summer outside Brownsville for another reason.

A few years ago, when he was about fifteen, Sharron discovered a principle familiar to those who crave celebrity. He found that the less he was seen around the neighborhood, the more he was admired. That year, through his friend Terrance, he got a job cleaning up and doing light clerical work for a small law firm on Fifty-seventh Street in Manhattan. While the job lasted for only a year or so, it gave the aspiring star money and kept him out of the daily mix. He could see a flicker in the eyes of the local cutie-pies when he reappeared after working for a weekend or a couple of afternoons in a row. The $100 a week he was carrying around gave him the means to buy some clothes — Guess jeans, Polo sweaters.

The quest for clothes took Sharron into the company of a loosely organized and far-flung group of young shoplifters who call themselves the LoLifes. At first Sharron and Terrance would head over to the Unity Houses, where a contingent of LoLifes lived, to purchase purloined Polo clothing. It was always Polo, because Polo was the trademark and inspiration for the name LoLifes.

"I don't know if the statement 'the clothes make the man' truly exists anywhere else," Sharron wrote, "but in Brooklyn it is considered a motto. With this in mind I have no problem admitting my being materialistic. I was seldom given credit for the things that I had done except for my vocal talent. When I had gotten into clothes it gave me character, so to speak."

There are straight-arrow young men in Brownsville, boys who have never had a whisper of problems, who go straight to school and home. But they remain outsiders, curiosities, sometimes targets. Sharron Corley doesn't want that profile, doesn't want to walk close to the curb and stay inside after dark. His relationship with the LoLifes is complex. A clear step in the wrong direction, it has also been a factor in his blossoming. "Sharron did not become Sharron until he got with the Lo-Lifes," an old girlfriend attests.

Like many street gangs in Brooklyn and throughout the New York area, the LoLifes are not a gang in the traditional sense of an organization that has a set membership and turf. There was no ritual initiation for Sharron, just a casual shift from outsider to LoLife. Each member of the crew receives a street name that is a combination of the initial syllable of his first name and the suffix "lo." Sharron is Shalo; his two best friends, Frank and Terrance, didn't fare quite as poetically, as Franklo and Terrlo. But they are LoLifes, as is a slim fifteen-year-old from the Linden Houses named Ian Moore, who signs his graffiti moniker, E-lo, all over town, and the Crown Heights boosters Jaylo and Marco Polo. If a member of the group has a girlfriend who shares the Polo mania, she is a LoWife. Silly names and name-brand gear — trivial stuff in most places, but in "the Ville," mystique can be a life-and-death matter.

"If you are nobody and somebody shoots you," Sharron says, "then nobody is gonna come back for you. You just go out. Simple. But if you got props, you got respect and you got a crew. People think twice about cappin' you, 'cause then there are people who are coming back."

"What makes Polo so appealing?" Sharron wrote. "It has style, originality, uniqueness, eye snatching designs etc. To the LoLifes it is more than a piece of clothing. It is what represents us as the best dressed group of guys in our environment."

Sharron remembers fondly the first time he boosted as a Lo-Life. He had stolen candy bars, bubble gum, and notebooks, but this was different. He wanted the merchandise, but more important, he wanted to feel part of something. He was nervous but ready. He knew each time you boost something, the more props you get, "like stripes on a soldier."

It was a Sunday morning last fall, just before Sharron was elected homecoming king. Sharron, Terrance, and Frank had been planning their caper since Friday. On the empty #3 train to Manhattan, they put the final touches on their strategy. They planned which entrance they would take into Bloomingdale's to avoid being "sweated" by the guards, how they would quickly remove the pop-off plastic alarms and make their way out of the building.

The threesome threaded their way to the Polo department on the basement level. There were no "DTs" (store detectives) working on Sunday, something the LoLifes anticipated. Sharron was jumpy and lightheaded. His eyes swept the store. He had an almost uncontrollable urge to look over his shoulder for guards, so he locked his gaze ahead, on Frank and Terrance. Then he began to worry that his attachment to his two friends was too obvious, so he drifted behind a display of Polo sweaters and sucked deep breaths. While he was pulling himself together, his two friends, out of his sight, were "gettin' busy," stuffing shirts into the bicycle shorts they wore like girdles under their baggy jeans. Sharron emerged and began rummaging for a sweater he had seen on a previous visit. By then Frank and Terrance were clearly nervous. The look on their faces told Sharron they had seen a DT, so Sharron dropped the sweater he was fondling and the boys headed out of the building. Frank and Terrance gave Sharron a "steaming out" look just before they reached the door. Sharron couldn't figure out why, unless the guys had stashed items without popping off the alarms. As the boys blasted into a dead run, the alarms went off. But the LoLifes were already in the wind, six blocks away in just over a minute.

When Sharron found out the others had stashed, he felt a dreadful sinking sensation. He begged them to go back with him, but Frank and Terrance didn't want to risk it. Sharron felt compelled to return to the store and prove he could "catch" something, prove that he was "able to be down with this three-some, worthy of being a LoLife." So he told the others to meet him on Fifty-seventh Street, where he and Terrance worked for the law firm, then stalked back to Bloomingdale's alone. He was determined to come out of the store with a Polo sweater, no matter what. He was full of heart. "If I get caught, I just get caught," he said to himself. Nothing was going to stop "his quest."

Sharron hunkered right down to business. No lurking behind display counters this time. He grabbed the sweater he had held in his hands before, a white Polo with an American flag covering the chest and "Polo USA" stenciled under the flag. He folded it quickly into a tight ball, stuffed it up under his knapsack. As he neared the door, he knew he had not popped the alarm, so he was ready to steam out into the street. But the alarm failed to sound. Elated, Sharron loped down Lexington Avenue anyway, ducking and bobbing through the pedestrians on the sidewalk. Like a farm kid who has just caught his first fish or a suburban boy after his first home run in Little League, Sharron ran to tell.

When he arrived at the office building, the guys were in the back room, detaching the alarms from the sweaters. Sharron walked in with his head down, pretending to have failed in his mission.

"Yo, Sha, what's up, son?" Terrance asked.

"It was rough, son," Sharron returned slyly. Then he banished the hangdog look and broke into a howl. "I caught the big flag."

The boys were so happy they cavorted like fools around the supply room of the empty law office. Terrance jumped into Sharron's arms and the two swung madly. While they were twirling, Terrance cut himself on a broken light fixture on the wall. But the wound was hardly noticed in the giddy celebration. The boys were just so happy with one another. Sharron had proved to himself that he was indeed one of the group. Many times he had felt as if it were Terrance and Frank, with him as an outsider. No more. "It will always be this way," he believed, "the three of us so tight, acting the way we can only act when we are alone with each other." He stepped back and sat on a desk in the corner of the supply room. "I love these guys," he decided. At the same time, he began to see himself as the smoothest character anywhere, as if he could never do anything wrong again, ever.

Even though he came into the Summer Youth Employment Project a week late and was an hour tardy for his first day of work, it seems as if things are going to work out. Aubrey, the lanky

director of the Brooklyn Youth Outreach site on East Street, is
on the phone when Sharron appears in the doorway of his office.

"C'mon in." Aubrey gestures for Sharron to sit and studies
his new worker while he listens to the voice on the other end
of the line with mounting impatience. Then he moves the receiver away from his ear and rolls his eyes while the person
continues to talk.

"I've heard a lot about you," he begins, still holding the
squeaking receiver away from his ear. Aubrey, Sharron has
heard, is from uptown, Harlem, and is slick and funny.

"Will do. Will do," Aubrey assures the person on the other
end of the line, without returning the receiver to his ear. He
hangs up the phone and addresses Sharron. "Do your job and
we'll be cool. We'll be cool. I know about these things." He
steps across the room and places a large bony hand on the boy's
shoulder. A wave of tangy aftershave floats with him. Though
Aubrey is an inch under six feet and of average build, Sharron
can't believe how big he seems, standing close, how heavy his
hand, how deep and comforting his voice.

"Cool," Sharron whispers.

"You aren't going to be just a worker, you're a site monitor,"
Aubrey says. "Which means you got responsibility for more
than just yourself. After you get used to the job, you'll give ori-
entation talks to kids and you'll break in other monitors. That's
if you show you can handle yourself." Aubrey pauses, backs up
a step, and studies Sharron, who makes full eye contact. Then
Sharron glances quickly at a jar full of pencils on Aubrey's desk.

"Should I write stuff down?"

"Nah, not right now." Aubrey chuckles at his bright new
charge. "You're gonna be all right."

Sharron's immediate job is to travel around to various youth
employment sites in Brooklyn, picking up time cards and
checking on site conditions. The very first afternoon, he finds
himself traveling in the hot sun from the Brooklyn Navy Yard
to Long Island College Hospital, over to Columbus Park on Jay
Street. Everything is fine until he gets off at the wrong stop on
the #2 train and finds himself beneath the crumbling St. George
Hotel in Brooklyn Heights. When he steps out into the daylight,
he takes a turn west and sees nothing but white faces. "Damn,"
he thinks as he checks the street signs. "Pineapple Street? Cran-
berry Street? Got to be a white folks' neighborhood."

Sharron makes a left at the corner. A woman walking her dog strains her ocular muscles to their very limits, using every single degree in her sweep of peripheral vision to watch Sharron without moving her head as he makes his way down the other side of the street. Three more blocks of cheery brownstone buildings with sparkling clean, unbarred windows at street level. No police cars in sight. No people now. Strange sights. Another two blocks, and Sharron stands frowning on the famous Brooklyn Promenade, which looks out over the harbor at the Manhattan skyline. But Sharron isn't interested in the sights or the roller skaters or the people strolling in the sun "actin' like nothing could go wrong."

"No, son. You want Carroll Gardens. Now that is a walk. But you're *young*, aren't you?" a hard-of-hearing gentleman observes after Sharron shows him the address of the old-age home he is looking for. Fifteen minutes of brisk walking and Sharron is at the site picking up the time cards, just as Jerry told him to.

Sharron is young, and $320 will come in every two weeks from his new job. He has his own modest welfare budget, but that goes to his mother, Gloria, to pay the rent and cover food and utility bills. In Sharron's view, this job is just right, because it has respect, props. It's one thing to be a senior monitor, checking on things, quite another to be packing bags in a supermarket or sweeping the back room of some business.

One rainy summer day Sharron asks Aubrey for a couple of hours off to travel with Ms. King to an open audition for young actors in Manhattan.

"All right, but I don't want to be seein' your name in lights just yet," Aubrey says. "We need you around here."

On the #3 train, a whippet-thin boy with a chevron carved in his fade widens his audience across the aisle of the half-empty car to include Sharron. Ignoring Ms. King, he continues his account to his companion of a subway mugging in which he and another kid took part. The boy is a born storyteller.

"Check this out. Dude's in the last car. Briefcase an' shit. We check him out, an' like he knew we was clockin'? So he tries to reach in his coat. I come in his face an' ask him all cold, like 'You got a weapon, sir?' Ah-ah."

Slam, he demonstrates how the man was pinned and stripped of his valuables. *Crash*, he staggers to show how somebody in the car pulled the emergency cord, jamming the train to a halt. Then the kid shows how he slithered off the train between cars and hit the tracks, how he fled down the tunnel straight into the arms of the Transit cops, who trained their big guns on him. Big fun. He leans toward Sharron for affirmation, the ritual touching of hands. But Sharron's loyalties are divided, and he is scrupulous not to disrespect Ms. King by putting his stamp of approval on such a roguish adventure. He waves a perfunctory hand in the direction of the storyteller as the boy reaches for a righteous slap from his original listener.

In the Times Square office of the casting agent, a thick orange shag carpet fails to muffle the racket of automobile horns outside the sooty second-floor windows. An assistant in a bulging striped vest and gray patent leather shoes is ill-tempered and rude.

"Are you auditioning?" he asks King.

"No, I'm with Sharron."

"I thought you were Sharon."

"I am, but this is Sharron, and I'm with him. I'm his teacher." The man raises his pale eyes to the ceiling.

"Have your glossy ready," he says, referring to the photograph actors hand over at auditions. Sharron glances at King. He does not have a picture to submit.

"No picture. Ahhh." The man groans. King's eyes glint. The assistant is about to get cursed out. Sharron reaches across and lays his hand on King's arm. The assistant spins to the crowded room and raises his voice. "Absolutely no talking. Do you understand?"

People in Brownsville and East New York are much more careful about whom they disrespect, more conscious of the possible consequences of any personal interaction, than people in most other places. If you are insulted in the Ville, you can be sure that it is personal and that it is on purpose. In this white world, it seems to Sharron, slights and insults are served up carelessly. He accepts the disrespect goodnaturedly. Somehow this man does not count.

Sharron sits next to King on the cracked Naugahyde couch and looks over the pages of the script. He will read the part of Terry Malloy in *On the Waterfront*.

"Not my night? Not my night? I coulda torn Wilson apart.

But you, Charlie. You and Johnny, youse went for the price on Wilson. He gets the title shot in the Garden and what do I get? A one-way ticket to Palookaville."

Before he enters the room for the audition, which will take two minutes, Sharron turns to Ms. King and asks, "What's Palookaville?"

"GET OUT OF BROWNSVILLE"

t is five o'clock on a Thursday in the first week of July. Ninety degrees, the first real heat of the summer. Sergeant Jimmy Priore has just changed over from two weeks of day tours to the four-to-twelve. Hammil is his driver today, and the two are headed to Brookdale Hospital, where Priore has to check the paperwork on some white kid from Brentwood, Long Island, who was shot in the head while making a cocaine deal in Unity.

The emergency entrance of the red-brick hospital opens like a wound onto busy Linden Boulevard. A two-foot loading dock sits at the head of the small parking lot so the EMS people can roll the damaged goods right into the hallway. Beside the dock is a ramp. Priore strolls up the ramp with a handful of papers and a happy smile. Hammil, less enthusiastic about the day, takes up the rear. Just inside the door to the emergency area, Priore pauses near the white kid, who lies on a gurney in an alcove, barely out of the traffic in the emergency room hallway. The young man's name is Gilmore. He has a rose tattoo on his forearm. A glowing dot hops like a mountain goat across the dark screen of a monitor above his head. He is brain-dead.

"They're gonna use him for parts," Priore says, still smiling. "The word was that a fourteen-year-old kid was the shooter. We had a tip where the kid was. We didn't know his name. We end up talking to his father. The father says, 'Yeah, my son? He's right over there,' and we arrest the kid. But before we can cuff him up, he punches his father in the face. Drops him right to the pavement." Priore mimes the punch and the falling father.

"The kid says to his father while he's on the ground, 'You gave me up, you fuck. I killed a guy.'"

As the sergeant and Hammil leave the hospital a few minutes later, there is a radio call. Priore slaps his radio to his ear. Hammil slows the car and waits.

"Shots fired, in front of 393 Dumont Avenue."

"Check the callback," says a voice from a radio car in the area, requesting verification and further information.

"We have a callback, K. One male believed shot at that location. Housing sergeant respond. K."

Priore moves the radio to his mouth. "This is the Housing sergeant, Central. We're on our way."

When Priore and his driver pull up to 393 Dumont, a cluster of blue-and-orange Housing patrol cars are arranged in a fan on the broad sidewalk in front of the twenty-one-story building. Twenty-five women and children with opaque eyes shuffle close to where a man in his mid-twenties lies, a foot from the wrought iron fence that lines the walkway. The fountain of compassion here is as dry as powder. You can see it with police officers and with the residents. This shooting is nothing special. There is no child on the pavement, clutching a teddy bear. No one has used a baby as a shield. The newspapers will not arrive.

There is a thickening puddle of blood by the victim's shoulder. He is lying on his stomach, with a dingy plaster cast on his right forearm. His brother squats on his haunches on the far side of the hip-high fence. "Breathe easy, breathe. Just breathe slow." Like a partner in a Lamaze birth, he is coaching, helping his brother stay alive until the EMS arrives.

A little boy strides up to Priore. "I'm Born Son's brother," he lies. Then the child offers some unsolicited opinions on the conflict between Born Son, a local drug dealer, and Bobby Schulman, a Housing cop who has been trying to lock Born Son up. "Schulman isn't shit," the kid pronounces. "Schulman just wants to steal Born Son's Jeep."

Priore looks at Hammil and rolls his eyes.

The cops stand by, as numb and inactive as the residents, making halfhearted attempts to keep the curious away. Only the brother acts as if there is anything more than a dying pigeon on the pavement.

"Stay down. Breathe," he repeats, holding his arms straight out with his palms down, the signal baseball players use to tell a base runner to slide. It is late afternoon and a shadow spreads over the scene as the crowd waits for the bus. The pool of blood on the pavement congeals.

"Oooo, is that liver?" a little girl wants to know.

As the bus pulls up, the brother, alone spurred to haste, vaults the fence and clears a path through the crowd, pointing to his bleeding sibling. The shooting victim is hoisted onto the tight white sheets of the gurney and rolled to the ambulance. With a whoop and a holler from its siren, the ambulance pulls off. The crowd quickly melts back to its early summer business. A boy bounces a basketball off to the right.

Back in the station house, Sergeant Priore remains in fine spirits. "Man down at 393 Dumont. Not likely," he tells the officer, a lieutenant, behind the desk.

"I hope it was Gilliam," the officer muses.

"It was," Priore is delighted to inform him. "Hey, lieutenant," he jokes. "We don't have a scrip on the shooter. It was probably *you*." He leans over the desk and performs a mock frisk on the duty officer. "Let me take a look at your gun."

A moment later the barrel-armed weight lifter Jeff Desimone walks up to the front desk with a prisoner who looks to be thirteen.

"Hey, wha's up, K.K.," a detective leaving the squad room says, greeting the kid.

"I thought you said you were never arrested before," Desimone says to the boy.

"I said I never been arrested for stealin' no *car* before."

John McMullen, a wisecracking Irishman, is standing near the glass front door in his street clothes. He is in a grand mood, about to walk out the door for a two-week vacation. But first, he has something on his mind.

"I've been meaning to ask you." He addresses Desimone, who is staring at his tiny prisoner, shaking his head.

"Yeah?"

"How big are your arms?"

Desimone twitches. It would take McMullen to ask such a question. Querying Desimone about his arms is a scary thing to do, like asking Cyrano de Bergerac about his nose. Luckily for McMullen, Desimone appears disposed to answer. He leans against the gray restraining bar and takes a long look at his right arm, where his bicep is laying siege to the fabric of his short-sleeved uniform shirt.

"Last time they were measured?"

McMullen nods. The lieutenant stops writing and listens. A hush descends on the front room of the PSA.

"Nineteen and three quarters."

Ten minutes later, after Desimone has led his young charge to the holding tank, there is another call from 393 Dumont. "Retaliation," Priore speculates.

But it isn't. The front door of an apartment on the seventh floor is smeared with blood.

"Don't touch the door, boss," an earnest-eyed uniformed cop says to Priore as the sergeant steps from the crowded elevator.

Domestic dispute. Like the residents of Brownsville themselves, the police pronounce the word "*dis*pute," with heavy emphasis on the first syllable. Hammil comments, "My wife asks me what the hell is a *dis*pute?"

Inside, there are three rooms full of police officers and family members contemplating the crime and the victim, an under-grown forty-year-old woman dressed like a teenager. Her wispy but strong body offers a contrast of weakness and strength, health and decrepitude. The woman is either a marathon runner or a substance abuser. A friend, a woman who has fled the scene, slashed her from the spot where her jawbone meets her neck to her clavicle. The wound is dangerous, but the woman is resisting aid, waging a mighty battle against the state of shock that descends on her as the EMS workers try to persuade her to ride in a wheelchair down the hall to the elevator and out to the ambulance.

"Assault one, disfigurement," Priore announces to Hammil as he documents the crime in his thick black memo book. Priore is the very picture of professionalism. There is a benign symmetry to his features. His dark hair and gleaming black mustache go perfectly with his hat, when he wears it, and with his uniform. He is a remarkable police officer, but his attempt at irony falls short. All he can manage is the tone of cheap complaint that is the one-note song of the New York City police officer. "Probably plea-bargain to disorderly," he says.

Finally the wounded woman allows herself to be rolled out.

She presses a piece of gauze to the wound. Between great shivers, she mutters threats: "I swear to God I'm gonna fuck her up." The woman is more worried about her role than about her wound. She refuses to see herself as a victim, refuses to be seen by others as such.

The performance doesn't work. Two women in their warm weather outfits, a white-and-red-striped sunsuit and an orange tank top over biking shorts, take a moment to observe the severity of the knife wound as the victim moves the hand with the gauze away for a moment to step up into the ambulance.

"Oooo. Somebody cut me like that, it's time to shoot to kill," the one in the sunsuit observes.

"I'm gonna get the fuck out of Brownsville this summer," says the other.

J.R. JUNIOR

The next day Gary Lemite is on his meal break, seated on one of the old couches in the officers' TV room across the hall from the locker room. No one else is in the room. The mounted television is silent. The only sound is the clink of metal on metal, somebody doing fast repetitions in the weight room next door. John Reynolds, nicknamed J.R., an ultra-savvy street cop who was one of Gary's training officers, strolls in and settles across from him.

J.R. is something else. He has a WASP name but the jet-black hair and raven mustache of a Mediterranean, the dark eyes of a Valentino. He has nine years on the job. His father was a city cop. According to the NYPD way of looking at things, Housing police is a second-class department that works in third-class neighborhoods. Appointment to the Housing police means that an officer will spend his career patrolling the projects where, according to the Housing police union, he is five times as likely to be shot at as NYPD cops throughout the city. When the city started assigning officers to the Housing police by lottery, a wave of fear went through NYPD families like J.R.'s.

J.R. had read every book there was about New York City police. He could recite the names of officers killed in the line of duty as if he were quoting Scripture. But the Housing police it was. On the first Thanksgiving after he went on the job, his old man looked down the groaning table and frowned at his son. "Pass the gravy, *Housing*," the old man snorted.

Today J.R. has something on his mind. "I just resigned from OSC," he announces to Lemite, referring to Operation Safe Community, his plainclothes unit. "Too much bullshit. I'm going back to uniform. Midnights." Midnights, haven for lost souls, promised land for the easily annoyed. "Eleven years of midnights and out," he repeats.

Lemite nods. J.R. has a glittering reputation he gained as the PCO assigned to the Howard Houses, a complex just three blocks from Sharron's Saratoga Avenue address. J.R. walked into Howard like a sheriff in a western town. He got to know the people, the old ladies trying to make it to the store for some household items, the single mothers trying to raise their kids. Then he went head-to-head with the mad agents and the slingers who were making life hell for everybody else. He simply intimidated the perps until they folded up shop and moved their business somewhere else.

"I'm gonna need a partner," J.R. adds.

Gary slows his breathing and cocks his head, trying to appear cool. He knows he is receiving a most flattering proposal.

"My last partner was the baddest guy in Brownsville. He hit a guy once, the guy's feet went six inches off the floor. My partner's fist was under his chin the whole ride up. I need somebody, above all, to watch my back. Can you fight? Have you got balls?"

"Yeah," Gary answers without hesitation.

"How do you know?"

Gary thinks for a moment and shrugs. J.R. is satisfied.

Midnights. It is 12:30 A.M., the beginning of their shift. After a few days of riding with J.R., Gary knows the routine: the rookie gets the dirty jobs. He circles the RMP, checking for dents. Then he leans in and removes the back seat. He scoops up a handful of newspapers and a soda bottle and pauses to check for any drugs and weapons that were "offed" by a prisoner during the previous shift. The drugs could get somebody in trouble. The weapon could get somebody killed. Gary replaces the seat, slides in the front, and turns the engine over. He checks the gas gauge, feeling behind the sun visor for the gas card he will need to refuel.

The radios are quiet, so the partners ride over to the Greek coffee shop on Fulton by the bus depot for a cup of coffee. When the girl at the cash register tosses her black hair and beams at Gary, J.R. issues his first directive.

"I don't care if you flirt with her for twenty years. Don't screw her. She'll end up pissed off. And I don't want anybody fucking with my coffee."

Then it is the streets for eight hours. Night after night, the midnight streets, with Reynolds teaching, Lemite listening, watching. "I foresee a plethora of good arrests," Reynolds predicts. He's right; the collars start pouring in. If Lemite has a hunch — "Hold it. J.R., back up. I think that kid is carrying something" — Reynolds respects his instinct. More often than not, Lemite is on the money. In the mornings, Lenti and Kammerdener look at the arrest reports and shake their heads.

"Somebody has got to do something about these people," Gary says, looking out over the windy dark streets of Brownsville one night a week after his partnership with J.R. has begun.

"Who are *these people*?" J.R. asks. "It doesn't work like that. Remember that it doesn't matter if a guy is an asshole. If he's not acting like an asshole *today*, he's not an asshole *today*. Tomorrow, things may be different. But today you treat him with respect. The only thing a person out in Brownsville is looking for is a fair shake. Like in a fight. You know how you ask for a fair one? That's what I give them, a fair one."

It is 3 A.M.; a call comes over about shots fired by two males in a burgundy Lincoln. J.R., driving across Sheffield at Glenmore, spots the car on Blake, and with a howl of his siren hooks a half-turn so the RMP sits headlights to headlights with the suspects' car. Gary leaps from the RMP with his gun pointed.

"Show your hands out of the car. Put them on the roof where I can see them," he commands, striding toward the vehicle.

A search of the Lincoln produces no weapons. After the men have driven off, J.R. drives around the corner and stops in the dark beyond a streetlight. He stares at Gary.

"You're embarrassing me," he growls. He reaches into his shirt pocket and lights a cigarette. "What did I do?"

Gary is quiet. But J.R. wants an answer.

"Where did I stand?"

"Behind the door of the RMP."

"Why?"

"Cover."

"Always do your talking from there." J.R. blows smoke out into the summer night. "When you approach a car from the rear, tap on the trunk to make sure it's closed. There could be a shooter in there. Remember, when you're dead, I'm the one who is gonna have to knock on your door and tell your wife."

A few days later, a man slips out of Gary's grasp after a street pursuit. "Don't grab the guy by the shirt," J.R. advises with a grin. "He can run out of his shirt, but he can't run out of his hair."

The next night J.R. stands in the doorway of a kitchen, next to the refrigerator. The partners have been called to the ninth floor of a building in the Tilden Houses for a domestic dispute. A mountain of a man has violated an order of protection against his ex-wife, punched her, terrorized the kids. The man is stand-ing, foam-flecked and ready to rumble, in the kitchen, the worst possible place to try to effect an arrest. There are all kinds of weapons within the guy's reach. J.R. nudges Gary gently out of the room and addresses the problem.

"Let me tell you how this is going to be," he begins. "I am going to place you under arrest for violating an order of protec-tion against your wife, who called us. You punched her and you are definitely going to jail."

"Step on," the heaving bruiser challenges. Gary is behind, un-sheathing his baton, ready to do his part. The wife and kids have fled to a friend's apartment. The boldest of the neighbors are craning their necks in the open front door of the apartment to see the fight.

"No, no, wait. I haven't finished," J.R. says, raising his eye-brows and waving Gary back. "As I was saying, I am going to place you under arrest. You may resist. We may fight. I have no doubt that you can kick my ass. But my partner is behind me. He will jump in. Before he does, he will radio for help. If neces-sary, we will bring cars from Manhattan till this room is full of cops. Make no mistake, you *will* be arrested. Now turn around and place your hands behind your back." The cuffs only close one click around the man's huge wrists. J.R. looks over his shoulder at Gary and rolls his eyes.

As the cops escort the man down the hall, J.R. puts a hand on the head of a five-year-old who stands weeping near the eleva-tor. "Daddy's all right. Everybody's gonna be nice now," he says.

As they walk the man out the front door of the project to the patrol car, a voice taunts the arrested man with a rhyme from behind a curtain in an upper window. "See ya. Wouldn't wanna be ya."

Dealing with people in Brownsville, where nerves are frayed so fine they can be lit by a hot glance, is not a simple job. J.R. is a master, but many of the cops in the PSA don't have the easy touch.

"It's not only that they don't know anything about black people, or that they are not sensitive," a retired black Housing cop says. "It's that they have no humility. When I first walked into a family dispute and I looked at this old gentleman who was on the edge with some family problem, I said to myself, 'Who am I, a kid, to tell this man who has seen and been through so much how to deal with his problems?' I was humbled. Some of these fools walk in like they own the place and start telling people where to stand and how to talk."

After the big man is safely locked up in the back room of the PSA and the paperwork is done, J.R. and Gary ride out for a last cup of coffee. Their shift is nearly over. It is almost eight o'clock in the morning. As their sector car rolls down Sutter Avenue, dozens of junkies are showing up already for their methadone a hundred yards from a day-care center on Powell Street. On the opposite corner, Rony Shoman and his brother, Zaid, are rolling up the steel gates that blanket the windows and doors of their supermarket. Rony casts a jaundiced eye over his shoulder at the congregation of dope addicts, who will soon shift across Sutter Avenue to spend the rest of the morning in the parking lot of his store. There they will socialize and sell various forms of pills among themselves, including "spitbacks," doses of methadone that are dispensed into the mouth at the clinic and, as the name suggests, spit back into a container for sale.

Balancing a Styrofoam cup on his clipboard, J.R. lights yet another cigarette and explains his philosophy of police work to Gary as the two cruise past the supermarket back to the PSA to sign out.

"You don't look for trouble. If you can, you talk your way through. If a guy could kick your ass before you got the gun and badge, he can still kick your ass. But if a guy tries to hurt a cop, you make sure he doesn't go to the lockup. He goes to Brookdale."

Gary takes the message to heart. Just a few nights later, a 10-13 comes over from Transit. When J.R. and Gary pull up on Junius and Livonia, a handful of officers are struggling with a strapping twenty-five-year-old male who is pinned against a sagging chainlink fence. The officers cannot seem to get handcuffs on the thrashing man. The Transit cop whom the man sucker-punched, starting the incident, is stumbling around in the street, holding his head and moaning. Suddenly Gary lunges into the group and cracks the suspect across the neck and shoulders with his nightstick. Incredibly, the recipient of the blow stays on his feet, defiant. He cannot see who hit him, but he can guess. "Who was that? Transit? You punk motherfucker. Transit punk." Cuffed and in the back seat of the police van, the man is still shouting challenges as Gary and J.R. drive off.

"Hurt a cop," Gary says. J.R. nods.

It's difficult to stop a man from doing something that he thinks may save his life. The police have seen too much of the justice system to believe that it can protect them. They have seen the dozing grand juries, the incompetent, inexperienced assistant district attorneys, the sneering defense lawyers, and they have decided to protect themselves. It seems simple.

But just days later, it becomes more complicated for Gary. Early in the shift a call comes over. The dispatcher's voice is high and tense as she reads the job even before all the information is in, something done for 10-13s and other emergencies.

"10-13," Central reports — a robbery in progress. "Howard and East New York. Awaiting further. Who's going?" Central is buzzing. "Who's going," she demands again.

"73 Adam." The A sector car is going.

"73 Charlie."

A moment later Central has more information. "The perp is a male black, twenty-five years of age, green fatigue pants, white baseball cap."

Then a unit on the scene reports, "Central, be advised the perp made believe he was stranded. When the motorist attempted to assist him, he jumped him and pistol-whipped him. White Toyota Maxima. New York reg. Henry, Lincoln, Charlie three-two-one. Suspect is five-nine, one sixty-five, wearing army pants."

"10-5 the plate number, Central," J.R. asks, scribbling as Central repeats the number of the license plate and adds that the victim of the carjack was beaten and stripped of his clothes.

"Fucking carjacker," Gary mutters. "When I drive into Brownsville, like now, in the summer? I roll up my windows and keep my off-duty on the seat. Shit."

"Why the gun? Nobody wants that '72 Dodge you drive," J.R. scoffs. "Especially with blue carpet glued to the fucking dashboard. Who had that bright idea?"

"Guy I bought it from. I didn't do that."

The officers continue their patrol, tensing slightly every time they see a white car. An hour later, the radio reports that a white Toyota has sideswiped another car on Hinsdale and left the scene of the accident. "New York plate Henry, Lincoln, Charlie three-two-one."

"Take a drive by the Complex," J.R. directs. The Complex is a series of connected projects that run along Dumont and Livonia avenues and includes the Brownsville, Tilden, and Van Dyke Houses. Ten minutes later, J.R. stiffens like a hunting dog. A white Maxima is parked in front of the Brownsville Houses.

"Don't get too close. Just so I can get the plate," he says as Gary eases the sector car down the street. "That's it," J.R. snaps. "Stop."

The two Housing cops back around the corner and wait for the perp to show his face. Just ten minutes. A man in billowing camouflage pants appears, strides up to the car, and reaches for the driver's side door handle.

"Go."

Gary guns the RMP and nails a screeching stop beside the man. Doors fly open and the chase is on.

Gary is in the lead. J.R., behind, calls the pursuit over the radio. The two cops trail the man down a walkway through the deserted project grounds. The suspect is wearing sneakers. Gary and J.R., weighed down by bulletproof vests, gun belts, and radios, lose ground. The chase goes around a cluster of buildings and then around again. On the third lap, just as a 73rd sector car and then another arrive, the suspect plunges into a lobby and disappears.

J.R. and Gary pause at the base of the stairs to catch their breath. J.R. points upstairs, and four fresh-legged white NYPD cops charge up the steps. A minute and a half pass. As the rejuvenated Housing cops trot upstairs, the NYPD cops are already on their way down. One cop gives Gary a big wink and points to the roof. When Gary and J.R. reach the suspect on the pebble-strewn roof, he is semiconscious. Blood trickles from his right ear.

"Damn," J.R. says, pursing his lips with disapproval. "Get a bus."

The hospital report reads that the prisoner has a broken femur, a bruised heart, and a fractured jaw. The arrest report surmises that the injuries were received in the earlier car accident. But Gary has been on the job long enough to know that he has seen for the first time what the cops call a "freebie." When a crime involves a car accident, some police officers respond enthusiastically, at least in part because they know they can administer a beating and blame the injuries on the collision. The NYPD officers had most certainly arrived under the cover of silence, never reporting that they were responding to the call. Officially, they had not been at the scene.

Gary and J.R. have been together on the midnights for over a month. It is midsummer.

"Well, if it isn't J.R. Junior," Hammil cracks as Gary walks from his dusty blue Dodge to the PSA one night. The quick-study Lemite is not offended in the least by the nickname. Not for now. Tonight, he and J.R. ride down Dumont Avenue, past the Complex. It was here, in the Tilden Houses, that Willie Randolph, long-time shortstop for the New York Yankees, grew up, and here that Housing police officer Anthony O. McLean was gunned down in 1988 by Johnny Ray Robinson, a mid-level operative in the Baby Sam gang. The Housing police had been searching for an eight-year-old girl, missing for a day. The detectives had knocked on Gita Malave's door and questioned her daughter, Tashana, a friend of the missing child, but both Gita and Tashana shook their heads. The child had vanished. When McLean, a uniformed officer, started his vertical search of another building in the Tilden Houses, he surprised the armed Robinson in a stairway. "A freak accident," one of the locals called it. The girl was found at an aunt's house the next afternoon.

J.R. slows the car at 340 Dumont Avenue and, as he does most times he passes the spot, remembers. J.R. remembers everything. Sometimes his memory is a curse. J.R. sees a smiling

Tony McLean in his blue uniform and the dull gold inscription under his memorial plaque. The dark circles under J.R.'s eyes deepen; his face seems to sag. There is a shout, and J.R. turns to the other side of the street, his sadness swept away by a scowl. Across the street is 295 Dumont. J.R. and the "children of God" of the PSA 2 are not happy with what is going on at 295 Dumont Avenue.

At that address, at all hours of the night and day, a lookout stands like a cardboard cutout in the fifth-floor window. The figure, one of the Worthy clan, which has occupied the connected apartments 5A and 5B of the building for more than a decade, is watching for the Housing police. According to Housing cop Bobby Schulman, the family is nothing but a drug gang. There is no back entrance to the building, so the police can never enter without alerting the lookout, can never effectively raid the premises. "Like they built the place for the perps," Schulman laments.

The Worthys are working for a new gang that has taken over the crack trade in the Complex. The group is run by a personable twenty-three-year-old basketball whiz named Born Son, a kid who grew up under J.R.'s watch in Howard. The crew has been making life miserable for some people, good for others. Among the miserable are the people who live in the building. "We can't go on like this," a resident moans. Among the happy ones are some teenagers. "Born Son employs a lot of people in this project," says plainclothes cop Lonnie Hayes, who grew up in Brownsville. "When Born Son goes down, he's taking the eight-to-four shift and the four-to-twelve shift with him." So far the cops haven't been able to do anything but harass the operation.

In the middle of their shift on this starless summer night, J.R. and Gary take a walk up the five flights just for the hell of it.

The project stairways are known for sudden meetings and ricochets. These cinderblock passages are an unnerving combination of public and private places, places for a stolen kiss or a brutal robbery. Here the walls are freshly painted in Housing Authority yellow or beige but covered with boasts and warnings, territorial markings of young hands; "International Rude Gal," "The Gucci Girls in Full Effect," with a roster of members' nicknames below. Other stairways proclaim "Decepticons," "Crack Busters," "Dirty Bunch," "Wyona Dogs," and the phrase "LoLife$ Get Paid."

J.R. and Gary are ready for trouble as they crunch red-and-blue crack vials underfoot on their way upstairs. But neither has his gun drawn. And neither is the slightest bit afraid. Comradeship is an antidote for fear. Besides, they are the hunters, not the prey.

"You looking?" J.R. asks, wondering whether Gary is interested in making a collar, as they reach the third-floor landing.

"Nah," Gary says. "Got marriage counseling tomorrow."

J.R. jerks his head back. He has never seen Gary value anything above a collar before.

Before the officers reach the fifth floor, J.R. politely detains a cherubic young mother of three and her smiling blade-faced girlfriend on the staircase.

"Live in the building?" J.R. asks. The plump woman claims to be visiting a friend.

"At three o'clock in the morning?"

The questioning seems unnecessary. But the women endure the search of their pockets by the deferential J.R.

"Anything in here that's going to stick me?" J.R. asks, ever wary of the threat of the AIDS virus.

"No," the woman answers sweetly, her voice rising like the chiming of small bells.

Surely this is why the police are so disliked in the neighborhood. They don't go after the fearsome Born Son and his boys, Tai Stick, Supreme, and Bang. They harass good people trying to make a casual social visit.

J.R. rifles one pocket and then the other, sifting the contents like an archaeologist while Gary watches. The woman and her chatty friend seem to have no end to their tolerance for the policemen. As the search goes on, a teenage girl walks out of Apartment 5A. A scab on the top of her left ear marks the spot where a hot comb strayed. A skim of grease pins a tab of stiff bangs to her forehead. She has a smattering of pink scratches in the flesh over her cheekbones.

"What's up, Tanya?"

"Nothin'."

J.R. greets her casually, as if they have known each other all their lives. She is neither surprised nor upset to see the police, though she is a fugitive in some sense. Only sixteen years old, Latanya Worthy is a runaway, a dropout, and a petty thief, designated by the courts as a PIN, a person in need of supervision. Even the other Worthys describe her as uncontrollable. She skips down the stairs and out the front door.

"Ah-ha." The cheerful staircase hoppers are crack smokers. J.R. turns the cloudy crack pipe over and over in his hand. With his eyebrows raised, his lips pressed together, and his head cocked in gentle reproach, he looks like a kindly grandfather. In one woman's handbag are three Bic lighters, two green and one red. J.R. lets the women go with a warning. They appear embarrassed, but are probably disappointed at being barred from Apartment 5A at this late hour. They head downstairs, back to their own building.

As J.R. and Gary leave the building, they pass a couple of plainclothes cops. The next stairway hopeful hasn't been so lucky. He can't name anybody in the building he knows. His stretched skin and deep eye sockets mark him as a pipehead, a "stem." Neither of the plainclothes guys really wants the collar.

"Name three states and we'll let you go," the dark-haired cop offers.

"Rochester" comes the quick reply.

"Cuff him up," the second cop says, lounging against the chipped cinderblock landing.

"Rochester's a state," the man protests. "My brother lives there."

"That don't make it a state," the first cop instructs as he click, click, clicks the cuffs on.

PROPS

Sharron is waiting patiently in the lobby of the elevated station at Saratoga Avenue. His date is forty minutes late, but he is confident she will arrive. If she wanted to play him, why did she go to the trouble of passing her telephone number out of a moving bus on Belmont last week?

Frank witnessed the exchange. "Damn," he marveled at the time. "I didn't even know the windows of those new buses opened like that. I thought they was all air-conditioned."

Still, the new girl is nowhere in sight. The buzzer indicating another approaching Manhattan-bound train sounds its tone. Then, with a flurry, she appears, dressed in shiny black pants and a white blouse. Her shoes and fingernails are pink. Sharron slips in past the turnstile without paying as his date hands over her $1.25 for a token. It isn't that Sharron doesn't have the money. He has $40 in his sock for this movie date. It's that he does not want it to be said that he has gotten soft enough to pay his way on the train like a sucker.

In the same spirit, he refuses to scamper up the stairs, and the train pulls out of the station, leaving the two young people to face their first real conversation.

"You're crazy, Sharron," the new girl says. "I like your eyes. I'm glad you didn't wear the sunglasses."

Sharron doesn't have much to say. He lets the new girl do the talking.

"My friend seen you when we was on the street. And she said that I was scared to speak. And then the bus had came? So I just wrote the number. And gave it to you."

50

Soon the single headlight of the #3 train coming in from East New York appears. The platform shudders faintly as the cars slow to a halt. But Sharron and his date are at the end of the platform. This is a Saturday, and the train is short. The last car sits fifty feet away. Once more, a run is necessary. Once more, Sharron refuses to hurry. Wearing an oversize shirt draped over droopy straw-colored jeans, he walks with a dip and a slide. He glances over his shoulder to make sure that no one is watching before he deigns to trot the last few steps to where the new girl stands holding the closing door. She reaches out and yanks Sharron toward her. With an involuntary laugh, he swings into the train and into her arms and kisses her lightly on the neck.

When the gay couple turns to find seats on the all-but-empty car, Sharron is greeted by a most unpleasant sight. Seated directly across the aisle is his nominal girlfriend, Sheryl, shoulder to shoulder with a clean-cut boy who looks like some kind of college guy.

True, Sharron has not called her in over a week, has not been to visit her in the Linden Houses, to charm her mother and grandmother, since the play closed. But this is too much. He does not flinch or speak. His brown eyes lift over the offensive sight, and he leads the new girl up the train into the next car. Even when the train snakes around a bend at the Borough Hall stop twenty minutes later, he does not look back to the last car to see what is going on.

Sharron writes the romance off. It is just lucky, he thinks, that the new girl does not know Sheryl, that the scene was not witnessed by anybody from around the way who could spread the story of his being played by Sheryl.

On the way home from the movie on Forty-second Street in Manhattan, Sharron leads his date off the train at the Clark Street stop, where he got lost two weeks ago.

"Where we goin'?" she wants to know.

"Chill. I got a spot I know you're gonna like."

Sharron walks his new friend down to the promenade. The deep summer night rides over the harbor. A sailboat drifts in the distance, and the lights of the Manhattan skyscrapers flash like tiny diamonds. The girl at Sharron's side stares at the strolling people. No one on the promenade is looking over his shoulder. There is no sense of threat.

"Don't even feel like we're in Brooklyn. I feel like I'm in Hollywood," she says.

Sharron nods, and places his arm around her shoulder. She looks up at the mysterious young man at her side and wonders how he knows of such a spot, and what other wonderful places he has been in his life.

In fact, Sharron has never left New York City. He was born in Kings County Hospital. "My, that's an ugly child," Sharron's grandmother, Tina, said when she first laid eyes on the baby. "And it's no damn surprise, either, nasty-lookin' as that man is." "That man" was Sharron's twenty-three-year-old, dark-skinned, gap-toothed hustler of a father, who had already begun to melt into the maze of Brooklyn streets. To complete the cycle of foolishness, Sharron's daddy's people did not like Gloria's looks. They thought she was the ugly one.

One of Sharron's earliest memories is of a day when he was five. He was playing outside in the street when his mother called him from the window. He bolted across the street into the path of a car, which screeched to a halt. The driver emerged, looming and angry, loosening his belt to administer a whipping to the boy he had almost hit. He was a huge man, the image of a father who had not lingered long enough to dispense either love or anger. Sharron might actually have received a beating if his mother had not threatened the man from the window. But Sharron never forgot that incident. He remembered so well that another time, when he was actually hit by a car, sent tumbling through the air with his bicycle, he popped up and pedaled home on a bent wheel without looking back.

When Sharron was six, he lived on Hancock Street in Bedford-Stuyvesant, a vast black area of Brooklyn known in the seventies and eighties as a hellhole. "Bed-Stuy, do or die" was the motto of the youngbloods from Gates and Stuyvesant, from Boys and Girls High School. But Bed-Stuy, as tough as it was, never had the capacity for urban terror that Brownsville has now. The difference lies, at least in part, in the architecture. Bed-Stuy, like Harlem, was once home to the affluent and the middle class, who left their wide streets and brownstones behind. The apartment Sharron, his mother, and his sister shared on Hancock was a reminder of that earlier time; it was a comfortable five rooms.

More important, it was a haven from Gloria's overbearing mother. Ever since Gloria gave birth to Shawanda, things had not been right living with Tina, over on Herkimer Street, a few blocks away. Grandma had a good heart, all right. When Sharron got hit in the head with a metal stickball bat, she flew to St. John's Hospital with him in her arms. But after he was stitched up, when it was clear that he was going to be all right, she turned her anger on her daughter. "Where were you?" she yelled. "How come you aren't here for your children? These are your children. These are *your* children, these are not my goddamn kids. I raised my own kids."

Tina had not been ready to be a mother; now she was a grandmother, and she did not like it. "She had a terrible temper," Sharron remembers, "and she didn't like my father. Mommy and her were fighting all the time." The apartment on Hancock had changed all that. The relentless friction was gone. Now there were just money problems.

A year later the problems worsened. One day, when Sharron was seven and Shawanda was nine, they found themselves alone. Gloria was out paying some bills. All morning Shawanda tried to fix the blurry triple-vision TV set. She was aggravated, but she never stopped trying. Sharron was under the couch, where he found some matches on the floor. He took a deep breath and blew some hanging strings until they lay flat against the bottom of the couch. When he ran out of breath, they swung down again. Then he struck a match. It flashed and he threw it on the dusty floor. He struck another and fired one of the dangling strings. Shawanda spotted the flames as Sharron scrambled out from under the couch and ran into the kitchen to get a cup of water.

"The fire began to spread and spread until it was dangerous and uncontrollable for anyone but the Fire Department," Sharron recalls. "Everyone was out of the building but Shawanda. Then a man went inside and came out with Shawanda in his arms." Sharron was mightily relieved, but then Gloria arrived to watch the apartment gutted by flames. "She grabbed us, hugged us, and kissed us. Then she went into strong worry about our next stop." When Gloria found out that her son had started the fire, she couldn't even look at him. "I got beaten and punished for a long time, but that didn't make me feel as bad as knowing that Mommy's last resort was Grandma's house. Just knowing what I'd put Mommy through was taking a toll on my feelings."

As bad as things may have been for Gloria back at Tina's house, they weren't that bad for Sharron, who remembers his time there as "the days of my exceptional childhood." "I didn't have to worry about clothes or making a name for myself. All I had to worry about was having fun."

While Sharron was running around with his friends, having rock fights and climbing fences, Tina was holding little card parties and drinking hard, "to get away from her problems," she told the boy. "She would raise all kinds of hell once she got aggravated. To our family and friends she was known for her quick temper."

It seemed to Sharron that Gloria was hardly ever home. She was looking for a place to live, on a mission to get out of Tina's house. Then she found Brownsville. The four-room apartment on Saratoga was simply heaven for Gloria.

It was not long before she met John Hill, Jr., a member of a Brooklyn religious sect known as the Five Percenters, who called himself Alleke. Alleke hustled for a living, but he was a family man at heart. Every time he had even a little money in his pocket he would come to the apartment with brown bags of groceries so big he could hardly carry them. Sharron would spy him from the window in Gloria's bedroom, struggling with the bags down on Saratoga, and rush downstairs to help. Alleke would set the packages down and hand a few of the items on top to Sharron to carry. Soon he was living with Gloria and her children and Sharron was calling him Daddy.

But Alleke had a drug problem. He would stay away for several days at a time. More than once young Sharron saw his stepfather standing on the sidewalk somewhere in the neighborhood, knees bending slowly, head sinking to his chest, eyes half closed, in the throes of the telltale heroin nod. Sharron's stepfather no longer takes drugs. Nowadays Alleke dons his worn navy pea coat and a pair of Sharron's old sneakers and shambles over to a pocket park on Pitkin, where he drinks some and sits, slack-faced, with his cronies. His hustling days are over; even his days as an angry Five Percenter are gone. He just hangs. He is forty-five years old.

Sharron's relationship with Alleke is complicated. "The man took very good care of us when Mommy was spending time hanging around with the pretty boys. I give him respect in the house, but if I was to see him in the Burger King I wouldn't speak." Sharron admits that if his gaunt and shabby stepfather approached him in the street, there might be a problem. "If I was trying to talk to a girl I would react [negatively], 'cause he knows it is not about that. He knows."

"Me, myself," Sharron writes in "The Story of My Life," "I've been through a lot of incidents that weren't all that pleasant. I've always had, to put it in the least, to prove something. It could never be simple, no matter what the circumstances. Like being able to get the attention I felt I needed with peers, or girls, or being compatible with the homeboys around the way."

From a very young age, Sharron would do almost anything for adulation. He was nine years old when he tried to outdo some strong swimmers by launching a back flip from a spot too far from the edge of Betsy Head Pool, a block-size oasis of green water below the #3 train on Livonia. When he flipped over, he smashed the bridge of his nose against the metal edge of the pool. When he came up, his nose was broken and there was blood in the water. The girls were gasping and holding their hands over their mouths. "I guess it just wasn't meant for me to have it going on that day. The trick couldn't have backfired any worse than it did." The accident left a short, crooked, deep scar on the bridge of his nose, so deep that Sharron would say later that he was lucky it didn't scare the females away. It was not the last scar that he would earn, and the pool accident didn't teach him much about the perils of trying to impress people.

Sharron's urge to make an impression was not restricted to his peers. "When I was with my friends and we were doing something, I would always stop so the grownups would think I was a good kid. I always wanted to be good. I have a whole lot of uncles and stuff and most of them are in jail. I was going to be better."

It was at the age of thirteen that Sharron broke into song. A junior high school teacher, Miss Morley, noticed him hitting all the right notes when he was singing with the class and asked him to stay after school. She played the piano, hummed, and nodded to the boy. Sharron began humming along with her. Then he started to sing. But Morley's encouragement dried up one day, and she lashed out at Sharron in class. "She yelled at me, all nasty and mean, said I was taking advantage of our relationship. And then when she called my mother she told some lies. She said I had talked back to her, which I never did. So I haven't talked to her since that day."

When Sharron found he could sing, when he found he had the tools to turn the girls' heads, he went to work and never stopped. "I hadn't actually been confident in my features until guys who in my book had it going on started calling me 'pretty boy.' Sometimes they may not mean it in friendly terms. But all in all, it is being said."

There were still obstacles. "It was never easy." Sharron sighs. What he calls "the drama," danger and trouble, "started up early, and it kept going on. All day every day, twenty-four seven. Maybe I should take lessons on living a monotonous lifestyle, because I just can't seem to do it."

Sharron Corley is a son of Brownsville. In the Ville, it is almost impossible for a young man to behave in a way that will keep him untouched by trouble. It is not healthy to stay in the background and appear passive. But it is not such a good thing to stand out on merit, to excel with the girls, to dominate on the basketball court or in the classroom, either. The kind of admiration young men want most is that which is mixed with traces of fear. Sharron is doing quite well by Brownsville standards. On the street, he is known widely as a pretty boy, and not one who just runs his mouth. He is known as someone who "gets paid," who shows up with impressive stolen gear, as a result of his LoLife affiliation. Sharron's props have been further enhanced by the school play and his growing reputation as an actor and a singer.

THE SCREAM

Metal on metal. The front door of 380 Dumont Avenue in the Tilden Houses blasts open, colliding with its frame, and Powerful charges out. The two men who slipped in the back door and surprised him in the lobby are twenty feet behind, firing their guns. A white puff of cement fragment kicks up from the sidewalk beside Powerful's foot. He ducks into a crouch and flees like a crab out onto the sidewalk, waddling furiously along the low iron fence. From the first shot, Powerful and everybody else outside knows this is no joke. This is a hit, an assassination attempt.

The previous April, more than one hundred wild shots were exchanged across the street in a running gun battle between the Young Guns, from the Brownsville Houses, and Ninja, Powerful, and the boys from Tilden. But these shots are coming from behind, and the shooters are only steps away.

"You have to remember about these kids and guns," Lonnie Hayes says, "they don't really know what they're doing. They run up and *pow, pow, pow,* they run away. They use dirty bent-up bullets, anything they can find for ammunition, and they have no training. They don't know how to deal with another armed man. One time we had a guy that was actually aiming and shooting guys and then coming up and shooting them again when they were down to finish the job. I had the perps coming to me saying, 'Lonnie, you got to do something. Who the hell does this guy think he is, an Italian?'"

This time somebody knows how to shoot. Powerful is nailed in the leg. He crawls a few feet and is hit again and again. Then silence. Everyone on both sides of the street is running. It is hard to tell where the shooters are. Just eight shots and Powerful lies dying in the gutter on Dumont Avenue. The word on the streets is that Tai Stick has been trying to set Powerful up. And when the running stops, all eyes look across the street at the Worthy family.

When twenty-two-year-old Nikia Vinson, granddaughter of Kate Worthy and cousin to the brood of Worthys at 295 Dumont, captured the heart of young Bobby "Born Son" James, the charismatic basketball player from the Howard Houses, a coalition was formed. Born Son and his buddy Supreme came together with a slickster from the Brownsville Houses, Chris Muncie, nicknamed Tai Stick, and the many Worthy brothers. Born Son was the boss, Tai Stick his lieutenant. Supreme took care of security, and the Worthys peddled the drugs, much of it out of Apartment 5AB. Business got so good that the crew needed more muscle, so they recruited a slope-shouldered bad actor named Billy Odums, known in Brownsville and the Coney Island projects, where he had just beat a homicide charge, as Bang. Odums had been in a California junior college on a football scholarship. When he hurt his knee, he came back to Brooklyn to handle a burner for the gang that was now calling itself the Young Guns.

But the local dealers from Tilden, across the street — Ninja, Justice, and Powerful — were not happy over the rise of the Young Guns. At first the two groups tried negotiation. There were half-a-dozen meetings to settle on rules for sharing the crack trade in the Complex. There were beefs and counterbeefs. "Like they would make a deal at a meeting with some of the guys from Tilden or whatever," a Worthy explains, "that they wouldn't sell treys [three-dollar vials], that they would only sell nics [five-dollar vials]. And then somebody would start sellin' treys and then the shooting would start up, and once it started it wouldn't stop for a while. Then they'd have another meeting about who was gonna sell where, and the same thing would happen all over again."

Then there was a personal argument between some of the girls, a "he say, she say thing." The Worthy girls — Nikia, Renee, Omean — were not backing down. The "girl thing" got violent. It came down to Born Son and his boys against Ninja, Justice, and Powerful. The war was on.

Gary and J.R. are a block away, on Mother Gaston Avenue, when the call about the Powerful shooting comes over. J.R. yanks the RMP around the corner. Gary is stunned by what he sees.

"Be advised there are hundreds of people on the block, Central. I want a bus now," he stutters into his radio.

In moments, Gary and J.R. are standing over Powerful, who is on his back between two parked cars, gushing blood into the street. Dead silence. Gary watches as the veteran J.R. swings into action. J.R. checks out the burgeoning crowd and leaps on top of a parked car.

"You. You. You. Let's go. We need a path for the ambulance." J.R. points to the biggest bruisers, guys he calls his parolees, guys with jail muscles, to help him. The heavyweights, eager for a function, any function, jump to their task.

In Brownsville, time and time again the scene is replayed. When there is an emergency, scores of alert young black men stand idle, strong hands useless at their sides. Other men show up in big black-and-yellow rubber coats to put out the fires, in green jackets to save the sick and wounded, and in blue coats to keep the peace. The jackets change color, but the men who wear them are almost always white. They have the training, the tools, the authority, the respect. They get paid.

A passing Fire Department ladder truck pulls up and the T-shirted firemen scramble to stop Powerful's bleeding. There is blood everywhere, no rubber gloves in sight. Still the firemen work furiously, battling to keep Powerful alive. EMS workers push forward with a respirator and an inflatable orange device that looks like a raft for a back-yard swimming pool. They struggle frantically to get the thigh-length pressure pants over Powerful's legs.

Gary is still wide-eyed, not so much at the wounds or the crowd of gaping, jostling people, or even at the shoving between some arriving NYPD units and people on the outskirts of the event, as at the contradictions. He has heard on the street and in the PSA that Powerful is a ruthless killer, and the firemen and EMS workers are going to extraordinary lengths to keep him alive. Despite his wounds, Powerful is still breathing when the ambulance wails away from the crowd toward Brookdale, with J.R. and Gary and Powerful's mother trailing in the patrol car.

Inside the emergency room, the two cops stand aside, J.R. with his memo pad at the ready. If there is a lull in the activity, he will tap a doctor on the shoulder, slide next to the bed, and lean close to Powerful, hoping to get an ID on the shooter. The pressure pants are removed. Gary winces and turns away as a catheter is forced up Powerful's penis. The EMS technician who worked so feverishly to keep Powerful alive on the street goes berserk at the sight of the pressure pants on the floor.

"You stupid fuck!" he screams at the doctor. "I had him stabilized. You just killed him." And sure enough, in moments Powerful is dead.

The doctor stares straight ahead and draws a deep breath.

A sergeant from the PSA appears in the doorway of the room and asks Gary, "Did you ever hear the scream?"

"No," Gary answers.

"Follow me."

Powerful's mother and his sister are waiting forty feet away, around the corner in the hallway by the nurses' station. Just as Gary and the sergeant arrive at the spot, another doctor steps up. "We did everything we could, but we lost him," he tells the mother flatly.

Powerful's mother releases a noise that Gary will never forget, a rifle-shot scream, the unique result of the unbearable collision between two elements of the world meant to remain far apart, young life and death. Then she faints, collapsing on the floor.

The next night a pair of young boys call to Gary and J.R. as they ride slowly down Dumont Avenue. The kids point to a clump of grass near where Powerful fell. J.R. gets out of the car and spots an old .32 revolver half concealed near the metal fencepost. J.R. guesses that Powerful ran past his gun because the shooters were too close behind. Everyone on the block knows the Worthys had something to do with the shooting. But no one is saying a word.

PAYDAY

t is going to be everybody-on-everybody-else's-last-nerve hot, no-damn-sleep-at-all hot. And it is just the end of July. On Fulton Street, in the downtown mall just off Hoyt Street, a blue-suited man is preaching. The man holds a hefty Bible in his right hand, a microphone in his left. The words from the microphone, alternately husky and metallic, ring out. Each sharp sentence is punctuated by a blast of air, a pneumatic period. "Do you think it's gonna be that easy? Huh. When you get shot in the head? Huh. When you get shot in the back? Huh. Do you think it's gonna be that easy to talk to Jesus then? Huh. Satan might be leapin' and rippin' through the land, huh. But payday is comin', huh. Who knows what day the check is comin'? Huh. Payday is comin', huh, payday . . ."

Sharron ignores the preaching as he walks over to the check-cashing place on Fulton to cash his first full check from Brooklyn Youth Outreach. With the $320 in hand he hustles over to the electronics store on the same street to buy a beeper. He forks over $75 for the device, an unusual white model, along with $8 for the first month of service. On the way out of the store, he breathes a long sigh of satisfaction. He is now connected. Sharron does not have the beeper for any illicit purpose; he has it for style and function. Mrs. Dukes, the Corleys' next-door neighbor, is nice enough to take emergency calls for the family, but she is not going to stand for social messages, especially the harvest of phone calls Sharron expects to be reaping soon. The beeper, visible on the waistband of his pants, may raise some eyebrows among adults. But Sharron doesn't care. He and his friends, like many young black men, have nothing to do with drugs, yet they don't seek to dispel the impression that they do, because dealers have props, they "get paid."

The roadway narrows and traffic is restricted to city buses on Fulton Street west of Flatbush Avenue, creating the Fulton Mall. The shopping area is dominated by a large department store on one side and lined with clothing and shoe stores on the other. This Friday afternoon the mall is jammed with people from all over the borough of Brooklyn. The sharp smell of incense drifts down the street from the card table where a man in a white robe sits selling bundles of the stuff.

Sharron is looking for a summer shirt. As he strolls through a small boutique, he is tempted to lift a brown-and-mauve-swirled Hawaiian shirt off the rack and stash it in his pants. But he doesn't have his bicycle shorts on, or his backpack, and the Korean store owner, seated on a high chair by the wall, is as wary as a cat. Besides, Sharron thinks, what is $22? In two weeks there will be another check. Two weeks after that, another $320. And later more money. It's great having a job, he says to himself on the way down Fulton Street.

In fact, Sharron has never minded working. When he was fifteen, he got the "legit" job in a Manhattan law firm. "Any street attitude from this point was controllable," he wrote in his life story for school. "I began to become familiar with work-related people, how to speak with them, how to act around them. I picked up work skills, to continue to work if needed."

A woman, Mrs. Jacks, an office manager at the job, took a special interest in Sharron, always checked to see that he felt comfortable, talked to him and Terrance with respect. That is why Sharron felt so bad when Terrance got them both fired. Things had been slow at work anyway, not much filing or anything else to do. The boys were going in only once a week. But Terrance had the keys to the office on Fifty-seventh Street. Once, after Sharron and his date and Terrance and his dizzy girlfriend left the movies in Times Square, Terrance got the bright idea to head over to the office. He and Sharron could show the girls where they worked and maybe manage to get some "skins" (sex) on the carpeted office floor. Terrance took the boss's room, with its big desk and conference table. He was laughing about it all weekend, telling how his girl's skin squeaked on the shiny wood. Big fun. Sharron just listened. He didn't get any skins, just some kisses in the front office chair.

The video camera did the boys in. Mrs. Jacks called Terrance's house on Monday and told him not to come in anymore, and then she asked him to put Sharron on the phone. "She asked me why we did it, but I couldn't think of anything to say. She sounded disappointed."

After that, Sharron tried a couple of other gigs. He even worked at a supermarket, packing bags. But he was so obsessed with his image that the job went up in smoke the day a girl in his class mentioned that she'd seen him working. "Didn't I see you packing bags at the Associated?" she blurted innocently in front of a bunch of kids. The blood rushed to Sharron's face. His fear of ridicule snapped in him like a giant trap. Luckily, no one on hand picked up the hint, followed up the lead and "woofed" Sharron for being a bag packer. Before the scandal could spread, he quit his job. He didn't even call the boss, just never went back.

Shortly after that, he began writing and recording songs with his cousin Morris, a promotion manager for Warner Brothers Reprise records. The two worked together on and off for two years without a professional breakthrough.

But Sharron was achieving another kind of stardom. He was elected homecoming king at Thomas Jefferson High School in what everyone around the school thought was his junior year — quite an honor. The truth was that in three years at Jefferson he had earned just nine credits. "I loved going to school. I loved walking around and getting all the attention. I loved *beamin'*. That's all I would do. Talk to girls and profile. When I got home I wasn't even thinkin' about no homework, I was all about hittin' the street and flammin'." Deep in his heart, Sharron knew that he was a fake. Like the emperor with no clothes, he was the king with no credits. Still, he couldn't help but devour the attention at the homecoming pageant. "My mother was there, my best friend, Terrance. I rode on the float over to the football field. I have pictures. The girl who was queen, Lorna Mae Silcott? Lorna was fine."

Lorna Mae was certainly that. She barely came up to Sharron's shoulder, and her hips ran to thick. Her hair was unremarkable, medium length and drawn simply off her forehead — no billowing curls, no lustrous sheen, no locks down her back as the boys favor. But Lorna Mae had the most seemly, symmetrical features, almond eyes that caught the light and held it just so, and priceless brown skin that made people shake their heads in wonder.

Sharron struck up Thomas Jefferson High School's version of the perfect romance with his queen. "People always said we looked good together. I was goin' with her for a while." But Sharron found out that fame has its price. "I got so popular that it was hard for any girl that would go with me. The other girls would always give her some trouble. We wore like matching sweaters one time and the girls in the school always had something to say, like 'She thinks she's all that.' It was too much pressure."

There was no confrontation. The approval of their fans had brought them together, and it was their public that pulled them apart. Soon Sharron and Lorna Mae stopped speaking to each other in the hallway, just kept walking, turned to other companions and passed each other by.

By Thanksgiving, Sharron's head had already been turned by a fifteen-year-old freshman named Chantal. Chantal had a generous ponytail and fetching eyes under glistening black eyebrows. She was very pretty, but not a star at Jefferson like Lorna Mae. She didn't go to class much — not something that would ordinarily disqualify her from the upper echelon at Jeff — but she was too eager to please, too tiny and tentative. She was not in the school play, either. She was just another kid, but she rang Sharron's chimes.

"Chantal is pretty, prettier than the average girl, maybe," Sharron wrote in the diary that he had been keeping for the past year to help his song writing. "But her attire didn't match her beauty as far as style and name brands. But I sported her anyway because I knew how she would be if I had fixed her up."

Chantal was undoubtedly Sharron's type; her immaturity was actually an asset to him. It allowed him to dress her and mold her in the way that he liked. Much of Chantal's wardrobe came from Sharron in December and January, when they were an item. "She was short, very short, up to my chest, a very attractive girl," Sharron wrote with quaint and wooden passion. "She had an awesome walk. She looked like a little woman, a woman who would soon be by my side, walking down the aisle of matrimony."

But sometime in the spring, as Sharron got deeper into his role as Danny, he ran out of things to tell Chantal, ways to shape her. As the romance began to wane, she started dropping hints about pregnancy.

One day in April, after school, Sharron was reclining on a table in the fifth-floor cafeteria. Chantal was all over him, prattling about a baby. "My friends thought I was playing myself by being publicly involved with her," Sharron admits. He was still attracted to her, despite the mixed reviews she was receiving. But she was getting annoying with this pregnancy talk. Sharron came right out and asked her if she was pregnant and she answered no. Just a couple of days later, Chantal heard reliable news that Sharron was messing around with Sheryl, who was in the play. She demanded that he tell her what was going on, but he just smiled and changed the subject. "I could always get her to forget what was on her mind and make her laugh."

The next day, while Chantal was making what Sharron refers to as her little debut in the second-floor hallway by the security guards' room, jabbing her finger at Sharron and demanding to know her status, another girl happened by and asked Sharron if he wanted to hang out for a while. It was Lorna — "Yes, Lorna," Sharron recalls with guilty delight. "The whole thing was so cold." Sharron walked away after Lorna. Chantal followed for a few steps, then stopped and watched her sweetheart glide around the corner, out of sight. Her brown eyes brimmed with tears. She fled to the nearest stairway and ran out the side door. After that day, little Chantal stayed away from Thomas Jefferson High, just slipped out of Sharron's sight.

Sharron stands for moment on Fulton Street with the bag holding the Hawaiian shirt in his hand, thinking. He has plenty of money left. He decides to make one more purchase. Carefully, he studies the display window of a store near the end of the block, then steps inside to pick up two gold fronts for his teeth. After, he heads downstairs to the Hoyt Street subway stop with almost $200 left from his check. As he waits for the train to arrive, he shoots a swift look around him and deftly shifts his cash from his front pocket to his sock for the trip back to Brownsville.

The sign on the front of the arriving train says the New Lots

Avenue stop in East New York is the end of the line. It is hard to believe somebody did not plan it that way. Sharron, standing in the first car, closes one eye against the glare as the silver #3 train rises out of the Utica Avenue station into the sunlight, a resurrection attended by barbed wire. On both sides of the elevated track, razor ribbon drapes walls and rooftops. The Sutter Avenue stop arrives and the train moves above Brownsville.

Brownsville begins at Ralph Avenue and ends at the elevated L train on Van Sinderen Street. From there to Conduit Boulevard is East New York. On the far side of the Conduit are the family homes of Ozone Park, Queens. Brownsville and its sister, East New York, loll against the rump of Queens, hemmed in by a maze of parkways to the east and by the white enclave of Canarsie to the south. Most areas of Brownsville and East New York do not look forbidding. There are flimsy stores on Pitkin and Belmont and sagging one-family homes on the side streets, but for the most part the Ville is dominated by the symmetry of clean and well-ordered projects.

Sharron knows that if he passes Broadway to the north, he will be out of the Ville and into Bedford-Stuyvesant. If he crosses Linden Boulevard to the south, he will be heading out. By the time he reaches Flatlands Avenue, he will be far gone, and he had better not dally after dark. As he stares absently out the train window toward Canarsie, he isn't bothered by the fact that a real estate office that tried to rent homes to blacks in Canarsie has recently been firebombed. He isn't thinking about prejudice or even about how nice it would be to be able to spend a summer day at the Canarsie pier on Jamaica Bay, just a neighborhood away. His dreams do not include a modest home in a working-class neighborhood like Canarsie anyway. Sharron is dreaming about convertible cars and cellular phones. He plans to be a star. Besides, it is hard enough keeping his props up to par on his side of town without worrying about all that black-white stuff.

At the Saratoga stop, Sharron skips down the stairs, turns north up Saratoga Avenue, and walks past the spanking clean one-story Nehemiah Homes toward his apartment building. Two kids from the block, Fonzo and Fitty-sen, the latter so named because when he was younger he was always asking people for fifty cents, nod as he walks by. Nothing about Sharron is lost on the two boys. They spy his new white beeper and make a note to acquire one like it themselves someday. They spot the package with the shirt in it and wonder why Sharron did not boost whatever he has in there. But mostly they just admire what they see and plan for the day when they will have the same props.

"NO, ROBO, NO"

Hey, Mac," Gary calls to John McMullen as their paths cross in the PSA. "They're lightin' up your project again. Last night somebody capped your man Jo Jo."

"You sure it was Jo Jo?" McMullen asks, fresh back from vacation and eager for any information about the Complex, his post for the past several months, where he has been riding the Worthys so hard they have taken to calling him Robocop.

"Yeah, his leg was twitchin' in the ambulance. I think he was hit in the thigh. Probably late for his lookout shift so they shot him."

"Fuckin' projects. Let 'em kill themselves," an officer nearby chimes in. "Like a self-cleaning oven."

When McMullen arrives on the block for his shift, he sidles over and uses a key to scratch "Robo is back" onto the door panel of Tai Stick's new blue Honda Prelude, a message to the Worthys. Then he walks away, smiling.

It's all about reputation in the projects, and that doesn't hold only for the kids. The cops slip into the same mentality. McMullen, a rangy twenty-six-year-old with a gray rug of a crew cut, starts right where he left off before his vacation. He locks up Randolph one day for slinging, and Jimmy Worthy the next. Then it's Edward, and Jimmy again. McMullen knows he can't clean up the Brownsville Houses, but at least he isn't going to allow his reputation to suffer as the place goes to shit.

Kate Worthy stands near the corner of Dumont and Mother Gaston avenues with one of her tiny great-granddaughters in hand and watches McMullen stroll along the walkways of the

Complex. "There was a time when I went down South to Bowman, South Carolina," she says wanly. "I had a little house . . . brick. It was so nice. But Brenda, my eldest, was having all kinds of problems and I came back and I just stayed. I had ten head at that time. Edward, Noren, Randolph, Carlton, and Lennie all stayed with me, an' two of my daughters and their babies."

Kate's husband died and she was left to deal with a growing brood that had become an outlaw clan. "They became uncontrollable," she says. "I have to get out of that apartment. I'm not gonna die like this."

For Kate, her children, and her grandchildren, the police are loudmouthed, ignorant yahoos who can be relied on to bungle their job and demean and brutalize people while they are doing it. The Worthys and their cousins the Asburys are going nowhere and they know it. But this is their home, and they offer up a daily ration of abuse to the police, as occupied people do everywhere. It must be no different in Belfast or the West Bank. Domination, disrespect, gunfire, and death.

Many of the best Housing police make their reputation by setting a project straight. They get to know the people and they learn who the bad guys are. Then, just like the marshal in the cowboy movies, they clean out the town. Of course, the "good guys," as the police actually call themselves, don't always come out on top. With the Housing police of the PSA 2, it isn't usually for lack of trying. The stereotype of the cynical doughnut-eating police officer doesn't hold for them. Though there have been several corruption scandals in nearby NYPD precincts, a massive drug-stealing and drug-selling mess at the 77th precinct, and more recently, front-page exposure of a rogue cop gang in Brownsville led by an officer from the 75th precinct, the Housing cops of the PSA 2 don't have those kinds of problems. They may go to the Dunkin' Donuts over on Flatlands Avenue to grab some coffee, but they do not gorge themselves on sugar-coated doughnuts, and they hustle back to the Ville. They do not want to give up the streets to Born Son. They do not want to give up the possibility of a promotion to a specialty detail, and they definitely do not want to give up the overtime.

The next afternoon, Ninja, one of the players in the Tilden drug trade, is involved in a brawl in the lobby of 320 Dumont.

McMullen jogs across the street, strong-arms his way through the crowd, and separates the combatants.

"I don't want you anywhere near this building for the rest of the day," he tells Ninja.

Ninja, who is about five-ten and maybe 180 pounds, walks toward McMullen with his hands open in a conciliatory gesture. He steps all the way up to the six-foot-two McMullen and places his hands on the 190-pound officer's shoulders.

"Wha's up with that? For serious, Robo? I got to get in the building," he whines.

McMullen starts to raise his arms to knock Ninja's hands off his shoulders. But as he does, Ninja leans back and rocks McMullen with a stunning right-hand wallop to the side of the cop's pink face. Like a jolt of electricity, the word travels up through the building and across the street.

"Ninja's kickin' Robo's —" The kids, town criers of the neighborhood, can't even get the last word out before they run back to see. A huge crowd gathers. One of the saddest sights in Brownsville is people sprinting from all sides to get a look at a fight. A fistfight is topnotch entertainment for young and old; a local tough fighting a cop hand to hand is almost too good to be true.

The circling crowd stays well back. They know Robo has a gun; they are not sure about Ninja. Robo has been shaken by the sucker punch but manages his own roundhouse to Ninja's head. The cop leaves himself unprotected with the big swing and absorbs another straight cracking shot to the cheek. Now Robo steps in to clinch. He grabs Ninja by the shirt with his right hand; with his left, he rains on Ninja's head. Ninja hooks his finger under the neck of Robo's bulletproof vest, hangs on, and pounds Robo with his free hand. Like two hockey players, the cop and the Tilden tough guy punish each other.

The crowd is beside itself. "Oooo," it moans when one punch lands, "Aaah," when the retaliatory blow arrives.

The battle wears on. Not everybody in the neighborhood is rooting for Ninja. Upstairs, people are calling 911.

McMullen's radio has been dropped and kicked into the bushes. "10-13. 320 Dumont. Numerous calls," the portable sputters. All over Brownsville, cops hear the dispatcher say, "Officer being beaten by a man at that location."

Though McMullen doesn't know it, help is coming fast; foot-posts are sprinting, radio cars are wailing, mounting sidewalks to get past traffic. Still, the nearest cop is more than a block away. McMullen starts to go down, his knees wobbling. In desperation he reaches behind, unhooks the silver handcuffs from his belt, and smashes Ninja over the head with the steel restraints.

"No, Robo, no." There are people leaning out of the windows all the way up to the top floor of the seventeen-story building, and many of them do not approve of the cuff-swinging maneuver. "No, Robo, no," they howl.

The tide turns with the jolting handcuffs. Ninja sags almost to the pavement. Stooped with exhaustion, his arms slack, eyes glassy, Robo stands over the crumpled figure. Then he looks down and shudders with horror. He cannot believe what he sees as Ninja shakes his head, snorts, and starts rearing back up. The rejuvenated young man yokes the dazed McMullen in a headlock and starts pumping uppercuts. The light of the afternoon fades to dark gray for Robo; the squeals of the crowd dim to a muffled hum. Beaten, he gives up the fight.

At that moment, Robo hears a sound that brings a faint smile to his battered lips: the rasping static from the radios of the approaching police. The fair fight is over. Two guys from the 73 fly in and grab Ninja. Then the Housing cops arrive. It takes seven officers to beat Ninja down.

"When he wouldn't go down after I hit him with the cuffs, I realized he was high. Fucked up," McMullen says. "When I heard the sound of those radios, it was as good as sex."

"Look at this." Bobby Schulman calls McMullen to the door of the detective squad room an hour later. He is holding a sheet of paper with the cross statement Ninja has given describing his version of events. McMullen reads out loud.

"'I deal drugs right in front of Robo's face and he can't do shit about it. And today I kicked his fucking ass. Signed, Ninja.'" McMullen tries to laugh but coughs instead.

THE FEDS ARE CLOCKING

What the fuck is that?"
Balding, lean Bobby Schulman swivels his chair around to face the six federal drug enforcement agents in their country-boy-clean jeans and glossy shoes, behind him in the smoky alcove of the PSA 2 detective squad room. He smirks. "You mean that sound?" Schulman asks. "I'll play it back."

Schulman has been showing the agents videotapes of the drug dealing in the Complex. Ever since Kammerdener got back from FBI school, he has been talking about getting federal agencies involved in stopping the drug traffic in the projects. Schulman knew somebody in a DEA enforcement group who was looking for a case in Brooklyn. Now the DEA people are in Brownsville to consider a cooperative operation. When Schulman replays the tape, the same repetitive popping sound is heard. He pushes the stop button. "Probably a nine," he says, and lets the picture roll again. The agents glance at each other. "Sounds like it's coming from 340 Dumont — probably Ninja. Doesn't get along with the Young Guns."

In the next sequence, one of the Worthy boys is seated on a bench in front of 295, servicing a stream of crack customers. Each time a person approaches the bench, Lennie Worthy hands him a cigarette and palms a bill in return. He glances quickly at the bill as his hand slips to his jacket pocket and comes out with a pack of matches. As he lights the customer's cigarette, he passes the vials of crack, all in one motion.

"Smooth," Mathew DeJong, a pockmarked, taciturn agent, says.

"As whale shit," Schulman answers.

DeJong has spent most of his career doing water rescues and special projects for the DEA. For him and the rest of the DEA agents crowded into the room, most of whom gained their law enforcement experience as state troopers stopping cars on the interstate, the videotape of life in the Complex is amazing.

"The stuff never stops," an agent says.

"Twenty-four seven," Schulman replies, twirling the tips of his handlebar mustache. "Besides 295, Born Son and his boys are dealing out of 265 Livonia, 285 Livonia, 345 Dumont, and 312 Osborn. They have that whole side of the Complex. We're getting sometimes three thousand vials going through there on a busy weekend day." Schulman pauses for a moment. "Yeah, and they shoot people. All the time."

Half an hour later the agents flinch as they stand in the front room of the PSA, preparing to accompany Schulman on a tour of the neighborhood. It is the same hollow popping noise they heard on the tape. Only this time it is coming from somewhere above — if not from the building above the PSA, then from very close by. A couple of uniforms hustle out the front door.

"Now that *is* a nine," Schulman says over his shoulder as he confers with the duty officer at the desk, "or maybe an oowop," he adds, using the street name for an Uzi machine gun.

Several days later, the DEA agrees to assign Mathew DeJong and several backup teams of agents to an operation designed to build a case against Born Son and his Young Guns. Schulman, DeJong, and several assisting teams of federal agents will concentrate on 295 Dumont Avenue. Kammerdener wanted the feds because they have the resources, the surveillance vehicles, and the clout to score wiretaps and warrants. More important, they brandish the heavy mandated federal sentences that the K-Master hopes will strike fear into the young slingers, who have been shrugging off the modest state sentences. And Kammerdener wants to take down the slingers in the Complex because that's where Tony McLean died.

Kammerdener gives the case to Schulman. Together with DeJong, he goes about the tedious work of putting an end to Born Son's reign in the Brownsville Houses. The team moves methodically, watching and taking pictures from their unmarked van, listening to telephone conversations. Somehow word gets to the Worthys that the feds are "clocking," but the Young Guns dismiss the rumors and go blithely on with their crack-peddling business in the Complex.

Schulman and Born Son already have a history. A year ago, Schulman stopped him when he was driving a late-model BMW down Dumont Avenue. While the officer checked the papers, Born Son turned and fled into 295 Dumont Avenue. Schulman was in hot pursuit, but he tripped and stumbled onto his knees in the street, which allowed Born Son to race upstairs and hide under a bed in Apartment 5AB. The Housing cops couldn't find him for half an hour, until they brought in a dog to sniff him out. Before the cops took Born Son from the apartment, through the throngs of curious tenants, they beat him up.

"It was eerie," Lonnie Hayes remembers. "It was pitch dark in there, and all the time Born Son was gettin' his ass kicked he didn't make a single sound."

Later, in the cell area of the PSA 2, the bloody Born Son raised all kinds of hell, laughing at Schulman for tripping in the street during the chase and cursing the police.

"Callin' Schulman everything but a child of God," Born Son's mother says. "And that's why Schulman hates my son, because he was shamed when he fell and Born Son talked back like that."

In a couple of days Born Son was set free, but the threats continued from both sides. The Housing police reported telephoned death threats against Schulman. The kids around the Brownsville and Howard Houses, where Born Son grew up, swear that Schulman put the word on the street that he was going to shoot Bobby James in the back. The conflict was in part about business — the Housing cops doing the job they were paid for, Born Son trying to stay in the crack trade. But it was also personal, about reputation. Bobby "Born Son" James had the biggest props in all of Brownsville.

Born Son, the son of Margaret James, is less impressive than his name and reputation. He is an unprepossessing five-foot-nine, 165 pounds, with the bark-brown skin of his mother. He has generous lips, which he likes to keep wet with his tongue. "I didn't let him out of the house until he was eighteen years old," Margaret avows. "I kept him in, and when I heard the guns going off, it was like the wolves were howling outside." J.R. remembers Born Son around Howard as something of a mama's boy, but also as a kid who was always in trouble. "He was a punk. He used to get his ass kicked every day."

"I told him after a while," his mother says, "don't come up here with no bloody nose. All his life people have been messin' with him. The same way they mess with me."

Margaret tried to be strict. But she was working, always. First as a cashier, then as a secretary. When Bobby and his boys would cause some trouble around Howard during the day, somebody would tell the building maintenance man, Charley, and he would tell Margaret. When she got home from work there would be hell to pay. "When we saw her comin', guys would just take off," one kid remembers.

Born Son didn't spend time in the house, despite his mother's claims. And he learned things out and around Howard. The locals remember him as a kid with so much style and class that he was imitated from an early age. "You know they got that commercial about Michael Jordan, 'Be Like Mike,'" a kid from Howard says. "Well, everybody wanted to be like brother Bobby. Talk like him, stand like him. I mean, Timberland boots made *money* from people imitating Born Son. He had heart, and people fear heart."

The guys around the way describe Born Son's charisma as a mixture of intimidation and kindness. If you were his man, he would do anything for you, give you anything. Hank Walters, a coach and amateur boxer who has worked at the Youth Athletic League center in the Howard Houses for the past twenty-five years and who took Bobby under his wing as an eight-year-old, remembers that "what made people fear him later on was that terrible temper, and the fact that he always did what he said he was going to do."

Born Son was also a point guard on the basketball court, with serious "ups," or "hops," as the locals call jumping ability. "We could play him at off guard or small forward even, because of his jumping," Walters says. "But I had to sit him down many times because of his lack of control. I went up to his school when he was just a little kid and I talked to the teacher's aide. She told me, 'Someday Bobby is going to kill somebody.'"

When Bobby was just fourteen, Walters heard that he was carrying a weapon. When the kid walked into the center one night, Walters searched him and came up with a forty-five. "I told him I was going to hold it until the end of the night and give it back. Instead I gave it to his younger brother, who took it upstairs."

Hold it till the end of the night? Take it upstairs? This was not a water gun. It was a forty-five. The decision to give the gun back does not tell you as much about Walters, a reasonable man, as it does about Brownsville.

The recollection of Born Son hurts Walters. "When I was coming up, with the Tomahawks and the Jolly Stompers and whatnot, it was bad in Brownsville, but this is much worse. The kids put a dollar sign on the value of a life." Walters remembers the bell of the gym door kept ringing during pickup basketball games, and Bobby would keep running over and answering the door. Walters would catch glimpses of hard-looking guys outside. Bobby was not one to volunteer for such things, so Walters became suspicious. "I said, 'I'll answer the door next time,' but Bobby insisted." Turned out Born Son was making some kind of transactions from the gym. "I knew he had taken the other way," Walters says, "but I didn't think that he would put the other kids at the center in jeopardy like that." It costs only a dollar a year to be part of the center. Walters had pleaded with Bobby for years; after that, he had to cut him loose, for the safety of the others. He gave Bobby back his dollar and told him he was not welcome at the center anymore. Hank Walters had lost his battle for Bobby.

There are several stories about how Born Son got into the drug business. Margaret blames Nikia Vinson. But the Howard locals remember things differently. They recall that when Bobby became too old to play in the "D and D" basketball tournament, a heavy dealer around Howard nicknamed Trip, a man with drug connections all up and down the East Coast, gave him a spot in the organization. Reportedly, Bobby was part of a triumvirate that included his cousin, Knowledge, and a fellow known as Rockhead. Street history says Knowledge killed Rockhead. He was convicted and incarcerated for the deed, and Born Son found himself in charge of Howard at an early age.

Walters made one last plea. When he was sure that Bobby was in the drug business and saw that his younger brother was getting involved, he pleaded, "For God's sake, turn your brother loose." According to Walters, Bobby complied. "I do respect him for that," Walters says now. "His brother is now in school, I heard. Bobby was such a remarkable kid. He had a scholarship to Laurinburg Prep in North Carolina, but I heard that when he went down there he just started with the Brownsville mentality, threatening the coach and all that nonsense, and the coach wasn't having it."

Back in Brownsville, contracts were being put out all over the place in Howard. If Bobby was not shooting people, it was said, he was influencing his growing passel of disciples to do so. "One thing I know," a local says, "is that he could never leave Howard Houses unless he had his people with him. If Bobby went past Langston Hughes or Brownsville Houses? No questions. They would start shooting at him."

Bobby did get shot. When he recovered, he got shot again. "I used to search their room for guns, but I never found them," Margaret says unconvincingly. "He wasn't into that mess with guns and all that. Born Son just kicked ass. He kicked natural ass."

BLOODY VALENTINE

My name is Sharron. I'm your representative from the Brooklyn Youth Outreach."

Mrs. G., the Youth Employment supervisor at P.S. 32, glances up from her desk at the young man brandishing a smile in front of her. Sharron extends his hand. "Hello."

As Mrs. G. reaches toward him, Sharron seems to soften slightly. He almost blushes. His eyes hurry to the floor. His handshake is as light as silk.

"I'm kinda new at this, but . . . I'm checking to see how many kids you have, and if there are any problems. Are the kids getting along?"

The middle-aged Mrs. G. pauses for a moment to consider the new site monitor. Sharron raises his deep brown eyes and levels them at her. Can he be flirting? Mrs. G. has to smile. "Yes, as a matter of fact," she begins, "I'm delighted you came by today. I've been meaning to call. But maybe you can handle it. I've got two girls, sisters, who have the flu. I asked them to stay home, but they just keep coming in. I'm sure they want the full paycheck, and I can understand that."

In a moment Sharron is handling the problem like a veteran. After a call to Aubrey, he escorts the coughing, sneezing sisters to the Outreach all-purpose room, where they will spend the rest of the week out of the mix of children at P.S. 32.

Sharron is one of Aubrey's favorite workers now. When the director passes, he squeezes Sharron's arm supportively. Sharron has picked up the routine quickly, even designed a persona for the position. "I present myself as a young man who is mannerly and can handle all technicalities and responsibilities," he tells Ms. King on the phone.

It's too late to travel to another site today, so Sharron hangs around the basement office of the Youth Employment Project on East Street until quitting time, then strolls to the subway to go back to Brownsville. On his way to the train station, he straightens and slumps his shoulders, experimenting with first this look on his face, then that. The late July sun dances beside the landmark Long Island Railroad building on Flatbush Avenue. The big clock there reads six o'clock. As girls walk by, Sharron mumbles. One slim girl in neon green culottes and a lime green T-shirt pauses.

"What'd you say?"

Ah! This is the way it was always supposed to be, Sharron thinks. A pretty boy loose in a city with thousands and thousands of girls.

"You say something?" she repeats. Sharron sidles up the sidewalk like a cat. He hadn't said a word. Why devise some witty phrase? If the girl wants to talk to you, he reasons, she will jump at the mumble.

"I said, I like your eyes," he whispers.

"I like your beeper. I never seen a white one."

Sharron allows himself a bare moment to revel. He has learned not to lose his head; anything can happen. The girl's boyfriend could happen by. Like an experienced salesman, Sharron knows it is important to close the deal. He quickly scribbles the girl's phone number on a scrap of paper like the three or four he has in his pockets and the dozen in the drawers and on the floor of his room. He writes his beeper number down and hands it to her. As he speaks, the sun blazes on Atlantic Avenue, delivering a fierce sting down the length of the scar on the left side of his face. As the girl studies his sincere brown eyes and his handsome wounded face, he sticks the pen back in his pocket, cups his hand over the scar to shield it from the sun, and smiles so she can see the two new gold fronts on his teeth.

Sharron got the scar around Valentine's Day, just before Sharon King tapped him for the drama program last spring. His wardrobe was down then, and that meant he was low. He had gotten caught in the rain with his white Polo sweater, and it was all stretched and messed up. Worse, either Shawanda or Alleke had made off with his jeans jacket. It was out of the question to ask Gloria for money to go shopping. She was out of work, had her own problems. And Sharron had his pride.

The LoLifes were on the move, what they call a "meow," an expedition. Franklo and Beklo, the crew. This would be a rush number. Eight LoLifes charged into a leather store in the Fulton Mall; Jaylo punched out the owner, who was the only security. The crew grabbed as many coats as they could and jetted into the Saturday afternoon throng. Sharron heard later that two guys got snagged by undercover Transit. Not Shalo. He floated home in the back of a gypsy cab, tired but happy.

There were four leather bombers, two for sale, one for a girl-friend, and one to keep. On the next Monday, Sharron headed over to Jeff to try to sell the two. The price, $100 apiece. The bombers were easily worth $300. No luck at the school, so Sharron jumped on the bus up Pitkin Avenue and got off in front of a laundromat around the corner from his house, where he used to hang out. Being seen in the neighborhood peddling stolen merchandise was nothing to be ashamed of. Sharron and others around the way often avail themselves of $100 sneakers for $20. It is just the way things work. In fact, selling stolen merchandise is a way to show that you are a person of substance, not just a front; that you do "get paid."

Inside the laundromat, Sharron shopped the leathers to several neighborhood guys.

"What's up?"

"Not a damn thing."

"I got some bombers." Sharron turned to the left and right to include the half-dozen people around. One of the boys, a guy he had seen around for years, somebody he knew just well enough to greet on the street, nodded toward Sharron's knapsack, and Sharron shifted it around in front.

The boy looked at a tuft of brown leather bulging from the bag and lifted his chin.

"A buck," Sharron answered.

His strategy of staying out of the neighborhood has disadvantages. His alliances on the block were marginal. He checked the faces around him. The vibrations inside the laundromat were no problem. But no one wanted to spend any money, so with his two leathers crammed into his big bookbag, he walked over to his apartment on Saratoga.

As Sharron quit the laundromat, two boys, one stocky, one lanky, followed him. The heavier one he used to hang with a while back. The skinny guy he had seen around a few times.

"Yo, wait up," they called from the corner, and he stopped walking. Maybe they had changed their minds about buying a leather. The situation did not look good, but there was no running away. Here, you deal with things as they come up. Besides, just maybe, Sharron thought, his instincts were wrong.

The stocky kid approached; the other lingered several feet behind. The first youth kept walking and headed into Sharron's building, where he stood between the outside and inside doors, waiting. Any fool could see it was a trap. Sharron bought time with a front. He reached his right hand into his jacket, placed the bookbag with the leathers between his legs, faced the kid in the street, and demanded, "Wha's up?"

The boy by the curb, about Sharron's size, said nothing. Instead, he gave a quizzical look to the boy inside. Something had gone wrong with whatever plan the two had hatched in the laundromat. Sharron turned his head to check the guy inside the door, and the kid on the street lunged for the bookbag, snatched it, and backed around a car at the curb. With one hand he shook the jackets out of the bag. With the other he brandished a seven-inch knife. His head disappeared behind the car for a moment while he stooped to pick up the leathers. Then he dropped the bag in the street and shifted to the far side of Saratoga.

The inside guy popped out, emboldened. "Give it up." He pointed to the shearling Sharron wore.

"You're lucky I don't blow your fucking head off." Sharron summoned his foulest scowl — his coldest grill. That part of the front worked.

The kid's eyes widened, his jaw fell slack. "I'm not really down with this," he sputtered lamely, and scampered across the street.

Sharron climbed the yellowed marble stairs to his mother's fourth-floor apartment, thinking. The situation was not a disaster. He had not lost his own shearling. There were still two leathers left. It had been a nerve-racking experience trying to peddle the things anyway. The real damage had been done to the reputation he had worked years to construct. Robbed in front of his own house by guys he knew. Something would have to be done.

Sharron grabbed the scratched and pitted gray-handled .25 Raven he kept high in his closet and strode outside with a great display of irritation. He traveled the stretch of Pitkin Avenue to the laundromat with the small gun held at his side, walked up to the steamy window, and peered inside. No sign of the robbers. No one could say that he had been robbed like a pussy. He had looked for the thieves with his burner in full view. Done. Sharron wrote the coats off.

The next day was the day before Valentine's. Sharron was looking good. His fade had taken a while to grow into its own since the last cut. Now it was the perfect length, glittering gold on top, rich brown below. He was looking so good he could not bear to stay in the house. Outside by the pay phone, his phone, he profiled, shooting handsome looks all the way across the avenue while he waited for the girl in front of him to get off the line. He was catching all kinds of attention. He would not call Chantal; that could wait till Valentine's Day. Even when he couldn't reach the girl whose number he had written on a tattered orange bus transfer ticket, he decided to stay on the corner as long as the damp wind would allow.

"Shit." The two coat-snatchers were crossing Saratoga on the other side of Pitkin. Sharron spun on his heel and hustled upstairs for his gun. This time he charged outside, lest it be said by anyone who was watching — and it is axiomatic for Sharron that people are watching — that he abandoned his spot on the corner at the sight of the two thieves. Besides, he was angry. It was one thing to match wits with the downtown department stores, he believed, something else to rob somebody around the way who has props. This was all so complicated. So much drama. Every move had to be timed, considered, and perfected. The spirit of the players had to be robust, the reflexes wired like a race car. If Sharron did survive this life, how would he ever leave it behind? How could he sit down with a book, laugh off a social slight, focus on long-range goals?

The two Pitkin Avenue rip-off guys were heading back from the pizza shop up the street when Sharron reappeared. "Walking around like it's O.K.," Sharron thought. "Mad disrespect." They had two other guys with them now. One was a friend of Sharron's, and as the group came toward him, that kid stepped discreetly off. Sharron stood on the corner of Pitkin and Saratoga, his soft palm pressed to the chill metal of the Raven in his pocket. The moment was howling in his ear.

"It would have been so much easier to be a girl," he thought.

There were three, but Sharron had the gun in his coat. His clammy palm tightened and loosened around the handle of the baby burner.

"Whatever," Sharron said.

"Whatever," the stocky kid answered. He was the one who had stayed in the building, the punk who had fallen for the gun front. He was not going for any front this time. It was Sharron's mistake to think that the next order of business would be a knuckle-number. Things had gone too far for a fistfight.

The only plays he had were to cap somebody, shoot right away, or step off. He waited. The stocky kid flipped his slice of pizza in Sharron's face. Hot oil and cheese to the bridge of the nose, to the eyes. As Sharron reached up to brush the pizza off, the kid made an arcing move with his right hand, a glancing blow to the side of Sharron's face. Sha dipped low to punch back. Then the blood.

The kid had struck with a razor, laying Sharron's face open from ear to mouth on the left side.

Sharron glanced at the horrified eyes of an onlooker in the street and sprinted off with his hand over his face, pressing the wound. He took the stairs two at a time and burst past Gloria to the mirror. What he saw — the howling gash, suddenly bloodless white — buckled his knees. In a moment there was blood over everything.

"Jesus Christ." Gloria fought tears as she bent over Sharron where he sat glassy-eyed on the edge of the tub. She pressed a towel to the torn flesh and stroked his forehead. She raised her wet eyes to the light bulb on the ceiling. "My baby." She felt a rising sob, and canceled it with a curse. "Dammit." She had always feared losing Sharron. "When you go to college, I'm comin' too," she always told him. "It's O.K.," she said now. But she was not sure.

Four hours later, after Gloria had rushed Sharron to Brookdale Hospital, where a doctor put fifty-five stitches in his face,

Sharron sat at home, staring into the dark. The door of his room was shut tight, the window draped with a blanket. He sat motionless on his bed all that night and the next day, thinking, the left side of his face drumming with every aching pulse beat. Like a brooding monk, he mulled over sin and salvation.

One side of the ledger was the grievous attack. The kid who cut him lived in the neighborhood, was sure to be seen again. He should be shot, at least shot at. Anything less would be a serious breach of Brownsville ethics. Sharron had the loaded Raven, hidden again, high in the closet. A short walk in the street to the laundromat would do the trick. Then, come what may. On the other side of the ledger was the fact that there could be a gunfight. He could be killed. Even if he whacked the kid, everybody would know who did it. There would be big-time beef, payback. If he played that off, avoided the avengers, he would probably be jailed.

Sharron had never committed violence for its own sake, was never one to express himself through the quick punch, the knife, or the pistol. He had other resources. His violence had always been tactical, designed to win friends and ward off future attacks. He was a singer, a pretty boy, or at least he had been. Alone in his room, he was frantic with worry over what the scar would look like. "What are your suggestions? We'd like to know." The sign hanging on his door mocked him. Angry, injured, and depressed, he stayed in his room another day, and then another. Sometime in those hours, as the droning sounds of endless TV game shows drifted in from the next room, he decided not to reach for the Raven.

On the third day, Chantal came running. When Sharron had not called or arrived with a card on Valentine's Day, she had been angry. But when she heard the news she rushed to his apartment and pushed on the door to his room.

"Sha, 's me. Chantal."

No answer. In the afternoon shadows, Sharron sat up on the bed and twisted his back to Chantal, the hood of his Champion sweatshirt pulled high. He was not receiving visitors. She worked her way slowly to his side, lifted his hand, and kissed it. She slipped her hand under his white sweatshirt and let her freshly lacquered pink fingernails ride across his back. Then she lowered his hood, touched her cool cheek to the left side of his face above the bandages, and placed her petal lips on his. Sharron sank onto the bed and pulled her down.

Chantal wasn't much good at anything but making love to Sha. She held him close and kept him warm, squeezed her eyes shut and clamped her teeth tight to keep from crying out. And when it was over, Sharron collapsed in a fit of giggles.

"It was beautiful," he says now. "I always remember that, 'cause that is the moment when I got my confidence back. After that moment I was all right."

In the way of things, Sharron's scar turned out to be an asset. Nothing could give a pretty boy instant credibility on the street, a permanent membership in the hard club, better than the looping scar that ran across his sweet face. The scar was not gnarled, jagged, or lumpy. It was almost graceful. It was danger, mystery, everything a scar could be.

THE TROOPS

How 'bout some cold ones tonight? Johnny Ray Robinson got thirty-five years. *That* you got to drink to." Gary is speaking out the window of his RMP to Eddie Hammil and Jimmy Galvin, who are standing in front of the PSA. "Those bad boys are gonna taste awful good after that warm piss Maritza serves." Twenty minutes later, he tries the hard sell on a young cop who has a new live-in girlfriend. "C'mon, how many nights in a row you think you can spend with the bitch before she gets sick of your ass?"

It's a Monday night in mid-July. Gary is beginning to feel he's nearing the end of his partnership with J.R. Rumors have been floating around the PSA that Reynolds will soon be offered a detective shield. Besides, word has come that Robinson, the guy who killed Tony McLean, has just been sentenced to thirty-five to life. By midnight, Gary has recruited almost a dozen bodies for his drinking party.

The heavy wooden front door of Katie Cassidy's on Woodhaven Boulevard deadens the sound of roaring engines of cars that make the traffic light outside and squealing brakes of those that don't. It is precisely one o'clock on a Tuesday morning, a time when bartenders in most places have seen their best customers come and go. But Cassidy's is a cop bar, and the four-to-twelve tour will be along soon. It is then that most of the PSA 2 drinking will go on. The troops sometimes assemble over by "the Wall," a secluded spot along a desolate stretch of Belmont Avenue, which the K-Master declared a "cooping prone location," an unauthorized resting or socializing spot. Other nights they drink at Cheap Charlie's in Ozone Park, or here at Katie Cassidy's.

The walls of the front room of the Queens establishment are decorated with wooden plaques marked "Roscommon," "Tyrone," "Kilkenny" — the counties of Ireland. In the center of the low-ceilinged room sits a rectangular bar; beyond the bar, a room with tables and a fireplace. The regular cops, in jeans, sneakers, and black satin PSA 2 windbreakers with white skulls and crossbones stenciled on the back, arrive and congregate around the side of the bar closest to the front door. One fresh-faced cop wears a T-shirt with the words "Attitudes adjusted while you wait." Shirts like this, including one with the slogan "Boys on the Hood" over a cartoon of a black youth handcuffed over the front of a patrol car, are popular with the officers. The detectives, in discount Sy Syms suits, stand in pairs on the other side of the bar. Cops and detectives rarely socialize, but the Johnny Ray Robinson verdict brings both groups out tonight. "That motherfucker's parole officer isn't even born yet," a detective rasps across the bar.

The detectives sit on barstools and talk softly. They smoke cigarettes and finger short glasses of hard liquor. The cops stand and drink beer. Tall brown bottles of Budweiser are everywhere. The cops scrupulously buy each other rounds of Bud. Not one officer drinks another brand. If one guy slows his drinking for a moment, he becomes the focus of derision. "What? You got empties. You weak shit. Beer for the man." Not single bottles but handfuls of Buds are pushed across the bar at the slow drinker. Stacks of soggy bills cling to the bar top.

"I'm callin' for an investigation," the young cop with the new girlfriend announces. Heads turn. "I'm wearing a condom. I get finished. I look down, and the fuckin' thing has disintegrated. All I got is a rubber band around my dick. So I write a letter to the company. They write me back, 'The condom has to be donned correctly.' I write back, 'I am an experienced condom donner, and I *donned* the condom correctly.'" He finishes to a roar of laughter.

Officers congregate not only to exchange stories and to feel the camaraderie, so strong it hangs in the room like a scent, but for the practical purpose of making sure they are not out drinking alone when a stickup takes place. Stories abound of gunmen who have come down the bar searching and robbing each patron. As the thieves come toward him, an officer has to make the life-and-death decision whether to draw and shoot it out or let the perps discover his shield and gun. With an eight-beer handicap, the cop is likely to make the wrong move.

Without effort, Gary is already one of the boys, though he is the only black man in the room. He listens while one cop revises the story of the Robo-Ninja fight to the satisfaction of the audience. "The guy who kicked Robo's ass was just out of Riker's." Everybody nods knowingly. "Just out of Riker's" is a compliment; it means that the person is a muscleman.

A detective overhears and gestures with his drink as he speaks. "It's a bitch when you take somebody to trial. These guys look like skels on the street. A couple a months in jail, three meals a day, lifting weights, a clean suit, and the jury is looking at this guy and saying to themselves, 'Why would they mess with this nice-looking fella?'"

"Look at Reynolds." Hammil points to J.R., who is grinning on the fringe of the group of Housing cops. "He likes these guys. Tell 'em about your amnesties." J.R. shakes his head. Two more beers and he'll be ready to tell some truth. Now he'll let the others take the lead.

"Fuckin' J.R., when he was the PCO in Howard and he caught a guy fuckin' up on a holiday, he'd let the guy go. A lot of times. One time J.R. checks this mope's ID and finds out it's his birthday and he lets him go."

"Birthday amnesty," J.R. concedes. "But what'd I do the next time we caught the guy?"

It's Hammil's turn to concede. "You launched him down the stairs."

"*And* gave him a dis con," J.R. adds, referring to a summons for disorderly conduct.

"What about the time the lady wanted you to make her kid go to school?" another cop interjects. "J.R. slaps the kid around and sends him to school, and then later he fuckin' *calls the school* to make sure the kid is there."

"What about the lady in Cypress that's afraid of ghosts?"

J.R. can't resist this one. "Lady is all fucked up. Second time in the night she calls me and Gary, worried about ghosts coming in her apartment. So I check all the rooms. She's followin' me. I check the windows, and then I tell her to bring me a bag of flour. I sprinkle the flour in front of her front door. 'What's that for?' she wants to know. 'This way,' I tell her, 'when the ghost comes back, he'll leave a footprint. *Then* you call us, and we'll have a clue.''

Confident in his storytelling, Gary leans into the center of the group and launches into an account of a recent experience with an emotionally disturbed person.

"I'm workin' with Paddy. We got a call in Unity, an EDP, and there was this guy on the floor by the door of the apartment. The guy has the most incredible build you have ever seen. He looks like a statue. Shoulders to here. Waist this small." Gary puts his half-empty beer on the bar to perform the identifying gestures. "This guy is lying on the floor of the apartment nude, and he has his arm around like this, and he has his thumb up his ass." Small bubbles appear at the corners of Lemite's mouth as he giggles. "No shit, he has his thumb up his ass, and I ask him what's up. He says, 'I've got it. There's a bug up my ass and I've got him.' No shit. This guy thinks there is a bug up his ass and he is holding it in with his thumb."

Gary takes a small glance over at his chuckling mentor, J.R. "So I tell the guy that his thumb and arm must be getting tired. You should have seen the size of this guy. He *musta* just got out of Riker's. I tell him that he should switch thumbs. He takes one hand out and goes to put the other thumb up his ass. I grab one hand, Paddy grabs the other, and we cuff him up. I swear."

Several hours and dozens of stories later, the party breaks up. As Gary turns the ignition and the old Dodge kicks over, he thinks to himself, *I love cops.* When he was asked on the psychological segment of the police test why he wanted to be an officer, he knew enough not to tell the truth. "I am interested in the good salary, the possibility of advancement, and the benefits," he said. He had learned from friends on the force that it would not be good to tell the examiners that he craved the action, had dreamed about being a cop since he was a kid.

Even in the middle of summer, he waits several minutes for the car to warm up. He has had eight beers. He double-checks over his shoulder before he pulls onto Woodhaven Boulevard and maneuvers carefully over the wet leaves on the dark and quiet streets of Queens toward home. A blue and white NYPD cruiser pulls alongside after Gary makes a very slow left turn. Not a flicker of concern crosses his face. It is virtually impossible for a New York City cop to get a ticket for drunk driving from another cop, unless there is an accident. This was the way he knew it would be: the respect, the adventure, the stories, the friends for life.

Gary is doing great on the job, but not so well at home. Just two days ago, on a dripping Wednesday afternoon while Gary was working a four-to-twelve, Lisa moved out. She took Erica and Zach with her to her sister's house and now refuses to come back. And there is not one person in her whole family who is sticking up for Gary, telling her that she should try to work it out. True, she is white and he is black, but color never seemed to make a difference before. Now Gary is beginning to wonder. How is it that her brother-in-law and her mother, whom he has taken to calling a "master hypocrite," can turn on him like that? It is as if they are glad to be rid of him. There have been arguments. Sure, Lisa was still mad because he stayed away the day that Zach was born after they argued over the boy's name. But you'd think that should be washed away by now. Then there was that time in the spring when he had the collar with the two teenagers he chased into an apartment. He had the perps, but no stolen property, no weapon. He called one of the kids' mother at work and she told him he could search the apartment if an adult neighbor was present. He found the stolen wallet. He found the gun. That collar was too beautiful to hand over to another cop, wedding or no wedding. But that was all in the past.

Gary parks the Dodge on the silent street and walks up the driveway to the side entrance to his empty apartment. He scoops up Erica's tricycle with one hand, unlocks the door with the other, and steps carefully down the steps in the dark.

The separation stretches from days to weeks. It's not fair. Lisa has no responsibilities at her sister's house. No wonder she likes it there. A lot of her problems have nothing to do with him, he reasons. She had a tough childhood. Gary remains supportive. Whatever she wants to do is all right. He buys a book on codependency, goes for a visit with Lisa to her grandfather's grave. What good does it do? It seems that every week they are getting further apart.

When Lisa first left, Gary sampled the single life, and didn't like what he found. There were a few halfhearted interludes, a cute Dominican woman in the Brookline Houses with a white Caddy and a big laugh. Gary is young, good-looking, a little shy. He will do all right with the girls, just as he did before. But he is a family man now. He pines for the folded clothes and the meals on the table. He wants nothing more than his wife and kids, happy and under one roof.

That will take money. Collars for dollars.

J.R. is gone too. An interview he had taken for the detective squad two years ago bears fruit, and he is off the midnights and bound for the Bronx squad. Gary calls over a couple of times and leaves a message, but gets no call back.

One afternoon at the PSA a week after J.R.'s transfer, Sergeant Priore hollers over to Gary, "Hey, you see J.R.?"

"No," Gary says.

"Yeah, he was here to pick up his check. I told him you were downstairs."

"Really. That fuckin' J.R."

EDDIE ON THE BACK

Three A.M. in an apartment on the third floor of the Van Dyke Houses. Forty-five teenagers are squeezed into a pitch-dark living room. A huge gray tape player on the floor by the open window is humping a question to a hip-hop beat by the group Naughty by Nature: "Are you down with OPP? Yeah, you know me." Over and over the song asks, "Are you down with OPP?" meaning other people's property, props, or pussy. The tile floor is slippery with spilled beer. But it's too crowded for anyone to fall down. The raw smell of reefer floats from the bathroom. Shouts and laughter almost drown out the music, which is now a speed-word rap song, "Ghetto Bastard," also by Naughty by Nature.

When the woman who rents the apartment scheduled a weekend trip to Atlantic City with a couple of her card-playing girlfriends, her sixteen-year-old daughter began some preparations of her own. A sophomore at Thomas Jefferson, she couldn't resist the idea of throwing herself a belated sweet sixteen party. She spread the word. Kids in the school were talking about the upcoming affair for a week. The girl is not totally irresponsible, though; she has put the gold-painted table lamps in the hall closet and slid the couch into the bedroom and turned it against the wall so nobody can sit or spill anything on it.

A jam blocks the open front door and kids trail down the hall to the elevator. People are still arriving. There's been no trouble so far. Then the stairwell door swings open and a pride of young lions step into the mix. Bashim and the Howard Raiders are in the house. These are not even the real tough guys from Howard; Born Son and his Young Guns are too old for this kind of stuff.

This is the next generation, the ones who stood by, leaning on their bicycles, watching as Born Son fought his way to the top of the Howard heap.

Bashim, a "cock diesel" or burly, streetfighter, has cooled out in the past year. Always a smart kid, he is starting to show it after six years in high school. At five-eight, 240 pounds, he has finally found something to do with his bulk besides kick ass. Last spring, Carol Beck got him to join the football team and go to class. He's not starting trouble, and he is not carrying a gun anymore. But his boys are. Of the ten who arrive, seven are "strapped."

Before Bashim and his friends can get through the front door, there is some kind of trouble. Someone has brushed against someone else.

"I didn't say you *touched* me, son. I said you *stressin'* me," one of the originals at the party growls to one of Bashim's boys, and the Howard crew backs out, nice as you please. For once, the presence of so many guns seems to have a pacifying effect on the situation. Outside, one of Bashim's group decides to try out his burner. "When you get a new bis you wanna shoot it," Bashim says. "We go on the roof, in the park, wherever."

Bam bam bam bam.

It is 3:20 A.M. Gary Lemite is with his temporary partner in the Eddie sector car, three hours into his shift, cruising Brownsville looking for a collar, when the report of "shots fired" sings over the radio. The call is redundant, because shots are blasting through the limp air above the patrol car.

Some of the officers — sons of cops, like J.R.; grandsons of cops — were born to this business. Gary feels he was called to the job. A new rule says you have to have a couple of years of college to be promoted to sergeant and lieutenant, even if you place high enough on the test. Gary is not a good student or a good test-taker. He has no "hook," or connection, in the department. The only other kind of promotion open to him is the detective path, by appointment. He has decided that he's simply going to collar up so many criminals that the brass will have to reward him. The strategy has drawbacks. This is not a professional sports league, where performance is carefully calculated and rewarded. There are racial politics and jealousy, and there are the bullets.

Beep beep beep. On the tail of the staccato radio alert, used for 10-13s and serious crimes in progress, comes the voice of the dispatcher: "Numerous males with guns. Blake and Powell, no callback. K."

Before the fluttering message has died in the sector car, a flock of preteenagers spill out of the breezeway between the project buildings and scatter across the street. They bound like young deer. Then the automatic gunfire comes again. The sound is almost festive. The scene is like a carnival. But the *hut hut hut* of the gun is too mechanical for real fun. It is the chuckle of a cruel machine, a robot's laugh.

Two cops from the 73 who pulled up on Bashim and his boys around the corner are in pursuit.

"Adam-Boy, we're behind 'em . . ." The voice of the running cop from the AB sector car comes over the radio, weak and thready, as if he's crying.

"10-5 that location, Adam-Boy," Central responds. "You're breaking up," the dispatcher warns as the cop on the street begins losing contact.

"Eddie on the back," Gary hollers into his radio as he jams the Eddie sector car to a rocking stop to back up the cops in the AB car. He rolls out the door and sprints across the sidewalk, headed toward where he thinks the shots are coming from. The canyon walls of the clustered buildings produce echoes, and he is not sure exactly where the guns are until he sees a muzzle flash. He has learned not to run with his gun drawn unless he has to. Head up, right hand at his side, pinning his holster to his leg, and left hand holding the radio ear high, he charges into the flat face of gunfire.

A number of factors contribute to the strange sight of cops running into gunfire without taking cover. There is courage, and the fact that if a cop does it several times, he begins to feel he'll never be hit. There is also the fact that the kids most often do not fire at the police. They shoot at each other. They run from the police. The rule is not iron-clad.

Lemite continues his headlong plunge through Van Dyke as the last of the shots are heard ahead. A voice drifts down from a window high above: "Fuck the police." Life is so tough in Brownsville that people don't have the luxury of prejudice. If someone can be trusted, is willing to help, that person, white or black, cop or drug dealer, is quickly known as "good people."

Nevertheless, police as a group are simply despised here. The slightest confrontation brings the mantra *"Fuck* the police, fuck the *po*lice, fuck the po*lice."*

Gary Lemite, in search of a future for himself and the family he wants to keep, and maybe of an intoxicating rush of adrenaline, charges down the walkways in pursuit of youths unknown.

Two kids fly through the back door of a nearby building with the 73 driver right behind. "Goin' in. Blake and Powell. 85 forthwith," the driver hollers, indicating that an officer is in need of immediate assistance.

"10-5 the *address,* Adam-Boy," Central yells.

The driver's partner, Sergeant Marino, dashes around to the front of the building to head the kids off if they run out that way. At the corner of the building Gary runs into him. Marino has worked this twelve-to-eight shift for the past decade. He is the best, a legend; they call him the Ghost, because every time there is a shooting he appears.

The shooters are inside. Marino's driver is bounding up the stairs from the back entrance. With guns drawn, Lemite and the sergeant wheel and barge into the lobby of the fourteen-story building. The sergeant heads straight to the stairs. As he enters the cinderblock stairwell, there is a clatter of steel on cement. A bull-necked youth with droopy eyelids emerges from the stairway and begins to walk casually out of the lobby. Lemite connects the clatter to him and orders him against the wall.

"Got a gun," Marino yells to Gary. He has scooped up the discarded weapon, and he continues upstairs. Gary tries to cuff the mumbling youth as Marino takes the stairs two at a time. In the second-floor hallway, Marino's driver is kneeling on the back of a small-boned teenager with his gun to the back of the breathless youth's head. The driver knows there is more than one gunman around, and he hasn't heard or seen his partner in half a minute. He howls, "Raise my partner, raise my partner" into his radio, like a man searching for his wife in a shipwreck.

Downstairs, Lemite is having trouble with his prisoner. There is the smack and thud of bone on flesh, grunts. Gary's partner arrives and dives on top of him and the kid, and they wrestle on the floor. Soon reinforcements flood the lobby and the pile gets larger. In an attempt to get a shot at the kid, the cops on the outside throw stomps and wild punches. Gary and his partner get the worst of it.

Bashim and his boys gather outside to watch through the window. Their guns are safely hidden on top of car tires, where the cops don't look. Twenty black youths study the fifteen white officers and the café-au-lait Lemite.

"Those vests won't stop a .357," a kid warns a pair of cops who are just arriving.

The kids eye the heavy youth who is being dragged roughly to his feet. The second teenager is brought downstairs by Marino and his driver. Marino produces the gun, a futuristic semi-automatic .22 Intratech machine pistol with holes in the barrel, ostensibly to cool the weapon down but really, as one Housing officer puts it, "so that when the guy starts pumping it on the corner, all these sparks start coming out and he looks like a real gangster." There is also a cracked plastic banana clip with thirty rounds in it.

"You ain't had a burner," Bashim yells, hefting a forty-ounce bottle of beer in one hand and pointing with the other at the slender youth just brought down from the second floor. "Punk. Lettin' the cops think you got a gun. I'm gonna fuck you up." Bashim curls his scarred upper lip. Later he will say, "I just said that shit to throw the police off."

All eyes are on the gun now. The officers handle it, and one cop seems to adjust a broken piece on the clip. "They broke it. It's inoperative," one of the Howard boys outside announces, with the implication that the inoperability of the gun is crucial to the charges its possession will bring. "They tryin' to fix it." The onlookers are right. If the gun cannot fire a bullet, the assistant district attorney will reduce the charge from a felony to a misdemeanor.

"Why cops always want to beat people up?"

A cop near the door overhears. "We're not here to trade blows with you people."

"'Cause they can't fight" comes the answer from one of Bashim's boys.

"Cops don't fight. They kick ass," the cop replies.

A thirty-year-old woman walks through the lobby as the police prepare to remove their two young prisoners. She turns to the gathering of surly boys. "Why don't you boys go out and look for some girls? Where are the girls?" But the boys are not interested in girls just now. Their eyes are still on the gun.

Bashim, cradling his bottle of brew, pretends he cannot get over the fact that the slim kid is getting credit for being a gunman when he isn't. "You think 'cause the cops got you, everybody think you got a burner," he scoffs.

A burner, a jammie, a bis (for "biscuit"), a kron, an oowop — there are a score of ever-changing names for the gun, the most recent scourge of Brownsville and East New York, the one single element that has changed a desolate existence to a nightmare. The gun is the drug of choice for the young here now, giving them release from the shadows of doubt to the white light of power and respect or death.

The herd of big young cops in dark pants and pale blue summer shirts moves out of the lobby and through the growing crowd of teenagers and residents. The cops have a hundred feet to go before they reach their cars.

Pop. Whoosh. Pop. Bottles are flying off the rooftops of the twelve-story buildings, shattering to fine dust on the pavement. The officers break into a trot, dragging their prisoners with them. "Brownsville ticker tape," a cop mutters as he guns his patrol car away from the project.

It's four o'clock in the morning. The PSA is deserted. Behind the steel bar at the front desk, Lemite's collar is playing the hardrock, won't give his name. The desk officer puts it simply: "You act like an asshole, you spend an extra couple days in the system. Put him in as a John Doe." The officer leans closer. "Who stepped on your face?" he asks.

"The kid saw everybody run upstairs, and he rolled off the wall before I could cuff him up," Lemite says simply, and leads the kid into the cell area.

Lemite then sits and fills out the endless papers, the voucher for the gun and ammunition, the on-line booking sheet, the complaint report, and a lab analysis form, used when the gun is to be tested to see if it can fire a bullet. He is methodical. He wants to be known as a cop who can do it all, not some street cowboy who can't handle his paperwork. It's almost 6 A.M. when he stands, flexes his knees, and snaps a Polaroid of the gun and the rounds piled up on the gray desk. It has become custom at the PSA with gun collars to display pictures of the guns, especially exotic weapons like the Intratech machine pistol, in a glass-framed board on a wall in the front room.

Gary is a young man, but the signs of middle age are already there. He's not a weight lifter like his tightly wound younger brother and cops Del Migliore and Jeff Desimone, and he is no runner like Kammerdener. In a couple of years he's going to be broad in the ass and fleshy, unless he has a change of habit. Tonight he's satisfied. After securing his gun in his locker downstairs, he hitches up his gun belt and strides across the room to where the young gunman is standing in his cell. Time for fingerprinting. Like young lovers, hand in hand, Gary and his prisoner cross the room to the alcove where the printing is done. There Gary's pale hand guides the kid's dark hand, pressing each finger in turn onto the fingerprint pad.

Next comes the ride down a deserted Atlantic Avenue to Central Booking, on Gold Street, near downtown Brooklyn. The kid in the back seat says nothing. Every few minutes he winces. His cuffs are fastened behind him, and they are tight, digging into his wrists every time the car lurches over a pothole.

There are dozens of prisoners on the benches in the second-floor holding area at Central Booking. "Step along. Go to the door and stop," an officer orders a row of men who are handcuffed to a long chain. They are heading out of the building to be arraigned.

It will be afternoon before Lemite meets an assistant district attorney, who will determine the charge in the case. He knows enough to make his account short and sweet. If the kid has warrants, he will remain in the system. If he has no warrants and the ADA does not like the gun-in-the-stairwell story, he might be on the #3 train back to Brownsville by nightfall.

At 3 P.M., Gary is asleep on a sheet of newspapers on a bench in a waiting room. There is a hit on the fingerprints. An old rape warrant drops on the kid, who turns out to be seventeen years old, and the ADA decides to stick with the gun charge. Gary smiles faintly as he trudges over to the A train stop. His feet are hot and damp, his eyes dry and red. He has been awake for more than twenty-four hours, and he will have to change trains to get back to Brownsville. But he got eight hours' overtime and he caught a bad guy.

Gary is scooping up guns off the street at a rate that has some cops calling him Magnet and others Lead-ass, because they are sure he is going to get shot. But Gary is not about to make any stupid mistakes. And because they are best for overtime, he sticks with the midnight tours, when Kammerdener and Lenti are home with their families. But the numbers are speaking for themselves, and Gary is given the quarterly achievement award for excellent police work. A color photograph of him in full dress uniform hangs just inside the front door of the PSA.

OLD-TIMERS

Outside, it is breezy-warm. Inside, the Brownsville Recreation Center gym is flush-heat, full-sweat. It is late Saturday afternoon, in the third week of July. There have been five basketball games already, from the Pee Wee to the Legends Old-Timers game, and now the finale, the Pro Am, where the young stars of the neighborhood and players who have not made it to the NBA, who play in the minor league or in Europe, mix with the famous guys. Together, they strut their special moves for the hometowners.

Fly Williams threads his way down court, pounding the basketball on the golden gym floor. With a grimace, he pushes his ruined body into the air and casts an arcing jump shot toward the basket. The ball careens off the rim. As both teams charge past him toward the other basket, Fly stands rooted, glowering at the hoop of iron as if it has wronged him grievously. The packed crowd roars approval of his antics while Fly heads to the sidelines, calling for a substitute. He settles on the bench with a backhand wave to his admirers.

"He only has one lung, you know," a grandmother tells the people in her area of the bleachers. Like Rasputin, Fly is mad, connected to a higher power, and indestructible.

The game is the highlight of Old-Timers' Week in Brownsville, seven days of events that begin with a parade from the Betsy Head Pool to the storied Brownsville Recreation Center on Linden Boulevard and a "reunion night" featuring impersonations of Nat "King" Cole, Sam Cooke, and Billie Holiday. No rap songs or hip-hop. This is the generation born to the folks who led the black migration to Brownsville in the fifties, the women and men who grew up in the Ville when it was a mixed neighborhood.

This basketball tournament is sponsored by Jerry "Ice" Reynolds, of the Orlando Magic. The shirts he donated for the occasion bear his name. Earlier in the day he emerged from his Lincoln Continental, a six-foot-eight prince bouncing a baby in his hands.

But if Ice is a prince, then the king, the failed and wicked genius of the basketball court and of the Ville, is Fly Williams. At his best, in his prime in the 1973–74 season, the Fly was the third leading scorer in the country, when he played for Austin Peay State University. At six-foot-five, he was quicksilver. He could rise off the ground like a fool, extend like a rubber man, and shoot the ball like a machine. He had long arms and moves unknown. But like Sharron Corley, Fly was addicted to attention. As his short professional career with the St. Louis Spirits, of the American Basketball Association, crashed, he continued to unfurl his streak of insanity like a banner.

Insanity plays differently in places like Brownsville, where the authorities are uninvolved in the commerce of daily life. When people are poor and live in close quarters, when the perks are few and the competition great, there is an undeniable advantage in being known as crazy. It grants a person space. No one wants to lock horns with a madman. There were times when Fly would drive his Rolls-Royce to the Howard Houses basketball court and leave it in the middle of the street, creating a traffic jam while he watched a game. Whether it was an act or not, the folks in the Ville appreciated the virtuosity with which Fly played the part. They simply loved him and his game. Fifteen years later they still do.

Fly is here to play, but just a little. On the bench, he is still gasping for breath after five minutes of rest. He is beloved not because he was a success, and not even because he was such a spectacular failure. Like Leonard Bernstein in a crowd of music lovers, Fly draws people to him because he was once *chosen*, once stood with the gift glowing in his hands, and everybody remembers.

It is easy to believe that Born Son and his Young Guns are devoured by the love of money. They themselves will say that cash money drove them into the street with their "eightballs," brown paper bags full of crack vials, and their semiautomatic weapons. The motto of Sharron's LoLifes, scrawled over court-house stairwells, is "Money, ho's [women], and clothes." But it's not the truth. Ice Reynolds, still out on the Brownsville Recreation Center court running like an antelope, is a millionaire and a successful pro ball player. But he will never have the aura in the Ville that Fly has. Now, after becoming addicted and surviving a shotgun blast to his back, Fly sits on the sidelines, wizened and stooped but still deeply admired for his gift, and for the fact that he never really showed that gift to the world. He cared more to flaunt it in the Ville.

Waves of admirers flow Fly's way as the game continues, and there are a hundred small claims on him. He folds over in pantomimed collapse. "I'm takin' names," he says. "I'm not kickin' ass, but I'm takin' names."

He can talk that talk, but he cannot play that game anymore. He contents himself with shouted bons mots from the bench. A claque of spectators is more interested in his reaction to the game than the court action itself. A diesel-powered six-four forward vaults to the rim. "The parade passed you by," a fan shouts to the slouched Fly. "I seen that. I seen that," Fly assures the crowd. The move was nice, though nothing like the buccaneer game Fly used to play.

One fan, sucking on a forty-ounce beer in a wet paper bag on the far sideline, isn't having it. He strides across the court during a time-out and confronts Fly. He is angry, and it doesn't have anything to do with Fly's decrepitude. Everybody falls apart. The harder you live, the faster you crumble. Apparently, the man is upset about truth. In Brownsville the truth is important. The wider world is full of hype; people with nothing to offer get rich and famous off the lies. But Fly Williams was always the real deal. Now he isn't. He should not be playing the game.

"You're a fake," the man sputters to Fly's face, "a fucking fake."

Fly screws up his face and waves the man off. He is too old, too cool, and too tired to deal with this.

"That's an old-timer now," a fan yells in Fly's defense.

"I can't hang out," Fly announces to the crowd. "I'll leave the drivin' to y'all." With that, he retires from the court and heads out the door, followed by three or four fans, who keep a respectful distance.

The weekend is a revelation. The people in Brownsville, the folks of the previous generation, are warm and happy. There are hugs and laughs all around. "Don't be fooled by Brownsville," an old-timer warns. "If you take a fast look, all you see is bad things. You stay around a while, you'll see the good things. This is a community that comes out in shifts."

Most days Brownsville is no place for old men. Very few elderly or even middle-aged people ever walk the streets here. The ones who do shuffle with children or sit on benches. The church folks, slow-moving gents and women in exultant hats, come out on Sunday mornings, and in the summer, here at the old-timers' activities, the giddy survivors emerge for an entire week. Whenever these people gather, an observer would swear that he was in a small happy southern town where the conversation is about family and barbecues. These are people who have arrived at this time and place with epic dignity and uncommon good cheer, who know more about right and wrong than an army of police and legions of judges.

Old-Timers' Week is the time when the history of the neighborhood comes to show its face to the present, like a vigorous grandparent leaning over the bed of a dying child. A block away from the newly renovated and spanking clean Recreation Center is New Lots Avenue, one of the most lawless and dangerous places in the country. The street is an unending drug bazaar. The ramshackle subway station above, New Lots, is a study in peril. Transit police rate the station one of the very worst in the city.

Basketball player Tony Jackson, the legendary St. John's University jump shooter, knows better than to venture onto New Lots. He and a retinue of his admirers gather around a fan of cars across Linden Boulevard and hold a tailgate party. But when guys like Smiley Smith, Big John Jocko, and Leroy Wright walk over to get a six-pack at the bodega on New Lots, junkies beg them for money as if they are tourists. These rare robust middle-aged men are outsiders in their own community.

Gita Malave, a lovely forty-three-year-old redhead with lofty cheekbones, is here with a boyfriend who coaches the old-timers' basketball team. She has lived in the Ville for twenty-three years but remains aloof from the palpable good cheer. She is standing outside on the cement ramp to the gym when her sixteen-year-old son Kendall appears, his T-shirt soaked with sweat and his eyes glittering with accomplishment.

"Mom, who am I?" he demands.

"You mean, what are you?"

No, no, Kendall presses. "Check out the hat. Who am I?"

Gita eyes her son's cap, with a Chicago Bulls emblem bordered by glittering rhinestones. Kendall has fifteen or so different sports hats he has decorated.

"You're a clown?"

"Don't fool around, Ma. I'll give you a hint. I was bustin' dudes at the park. Goin' between my legs with the ball and usin' dudes." Kendall pauses and points an index finger at his chest. "The kid was just usin' 'em. Couldn't nobody hold me."

"Ahhh." Gita sighs, lighting a cigarette.

"Don't be smokin', Ma. Secondary smoke is gonna shorten my career. Who am I?"

"O.K., you're Michael Jordan, all right."

"You're close. I am Jordan, yes. But they call me *Baby Jordan*." Kendall howls and sprints off into the afternoon sun.

"How come they don't have something like this for the kids?" Gita grumbles, watching her son move off. "All this food around and they don't even have a free hot dog to give to a kid. Half these people don't even live here anymore."

Gita is not really thinking about recreation anyway. Ever since she started college, she thinks about little besides her courses in legal studies and her six children, aged thirteen to twenty-four, all of whom live at home.

There is a bittersweet taste to this week. It isn't just that these people have lost what used to be a hometown; that has happened to almost everybody. It is not even that the ones who have stayed here live under the threat of the gun. It is that the youths who are growing up, the ones who skulk around the edges of the proceedings, hanging around, who keep showing up at the Summer League games run by Jocko Jackson, looking to make their mark, trying to find a place out of the line of fire, will never have the memories that these aging men toss back and forth, that they live from. For the boys who survive, what will there be to look back on?

"They're animals," Eddie Hammil says as he drives by 295 Dumont, casting a cold eye up at the lookout in the fifth-floor window. "And the grandmother is the worst of the lot."

Kate Worthy is not at the old-timers' festivities. Instead, she is sitting on a bench in front of 295. She and her husband moved in 1951 from a small town called Walterboro, near Charleston, South Carolina. They settled in Brownsville, and when their entire street was condemned they relocated to Bed-Stuy. They headed back to Brownsville as soon as an opening came up in the projects in the late seventies.

With her pastel pants suit and sensible crepe-soled beige shoes, Kate looks like any other retiree. She is not a large woman, nor is she slight. She keeps a pack of Kools in one pocket of her pink double-knits, a supply of heart pills in another. She is quick-witted and feisty, nobody's fool. Her coppery face droops; her eyes are suspicious slits. But Kate can be charming.

The cops have another view. "She's a perp," Bobby Schulman insists. "We have her name on the registration of at least two of the vehicles the gang has, an Audi and another one."

Kate is probably not actively involved in the crack operation, as the Housing cops say, but her loyalty is to her family, hard as that may be. "I don't know what happened," she moans. "They just won't listen. They're always running in and out. I told them so many times to keep the door closed."

"Keep the door closed" — a pitiful solution, to be sure. But even the Housing police have developed a mania about the front door of Apartment 5AB. They have tried everything they can think of to slip past the lookout and burst inside to catch the Worthys with the goods. A couple of times they have been successful. A bantam rookie actually scaled the bricks in the back of the building like a rock climber, surprised the lookout, and barreled inside. He didn't find the cache of drugs he was looking for, but he was the talk of the PSA for months.

While the cops are trying to get in, Kate is trying to get out. Her application for retirement housing out of Brownsville is on file and she can hardly wait.

"It's just crazy," she says. "I went to court four times this week. Everybody's in and out of jail — Lennie, Edward, Randolph. They send me letters. When I have a little money, I send it to them for commissary. I do love to go to Atlantic City with my little money, though. I haven't been able to go for some time. Those slot machines talk to you. They do," she says with a sly smile.

Kate seems resigned, strangely removed from the collapse of her family. When did she lose control, what did she do wrong? There was a series of shockwaves. While the rest of America was living through the Vietnam War, a heroin epidemic was lashing the black ghettos. The future was written for the Worthys when Kate's daughter Brenda married a heroin user named Ray Asbury. The change from hope to daily disaster came on fast. Soon Brenda was an addict. The couple had five children: three boys and two girls, Renee and Omean, both of whom had children before they were fifteen. All those kids grew up in a festering world of syringes, dope buys, strangers, and stupefied parents. The second wave was AIDS, which killed Ray Asbury at the age of forty-two in 1988. Brenda was stricken with the disease a year later. Renee and Omean and their children were on their own. The third wave, crack, blew the doors down. Into this chaos rolled cars loaded with weapons purchased from gun stores in Virginia, brown boxes packed with guns delivered by mail order.

"I can never get a good night's sleep," Kate says now. "They come running up the stairs. There are so many faces I don't know who's who."

Kate is interrupted by one of her granddaughters, who is sitting beside her on the bench. "Tell about the time they was gonna shoot Randolph."

"Couple of guys," Kate recalls. "I never saw them before and they came upstairs and they had Randolph on the stairs, pointing one of them big guns, I call them cowboy guns, at him, talking about they were gonna kill him. I told them to get their behinds out of the building." Miraculously, the gunmen obeyed the seventy-year-old Kate.

The contradictions of living with the bitter smoke of the guns are stunning. Teenage gunmen are sent on their way by unarmed grandmothers. Even Kammerdener exploits the maternal factor. The "safe homes" antidrug program changes locks and provides some police presence in targeted buildings, but the linchpin of the initiative is the tenant representatives, most often mothers and grandmothers, who are stationed in the lobbies. Their job is to tell the drug dealers to move on. A lot of the time it works. The women have known the kids since they were little, and the natural instinct is to take the business somewhere else.

But Kate isn't even holding her own. She knows the chronology but not the reasons. "It all started with Noren and the mailbox. The drugs. The kids just got used to it."

The following Monday afternoon, DEA agent DeJong and Officer Schulman, dressed in white overalls and caps, disguised as Housing Authority painters, heave a large plastic bin on rollers up the ramp into the lobby of 340 Dumont Avenue, in the Tilden Houses. No one pays them any mind. Painters go in and out of the building regularly to work on vacated apartments. But Schulman and DeJong don't have paint supplies with them. Instead, another federal agent sits in a fetal position inside the bin. Upstairs, in an empty eighth-floor apartment, Schulman, DeJong, and the third agent set up shop. Schulman adjusts the video camera, DeJong squats on an overturned twelve-gallon drum and produces a notebook to record drug activity, and the third agent watches the door for trouble. There are no tables, couches, or mattresses in the apartment, just four walls and a window that looks directly down on 295 Dumont Avenue, across the street.

"You say you wanted to see what it's like to live in the projects?" Schulman quips to DeJong. "Now you got your chance."

For twenty hours, Schulman intermittently tapes the drug traffic at the door of 295 Dumont. But he isn't just looking for sales. He has plenty of those. He is watching for Born Son, Tai Stick, Supreme, or Bang, trying to build a case to prosecute the Young Guns as an ongoing criminal enterprise. Hour after hour, he witnesses nothing but a numbing parade of crack customers. Every six or eight hours, one of the younger Worthys shows up on a bicycle or in a gypsy cab, presumably to resupply the dealer on the bench with crack vials, delivered from the spot where the drug has been cooked and packaged.

The room where the cops wait is stifling hot. Schulman is

propped on a beach chair by the window, shirtless but wearing a sweat-dampened powder-blue bulletproof vest. "Where the fuck are they carryin' the bombs?" he wonders, using the street term for resupply packages.

Halfway through the shift, a black federal agent, who has an easier time than whites getting into the building without arousing suspicion, arrives with a bag full of Chinese food.

"You couldn't think of anything else?" Schulman asks.

"That's all they got around here. Besides," the agent says, glancing out the window, "you got to live like the people you're investigating. Look."

Outside, across the street, a Worthy is arriving with a white plastic bag with red lettering, identical to the one the agent has placed on the floor. Schulman crouches by the window and trains his binoculars.

"I think Born Son and his boys are addicted to Chinese food. That's the third time today," DeJong says.

"Yeah," the agent guarding the door adds. "They're always going in and out of the Chinese restaurant in front of the Albany Houses, too."

"Fuckin' A!" Schulman exclaims. "They're bringin' the bombs in the *Chinese food containers!*"

For their next shift, two days later, Schulman, DeJong, and the third agent slip in the back door of the project building and head upstairs. Within an hour, they get good stuff. The cops have not only been trying to connect Born Son to the sale of drugs; they want evidence to prove that he is the manager of the operation. Bobby has been smart enough to stay away from 295 Dumont, but not today.

Schulman whistles. "Born Son himself."

Just before noon, as an insistent wind tells of an approaching squall, Bobby's black Pathfinder rolls down Dumont and stops in front of 295.

"Born Son . . . and out comes Tai Stick, and . . . holy shit, Bang," Schulman reports. A blue Honda Prelude pulls up behind Born Son, and the bruiser who has been handling security for the Young Guns steps onto the pavement. DeJong scribbles names furiously in his ledger while Schulman adjusts the camera and narrates the action.

"They're having a board meeting right by the bench. This is too much."

Bobby is talking and the others are listening.

"I'll bet somebody is runnin' right now to tell Ninja and his boys. This shit here is a message," Schulman explains. "Bobby's lettin' everybody know, 'Make no mistake, I am the man.' We might see some shooting."

But there is no trouble. The only commotion is caused by the police. Five hours later, in the early evening, as DeJong, Schulman, and the third agent prepare to quit the observation post, Schulman places a call to a sector car in the area. "Eagle's nest OP requesting a car stop on Dumont."

The Housing sector cars in the area know the deal. The patrol sergeant told them at roll call that Schulman and the agents at the so-called eagle's nest observation post might call for some kind of diversionary tactic so they could get out of the building unnoticed.

"9711 on the set. We'll make that stop. ETA 17:40."

In the middle of Dumont Avenue, just a few doors down from 295, the driver of car 9711 flips on his roof light and pulls over a hapless law-abiding Transit worker. Both officers approach the car with guns drawn. They order the occupant to step out of the car and place his hands on the roof while they make a show of checking his driver's license. Folks standing in front of 340 Tilden wander over to see what's going on. A handful of children trot out of the Complex to see. Even the slinger on the bench at 295 looks up to see what kind of mischief the "Five-O's," the cops, are up to now. All eyes are on the humbled driver and the two officers in the street as Schulman and DeJong and the other agent slip out the back door of 340 Dumont.

Old-Timers' Week is over but the summer is not. There is a huge tent going up near Sutter Avenue for an outdoor revival meeting. And a week later, National Night Out, a gospel fest on the floodlit ball field at Betsy Head Park, is sponsored by the 73rd precinct. The theme of the evening is "We've come this far by faith." Two hundred people venture out. Children frolic and tumble on the illuminated grass while local choirs and a visiting contingent from out of state kick up a holy ruckus on the temporary stage. The guest choir, some forty strong, ends the night. The rich and reverent tones of the group are interrupted by individual members seized by the spirit, who bound onto the center of the stage, inspiring the chorus behind to a devoted frenzy. Soon the plywood stage under their feet is threatening to buckle. No less than a hundred police officers from the 73rd and 75th and the PSA 2 stand guard. The lights are still on when the out-of-towners' charter bus rumbles away and the police pack up and roll off. But no one lingers in the park.

"I NEVER MET THE MAN"

Gary is at roll call, chatting with Marlene Pemberton, a short black officer with her hair twisted in braids and a talent for bawdy language, which makes her popular with the troops. Marlene leans to Gary's ear.

"I heard that guy is in the Ku Klux Klan."

"Who?"

"That guy, over there, anticrime, the one with the long greasy blond hair. He's got a key chain with like a KKK emblem. No shit. Check it out."

Gary shrugs. "Really?"

"You goin' to the Guardians meeting Friday?" Marlene asks, referring to the black police association.

"Where is it?"

"It's uptown, in Manhattan. You should go," she advises. "You know we got no hook. I don't know about you, but I want somebody watchin' my back on this job."

"I'm watchin' your back, baby."

"I'm not talking about my beautiful ass, Lemite."

"When they hold the meeting in Brooklyn, I'll go," Gary promises.

The sergeant is talking. "Take the riot helmets with you to your post, have them in the RMP. No excuses. And there will be inspection tomorrow. I have said it before, and I will say it again: anybody with the Indian head missing from his hat is getting a complaint." There are snickers from the assembled officers. On the front of each officer's hat is a silver medallion with the figures of a pioneer and an Indian. In an obscure protest gesture, possibly in the spirit of ethnic solidarity, some cops have taken to decapitating the Indian.

PSA 2 is not a Fort Apache, not a crumbling antiquated wreck of a structure, staffed by cynical, burned-out, cooping racists. Instead, it is a crisp, well-lit place, which under the administration of Deputy Inspector Kammerdener is known for its cleanliness. "You can eat off the floor in the officers' lounge," a visiting captain gushes.

When Officer McLean was shot, Kammerdener knew that the brass would be arriving for the memorial. The heavy hitters would be there. So he arranged for the walls of the PSA to be paneled, but only as far back as the brass would be likely to walk. Downstairs and around the corner, where the officers' TV room and lockers are, the paneling peters out. For the memorial, Kammerdener had someone research, write, and frame short histories of the Brownsville landmarks on which the projects are built. One plaque says that the Howard Houses are built on a spot where a man named Howard ran an inn that served as a stagecoach stop in the eighteenth century. Kammerdener also made sure that the chiefs were fed. According to the grumbling rank-and-file, one of the female officers was given time on the clock to bake cupcakes. When they proved a big success, she was given a department commendation for her "police work."

The Housing police force has a history that is starkly different depending on whether it is told by a black officer or a white one. In the opinion of many of the white officers and a segment of the public, the original, almost all black Housing police were unmotivated and undisciplined. According to this way of thinking, the PCOs, or foot patrolmen, assigned to the various project complexes were ne'er-do-wells who signed in, headed over to their project area, and either read the paper for their entire shift or hung out with their girlfriend. The aim for these guys, the story goes, was to blend into the background and avoid trouble at all costs.

Larry Phillips, a retired black PCO and former community affairs officer at the PSA 2, is livid over that reputation. "What is the stereotypical black man like? Lazy and incompetent. What were the Housing patrolmen supposed to be like when the force was predominantly black? Lazy and incompetent. C'mon.

Nobody is going to buy all that. Now, when the force is more and more white, it's getting more and more competent and more dedicated. Blatant racism. Every time the white men show up, they call it a renaissance."

Phillips rankles when people talk about community patrolling. "We were out there alone in those days." The officers did not have the radio communication they have now. Even if they did, according to Phillips, they were reluctant to use it. Phillips explains that the white officers in the old days were not often PCOs. They were in the car, riding around with the sergeant. "If we called for assistance, an 85, we did it rarely, because when these guys showed up they didn't know how to treat people, and they made matters worse. We were alone, like a sheriff. We had guys who were the best. But they didn't go up the ladder because they didn't have the hooks. Same story all over. Ask people about Al Lane," Phillips says, referring to a legendary black detective. "Kammerdener was always second to Al Lane, and it still drives him crazy."

When Gary Lemite made out his wish list at the police academy, he used all his wits. He had heard that you don't usually get your first choice, so he picked a precinct that was near his Elmont home, just across the Queens border. His real desire was for the superactive PSA 2, so he put it second, and it came through, just as he thought it would. It was the first of many plans that have worked out for Lemite in his short career as a Housing cop.

The cops at the PSA are not sure how to treat the easygoing Gary. "Hey, that guy Lemite," a white sergeant wonders, "is he black or what?" Gary's mother's father was Lebanese, her grandmother half Italian, half black. Gary's father was one quarter Indian, one quarter French, and half black, looked like a Spaniard. Both his father and his mother emigrated from Haiti in their late teens.

Gary grew up in Island Park, a white community on the south shore of Long Island, just north of Long Beach, between the Oceanside dumps and Reynolds Channel. "The place is one hundred percent white," jokes Mike Scully, a real estate agent in Island Park who was one of Gary's boyhood friends. There is more than some truth to the statement. Gary, his mother, and his brother could easily be taken for Cuban or Lebanese. The Lemite family was tolerated in Island Park because they had money and they were so light-skinned. There were other reasons why the Lemites got along so well. The assertive Serge Lemite spent hours on the telephone, wrote letters, and stood up at town meetings to speak his mind with his exotic Haitian accent. "Nobody wanted to take him on," Mike Scully's father remembers.

"We never thought of Gary as black," Mike's mother insists. "We really didn't. He was just one of Mike's friends. That was it. The only comment I ever heard was when somebody said, 'Who is that beautiful black woman living over on Long Beach Road?' That was Gary's mother."

Gary's mother has the same sand-pale skin as her son. From the frozen cleanliness of her upstairs quarters, it is apparent that Mrs. Lemite is not an easygoing woman. Whenever she came down to Gary's basement apartment before Lisa left, she leveled a dangerous eye at her mischievous granddaughter, Erica. "When we were kids and me and my brothers did something bad," Gary recalls, "my mother would make us get on our knees in the bedroom and stay that way until my father came home and gave us the belt. All we could do was stare at the floor and wait."

Gary's father had a successful construction business, Lemite Building Co., with a dozen trucks. Gary remembers that his father used to carry two bundles of shingles on his back, when most roofers could only handle one. "And he always had a wad of bills that he would pull out. Just like a drug dealer." Serge was busy, but he found time to ride bicycles and play soccer with his frisky sons in the back yard.

Gary spent his summers playing at a tranquil beach a block from his home, so close he could hear his mother banging a fork against a can to call him home. He passed the days with his friends, swimming underwater from pier to pontoon, playing shark and games of tag. "I could hold my breath forever. I would just wait at the bottom at low tide, about ten feet down. Then I would just go right past. I was a fish." As he got older, Gary took to the boats. His friends worked at the marina, and he would go joy-riding with Jamey, Marty, and Mike on the customers' boats when they were not around.

Gary gets along famously in the PSA because he has been running with a bunch of guys just like the officers since he was a teen. "Nobody messed with me and my boys in Island Park 'cause we were tight. It's such a small place. We used to go over to the Nathans' on Long Beach Road and kick the shit out of the guys from Oceanside, which is much bigger. We got over 'cause they had all factions in that town. We stuck together."

Gary grew up with almost no idea of prejudice in the middle of a racially restrictive community. In fact, for Gary, racism is mainly a curiosity. The only time he felt he had been discriminated against occurred when he and a friend were drinking beer behind the city building near the railroad station. One cop said they could drink there, but another cop gave them a summons. The town held a kangaroo court. Gary was ordered to pay a $50 fine, and the other kid got community service, cleaning up the sink at the fire station.

Sometimes Gary heard door locks click down when he walked through the parking lot of the Times Square Store near his house. "But I didn't blame them. None of it bothered me."

Island Park had no blacks, many people believed, because Senator Alfonse D'Amato kept it that way. When money was first allocated to Island Park by the Department of Housing and Urban Development, it was earmarked for minorities. D'Amato turned it down. Somehow, he managed to get the housing money designated for Island Park residents only. "Of course, there were no minorities in Island Park, so the houses went to people who knew somebody," Mike Scully says. "Simple."

D'Amato and others worked hard to keep Island Park white. It was one of the things that kept the senator popular. "There used to be houses with black people in them," Scully remembers, "but Tippy — that's what we call D'Amato — got rid of them. He did all kinds of things."

Newsday reported that in 1971 D'Amato and Mike Massone, Island Park's superintendent of public works, conspired to get rid of twenty-five tenants they considered undesirable at 93 Quebec Road by using the excuse of a small fire to condemn the building. A bus was parked out front to pick up the tenants and take them to the Nassau County Department of Social Services, in Mineola. Scully recalls, "Massone ran through the building with a megaphone telling the people to get on the bus because they were going to get some kind of a payment from the county. The building was bulldozed within hours."

The people in the bullhorn eviction were not black, but the modus operandi of Tippy D'Amato was established. In 1975 twenty-one poor black families were evicted from 347 Long Beach Road after Island Park blocked the landlord's attempt to rehabilitate the property. There were more demolitions. The result was to reduce the black population in the town from 116 to 35 between 1970 and 1980, according to U.S. census figures, in a total population of 4,100. New York State Board of Regents data show that now one tenth of one percent of Island Park's school population is black: one student.

The only trouble the prosperous Lemite family ever had with the D'Amato-dominated town was when there were complaints about the Lemite Co.'s fleet of trucks being parked on the street. Serge Lemite would move the trucks into a parking lot until the pressure eased, then start leaving them on the street again. "D'Amato came to the house and my father gave him handfuls of money. That happened a number of times," Gary recalls.

Serge had a lucrative business and a summer house in Long Beach. But when he was in his early forties, things started to go terribly wrong. At first it was small things. Serge was forgetful and distracted. Then he started to hear things. He began to believe he was Jesus. There was a short stay in a hospital, and life went back to normal for a while. Then there was another episode. Serge began wandering around the neighborhood knocking on doors, praying on people's front steps. He sent telegrams to the president. The stays in the hospitals got longer, the periods of sanity shorter. Three years between breakdowns, then two years, then just months. Customers and suppliers started taking advantage of the frequent lapses, and the construction business went into debt. The business was lost. Gary's father succumbed completely and entered a home. Gary was eighteen.

Gary Lemite has the Long Island accent and body language of a white cop. His legs hyperextend when he straightens them and he fondles his small potbelly. "Gotta go on one of those Slim-fast diets," he says unconvincingly.

In this society, he is called a black man. But he doesn't see things that way. "Gary doesn't identify with his race," a sergeant at the PSA remarks. Gary wants to make it on his own because he's the best cop, not because he's a member of a minority group.

It's difficult to sort out the right and the wrong of his attitude. It is an affront to some of the black cops, especially the older ones. "I have heard about him — he's a hotshot," a retired black cop says. "I'm glad I never met him." For black people conscious of their second-class status, defections like Lemite's are simply unforgivable. They believe he is simply currying favor with those in power. Lemite, whose buddies are both black and white, insists that he is refusing handouts because of his race. More important, he feels he has talent. He is sure of his memory, his eyesight, and his judgment. "He knows a hell of a lot for a guy with as much time on the job as he has. But he doesn't know as much as he thinks he does," a supervisor says. Maybe the best way to understand Lemite's position is to imagine an art lover who finds that he has the gift of color and stroke, a connoisseur who discovers that he can create. Gary is a police buff who believes that the potential to be a great cop resides within him. How can he be faulted for dismissing group politics and special-interest considerations? Perhaps his great fault is that he has no sense of tragedy — a gift he may be better off without in Brownsville.

When Gary does attend a Guardians meeting, he sits quietly in the back row, behind Lonnie Hayes. When it is over, he walks out mumbling. "All they did was complain about 'the man.' Who the hell is this man? I never met the man."

After the meeting, he heads over for a couple of beers at Cheap Charlie's. It is three o'clock in the morning when he pulls in front of his mother's house in Elmont in his faded blue Coronet. He stoops slightly to enter the basement door. Inside, he digs his .38 service revolver from under one side of his belt and his .38 backup gun from under the other side and lays them on top of the narrow glass-doored cabinet in the living room, where Erica and Zach cannot reach them. Lisa never liked the spot. "If somebody breaks in the house when we're asleep," she always said, "he'll have the gun before you do."

Gary would like nothing more than to move his family back to Island Park. Last year Mike Scully offered a deal, $130,000 for a handyman's special. Gary could have rented out the top floor to a tenant to defray the mortgage payment. But he needed a $15,000 down payment, and he just didn't have it. Within a year he should have enough for a deal like that. It would be great there. No crime. Then Gary remembers that his wife may never come back. He sits on the side of the bed for a long time before he switches off the light and tries to sleep.

HELL NIGHT

A Saturday night in late August, just before 1 A.M., and according to Vanessa's way of looking at things, the party is a drag, the boys in attendance hopelessly uninspiring. There are two parties in the neighborhood tonight; coming to this one was Vanessa's cousin's idea.

"This is corny," Vanessa complains.

"We out," her cousin replies.

The two girls prepare to leave the party and walk several blocks to the other one. But as Vanessa and her cousin step out the door, they catch sight of hazel-eyed, dreadlocked Frank, Sharron's friend and fellow LoLife, heading in. The girls reach the sidewalk and slow their step.

"Did you *see* him?" Vanessa gushes. "Girl, I ain't goin' nowhere, if it's somewhere where *he* ain't there." The pretty teenagers double over with laughter. They delay a few moments in the night air, composing themselves, disguising their eagerness, before strolling back into the house.

Vanessa has been partying seriously, making the most of the fading summer vacation. She has not been getting much sleep; "been up for about two days," she tells her cousin's friend, the hostess, as she reenters the wood-paneled basement of the house on Saratoga Avenue, just a block from Sharron's home. Though she looks fine to everyone else, Vanessa is not at her best; she is raggedy and unkempt by her own standards. Her hair is losing its signature flip, her red-on-red nail polish shows tiny chips, her glowing white Fila sneakers are imperceptibly smudged. This is a girl who likes to do things right.

Vanessa attended Catholic school for all except the past two years. Now she is a senior at Wingate High School, and a pretty fair student, with college aspirations. But she is also an associate of the LoLifes, and though never a LoWife, she was a good friend of several members of the Crown Heights contingent before she moved to Brownsville. "I do feature Polo," she concedes, "but I will wear Guess."

Vanessa slips back into the party and dips into the bathroom, where she confers urgently with a friend. Her enthusiasm for Frank has been overwhelmed by even stronger stuff. "I walk in, lookin' like this, and there is this *Sharron* standing by the wall with his shirt off." Vanessa has known Sharron from around the way for the lady's man he is. Though she once did ask a friend to deliver a message to him that she liked him, she has never spoken to him directly, and believes that she is not really interested in him. "I have like five guys. I'm like that. I *keep* a lot of guys. Forget him." Still, she cannot explain why the party, which just a half-hour before was tired, the music beat, and the presence of supervising adults upstairs stifling, has taken on such an exhilarating flavor of possibility.

Soon Vanessa is dancing in the center of the low room, just an arm's length away from where Sharron lounges on the sidelines. Sharron makes eye contact, beckons for her to come even closer. She is tempted to comply but delays the move. "He's callin' me on the down low, so nobody can see," she whispers to her cousin. Sharron's idea is to make it look as if Vanessa has approached him unsolicited. More props. He keeps beckoning and Vanessa continues to resist, though the outcome is inevitable. When Vanessa does slide over and the two start dancing together to a reggae song, Sharron moves in very close and commences to sing. He doesn't sing along with the record. Instead he sets out on his own, crooning the words to a Bell Biv Devoe hit. "Tell me when will I see you smile again," he harmonizes, the notes struck softly an inch from Vanessa's ear. "I thought it was funny," she confides to her friend later. "I think Sharron is crazy."

Crazy enough to receive her telephone number. Sharron writes the number with an eyebrow pencil on a torn piece of notebook paper. But he doesn't call for five days. When he does, his voice sounds much deeper over the phone and Vanessa is not sure who it is. To remind her, Sharron sings again.

But the romance stalls. Not because of Chantal or Sheryl. Sharron has not phoned Sheryl since just after the time on the

#3 train when he came eyebrow to raised eyebrow with her, sitting with that boy she claimed on the phone was her cousin. Sad little Chantal is long gone. Friends of friends say she moved down South. It's that Vanessa feels that Sharron isn't serious. She just likes his company. "I'm not *talkin'* to him," Vanessa explains to her mother the Friday before Labor Day, as she prepares for Sharron's first visit, "and I'm not *with* him. I know what he's about, so we're just friends."

Sharron lives only two blocks from Vanessa, but when he leaves her house an hour after midnight on Saturday morning, he takes the long way around, so he does not have to walk past the Howard Houses. The golden moon above the project rooftops is cleaved precisely in half. The night is quiet, save for the low rumble of an airliner lumbering for Kennedy Airport to the east. In a few minutes, Sharron is safely home, the dangerous summer months all but gone.

A block and half from Sharron's home, Housing cops Danny Horan and Jimmy Galvin, a couple of Gary Lemite's friends on the midnight tour, are beginning their shift, sitting in their patrol car talking. Horan is a likeable, knowledgeable officer who should have become a sergeant or a detective years ago. He has white hair, a pockmarked face, and a family.

"I've been trying to save up money for a house, and I might not make it," he tells Galvin. "I'm coming to grips with that idea, but I gotta tell my wife and I haven't done it yet. Last week she tells me we're going to spend all day on Saturday shopping for furniture for the new house that she doesn't know we don't have the money to buy. So I start to tell her and all hell breaks loose. Ah, what the hell." He sighs. "What're we gonna do for dinner? You feel like Italian?" he asks after a pause. "You want Italian — pizza?"

Galvin ponders the proposal.

Horan is hungry. "What? Hamburgers?" he presses.

Galvin continues to consider.

"Possible 30," the radio blurts. "One male black armed with a sawed-off shotgun at Wendy's, Linden Boulevard . . ." Horan shrugs. The call is too far away for a quick response, and it's off-project. "So it's pizza then," he concludes.

Horan is heading down Sutter Avenue when a group of bare-chested Hispanic youths stampede past. They are in full flight.

A breathless runner carrying an aluminum baseball bat in one hand points behind him and yells, "Amboy" — Amboy Street, the home of the infamous Amboy Dukes. Amboy Street was the hard cradle that rocked Mike Tyson. At 176 Amboy is the building where Tyson grew up and raised enough hell to get locked up scores of times. But Amboy Street has calmed down. A number of buildings have tenant patrols. There is even a contingent of unarmed private security guards who watch over select buildings. Tonight none of that matters. Somebody is shooting bullets on Amboy.

At the light on the corner of Sutter and Hopkinson, Horan stops just two feet behind a car. It is a mistake for a police car to get that close to the car ahead at a light; in an emergency, it will take several moves to get around the vehicle. Both Horan and Galvin breathe quickly and hunch toward the dashboard, their eyes slicing at Amboy. Neither man speaks. They hear shots. Afraid that the siren will warn the shooter, Horan flashes the roof light, but the car in front doesn't move. Seconds slip by. Whoever is pegging shots on Amboy, a hundred yards away, won't be there long. Still Horan flashes the light. Danny Horan is simply not hell-bent. He favors what the police call "controlled response." Gary Lemite and some others — Del Migliore, for one — would have jacked that RMP backward and roared down Amboy Street looking for bullets. Horan himself would have done that if the call were a 13. He has medals to prove he is a brave man and a good police officer, but he has been answering these "gun run" calls nightly for ten years, and may well answer them for another decade. He is primarily concerned with going home to his family after work.

It's five seconds before the car in front moves up and Horan sweeps down the street to the site of the shooting, where a chubby young man is sprawled on the sidewalk, a puddle of blood around his head like a dark halo. No one else is on the street. The sweet smell of burned tire rubber lingers in the air.

Soon the residents of Amboy Street slip slowly back out onto the sidewalk they quit so quickly minutes before. No one speaks to Horan or Galvin. They whisper among themselves. The children talk loudest. The story comes out.

"Just rolled up and . . . sh', I ran."

"Why they gotta shoot up the whole street?"

"Witnesses. You spray, you run 'em off."

There is a grandmother upstairs with a superficial wound and a young girl who broke her ankle with a dive into a lobby.

The EMS people arrive and roll the body over. The man is still breathing, but the crowd lets out a "whoooo" of dismay when they see that the back of his head has been blasted loose. The victim wears blue jeans but no shoes. He lies directly under a sign that reads DRESS UP YOUR NEIGHBORHOOD — CONTEST WINNER — 1985.

Several youths use the top of a car like a high table and converse across the space. "The guy with the scar flipped on him," a kid says.

A purple banner with gold letters, drooping in the still night air, is strung across from second-floor apartments on either side of the street, welcoming people to the big end-of-summer block party the next day.

"People think you're a white cop from Suffolk you don't care," Horan mutters. "You see this, you care."

Twenty-eight-year-old Euston Brown, the "vic," is carted to Brookdale. Horan and Galvin sit on the crime scene and wait for the crime detectives to arrive. It will take some time. Somebody says that there are already five shooting victims in Brookdale Hospital tonight.

"I was over at Brookdale last week," Horan begins, lighting up a Marlboro, "and I saw my doctor there. This is *my* internist, the guy who I send my family to, and here he is in this fucking zoo. Right away I get worried and I start to wonder. I thought he was a good doctor. Now I'm starting to think he's a butcher. I go up to him and ask him what the hell he is doing. And he says he only has this one patient and the guy was admitted to Brookdale, so he makes the trip. I was relieved. Did you ever see what goes on there?"

Scalia pulls up. This is a half-pint sergeant who, the story goes, turned out the lights, put his feet up, and fell asleep behind the front desk in the Coney Island station house. Scalia was sound asleep when a shooting victim, trailing blood, staggered through the PSA and collapsed in the sergeants' locker room. Scalia was transferred to PSA 2 for his lack of vigilance. But tonight he is on his toes. In fact, he is on a little rampage. He walks past Horan to Galvin.

"Did you call me a dick on the radio?" he asks. It is the same question he has been leveling at the more irreverent officers on the midnight tour all night.

"No, Sarge, I've only got three years. I don't even know about doin' shit like that," Galvin answers earnestly. Scalia listens intently. Perhaps he is listening to the timbre of the voice rather than to the content of the denial. There is a small chance he isn't as stupid as he seems.

At five o'clock in the morning, the crime scene station wagon shows up and Jacques, a towering bald detective with a deep-sea voice, steps out of the car. There are still a handful of people on the street waiting for the festivities to start. The detective stretches and burps loudly. He stretches a long hairy arm and points his index finger straight down the street toward Livonia. "First Fortunoff's, right over there on Rockaway." Then he goes about his business. "Waited for him to flat-line. The kid went DOA at four," he announces as he heads back to his vehicle to get his gear. In a few moments, he's picking a spent round out of the tire tread of a parked car.

But the shooting isn't over tonight. There is a DOA at 315 Fountain, in the Cypress Houses. And, at the first touch of dawn, a call to the Brownsville Houses. Renee Worthy is sitting on the bench in the middle of the Complex. People are lined up behind the green benches. There is no banter. James Awe, twenty-two, nicknamed Boy, has been shot dead beneath the window of his mother's third-floor apartment. Plastic yellow and black crime scene tape, the hideous funeral bunting of Brownsville, mocks the death. "He don't never bother anybody," Renee says. The victim's stately, long-necked sisters stalk the grass around the body like Furies. His mother, a great crumbling woman, is on her knees. "What's going *ooon?*" she howls.

"They killed Boy," Renee announces softly to a late arrival. "Six people got killed this summer here. Spider, Mousey, Tango — you heard about Tango. They shot him in the mouth with an AK-47, some guys from Cypress. People shot Sean, Clinton, and now Boy. Six. He don't bother nobody. All he want to do is drink beer and joke around.

"They took him to Brookdale," Renee tells a woman in a white and purple sweatsuit.

The woman frowns. "Brookdale ain't shit. You take your baby over there, you wait from 8 A.M. to 8 P.M. on a chair in emergency. Nobody helps you. By that time, the baby's all better and you go home. Fuck a Brookdale."

"He dead? Oh, no." A woman passing by at 5 A.M. flinches as if she has been backhanded. There are people here who are numb, people who pull the triggers and sleep like babies, but others, the mothers and the sisters and the brothers, the fathers and the friends, hurt again and again.

Nine young men have been shot already in Brownsville and East New York tonight. Four are dead. A sickly sun is up now. Shots pop in the distance. Nobody moves. A woman approaches half a dozen uniformed Housing officers.

"There is an apartment. And there are these crackheads in there?" The woman pauses to see if the cops are following her account. No one nods or encourages her to continue. "And they have my fifteen-year-old daughter and they want her to suck their dick. Or they won't let her leave."

The cops slouch in careless fatigue. "Call 911," an officer tells her, and yawns. "Probably they wouldn't give her any crack," the cop says as the woman walks away.

The morning air is moist and sad. Unbelievably, there are more sirens. The cops stoop and cup their ears to their radios. A shooting at 1750 Prospect Avenue.

Officer Fahey and his partner take a ride over. "I hate Prospect," mutters Fahey, a square-faced cop with a crew cut who was almost killed last year by a perp whose gun jammed. "I call it NASA 'cause they're always throwing bottles off the roof."

When the two Housing cops arrive, the bus is just loading. Two hundred people congregate on the sidewalk in clusters of ten and fifteen. It is twenty minutes after a drive-by. Automatic weapons this time. The victim is not likely, but he cannot go to Brookdale. Brookdale is now full, closed to gunshot victims. The wounded youth will take the ride to Kings County Hospital.

Fahey pushes his way through the crowd and stands by the lobby door. More people drift outside and stand in eerie silent communion. Above, black faces fill a dozen windows high over the cement approach to the building. Fahey sneers. His arm snaps outward to describe the expanse of Brownsville. "They should dynamite this fucking place." Then, looking up at the faces above, he shakes his head in a spasm of disgust. "Fucking baboons."

KIDS' STUFF

It is Labor Day in the Cypress Houses quadrangle. The September sun is flashbulb bright. The picnic on the grass at the foot of the seven-story building at 1260 Sutter Avenue is just gearing up. Thirty-seven-year-old Nettie Epps and her mother, Connie, have done most of the cooking. Two card tables sit laden with chicken and potato salad, bottles of hot sauce and mustard, collard greens, hot dog rolls, and several huge bottles of discount orange soda. Husky chest-high speakers by the side of the building kick out the beat. The young girls walk around, arching their necks and rolling their eyes at the boys, whispering to each other. Trevor Epps and his friend Marcus McClain absorb the attention and rededicate themselves to music production. This is the way things should be. Sunshine, food, and family, good times under the eye of the elders.

Grandmother Connie stands in the midst of her friends, thinking how much she is going to miss the place. But she has been having such hard times. Six months ago she lost her husband. Now Nettie's sister is getting ready to die. "Has the cancer from the AIDS," Nettie reports flatly as she fires up the barbecue grill. "Been smoking crack for eight years. She couldn't stop crying when Mama left her in the hospital. But I told her, if you stay here and you start eating and you get your weight up, Mama will take you back. You ever see *Tales from the Crypt* on HBO? That's what my sister looks like." Connie just wants to go home to South Carolina. "She's a strong woman," Nettie says, "but this is too much." Connie can't take it anymore. This is to be her last day in Brooklyn. Tomorrow she will move down South.

The smell of charcoal and barbecue sauce wafts to the upper windows, and more kids and adults float down to the picnic. "Where the hell are those police?" Nettie whispers to Connie.

Nettie Epps has two sons. Donald is eighteen years old, Trevor sixteen. These are the dangerous years. Nettie has lived in Cypress for thirty years. She was in the sprawling fifteen-building complex when there were white people here, when you could get a ticket for throwing a piece of paper on the grass or shouting out a window. She raised her family here through the late eighties, when the A Team ran Cypress, when the building at 315 Fountain Avenue belonged to the gang, not the Housing Authority. The members of the A Team would double-park half a dozen brand-new Hondas along Sutter Avenue and go about their drug-dealing business, until one day a rival dealer, Chris Moore, firebombed the row of cars. "You could see the smoke all the way to the 81st," a cop from that Bedford-Stuyvesant precinct remembers. Then someone, perhaps Chris Moore himself, offered information to the police that sent the leaders of the notorious crew either to jail or, in flight, to Pittsburgh.

Moore seems comfortably situated now as the man, the owner of a lingerie shop on Euclid and Belmont, around the corner from Cypress. He keeps his gleaming white Jeep parked there and runs drugs through the projects the same way the A Team did a few years ago. Moore makes it all look easy, but nothing is easy in Cypress. A group of young pistoleros who call themselves the New A Team, including a kid named Nephtali, has been giving Moore trouble, taking shots at his slingers. As the A Team started to disintegrate, when the big guys went to prison, they put what was left of the drug business in the hands of young bloods like Nephtali. Sergeant Priore explains, "They tell a kid with no business experience whatsoever to run a complicated cash operation. Every time the kid has a problem, he shoots somebody."

If you ask a kid in Cypress if he is afraid he will be shot, he laughs. Many of the young men here have already been shot. Nephtali, who came up as a gun bearer for the A Team, has been shot three times. "We got teenagers walking around with colostomy bags," Priore says. Sometimes the cops come across youths with leg wounds but no bullet holes in their pants. They don't have holsters, and they simply shoot themselves by mistake.

*

Later this afternoon the #3 is a ghost train as it squeals to a halt at Pennsylvania Avenue. The breeze wafting in the doors of the subway cars is cool. The only person on board is Nigel, nicknamed Indio, a cook in a Caribbean restaurant in Manhattan who is coming home to his place near the Cypress Hills Houses after a night of partying in the Manhattan clubs. Pink-eyed and bone weary, Indio nips into the corner bodega for a moment. When he comes out, he stands beneath the elevated tracks and studies the meager traffic for a cab, any kind of cab. He's careful how he waves for a ride. With half his paycheck left in his sock, he doesn't want to attract attention.

When Indio arrives on Sutter Avenue, he can hear the music from Nettie's picnic. He's careful not to let anyone see him handling the change from the $20 bill he has given the driver. Indio knows all about the Cypress Houses and East New York. He even knows Yellow Man, an albino who was arrested for popping off eight rounds when Mayor Dinkins appeared to talk about gun control on the grassy common of Cypress last spring. "He went out duckin' like everybody else," a resident told a reporter.

Indio, who comes from Westmoreland in Jamaica, speaks with a billowing lilt, different from the Skilsaw whine of the cops and the shock speech of the youths here. "It is ruf dung deh," he says of Jamaica. "*Reeel* ruf. Di police come and beat ya up, and ya cyan sey nuttin'." It isn't the police Indio worries about here, it's the locals. He keeps his gun in that twenty-four-hour bodega near the subway stop. Picks it up when he comes back from Manhattan. Drops it off again when he travels back into the city.

When Indio is asked if he is scared he will get shot in Cypress, he shouts, "Mi *been* shot, don't you know? I shot in the leg, mon. Mi ride me bike an alla da leaves start shake. It neh because a de wind. A wen da bullets. Bwoy in front get sixty shot inna im." Indio nods up and down vigorously to bolster his fantastic bullet count. He says he and his friends in Jamaica have a saying: "If ya wan dead, go a Cypress."

Indio is headed upstairs to sleep, but Nettie Epps isn't tired. She's in high spirits, presiding over her glorious picnic. Sergeant Priore, just starting his four-to-twelve tour, is on his way over to provide some security. "There was a party over there on Friday night and we had a man on the roof. Everything went all right," Priore muses on the ride over. "We'll just stop by for a couple of minutes."

The Labor Day picnic has been a righteous farewell to Connie. Nettie is delighted as she starts the cleanup, wrapping a piece of tinfoil around a package of uneaten hot dogs. The good food has slowed the kids down a bit, quieted the laughter too.

Three kids from the building across the sidewalk from 1260 Sutter show up quietly and assume position on the sweet-smelling grass under the sycamore tree fifty feet from where the big speakers are doing their work. Quani, a fifteen-year-old wild child, opens fire. *Bam bam bam bam;* the shots echo off the brick walls. Trevor Epps spins away and dives through a doorway as bullets chip off pieces of the brick face of the building and punch through glass in the front windows. Mothers and grandmothers dive and crawl, roll and run. But Marcus McClain is caught in the open. He yanks his own silverplated .45 from under his oversize T-shirt, but it jams. Probably a bad bullet, one of those refilled casings he bought cheap. He doesn't know how to rack the slide on the gun to eject the defective bullet and chamber a new one, so he pulls the trigger again, and again nothing but sickening clicks. The barrage takes only seconds. Quani walks over to a spot in front of the bullet-pocked speaker and fires one shot into McClain's head. Then he runs.

In just a few minutes Priore is on the scene. The shooters are out of sight, but they are still somewhere in the projects, and Priore orders a vertical search of the nearest buildings. Cypress has fifteen buildings, five thousand residents. Fifty officers are on hand in minutes, milling about. The body has been whisked away, the building entrance draped in the familiar crime scene tape.

"Excuse me," a girl asks matter-of-factly, "can I see if that is my brother in there dead?"

"Nobody's in there, ma'am," Priore answers.

Nearby, a nine-year-old boy whispers to another, miming the action shooting.

"Goin' on? Goin' on?" A young Hispanic woman with sweeping black eyelashes snorts at a young cop. "Smoke 'em up. Shoot 'em up. Beat 'em up. That's what's goin' on."

A slate-blue Plymouth Fury rolls across the sun-dappled

grass. The DTs get out. The black detective is wearing a gray suit and a salmon tie. Cypress sits innocently under the gaze of the DTs. Then Charlie Kammerdener, recently promoted to inspector, shows up from his home in Queens, just minutes away.

The residents are veterans of this kind of thing, but today they are shaken. Some reflect on the nature of things. A bearded man is distressed enough to look to a cop for the answers. He asks in Priore's direction, "What would you do? As a Caucasian man, you would know what to do."

The bearded man's friend shakes off that kind of thinking. "All black people aren't illiterate and all white people aren't intelligent. It just looks that way. We are not animals." He points at Priore. "They the ones who cover this shit up. Housing don't care."

A bruiser approaches the yellow tape and spits. "Little punks. This shit is outta hand."

Nobody knows what to do but Kammerdener. He eyes the complex craftily and points at a building. Three uniforms hustle over to search it again.

Everybody has had enough, but Trevor Epps is the one ready to do something. He steps up to the white detective. "I know who did it. It was Quani." He coughs the name up like a piece of spoiled meat. In a moment he is in an improbable position, sitting for all to see with his grandmother in the back of Priore's sector car, on the way to the PSA to give a full statement. He doesn't speak in the car, just rocks back and forth. Connie stares at the back of Priore's neck and moves her lips silently. The police car pulls off down the walkway as the assembled residents watch and wonder if the Brownsville aphorism "Snitches get stitches" will hold.

The sergeant drops Trevor Epps off at the PSA, where he disappears into the squad room with his grandmother. The black detective pulls up and heads toward the front door to interview him. Before he enters, he pauses on the street beneath the American flag. The detective is close to retirement. He straightens his stiff tie and thinks about days on a boat on a quiet river somewhere. "Hired in my twenties. Retired in my forties. Can't touch this," reads a police union bumper sticker on his private car in the officers' parking lot. But the detective will never be able to forget, really forget, Cypress. "Society has to know about this," he says before he leans on the glass door and disappears inside.

Priore returns to Cypress. When he gets there, Charlie Kammerdener is standing stock-still, squinting at the walls of Cypress as if he has x-ray vision. *Crash;* a shirtless youth bangs open the front door of 1200 Sutter, the building Kammerdener ordered searched, and flees across the grass toward Fountain Avenue with a cadre of heavy-legged Housing cops in hot pursuit. Priore jogs to his car and roars out of the narrow walkway onto Fountain Avenue.

"One male black. Fleeing on foot," Central repeats. "Can I have a location, K?"

Scores of cars from the 75th and PSA 2 sift through the streets around Cypress, but the kid has disappeared. "Perp magic," Priore mutters. The radio leaps; the kid bounds across the street ahead. You cannot help but admire his heroic stride. He wears state-of-the-art sneakers and blue jeans.

Gone again. Priore backs his car at breakneck speed down Sutter Avenue, peering down cross streets with the radio kicking out sightings.

"Belmont and Pine."

"Belmont and Euclid."

Suddenly, a cop who must be on foot is heard. His shouts are breathless.

"You're breaking up, K," Central says. The dispatcher cannot get a location of the foot pursuit through the barrage of static. There are jumbled shouts on the radio. The dispatcher commands, *"Units stay off the air."*

The kid is possessed by speed, covering a quarter mile in less than a minute. The radio is quiet for a moment and then it spits again. "He is on Pitkin. We've got a call from a resident. He's in a lot."

Then he is out again. The cops get fleeting glimpses of him between the one-family homes along the side streets. He is in the back yards. The police cars back up and squeal down another street. And then they get him.

"One under, Central," comes a voice as calm as the sky. A car from the 75th has him, with no shots fired. He's standing with his hands on the roof of a parked car, at the entrance to an open lot. His eyes are wide, his skin polished to a high glaze. He is surrounded by twelve white cops, all in uniform. A call comes over that the boss wants the kid to be held. Twenty seconds later, an unmarked car pulls up and a stooped man with dappled skin and gray hair gets out. His neck juts forward from his shoulders instead of up. He is an NYPD captain. He walks to where the kid is held, stands inches from the youth's face, and stares as if he is examining a specimen. The white man takes off his glasses and peers again. The kid, rankling under the insult of such clinical study, pulls his head back.

"Remember me?" the old captain asks in a sick, soft voice.

The kid shakes off the dripping intimacy. "I don't know you."

"Take him," the captain says, jerking his head toward the patrol cars.

"Have a nice life," a cop yells.

It isn't Quani. Instead, the cops have come up with Eric Lema, one of the two boys who was with Quani. He sits with his hands cuffed behind him and stares straight ahead. The officer who has the collar sits next to the kid. "Good eyes, Jimmy," Priore tells the fleshy young cop. Lema just stares. Nobody pays him much attention.

That night Priore gets the word from the street that even though McClain was Chris Moore's operative, the shooting had something to do with a loaf of bread. For Nettie Epps it doesn't matter what the cause; the shooting has changed things forever.

"I'm so proud of Trevor for doing what he did," she says as she tries to squeeze an antique suitcase closed over a mound of Trevor's clothing. "But he's going to have to go with Ma when she leaves tomorrow. I had a dream somebody came out and took a shot at him when he was packing up the car."

It is after midnight. "Quani is the devil in disguise," Nettie says wearily. A couple of years ago Quani's brother was shot dead. Nettie was looking out the window and saw him fall. People said it was guys from the Pink Houses. "Quani has been running amuck ever since. He steals people's wallets and bicycles. Basically, he does whatever he wants to do. He used to just shoot people in the leg and arm. But now this. He's gone too far."

Nettie forces a puff of air past her lips. "They were thinking of bringing the white people back. But after this, I don't know. Chris Moore told everybody to get off the streets tonight because retaliation is comin' down. It's going to be World War Three out here."

Nettie wants her older brother to pick up Connie and Trevor at six the next morning for the trip down South, but her son is adamant. "I ain't scared, an' I ain't sneakin' out of here. Tell him come at eleven. I got to say goodbye an' shit."

The next morning at a few minutes past nine, Trevor carries two shopping bags and a suitcase full of clothes downstairs and arranges them in the trunk of a waiting Buick. Then he returns to kiss his mother. None of his friends or enemies are awake to see him swagger outside the second time, pause beside the idling car, and take a last look at the Cypress Houses.

FALL

JEFF

Shalo is back. His skin tone has been deepened half a shade by a summer in the sun, his hair is trimmed a quarter inch, his shirt and pants droop with infinite precision. He stands alone just inside the front door of Thomas Jefferson High School, deftly brushing the extended hands of acquaintances and admirers as they file past on their way to class. It's the first day of school, and the freshly waxed floors of the school are gleaming. Shouts and peals of laughter echo off the walls of the first-floor hallway, the same way they must have in 1924, when Thomas Jefferson was built as a monument to the aspirations of a generation of Jews. The new clothes, the promise, the well-lit path . . .

Thomas Jefferson was constructed as part of the presidential series of Brooklyn high schools. With its worn brick facade, mixed bag of classical design features, and lower windows framed by brown steel security mesh, it looks like any other New York City public school built before the Second World War, only bigger. Inside the front doors, a life-size statue of Thomas Jefferson, painted a dull gold, sits on a pedestal. Around a corner, across the hallway from the small, neat library, is the honor board. Framed in dark lustrous wood, the board tells a story of Brownsville. Under the heading "Alumni Notable for Distinguished Achievement" are columns of names from the 1930s and 1940s. Next to each name is an engraved reference to the alumnus's field of excellence. There are physicists, scientists, and diplomats. Dr. Frank Field, meteorologist; Shelley Winters, actress. The board boasts leaders in the fields of journalism, literature, public health, government, science, international law, and education. The list goes on. That is, until 1960, about the time that Brownsville and Jefferson became predominantly black. After 1961, there are only two names on the board, John Brockington and Jim McMillian, professional athletes of some renown.

Sharron Corley walks past the honor board without a pause. He is at Jefferson today to arrange his transfer to another high school, in what seems a strange maneuver for an eighteen-year-old who has achieved the kind of popularity at Jefferson that Sharron dreamed of as a kid. But at Jeff, Sharron is dogged by both admirers and detractors. And here, the kids who do not like you do not just scrawl bad things about you on the bathroom wall.

Two weeks ago, on a late August morning, Sharron traveled to Chambers Street in lower Manhattan with his buddy Frank to look at an alternative high school, the Satellite Academy. It was Frank who was seriously considering the school. Sharron was along for the ride, checking the facilities and prospecting for a rich new lode of girls.

There were papers to be filled out, an interview with a counselor, entry tests to be taken, and at each stage there was a room more than half full of girls. Sharron squinted his eyes slightly, adjusted his new clear glass "lo frames" by Ralph Lauren as if something were troubling him, held his head at a tilt, and avoided eye contact. He appeared worried, and impossibly shy under his war bonnet of brown and gold hair.

To his surprise, just three days after the interview, he received notification in the mail that he had been accepted at Satellite. Sharron was admitted so quickly because he was a perfect fit for the "mid-risk" student profile at Satellite Academy: a student with reasonable academic skills and less than critical personal problems who was not progressing at his own school. Frank was placed on the waiting list; a week later he was accepted as well.

Today Sharron is at Jeff to soak up some attention and collect his transfer papers. The attention will have to hold him for a while. Satellite is a quiet, low-key venue, no place for a star. The school has about two hundred students and a faculty of twenty. Sharron likes the friendly vibrations there, the way the students call the teachers by their first names. He also believes he will be permitted to participate in the school play at Jefferson. If things work out according to plan, he will have the best of both worlds.

Though it came to pass by accident, Sharron's decision to transfer is neither capricious nor unusual. Things are so wild in the Ville and East New York that more and more students opt to attend school in distant communities, even in neighborhoods that are also rough, in order to cut down their chances of catching a bullet, either as a bystander or as the object of a vendetta. Mothers play a deadly game of chess with their kids. Some, like Nettie Epps, who has just delivered Trevor to South Carolina for the school year, send their sons South. Several years ago, Margaret James sent her favorite son, Born Son, to South Carolina to get him out of harm's way, but he couldn't stand the quiet and came back to Brooklyn and the worst kind of trouble. Others, like Gita Malave, of the Tilden Houses, across the street from the spot where Born Son would take his big fall, don't have the finances or the relatives to make such tactical maneuvers. So Gita watches her teenage children and worries, heads off to work and college at night with her fingers crossed tight.

The teenagers here are undereducated in most things, but they are connoisseurs of pop culture, ready receptacles for the jingles and scattershot imagery of television. Their speech is drenched in the verbal flotsam of television shows. The police are called Five-0's, after *Hawaii Five-0*. They know the stars of the soaps and sitcoms as well as they know their neighbors. Brand names tyrannize the classrooms; prestige cars are worshiped. The world Sharron travels in is a pure consumer culture; the LoLifes are more an outlaw consumer group than a gang. With a neighborhood unemployment rate so high the methods of measuring it are no longer valid, these youths are slated by society to be nothing more than consumers, and somehow they know it.

But they are also a driving force behind pop culture throughout the world, and one of the only charismatic protest cultures left in the United States. The project kids, the so-called homeboys, have been housed far from commercial and cultural centers, away from the white and the black middle class. They have an identity separate from the white, adult-monitored mainstream. Young white kids watch with rapt attention everything they do and say. If they wear their baseball hats backward, their trousers low and loose, kids in the suburbs are quick to swivel their brims to the rear. The designers and marketing machines register the trend and spread the word. In a year, lines outside trendy clubs in Paris and Tokyo are filled with would-be homeboys in backward caps and droopy pants.

The irony is that the young white kids are not rebelling against anything, and neither are the boys in the Ville. The young black men in Brownsville indict society by their total belief in it. They trust what they have been told about image, status, competition, hierarchy, and the primacy of self-gratification. Their faith is lethal, mostly to themselves.

Chantal, Vanessa, and their friends sacrifice the chance to display their feminine charms to dress exactly like the stickup boys because they are the ones in the Ville who get the most props. The media know and respect the homeboy because they know he cannot be ignored. He is original, dangerous.

Even Gita Malave copies the manner of speech of the rough-and-ready guys who hang in the parking lot and by her elevator. "Yo, what's up?" she likes to say, just like the kids. "Don't play yourself." She is only half kidding. One of the salient features of Brownsville is the simultaneous primacy and neglect of the children, especially the boys. This is a country where children have always been abused and worshiped. In Brownsville, they rule with a murderous innocence.

Here comes Chantal Redding, down the hall past the guidance office toward Sharron. Transfer papers in hand, the young king of Thomas Jefferson lingers in the hallway opposite the entrance to the auditorium, nodding to his faithful, granting brief audiences with his courtiers. Chantal moves on tiny sneakered feet, a gamine lost in a pair of baggy Guess jeans and a double-extra-large T-shirt. This is the first time Sharron has seen her since their spat in the hallway in March. She never had much besides her undeniable cuteness. Today she has news.

"Sha, wha's up?"

"Same old. I ain't seen you in a while. Where were you?"

"Down South. You still here?"

"Nah, I'm transferrin'. Too much drama."

"Word."

As Sharron speaks with Chantal, he absorbs the waves of attention that roll toward him. Slowly, he maneuvers the conversation fifty feet down the hall to a spot in front of a display case, opposite the statue of Thomas Jefferson. The location is his favorite in the school because in the back of the display case is a full-length mirror. The soft lighting in the hallway is just right to highlight his skin and backlight his hair. As his ex-girlfriend talks, he rotates his head this way and that. Life is grand. Not only is the girl he left behind making a public attempt to get back in his favor, and not only are the new and old girls in school "sweating" him big-time from all angles, but he is now in a position not only to gather the harvest of admiration but to watch himself receiving it. It's a shame to leave all this, Sharron is thinking. But a plan is a plan, and he knows better than anyone that familiarity breeds disrespect.

Chantal is telling about her visit down South. Her voice is soft, her consonants flabby, babyish, as she describes how quiet and dark it was in Fayetteville and how there "wasn't nothin' to do but chill." Her account is notable for its gaps. There is no mention of boys, and boys are what makes Chantal's world spin around and around. The first period of the school day ends with a droning five-second tone, and the second begins. Still Sharron and Chantal stand and talk.

Sheryl happens by and shakes her head. That unfortunate encounter on the #3 in June could be forgotten, she has decided. She has been considering a reconciliation. Sheryl knows that any girlfriend of Sharron's is going to have to deal with "shade" from the other girls. He is simply what they are looking for. Sheryl is realistic. She can deal with the shards of jealousy and with the relentless hopefuls, but she is not sure she can deal with reruns like Chantal, though that is exactly the role she is contemplating for herself.

When Sheryl passes by again twenty minutes later and Sharron and Chantal are still deep in conversation, she flushes, her breath quickens. "Chantal needs her little ass kicked." But when they are still head to head an hour later, Sheryl simply writes off her own comeback.

Sometime between second and third period, Chantal reveals her reason for leaving town.

"I don't know how to . . . tell you. Sha. I had a baby. Andre. He's yours."

"Mine?" Sharron looks over both shoulders and back at Chantal.

She nods solemnly. "He's so cute. He be sayin' things already. Talkin' almost."

"You *know* he's mine."

"Yours . . . I was gonna keep it from you. I know you got a future. I didn't wanna mess it up for you. Sha?"

Ah. Those carefree moments of youth are short, when all the world is right and all the doors are open. Sharron is jarred. He catches himself frowning in the mirror, quickly recasts his features, and mouths a policy statement.

"I'll do the blood test thing. If it's me, I'll take the responsibility."

Chantal moves several inches closer. Suddenly, a less calculated reaction grips Sharron. Later he explains, "She was standin' there, and I was lookin' down at her and she was lookin' up and she was looking so good. And I remembered how we were close. And she was wearin' a yellow Champion T-shirt with red writing and dark blue jeans. I was wearing a yellow Polo sweatshirt with red writing and dark denim Guess jeans. It was incredible. I just got this feeling — that we were meant to be together, that we were made for each other."

Sharron is so impressed that he makes a spur-of-the-moment decision. He had heard that Chantal had gone down South with some guy who is back in New York with her now.

"I'll do what I gotta do with . . . for . . . Andre. But you gotta stop dealin' with this dude."

Chantal nods and presses her small face to Sharron's chest to hide the big bubble tears on her cheeks. Sharron recoils momentarily and places his left hand over his heart so the back of his hand will stop Chantal's tears from staining his sweatshirt, then crushes her to him with his right arm. For the moment, he does not care who is watching.

Upstairs in Room 544, Sharon King is introducing herself to her third-period global history class, working her mojo on the sophomores and freshmen, who have never seen anything like her. She is dressed like a lounge singer, in shiny black pumps and a black skirt that accentuates a prominent behind, which she likes to call her "African rhythm section." Glowing with good looks and zeal, she is hip, hipper than that. She "knows what time it is," the kids who know her from last year whisper. She knows how to put a lesson together, too. Some of the other teachers are envious of her relationship with the students. "Hell, I don't blame them. I'd be jealous of me too," she says.

King has arranged the seats in her room in a rectangle, allowing for a center performance space in which she can do her own special brand of motivating and instructing. The first thing veterans in a tough school tell a new teacher is "don't smile until Christmas." But King pirouettes so students on all sides can see her smile.

"I want you coming in here every day with a notebook. Not some raggedy pieces of paper you borrowed from somebody five minutes before you walked in here. And cover your textbooks. If you don't have your notebook and your cover, talkin 'bout 'I don't have the money' or some shit like that, I'm gonna *give* you the money." The class titters. "Word up. I *will* embarrass you like that."

King has stacks of printed handouts on the desk behind her. Each of her lessons will be laced with lively role-playing. The twenty-five students relax visibly. They will not be left to their own devices.

"We're gonna get busy in here. Ask Theresa." King nods at a student who has been in her class before.

"Word," Theresa testifies.

The door swings open and fifteen-year-old Khalil Sumpter appears. He waves broadly to Dupree, his best friend, and Melvin Jones, another buddy, seated in the back row. Khalil is wearing a gold jeans jacket. He is five-ten and sturdy, a bad actor. He slides into the room with much fanfare, waves and touches hands left and right. Nothing terrible in that, just the classic tone-setter for a classroom in which nothing will get done. His boys slide apart so he can sit in the middle of the back row, leader of the opposition party.

King never has trouble with a class. Her package is too potent for all but the most disturbed kid. If there is a clown or even a cadre of ne'er-do-wells, she takes it straight to them, with the rest of the class as noncombatants. No one can take sides against Ms. King.

While King attends to some opening-day paperwork, Khalil

and his friends have plenty to say behind cupped hands. Khalil is the brightest of the three. His records show that he is a very smart kid who has decided that academic achievement is counterproductive to his goal of gaining and holding props.

Something else is bothering him. A year ago, Khalil and a kid named Tyrone Sinkler were arrested for stealing a kid's hat and lunch money outside nearby George Gershwin Junior High School. Sinkler, who had prior arrests, was packed off to Spofford for almost a year for his part in the crime. Khalil was turned loose with probation. After Sinkler was sent away, word began filtering back to Khalil that Sinkler was calling him a snitch. Now, after his release, Sinkler has transferred from Westinghouse High School to Jefferson. Khalil has already seen the hulking, scowling Sinkler in the hallway, and he is bracing for trouble.

Khalil and his boys in the back row giggle and "snap" (joke) about getting skins from girls. They believe they know what will transpire in this room. The asides will always be funny, the lesson always boring and meaningless. But the likes of Sumpter, Dupree, and Jones have never met the likes of King. The contradiction in their scenario is that in their closed adolescent society, their world of bawdy one-liners and guffaws, a curvaceous female like Ms. King is never to be ignored, cannot be excluded. From the opening bell, this will be a different kind of contest. When King steps back into the center space, she has their full attention.

"What's up, gentlemen? The three new wise men of Jeff. And the man in the middle, a day late and a dollar short." She nods at Khalil's bare desk. "Where's your books?"

Khalil loves the attention. "In the library, where books belong. Aaah, snap." He turns to his laughing classmates and raises his hands in recognition of their appreciation. There will be no unbearable boredom here. He will see to that, his gesture promises. This should be a good one. The classic disrupter and the strutting master teacher. Who will win?

"But there's no *skins* in the library," King retorts, with a saucy toss of her head and a wink. "So you hustled your behind up here. Good decision."

Sharron leans into the open doorway to catch King's eye. She breaks away from her class for a moment and steps outside to confer with him.

"Boo Boo," she coos, "I can't believe you're transferring. I heard it from Sheryl."

Sharron is embarrassed. "Ms. King," he whines, curling his body around an imaginary knife in his heart, "it's somethin' I got to do. I'll still be in the play. Just too much going on here."

King has already heard something of Chantal's pregnancy. "Yeah, sweetie, I've heard."

There is a burst of laughter from inside the room. King slips back to her class. She cannot afford to leave the stage to the pretenders for too long at this time of year. Later, when she has developed personal relationships, done important favors for every one of her students, when she has her merit system in place, she will be able to do almost anything. Right now she must keep the spotlight on herself, before Khalil and his crew gather momentum.

Minutes later, Sharron is heading out the front door. Cortez Sutton is walking in. Cortez is as dark and bright as a glittering midnight sky; a razor-featured junior honor student, he is also a wit and a basketball player, a left-handed point guard. He is headed to the main office to effect his transfer from Lafayette High School, where he was given a superintendent's suspension last June for brandishing a screwdriver at two white kids who threatened him. He lives near Sheryl on Pennsylvania Avenue, on the other side of Linden Boulevard, in the Linden Houses. Jefferson is the nearest high school, so it was the natural alternative when Mrs. Sutton decided to pull her son from Lafayette. This is a chance for Cortez to put the academics and the hoops together and grab a ticket to a green-shrubbed campus and the outside world. But Cortez won't be able to play ball for Jeff in the regular-season games unless the suspension is lifted. He knows all about Jefferson. He has plenty of friends here, including his buddy Ian Moore, E-lo. Cortez is smart, too smart it seems, always the guy with the quickest woof. That is what got him in trouble at Lafayette. But he is a comer. Maybe he can keep his mouth shut over here at Jeff.

Cortez is far less besotted with clothing and girls than Sharron, who is drifting down the street away from Thomas Jefferson like a sailboat. Sharron has already recovered from the shock of having a son, believes that the inconvenience will be minimal. The young grandmothers, Chantal's thirty-year-old mom and Gloria, will take care of the child. Life will go on without a hitch. But the alarms have been going off in Cortez's head ever since he got suspended. He knows that if he is going to prevail in the world outside the neighborhood, he is going to have to make his move now, keep rocking the books, and pray that he catches a college scout's eye with his left-handed sorties to the basket.

Principal Carol Beck stands on the front steps of the school. It is five minutes before the end of the first regular school day. A recipient of a *Reader's Digest* American Heroes in Education award, Beck is riding a groundswell of acclaim and positive publicity. The idea now is to keep the ball rolling, build on the success. In recent years, Jefferson had the worst reputation of any school in Brooklyn, perhaps in the entire city, and ranked at the top in violent incidents and dropout rate. Beck has slowed the heavy wheels of decline, and she is determined not to let them roll again. But the problem came right at her at 8:40 this morning, surging down the hall: five hundred new students, freshmen, from seventeen feeder schools. They come from all kinds of educational environments, many of them exquisitely chaotic. They have no idea about the new regime at Jeff.

Beck smiles at two security guards with walkie-talkies, turns, heads inside, and takes a position near the likeness of Thomas Jefferson, studying the freshmen as they leave the building. Dressed in a blue suit, and white sneakers for speed, she knows she can't control the school from the principal's office. Twenty years in the New York City public school system have taught her exactly what has to be done. It will take savvy and inhuman endurance. Luckily, through a freak of nature, the fifty-four-year-old principal has more energy in her veins than any three children. If she did not have this job, it seems, she might have to take tranquilizers or be restrained.

Beck grew up in St. Louis. She was a musical prodigy who came to New York City after college to sing in the Metropolitan Opera. When she found herself headed for the chorus, she took a job as a music teacher for the board of education. "I come from gangsters," she says with a mysterious arch to her eyebrows. "I know their pain."

From her position in the hallway, she manages to make eye contact with each of her veterans and new recruits. When

Michael T., back in school after an abbreviated stint upstate for pulling the gun on Gary Lemite, tries to slip by, she detains him with her hand, looks into his eyes, and shoots him a smile both sweet and lethal. Bashim Inman, the Howard Raider, is next. Bashim, another rambling heavyweight, has been attending Jeff for a long time. Beck has been principal for four years, and Bashim was at Jeff before she was. He started in an honors program at Martin Luther King, Jr., High School in Manhattan. But early years in the Howard Houses did not serve him well outside Brownsville. "I was always getting beef, carrying a gun, all that, so I got transferred to Jeff."

He did not want to come. Jeff is the arena where contingents from the various projects meet. Linden and Howard, oil and water. Bashim is a hardrock, a tough guy, but when he saw "Thomas Jefferson" written on the piece of paper, he said, "No way." "It was wild then," he recalls. "I carried a .32 Luger. And then a four-fifth. I loved that gun. My baby. Big thing. Stuck right in my pants. I had it all." Big Bashim talks about his guns with the affection some kids in the suburbs have for the used cars they once owned. "It was funny with all those guns," he remembers. "Guys had to start resorting to some other way to deal with things. Like you have a beef, you try to melt the other guy with the ice grill. If that don't work, we knuckle up."

Early in her first year, word of an impending "throw-down" reached Beck, and she summoned Bashim to her office. "Bashim, you've got to get your people under control. This is just not going to happen like this."

Beck's strongest suit is that she can deliver the message that she is more committed to order than the kids are to chaos. If they are willing to fight and shoot, then she is willing to die. She makes them believe that, and it might be true. "This is a tough age," Beck states, "but we love these children. They have one dimension of experience, and we are trying to make them bicultural. They have one channel, and we are trying to give them cable." Beck believes more in education than the kids do in the status quo of beefs and counterbeefs, violence for goods and violence for status, violence for entertainment, violence out of habit.

That first year, Beck was savvy enough to put her finger on the juice behind those "little bastard Smurfs who were running amuck on the fifth floor." After Bashim's talk with her, he headed upstairs and waved a hand over the waters. "It's chill," he said with his ice grill.

The same thing had happened on almost the same spot some thirty years before, when Smiley Smith, the six-foot-five leader of the terrible Roman Lords, had stood looking down at basketball coach Sam Beckman in the first-floor hallway at Jeff, listening. "Something clicked," Smiley says about the moment that changed his life. "I don't know what it was about that little man. He was kind of mean. But something happened and I started going to class." Smith became a basketball star at Jefferson and is now a community leader in Brownsville. Beckman had something. It wasn't pity or even concern. It was respect, and a plan for something different. Mr. Beckman and Carol Beck had more than good intentions; they had the gift.

Bashim Inman is a powerful ally. Beck watches him warily. He can control the action with his size and smarts, think on his feet like a barrister. But at nineteen, he has been in high school for six years. "I'm like a chameleon," he says. "I have game for any situation. I want to be a politician." The girls do not like him much; with his round pumpkin head and knuckle-gnarled upper lip, he looks like a classic bully, and he is. Even now, he cannot resist throwing his weight around a little. On this first day of school, near the guidance office, he spots a posturing would-be gangster, Khalil Sumpter, and makes a mental note to harass him the next time their paths cross. "If I can't be bad, then can't nobody."

"COME BEHIND ME"

A week after the opening of school, Born Son cruises to a soundless stop in front of Thomas Jefferson High School. It is 2:40 P.M., dismissal time. Born Son is dressed in a green iridescent suit over a black silk T-shirt, and the smooth dark skin of his neck is festooned with chains of gold: an inch-thick rope for weight, and a finely woven strand with an anchor-shaped medallion for style. On his left hand he sports a diamond-studded ring custom-made in Manhattan. He is seated in regal solitude behind the wheel of his jet-black Jeep Pathfinder. In minutes there is a jostling throng of a hundred profoundly impressed students.

Bobby James was always just a little smarter than the fellows around the way, could talk just a little better, always knew where the parties were. Everybody wanted to hang out with brother Bobby. A security guard tries to disperse the growing crowd and inspires more curiosity. A girl trips and screams as she fights to regain her footing. More students rush up to get a look at what is really just another kid. Throughout the mini-riot, Born Son, bathed in myth, sits serenely astride his Jeep.

What does Bobby have to make him seem such a prince? It is not that he makes so much money dealing crack — perhaps a thousand a week, probably less. He has some gold jewelry, a custom-made suit. But the Jeep he drives is not a fairy-tale chariot like a Rolls-Royce, just the middle-class vehicle of commuters and spoiled suburban kids. It is the things Bobby James has in contrast to the desolate lives of the people around him that make him seem so special.

Born Son shifts his Jeep into gear, smiles, and floats down Pennsylvania Avenue on a wave of heartfelt admiration. Like Sharron Corley, he cares far more about his image than he does about money, his future, or even his safety. The Worthys, especially Nikia, are not constrained by such abstract notions. When push comes to shove, when the feds flash their badges, it will be Born Son's loyalty that will be his downfall.

Sitting in their orange and blue Chevrolet Caprice on the corner of Dumont and Pennsylvania, Hammil and his partner cannot help but curse their station in life when they see Born Son's flashy car. "I got a fucking two-year-old Escort and this fucking mopehead is drivin' a fucking Pathfinder," Hammil whines.

"And you just know he doesn't have any registration. The papers are always fugazy," his partner concurs, using a cop slang word meaning phony.

Hammil cannot touch Born Son. He is Schulman's case, the subject of a federal investigation, immune to petty harassment. But when a white Mercedes-Benz with two young men in the front seat and two in the back rolls by a few minutes later, the car stop is inevitable. Hammil flips on his red roof light.

The scene is familiar. As the boys pile out of the car, black people walking by exhibit varied emotions. The older ones avert their eyes. The youths are probably drug dealers, they think. The middle-aged folks, the ones with jobs, sometimes share the perspective of the police. How, they wonder, have they worked all their lives and failed to acquire such a machine to transport their aching bones? When the teenagers leaving the high school see the flashing red light, the luxury auto, and the splayed doors of the police cruiser, they whip off their Walkmans and edge close. With jutting chins, hands on hips, they mutter loud enough for the police to hear, "Always fucking with a brother. Can't stand to see a brother with somethin'. Ain't this a bitch. That's why they get hurt. That's why somebody always shootin' they ass."

A couple of days later, Schulman is in a slate-blue surveillance van watching Nikki. His CI, as confidential informants are known, has given him the time and place she is supposed to make a pickup.

Nikia is the smartest of the Worthys. The police know it, and her grandmother Kate knows it too. "Nikki is slick. Always has been." She was slick enough to be somewhere else when her cocaine dealer boyfriend died in a stiff breeze of bullets in the Chelsea section of Manhattan in 1988. After that, she lived in a shelter until she moved in with her cousins at 295 Dumont. It was penny ante there until she met Bobby at an after-hours place for hustlers on Pitkin Avenue.

"I knew the girl was trouble the minute I saw her," Margaret James swears. "The minute I *heard* about her."

The bootleggers of the twenties had their speakeasies; the Brooklyn crack retailers had the Limelight. Everybody was frisked at the door. "The drug dealers all went there," Bobby Schulman says, "but they left their business outside. They didn't socialize with each other, just stayed in their little groups."

A Howard Raider remembers the night Bobby and Nikia met. "Bobby used to come in the Limelight with all gold and shit. He had serious props. He tried to push up on her and she wasn't havin' it. Bobby was sweatin' Nikki, and she was playin' him."

The story goes that Bobby told his boys to rob Nikki, relieve her of her jewelry. But the robbery did not happen. Instead, Born Son was smitten. "She had heart comin' in there," one of Bobby's young followers says. "Next thing I knew, they was together."

Nikki is not a lush young woman. At twenty-four, even after three children, she looks girlish. She is wiry, tough, built for the long march. Both earlobes show scars from earrings that were torn away in anger. She talks in a combination of sharp exclamations and warp speed mumble; her vocabulary is state-of-the-art street slang. Not for effect; she does little for effect. Whatever the street recognizes as cool is Nikki. Her intelligence has never been used for anything but the street. She can take the measure of a player quickly, can tell what is going to go down long before the guns start popping. She is brave but not vainglorious. Nikki can handle drug dealers, thugs, and just plain troublemakers with ease. Cops, prosecutors, and judges are not that much harder for her. "I'm goin' out to get me some money," she likes to say. She is everything that Bobby admires.

In Scarsdale, New York, among young people Nikki and Bobby's age, it is all about what college you go to, what fraternity or sorority you join. Bobby and Nikki had other credentials. He was the main man in Howard. She had been part of a crack operation already. She knew how and where to cook it up, how to add the baking soda and bag it. She had a steel trap for a memory and a head for figures. She was rough and ready. It wasn't long before Nikia got pregnant and gave Bobby a son; they called him Little Bit. The Young Guns had become a mom-and-pop operation.

But the good times are over. Schulman and his partner from the federal task force, Mathew DeJong, have most of their case. It is time to snatch up Nikki and force her to roll over. The plan is to bring her in on a state warrant and try to scare her into providing evidence for the federal investigation. This is the day.

When Schulman, DeJong, and a handful of backup DEA agents pick up Nikki at her mother's apartment in the Albany Houses in Bedford-Stuyvesant, she is unconcerned. Back at the PSA, Schulman begins to explain the situation to her.

"We got tapes, Nikki. Matt, get the videotapes."

"I don't want to see no tapes," Nikki mumbles wearily, rolling her eyes. She tilts her head down and shines the smudge off one of the studs on the sleeve of her $1,700 leather outfit. Nikki has been in and out of police stations all her life. She won't frighten easily.

"Nikki, we got sound tapes, talkin' about you runnin' things in the Complex while Bobby was stayin' away. We got pictures of you with money. *Beaucoup* drugs. We got people to testify."

Nikki levels her eyes at Schulman. "I'll give you a powder spot an' a homicide."

"That's good, I think we can work with that. Let me make a call," Schulman says.

He takes down the information and calls Robert Fineberg, the federal attorney assigned to the case. It's bad news for Nikia.

"Thanks for the powder spot, Nikia, and the other thing. We're gonna put you back on the street for a while. But the DA says you got to give up Born Son. It's like a game. We tag you. You tag Bobby." Nikia is silent.

In the next week, the task force breaks the Young Guns' operation down, getting warrants on apartments the crew uses on high floors so they will move the operation lower in the building and consolidate. The idea is that when the final arrests are made, the lower apartments will be easier to hit and likely to yield more drugs.

A week after Nikia's first arrest, Schulman and DeJong take her down again. This time they show her the federal arrest warrant. She twitches, puckers her lips, and regains her composure. The first time Schulman brought her in, she believed she was dealing with a state bust.

Nikia's lawyer shows up at PSA 2 and confers with his client for just a few moments. "I'm going to leave the room," he tells her. "I'm sure they'll do the right thing for you," he says, nodding at Schulman and DeJong.

The usually unflappable Nikia is worried. She taps her foot, drums her fingernails on the tabletop, and stares at Schulman.

"Born Son," the cop says.

"I got to testify in front of him? I don't want to do it in front of him."

"If it goes to trial, you'll have to testify in open court. He'll be sitting right in front of you. Nikki, this is no joke. You are in deep shit. You give us Bobby, the DA writes a letter to the judge and you're out in a couple of years. Otherwise, you don't see Little Bit till he's in his thirties."

Nikia nods slowly. Her voice cracks. But she does not weep as she tags Bobby James, the father of her baby boy. "You got it," she says.

It's time to take the whole operation down. Three days after Nikia agrees to testify, the Housing cops and the DEA grab Born Son and Tai Stick in their Pine Street hideout. They snatch Supreme and Billie Odums on the street.

Through a relative, Nikia manages to deliver a terse message to Bobby. If a deal is to be made with the feds, it must be made quickly. "Come behind me," she tells her lover. But Born Son and the Young Guns are still not deeply concerned, even after they learn what the federal charges are all about.

They should know better. They had heard rumors that the feds were involved for some time but had not heeded them. The maximum they would have served in state prison for the offense they are charged with is eight and a third years. Federal time is five times that. And there are the sentencing guidelines. As part of the 1984 Sentencing Reform Act, which went into effect in 1987, judicial discretion is severely limited in drug cases. Sentences are mandated based on a chart that takes into account only drug type, quantity, prior record, and role in the criminal organization.

Schulman and DeJong mention the possibility of a deal to Born Son if he gives up his connection. "Give us Chris Moore," Schulman offers, "and we can do business."

Dan Murphy, Bobby's lawyer, leans close and whispers vehemently in his ear. He is begging him to do himself some good. But Born Son has too much heart for that kind of thing.

"I don' know nothin'," he says with a jerk of his head toward the door of the squad room. "Y'all finished?"

The Housing police breathe a sigh of satisfaction over the arrest. The Worthys are out of business, and the four Young Guns are not just going to be locked up, they are going to be locked deep. Schulman and DeJong confiscate Born Son's Jeep, and right away Schulman begins using it as a surveillance vehicle in the new Chris Moore investigation, occasionally wheeling it past 295 Dumont — "to send a message," he says.

"STRAIGHT TO THAT HOLY HOUSE"

Lieutenant McGinty is downstairs in the PSA roll call room, briefing his sweep team.

"A message, Lieutenant?" asks Gary Lemite.

"That's right. A fuckin' message. Ever since Lavin left Fiorentino, the place has gone to shit. Yesterday some fucking mutt made a threat on Mike's life."

"Yeah," a team member affirms. "We had a gun run in there last week. All kinds of mouthin' off. Fuckin' mopes in Fiorentino are out of control."

"Today we go in and snatch some bodies," McGinty orders.

Gary Lemite, recently promoted to the sweep team, which concentrates on special conditions in the projects and so-called quality-of-life infractions, shakes his head slowly back and forth. Then he looks over at Mario Palumbo, his partner for the day. Mario points straight up, and the two officers head upstairs. The calendar says the summer is over, but outside the air is damp and oven warm. Gary reaches in his shirt, hooks a thumb under his bulletproof vest, and pulls the body armor away from his chest to let some air near his skin. Despite the heat, he would not even consider removing the stifling thirty-layer "point-blank" vest.

One sweep team member has to use the bathroom, and the sergeant has some paperwork to do. Those two will be along shortly. Gary pulls the blue van around the front of the PSA to pick up Mario for the ride over to Fiorentino, and the two young cops cruise through Brownsville in thoughtful silence, staring out the open windows at rows of silent dark young men.

*

The Jews who left have fond memories, but Brownsville was always a ghetto. During the Depression no area of the city had a higher percentage of families on relief. Jacob Riis called it "that nasty little slum." In the 1940s, the police credited it with producing more gangsters than any other neighborhood in New York City. It was said to be the toughest neighborhood in the United States. Poolrooms were three times as numerous as playgrounds. You could get a pretzel and an egg cream at Midnight Rosie's on Saratoga and Livonia. Between sips, you could also arrange for Murder Inc. to reduce the number of your acquaintances by one. There were twenty murders in Brownsville in 1939. When a local softball team played a team of inmates at Sing Sing, Murder Inc., also known as the Combination, supplied the uniforms.

Some say that it was a friendly ghetto, no doubt because of its homogeneity. The construction of the ramp to the Williamsburg Bridge uprooted thousands of Lower East Side Jews, who simply rode the soon-to-be-completed subway line over the new bridge and six miles out to Brownsville. In the early part of the century, Brownsville was almost entirely Jewish and self-sufficient, with a flourishing economy complete with "rotating credit associations," entrepreneurs, numerous small businesses, and manufacturing. It was home to a paper box factory, a staple manufacturer, U Bet syrup, and Holland Steel. It had its own shopping district. Pitkin had banks and fancy clothing stores, and people lined up for two-cent movies. Belmont had the open-air market with its pushcarts and the smell of herring and pickles. Saratoga Avenue was the place for junk shops, tinsmiths, garages, and stables.

There were scattered Italians and pockets of blacks living in shacks on the eastern border, under the elevated subway. One black old-timer recalls, "Back then we were accepted, even welcome in people's homes, because there were too few of us to be a threat." The neighborhood was dense, 140 people to a square acre. This was at once the new suburbia and a traditional shtetl. Around it were sleepy fishing villages like Canarsie.

Until World War II, the Jews did not go anywhere, not even to the next town. Those who lived in "Brahnzvil," as they pronounced it with their Yiddish accents, did not wander into neighboring communities. The borders of the surrounding German and Irish working-class areas were policed by gangs of youths. But the Jews did not have to travel. Every kind of good and service was for sale in Brownsville itself. New residents could always find work in the needle trades.

Many people were poor and even hungry. When a kid went to a fresh-air camp, the success of the vacation was measured by how much weight he gained. But the Jews of Brownsville prided themselves on the fact that they were the descendants of merchants, not peasants. They believed in the future. The homes were cheaply built and cramped, so the residents put their hopes in the schools and public institutions. Brownsville was the home of what was hailed as the first free public children's library in the world, on the corner of Mother Gaston and Dumont, half a block from where the Worthys live. Records show that on January 4, 1914, 2,645 volumes were borrowed from its shelves in four hours. A photograph from the 1930s shows a block-long line of dark-haired children waiting patiently outside the two-story brick building to exchange books. All you had to do was show clean hands and you could get two books for a week, one hard and one easy.

Thirty years later, the African American residents of Brownsville also wanted the best for their children. But the fruits of even a partial victory in the bitter controversy of the late 1960s over community control of the schools were sucked away by corruption and intractable bureaucracies. The credit associations and small businesses were gone by then. All that remained of the old Brownsville was its fearsome reputation. The neighborhood was so tough that the owners of Mr. Softee–type ice cream trucks saw fit to use the name Kool Man on their vehicles in Brownsville. In the 1970s, young Riddick Bowe, from the Noble Drew Ali Houses and Thomas Jefferson High School, walked softly around his Brownsville neighborhood because he did not want to run afoul of a local tough the kids called Bummy Mike, Mike Tyson. Both later became heavyweight boxing champions of the world.

In the 1980s, the East Brooklyn churches fostered a plan for private subsidies of one-family tract housing in Brownsville. The dwellings were called the Nehemiah Homes, after the biblical prophet who supervised the rebuilding of the walls of ancient Jerusalem. The one thousand Nehemiah Homes, offered to any family with a household income of $20,000, were quickly filled, mostly by city workers with good credit. The rows of private homes were an unqualified success. But the immaculate Nehemiahs, complete with driveways and back yards soon stocked with lawn furniture and barbecues, were simply too few to ease the misery of the projects, which stood above them like great poisonous trees.

Fiorentino Plaza, on Pitkin Avenue, is one of those projects. Reidus Saab, a retired female corrections matron, lives there, just biding time before she moves back to Clarendon County, South Carolina. "I'm a highland Geechee," she declares. "That's why you don't hear me talkin' all that stuff about 'Hey, mon,' like some Jamaican." Saab and the rest of the residents used to call Fiorentino PCO Brian Lavin "Sneaky," because of his stealth and persistence in apprehending drug dealers in the project. "That's my baby, Sneaky. He was a roof man," Saab explains. "Used to clock 'em good. Then he'd slide up on 'em all nice and smooth and put his hand on their shoulder."

When Officer Lavin was rewarded with a transfer to a plain-clothes detail, the residents held a party in his honor. A sixteen-year-old girl wrote a rap song in praise of his work. The lines of the song, written on the cracked keys of an old-fashioned type-writer, are tacked to the glass-covered photo board near the back stairway in the PSA.

> Lavin's his name. Sneaky's his fame.
> And this cop puts old Kojak to shame.
> They run and hide when they think he's around.
> When he's gone they come right back.
> But Lavin been hidin' he don't cut no slack.
> He pops right out and puts them on the wall,
> Till they start to bawl.
> This Lavin is like no other.
> He makes the drug dealers cry to their mother.

But Lavin is gone now, and as the young poet predicted, the dealers came right back. "I live on the first floor," Saab says. "I'm tired of payin' rent and sleepin' on the floor. Have gun will travel, that's this place here. So many bullets come in you be a fool to sleep in the bed."

So this steamy fall day, Gary Lemite and Mario Palumbo are

headed over to Fiorentino to do something about the situation. Gary has taken his first small step up the career ladder already, with this promotion to the sweep team. He is still in uniform, but from now on, no more sector cars. He will be sent out in a van with a group of officers on assignment.

Mario Palumbo is on the team, but one look at him and you can tell he is a free-lancer at heart. You can tell by the way he wears his hat, the way he stands and walks, the way he does, or does not, smile. Mario is tight and loose at the same time. He has the hot-wire moves and the balls, good instincts all around, but he has made a few mistakes. He was caught off-post once or twice, and he has been in too many shootings. They were good shootings, everybody, including internal affairs, Kammerdener and Lenti, and anybody else who matters, says. Good shootings. But good or not, Mario's record, his personality, and especially the gunplay make him a perceived liability by the bosses in the department.

An officer at the PSA tells about the time he sat in a car with Mario late one night in the parking lot in Cypress. A round went off somewhere nearby. Mario raised his hand to his partner with the index finger extended, as if to say, "I have just the right thing for this." He fished under his jacket and removed his unauthorized nine-millimeter automatic so he wouldn't have to use his service revolver, slowly rolled the window down, leaned out, and fired two shots moonward. "Scuds," he explained as he replaced the weapon. In a moment there were two more reports as the original shooter answered the challenge with a couple of ballistic rooster crows of his own. On the second shot the cops spotted the muzzle flash. In five minutes Mario and his partner had the kid and the gun in hand.

Mario and Gary are in Fiorentino Plaza to give support to the handsomest cop in Brownsville. It is not going to be an easy thing to fill Sneaky Lavin's shoes in Fiorentino, but Seeger, the guy with the wavy dark hair and professional good looks, whom the other cops call Matt Houston, is going to try. A handsome face does not count for much in Brownsville and East New York. The stress is so great here that people soon find out what is inside a person. The environment of a housing project is so hypersocial that people get to know each other fast and well. There are so many chances to do good, bad, or nothing that each person writes his résumé every day right in front of his neighbors. It is no different for the police officers. Matt Houston looks like a Hollywood cop, but he doesn't have the heart and style of Lavin, and the locals jump on him quick.

Earl Frazier, a Fiorentino fixture and small-time drug dealer, knows all about the sweep team, so when he sees Gary and Mario he puts down his half-finished forty-ounce and grabs the receiver of a pay phone on the sidewalk. He stands on the corner of Pitkin and Van Siclen, behind the stairway to the A train, and pretends to listen to a voice on the other end of the line.

Gary walks up on one side. Mario approaches from the other. On another day the incident might be over before it begins — a nod, a warning. Not today.

"I showed respect. I put the bottle down. I'm talkin to my girl," Frazier explains nervously. He knows the beer in his hand gives the cops the right to search him, gives them the keys to his pockets.

"I'm not askin' you, I'm tellin' you. Get off the phone now," Lemite orders. "Put the phone down," he growls, stepping closer, now chest to chest with Frazier. Mario stands a foot behind. But Frazier does not comply. He knows he is about to go to the wall for a toss and a ticket for public drinking.

"I didn't dis you," he whines. Then he spins, pushes Mario against the wall, and bolts across Miller Avenue toward the courtyard of the project. Gary is ten feet behind, charging for a quick catch. But as Frazier reaches the far side of Miller Avenue, just before he will make the turn and fly through the walkways of the project buildings, he digs in his waistband and comes out with a seventeen-shot nine-millimeter Beretta, turns halfway toward Gary, and pops four evenly spaced shots at him. Unhit, Gary draws and fires three quick shots back. There is no fear in him, just a massive dose of adrenaline from somewhere under his rib cage and a sensation of closure, the crystallized conviction that he will never see Erica and Zach again.

Frazier quicksteps toward the end of a wall along the sidewalk and the turn into the courtyard. Gary has not moved. Instead, after a moment, he fires three more shots. Frazier's right shoulder lurches forward, and his right arm swings away from his body as he wheels out of Gary's sight and sprints through the buildings toward Bradford Avenue. The kid is hit.

Gary is running, Mario right behind. Gary is having second

thoughts about pegging more shots at Frazier. Women and children flood the courtyard from the first-floor apartments. Miraculously, the barrage of gunfire is drawing people outside. There is swirling movement to Gary's right and left as curiosity becomes madness and people run toward the action. But Gary only dimly notes these people. His vision is funneled through the mud-brown brick buildings to Frazier, who is flying out the other side of the plaza onto Bradford. Gary stops in front of a sign that reads 340 Miller Avenue to jam a speedloader into the cylinder of his gun, a tricky maneuver that has always taken a few tries in practice and now requires just one pass. The speedloader slides in like butter; the empty cartridge rattles to the cement. To Lemite's left are doorways into the Fiorentino buildings; to his right, a small sunken playground with a green cement turtle and a frolicking red dolphin.

As Lemite, winded, resumes the chase, Palumbo sprints past and tails Frazier out of the plaza to the right up Bradford. Gary, now five paces behind, is on the radio spitting out the 13, giving cross streets. He fancies himself a radio man. Accordingly, he reports the location crisply, despite the lock on his lungs. Mario hears Gary say "Bradford" on the direct, but he repeats the location to Central as "Thatford," naming a street seventeen blocks to the west. There will be no backup cars soon. Mario is not a detail man. If you want somebody to stand post, stay in one place, don't pick Mario. If you need a partner in a shootout like this, he is just right. Mario lets a round go at Frazier on Bradford, and the chase continues. Most foot pursuits last only a few moments. This is a marathon, and it is far from over.

Reidus Saab hears the shots and looks out her window, an ill-considered maneuver that she can't resist.

"All them shots are ringin' and I see this officer right there. I guess God didn't have work for him that day 'cause he wasn't hit. I knew the boy who was runnin', sure. They shoot up this place all the time. Now when they come runnin' by that day, I know where that boy was headed. Straight to that Holy House."

As Lemite pushes himself up Bradford, he feels the presence of a narrow boy running by his side. Nothing in Brownsville and East New York is done alone. The people who live there know it. They have known it since the days when the Jews crowded these streets. The great and small moments of their lives are performed in front of witnesses. They know each other, they love and/or hate each other. They cannot get away from each other. The enforced intimacy is maddening. Lemite cannot guess the intentions of his frail shadow, but he doesn't have the energy to look closely or shout him off.

The chase turns onto Glenmore, again onto Miller, and back down toward Pitkin, as Frazier heads toward "that Holy House," a crack-blighted apartment building near the far corner of Pitkin and Miller. One last straightaway. Gary and Mario, thirty-year-old men on the heels of a twenty-year-old, suck in air that feels like ground glass and hang on to the kid like hounds. The streets are lined with people like the finishing stretch of a famous road race. The runners are old rivals.

Frazier tries to dive into a parked car on the corner of Pitkin and Miller, but the three men inside lock the doors. He flees around to the rear of the Holy House and disappears inside. Finally, help is here. An Emergency Service Unit truck is screeching to the curb. Cars from PSA 2 and the 75th are alighting on the street like great screaming birds.

"We'll take off every fucking door," a Housing sergeant is saying. It isn't long before a trail of blood leads to the wounded Frazier, who is found changing clothes in a second-floor closet.

Outside, Gary Lemite peels off first his shirt, then his bullet-proof vest, then his gun belt, which he drapes carelessly over his shoulder. Things do not seem to matter to him. He stands blank-eyed in the street. Behind him is the Xima beauty salon. On the wall beyond the salon is a mural with a motorcycle and the words "R.I.P. Manny." Nearby is another memorial, "R.I.P. Ant," and a picture of a gravestone, "Luis, 1979–1991."

The three men in the car Frazier tried to hide in have been detained. The fact that Frazier sought their help is enough to make them suspects. In their vehicle is half a pound of cocaine and $4,000. Gary is still dazed on the street. Chips of glass from bottles broken long ago sparkle at his feet. An open fire hydrant wastes a funnel of clear water in the oily gutter. A resident bellows from a window high above, "Let my people go," as Frazier, who has been bounced off a few walls on the way downstairs, is loaded into the ambulance for the trip to Brookdale. Still Gary stands.

Plainclothes Housing cop Gus Platt sidles through the crowd with a cheap smile. "Welcome to the club," he says to Gary. He means the shooters' club, for those cops who have been in gun

162

battles. This is the first time Gary has fired his gun at a human being.

But Gary is not listening. His mind has stalled. Too many thoughts have been stashed away in the past few minutes, too many considerations put off in the simple world of action; no more ideas can penetrate until the brain disposes of its workload. He stands with his knees locked, hips forward, staring straight ahead. Then he hears a voice.

The kid who ran beside him up Bradford and Glenmore, down Miller — guardian angel, thrill-seeker, perp, whatever — is at his ear. "The gun," the kid whispers. "Let's go get the gun."

The gun. An image leaps to Gary's mind. As Frazier turned off Bradford onto Glenmore, he heaved the gun in a lofty arc across the street into an auto lot. The Emergency Service, an elite NYPD unit, is called over to check the lot. The search is crucial, because a police officer has shot someone. Gary stands by, the kid next to him. ESU finds the Beretta.

Still Gary is unfocused. "La-la Land," he calls it later. It is Sam Tilly, a Housing cop who was shot in the arm in Harlem, who brings him back. It is not the pats on the back or the words of praise that do it, just Sam close by. For a year after his shooting, Sam was trapped in a never-ending replay of the moment. He watched the shooting in slow motion and real speed. He could even freeze the action at will, but he could not make it go away. Sam understands. One look in his eyes and Gary feels much better.

But not for long. The thing is over, but adrenaline has life of its own, and Gary can't relax, can't even sit down. He shot the kid. He is glad he hit the kid, but he is all twisted up anyway. He hit the kid.

Very few cops ever actually fire their guns, much less shoot a human being. For Gary, a veil has been lifted. What if he had been hit? What if he had killed someone? What? Then a mood swing. "I know I can shoot. If I had a chance to get ready, I would have punched his ticket," he declares.

An instructor at the academy told Gary, "Someday you will look back on what you did and you are going to freak out," and now Gary knows exactly what the man meant: pride, confusion, and a buzz that won't go away. Gary walks to a pay phone and dials Lisa at her sister's house. His voice quivers.

"Lisa?"

"Are you all right?"

"Sure," Gary says.

"Sure?"

"Yeah, I'm O.K." Gary minimizes the gunplay. He and Lisa talk for a minute about how Sam said that Gary should see the police psychologist before he goes back to work. Another half a minute. There are long silences, and Lisa begins to edge off the phone. Gary hangs up, stands for a moment, and calls again. This time Lisa hears his voice and places the receiver gently back in its cradle. This is not her world anymore. She will not be forced into the role Gary needs her to play now. She just hangs up. The buzz of the dial tone releases a flood of rage in Gary as he walks toward the corner of Pitkin and Van Siclen to the car, where Sam is waiting to drive him to the hospital.

Things are not going any better for Mario. Expecting a reward for his valiant pursuit, Mario tells the inspector who interviews him after the shooting, "I'd like NEU." As aggressive as Gary was, it was Mario who was on Frazier's trail like an Exocet missile. But the inspector tells Mario that a promotion to the city-wide plainclothes detective path unit is out of the question. The big boss lets Mario know to expect a move in the opposite direction — a transfer, at the very least. It is about numbers. Mario now has four shootings in four months. If he does something bad now, people are going to ask why the pattern was not seen, why something was not done. The brass will try to protect themselves from that kind of second-guessing now. It is unlikely that Mario will be back at PSA 2.

Frazier's arm wound is superficial and he is out of the hospital in hours. Back in the squad room, the detectives are not happy with Earl Frazier. He tried to kill a cop.

"You came in here with some information and your handsome face," a detective tells Frazier before the kid sits down to be questioned. "You're not leaving with both."

Even with that, Frazier cannot get his story straight. He tells the detectives and the circuit-riding ADA who takes preliminary statements in the local precincts that he carried the gun because some guys were looking for him. He ran because he did not want the gun charge, and as he fled, he passed two Spanish guys who were shooting at each other. One of their shots, Frazier says, hit him in the arm. His second story is that he took the gun out of his waistband as he was running and it went off.

As he thinks about the shooting in the ensuing days, Gary becomes convinced that the people who let Earl Frazier hide in their apartment should be charged. "If they didn't let him in voluntarily, as they claim, then Frazier should be charged with breaking and entering or burglary," he argues.

It seems that Gary has been making too many good moves on the street, stepping out of his place in the pecking order of the PSA. The good-natured kidding directed at him from the other officers has all but faded away, and in its place a vague wariness has arrived. Downstairs in the PSA, somebody has written "Knows it all. Does it all" on Gary's locker.

Two days after the shooting Gary still cannot sleep, cannot lasso the galloping adrenaline. At three o'clock in the morning, his eyes jammed open in the dark of his bedroom, his pulse roaring for action, he is on the phone talking with a friend about Earl Frazier, and about his wife. He has seen the police shrink, told the man he is O.K. But he still feels jumpy. Near dawn he gets some sleep, but he's gummy-eyed when he wakes. Frazier. Damn. It's not about Gary's performance on the job or his ambitions anymore; the shooting has released a swirling cloud of uncertainty. Gary has been cleared by the department doctor to come back to work later in the week. At noon, he calls the PSA to find out what his schedule will be. He discovers he will be out a day longer than he thought he would be. "They mean well," he says of the psychologists and supervisors.

As thoughts of the shooting subside, another tide of anxiety rises. Gary cannot stop thinking about how Lisa hung up on him. He has to get back to work. Every moment the telephone in his basement apartment sits mute on the wall, every silent meal he eats, makes the possibility of their reunion seem more remote.

The beat goes on. With no family to go to, no wife to call, Gary throws himself back into the streets. He is riding hard, watching every move of every kid, looking for bulges and quick step-offs. Some of the other officers have other things on their minds. One afternoon Gary spots a kid with what he is sure is a big gun. He tells the driver of the van to turn around and the cop just keeps driving down the road. Gary does not say anything at the time, but back at the PSA he vents his anger to guys he knows will tell the driver. The next day the driver of the van comes up and says to Gary, "I hear you're saying I'm the devil. Am I the devil?"

"Well, no. I wouldn't call you the devil," Gary says.

A couple of days later, Gary rocks a fresh-mouthed kid against a wall in the lobby of Seth Low Houses. It is the kind of thing that brought J.R. good reviews. But Gary is called back to the PSA within an hour of the incident. Lenti wants to know the story. The mother just called, complaining that Gary was drunk. Satisfied, Lenti sends him right back out, but it is not long before Gary learns that the mother has filed a civilian complaint over the incident.

SATELLITE

Sharron is standing slouched at the head of the small classroom, his wrists crossed in front of his genitals, hands loose, ready to move. His head is down, eyes up. He is fiercely nonchalant. Twenty students watch carefully as he speaks the body language of the street. This is a role-playing exercise. At Satellite, the school day doesn't begin with an anonymous homeroom but with a "strat," or strategy period, a counseling session designed to help students deal with personal distress. Strat can be a boring annoyance or, when a topic catches on, an opportunity to help students confront their own trauma. The man in charge of Sharron's strat is Neil, a tall, bald and bespectacled veteran instructor who is also Sharron's science teacher.

Today's exercise finds Sharron cast as a witness to a street crime. To the uninitiated, his posture indicates an insolent lack of discipline. In fact, it is both functional and articulate. The exaggerated slouch communicates to the thief that Sharron is not a regular citizen, a "vic," constrained by laws against possession of weapons. The placement of the wrists is a stylized martial arts pose, offering protection and potential for quick reaction. The tucked chin protects the vulnerable neck area.

In the scenario, an elderly woman has been robbed; the mugger bolts toward Sharron, who has an opportunity to rescue the woman's pocketbook, which holds her rent money. "Help me, help me, please," the girl portraying the victim wails. Like a matador, Sharron steps smoothly aside, and the thief is gone. His classmates nod approvingly.

"Go, *Sharron*," a girl in the back applauds. In the students' eyes, volunteer crime prevention is misguided and frightfully dangerous.

Like most adults, Neil takes a quick liking to Sharron. Things start in September on the right foot. The other students accept Sharron just as quickly. For his part, Sharron is not interested in cutting an astounding figure in this small theater. He is content to lie low. The pressure on his wardrobe will not be as intense; the clothes on his back will not be the subject of such rapt attention as they were at Jeff. Simply, there will be less drama.

Satellite Academy is housed on the drafty second floor of an old office building facing the back wall of City Hall in downtown Manhattan. The quarters are cramped and the equipment is limited. There is no gymnasium, auditorium, or library, no labs, few computers. But the classes are tiny, the teachers warm and zealous. "The students help make the decisions here," a henna-haired Hispanic girl says as she lounges by a desk in a reception area. "If you fight, you get kicked out, no matter who threw the first punch. So you don't see any fighting. And you can take a teacher to school court if the teacher gets all loud with you."

Sharron may have made the best move of his life going to school outside Brownsville. With the accelerated credit program at Satellite, he stands a chance of earning enough credits to graduate by June. When he accompanied Frank to Satellite High, he serendipitously placed himself on the cutting edge of instruction on the urban high school level. Carol Beck is a phenomenon, to be sure, and it would be difficult to conjure a teacher with more assets than Sharon King, but schools like Jefferson may well be obsolete. With eighteen hundred students, Jefferson is simply too large and impersonal for the kids it serves. When such schools were designed, centralization aimed at offering varied programs and specialized equipment that would be impractical for every small school. The large public high school could bring students together with teachers who had special expertise. It was a good idea for its time and place. Clearly, it does not work anymore.

In the future, educators and urban planners may despair that cities stuck with the megaschools as long as they did. The schools are like the projects themselves — a good solution to a bygone problem. The adolescents who go to Jeff need personal attention. The baby talk that Ms. King dispenses fills a personal and emotional void for her charges. These students fail to learn high-level reading skills not because they don't understand or can't remember — they manage to create and revise their own language every month — but because they harbor a mistrust of the words on the page and the teacher who introduces those words. What they need is an educational environment that is structured to make personal relationships between the teachers and students possible, so the kids can bond with mentors.

It will still be a tough year for Sharron. He faces courses in anatomy, ideas, interdisciplinary writing, and novels. And he will have to find a way to do some homework for the first time in his life. If he is to negotiate the land mines around him, live through the school year, and emerge with a high school diploma or on the verge of receiving one, he will have to stay out of the way of the bullets and the law. But there is more to his dilemma. Despite pledges to his mother and Ms. King, despite his words, there is something deep in Sharron that resists the passage out of Brownsville, the relinquishment of his hard-earned props.

If Sharron does graduate from high school in June, he will be the first in his family to do so. Shawanda dropped out in the eleventh grade, and Gloria stopped going in the tenth, when she had Shawanda. Even with his arrests, his shoplifting, and his fights, and despite getting left back in seventh grade, Sharron carries his mother's lofty expectations with him as surely as if he were the scion of a wealthy family.

Gary's sister-in-law, Melanie, and her husband, Bill, do their very best to make their own sunshine. They have a swimming pool with a sun deck and a hot tub and plenty of extra room in their airy childless house. Bill is a "can do" guy with a consuming desire to make his wife happy. Here, Lisa has her own room and much less responsibility than she had in the basement in Elmont. She can sit around the pool while her sister and brother-in-law fuss over the kids, even sunbathe nude on their enclosed deck.

Gary was never the ideal husband, or boyfriend, for that matter. When he first started to date the open-faced, blue-eyed Lisa, he treated her with the same cavalier approach he used with all his girlfriends. When he picked her up for a date, he would pull up in front of her house and beep his horn. Lisa's parents were irritated, but she was mad about her Haitian suitor with the body language and accent of a Queens construction worker. She would skip out to the car. But soon she had enough of Gary's self-satisfied ways and stopped seeing him. This first defection shook Gary in a way that he did not fully understand. He managed to conceal his mounting desperation and woo her back, but he never forgot the feeling.

Lisa still has a soft spot for Gary's smile. And after a couple of sea breezes at a local bar during their first attempt at reconciliation, her grievances over his mania for the job, his casual attitude toward her happiness, and the rabbit warren of a basement he calls a home lift magically away. All she can think of is lying down with him again. It has been a month since they have held each other.

When they get home, Gary undresses her in the half-light of their bedroom. She has not lost the weight she gained from carrying Zach. But that does not matter. Gary holds handfuls of her thick chestnut hair in his hands, draws them to his face, and inhales. After they make love, he reaches to the table lamp and switches on the light. Lisa is a quarter Cherokee; a red Indian head tattoo glistens on her shoulder blade, and her skin is soft and deeply, gloriously tanned.

Gary snaps his head back, drawing his chin down to his chest. "What the fuck is this?"

"What?" Lisa wants to know, her eyes round with innocence.

"You know what I'm talking about." Gary's voice quivers. "I told you about taking your clothes off. You can do whatever you want, but not with the kids around. I told you."

Lisa has been preparing for a moment just like this. "Neither you nor anybody else is going to tell me what to do. Understand that?"

The light from the small lamp beside the bed shows that Lisa's suntan is uninterrupted by spots where clothing might have been — should have been, according to Gary. The evening is ruined. After Lisa leaves, Gary sits in the kitchen with the lights off, plagued by images of her loose behavior in front of the kids, of family conspiracies against him, of Lisa's imagined infidelity. Why will no one put in a good word for him? Dammit, hasn't he helped every one of them at one time or another?

The only bright spot is the weekly Friday night visits Gary and Lisa are making to see the pastor at Lisa's church. Merle is a middle-aged midwesterner who can be very helpful when he is not rigging sides on volleyball nights or rubbing people the wrong way with his hypercompetitive play in all sports. He seems as if he really wants the couple back together, wants Lisa to think about giving the marriage another chance. The pastor advises patience and support.

Gary Lemite has jeopardized his marriage by his singular focus on his job, while at Satellite, Sharron Corley is risking his last chance at a high school diploma. He is having trouble making it to school on time. This day in October, after missing strat and his first-period class, on the brain, he strides into his interdisciplinary writing class, his face soft from sleep. Two energetic young team teachers flutter earnestly about the room, working with individual students. They accept Sharron's late entrance pleasantly, taking a moment to hand him the topic sheet for the writing assignment. After ten minutes, he has done no writing.

"Are you all right, Sharron?" one of the teachers asks.

"Yeah, cool." He smiles and adjusts the position of the assignment sheet on his desk. He stares at the paper. But his Polo frames fail to deliver a studious appearance as he yawns through the session, thinking about what kind of lunch period he and Frank will have. The two friends have taken to jumping the turnstiles, riding the train to Greenwich Village, and "taking lunch." Besides such mischief, he is bothered by an energy deficit. Even though he had endless patience for the Jefferson play, he seems now to be dragging himself through every school day. He has always gotten his spirit of perfectionism from the spotlight. But Satellite is no kind of stage, no fashion show. There isn't even a proper mirror anywhere in the joint.

At Jeff, Sharron's lateness and lethargy might be overlooked, but here at Satellite, Neil is watching. When Frank and Sharron slip up the back stairs after lunch, late for their class, the towering Neil is standing akimbo in the hallway. He does not say a word, just raises his arms over his head with his fingers spread, as if to say, "What's up? You guys are faking the whole thing here, and I know it."

Sharron slinks sheepishly off to class, but still he has other things than school on his mind. Following his conversation with Chantal the day he went to Jeff to get his transfer papers, Sharron determined to meet his responsibilities as he saw them. He hit Macy's and Bloomingdale's and began a boosting spree for his girl. On his second trip to Manhattan, he "caught" a brown and beige reversible goose-down vest for Chantal to wear when the weather turns cold.

When Sharron gets home from school, before he heads upstairs, he stops at the pay phone and places a call to Chantal. "Yeah, I miss you," he tells her. Baby Andre is babbling and cooing in the background. "Let me speak to Andre."

Chantal is reluctant. Sharron doesn't call every day, and she wants him to herself. "Oh, Sha, you know he can't say nothin'."

"You said he could talk."

"He *do* be talkin'. But you can't tell what he's sayin'."

"Put him on the phone."

Andre produces a variety of sputtering sounds into the phone.

"What you want? What you want? Why you spit so much? When you comin' to see your daddy?"

In a moment Chantal is back on the line. "Sha?"

"Andre says you been smokin' cigarettes, an' you ain't been goin' to school."

"Who says I . . . Oh Sha, stop. It's hard. How come I beep you an' you don't call?"

"Sometimes I be in the train. Or school. Or rehearsal." Sharron has been spending time in his cousin Morris's tiny sound studio, singing with Frank, who Sharron has discovered possesses a talent for rap, and a boy named Chris, whom Sharron has nicknamed "the choirboy."

"We sound mad good," he tells Chantal. "I got a new song, 'Nothing Can Go Wrong.'" He begins to croon the lyrics into the phone.

I've got a job to do.
Let's get it done, get it on.
It can only get better.
'Cause nothin' can go wrong.
Nothin' can go wrong.

*

A local in Unity aims a finger at Gary Lemite one day and asks Lonnie Hayes, "Who the hell does that half-white motherfucker think he is?" Hayes just shrugs.

The bleak landscape matches Gary's mood. His heavy hands are earning him enemies on the street, but his spate of gun collars is bringing him props in the PSA. The rumor mill says he will be promoted again soon.

Today he is still on the sweep team. It is noon. Five officers approach the van. Marlene Pemberton is at the wheel, Sergeant Billy Bright in the passenger seat. John McMullen greets Jimmy Galvin as he steps up to the vehicle. Each of the two cops has recently been called a major disappointment by the sweep supervisor, Lieutenant McGinty. McMullen snaps his hand to the brim of his cap in a crisp salute.

"Good evening, Major Disappointment."

"At ease, Major Disappointment," Galvin returns.

"How was it last night?" Galvin asks Marlene as the van begins to move.

"Good to me. Better to him." Marlene turns to Galvin and McMullen behind her, doffs her hat, and wiggles her eyebrows.

"Watch the road," Sergeant Bright admonishes.

"How many rounds?" McMullen wants to know.

"The distance."

"The distance?"

"Yeah, this golden pussy probably kill one of you needle-dicks."

"How can you say that, after you licked my pickle last week?" McMullen protests.

"Slow down," Gary snaps from the back seat. Marlene slows the van next to a group of kids. "Nah, go ahead," Gary instructs.

"Whaa, Gary, you see a bulge? Marlene, Gary saw a bulge. You wanna go back?"

As the van rolls down Rockaway Avenue, a youth makes steady eye contact with the officers in the van. "That's that asshole that we had on the dis con. The one with the bullets, a couple of months ago," Galvin remembers.

Police officers depend on their powers of recall, shine their memories up and roll them out like fancy cars.

"Nah. It was a holster. Black holster," Gary corrects.

There are problems for Gary with the sweep team detail. The

quality-of-life assignments they are sent on are often seen as harassment by the tenants, who call them the Goon Squad, and civilian complaints pile up. The sweep team is also trouble for cops like Gary because it forces them to sink to the level of their squad. Virtually everything the group does is agreed upon in advance by all four or five cops and the supervising sergeant in the van. There is much discussion, but limited spontaneous, instinctual police work.

Now the team is waiting outside the PSA for Sergeant Bright to emerge from the bathroom.

"What the fuck is he doin', layin' cable?" McMullen gripes.

One aspect of police work that cops like is that it has room for all types. An officer can shift from one profile to another at will. There are the hotshots, like Lemite and Lavin and Schulman, and the guys who never want to make a collar, who just walk through the motions. A guy can tear up the streets for a while. Then, if he thinks he's been screwed by the job or he goes through a change of life, he can make the transition to being a cleanup man. No questions asked.

The only advantage to driving around with five guys is the jokes. "You gap-toothed Irish bastard," Galvin says to McMullen. "The reason your father put himself in a home is 'cause he didn't want to pay your dental bills."

For his part, McMullen, formerly Robocop of the Brownsville Houses, who now insists on being called McDaddy, is delighted, giddy, to be back at work after a dreadful accident some months ago. He was searching a project rooftop for a suspected robber and climbed up a ladder to a wooden water tank. As he was coming down, the ladder snapped off and he fell ten feet to the graveled roof. He shattered his pelvis and was rushed to Bellevue Hospital, where he shared space in the intensive care unit with perps of all kinds. When Jeff Desimone showed up to visit, he whispered, "Wake up, asshole." McMullen roused himself from a haze of painkillers. There were intravenous tubes in his arms and a catheter in his penis. "Get me the sex crimes unit," he quipped. "I'm being violated."

Many police officers dream of getting out on three quarters, tax-free disability. The chiefs and the superchiefs routinely come up with some "job-related" injury or heart ailment that puts them in the comfort zone of a disability pension. One

NYPD chief got out on three quarters because he said he had incurred irreplaceable hearing loss at a Rolling Stones concert at Shea Stadium. Many cops dream of shedding the "blue burden" and going on to another life, but McMullen is not one of them. He is not as collar-driven as Gary — a bachelor, he does not depend on the overtime — but like Gary he loves the job. When he recovered, he came back to work. His first day back, it was all he could do not to skip down Sutter Avenue.

High-riding October clouds sail over Pennsylvania Avenue. Across the street from Jeff, on Dumont, opposite the drug house at 666, Michael T. stands near the center of a group of boys tossing Selo, a game of dice. It is just 1 P.M. on this school day. The cubes rattle against a cement wall and tumble onto the sidewalk as the sweep van pulls slowly to the curb. Gary is on the sidewalk side of the van in the back seat. The dice game is over. The boys back off slowly, except for Michael T. "That's the cop I almost clapped," the big kid tells his cronies, forming a gun with his index finger and thumb and pointing it at Gary. "Shoulda clapped him."

"Starts talking that shit again," Gary grumbles to his partners, "I'm gonna lock him up."

IN FULL EFFECT

The first bite of autumn finds Carol Beck harried. Her lower lip is dry and cracked. She wears a blue suit with a wide white tie and her Nefertiti brooch. She is moving down the hall at the head of a platoon of security guards, looking for class-cutters, interlopers. A handful of disappointed miscreants are caught in the open, herded into an elevator, and escorted to a holding room. "Run them through the computer," Beck snaps. Within minutes, a call will be placed to each child's home — that is, if the student has a phone.

On her way back to her office, Beck is summoned to a fourth-floor window. Five girls are standing on the pavement across the street from the school. With help from a guidance counselor, Beck identifies four of them. Their names are fed to the computer, the calls made. Within ten minutes, an irate mother is on the street, jawing at her daughter.

The two toughest seasons at Thomas Jefferson are the fall and the hot days of late spring. This fall is probably more difficult because of the triumphs of last year. There was the naive feeling that the battle had been won. But in a big city high school, the battle is never won. Suddenly, Beck feels she must sit down. "We can't schedule that meeting for second period tomorrow," she tells her assistant principal, who trails her down the hall, "because we have a sweep second period. This is like a war. I won't give up the hallways. And I won't give up the street outside my school. I'll take a bullet if I have to."

Bashim remembers when Beck was a brand-new principal. "She was standing up on the stage and giving out the rules and whatnot. You know, the do's and the don'ts that she had. It was a whole list of shit. All of a sudden some guy yells, 'Fuck you!' Beck comes down off the stage and smacks the shit out of the guy right there. All the people are sayin', 'Hey, we aren't havin' this. Nobody is gonna smack me, blah blah,' and we walk out. Get this. There's all these kids standing out in front of the school and Beck comes out and says, 'Get back in the school,' and people went back in.''

Another time there was a fight between a group from the Linden Houses and Bashim's Raiders from Howard. "It was wild — dudes was throwin' down right in that small space on the first floor. The security guards were like peekin' through the little windows at the end of the hall. Beck is right in the middle of it, pullin' guys off each other. There were razors flyin' through the air, whoosh, whoosh, and she was right there. Carol has heart. Everybody knows that.''

Still, Beck is under siege. There are about a hundred freshmen who are not adjusting. "They are like mercury," she observes, with a look on her face as if she has seen something new. "Half a dozen come together just to rob people in the stairway, and then just like that — apart. I had to throw eight of them out this week. They were jumping my football players in the stairwells.'' As she arrives at the door of her first-floor office, she adds, "We have a contradiction. We have the sweetest, the smartest, and the craziest." She shakes her head slowly. "They don't believe." But Beck doesn't allow herself to sink for more than a moment. In a flash, her face breaks into a wide, disingenuous smile. She often makes exaggerated faces so she can be read by the students more easily. "They shot Wesley in the barber shop," she says solemnly, and then, clapping her hands like a little girl, "We got land from the city to make a garden.''

Beck retreats into her meeting room and collapses into a hard chair, breathing deeply, resting. In front of her is a scarred wooden table large enough to accommodate a dozen people. But despite School Chancellor Fernandez's school-based management plan, designed to broaden the decision-making process, Beck is running this campaign alone. And in her own way. Behind her is a private bathroom, which she makes available to a steady stream of students, an astounding practice for a New York City principal.

A newly curvaceous sophomore enters. "I just want the transfer paper," the girl insists shyly. It seems she has had an argument with her mother, the guidance counselor has been prodding her to improve her attendance, and she wants to go to Thomas E. Dewey High School.

Beck is seductive. She stands and steps back, examines the student, and fairly blushes with admiration. Then she moves her hands in the air to describe the girl's new shape.

"You aren't a bucktoothed girl anymore. You have fashion. I see those hats you wear. You're a star, a born leader, smart and beautiful."

The girl is touched. She stares at Beck as though hypnotized. "Thank you, Ms. Beck."

Then the principal snaps the curve ball. "But in two years you will not know a single one of these people that you are trying to impress now. It's sad but it's the truth. We're up your nose now because we care. When we stop talking to you, that's when you start to worry."

The girl decides to stay at Jeff.

When she exits, Beck remarks, "A beautiful girl, and she's just finding where her zippers are. All that attention. I have to combat that with my own brand of attention."

A few minutes later, the revitalized Beck is lecturing a dozen boys in a small room used for music instruction. Seated in the ascending seats are the survivors of the final cut for the varsity basketball team. In the front row is Cortez Sutton, the quick-witted transfer from Lafayette, whose suspension will bar him from league games; behind him is Willie Brown, a four-square junior swingman who started on last year's team. Another veteran, Musbau Ogunyemi, a knobby-boned center who calls himself Nick, is on hand, sprawling at the end of the first row near the wall. Newcomers Jude Princivil, a junior forward, and his brother, Carl, a sophomore point guard, are positioned several rows up. The coach, George Moore, a six-foot-four, thick-waisted, light-skinned man with a short scraggly beard, stands by. Moore, about forty years old, is a corrections officer who doubles as security chief at Jefferson. He has been head basketball coach here for three years.

The glory days of Jefferson basketball have been over for a while. The National Basketball Association has had a handful of Jefferson players in its ranks of millionaires, including several, such as Sidney Green, who plays for the San Antonio Spurs, who are still there. The neighborhood courts are still brimming with talented players, but life is so tough here now that the best players from the Ville either drop out or go to school outside the neighborhood. If they do stay at Jeff, they have trouble sticking on the team. Beck has made it perfectly clear that the basketball team is a sidelight to academics in her regime. She will have no truck with superstar ne'er-do-wells at Jefferson. It is part of her plan to deemphasize basketball and highlight gymnastics, fencing, tennis, and swimming to erode the stereotype of the black male. She is tough with the ballplayers.

"I will not have you play for me and play with those Gauchos or Hauchos," she begins, referring to the citywide teams sponsored by private businesses. "Those are basketball entrepreneurs. They try to buy you with a pair of underwear and a pair of sneakers. If you play for me, that's all you do. I don't know what their agenda is, but if you can be bought with a pair of sneakers, something is wrong." Nick makes eye contact over his shoulder with Jude and nods his head affirmatively. *I told you Ms. Beck knows the deal*, he seems to say.

"We are not using you as a tax write-off," Beck continues. "We are here to help you become what you want to be. There was that kid . . ." She turns to Moore. "What was his name? The kid who got shot. He went to Jefferson as a freshman."

"Lloyd Daniels," Moore says, referring to a six-foot-eight playmaking *wunderkind* who was expelled from the University of Nevada at Las Vegas after he was arrested in a crack house. The players nod knowingly. Daniels was later shot in the stomach; after he recovered, he struggled through the minor leagues and made it to the San Antonio team in the NBA.

"Lloyd Daniels couldn't even write his name," Beck continues. "I want you to be like Bill Bradley." She stops and eyes her players. This time the squad comes up blank, except for Cortez, who whispers the word "senator" over his shoulder. "I want basketball to help you be what you want to be," the principal explains. "Basketball is too short a career."

Beck notices that rangy Jude Princivil is wearing a hat. "I don't want you with the hats." Jude snatches it off. "They don't sell those hats anywhere but East New York. I don't want people to know you're from Brownsville and East New York just by looking at you. Like that little monster from 176 Amboy Street who is getting ripped off by Don King." Nobody in the room has to mention Mike Tyson's name.

"We will check your eligibility," Beck warns. "You can count on it. We will not be slippin' and slidin'. You will have your proper average, and when the scouts come, you will have your transcript in order. And if it means I have to play with less talented players, I will do it."

Little Michael Washington looks at the floor. He is undergrown, has minimal court skills, and knows he is on the team only because he has been going to class and keeping his repertoire of wisecracks under wraps. Beck knows Michael well. "We will never be embarrassed that you went to Jefferson," she says in his direction. "Nobody will have to mention your name being involved in any foolishness. You are my leaders, my *men*. If I have to take your hat, I am going to be outraged. We are not wearing hats. It makes you look like hoodlums. You are not hoodlums. You are talented stars."

Beck finishes her speech and leaves the stage to the athletic director and the coach. It was a good speech; it showed the players the tone of the program, which is not about excellent basketball but about acceptable schooling. The one thing that Carol Beck perhaps did not understand was the purpose of the hats and the hoods. Kids like Jude and Cortez, and the instigator Michael, do not wear those accessories for their style alone. They wear them for safety. It is hard enough walking home through the Linden Houses to the Boulevard Houses, or walking past Unity, without wearing a sign on your back proclaiming that you are a straight arrow, with your eye on the future. The gangster look is surely protective coloring. The hoods and the hats serve the same purpose as the ski masks and goggles that the kids in Crown Heights have taken to wearing; they give the chilling impression that you don't want to be identified. The droopy-pants look comes out of the house of detention, where belts are confiscated to prevent suicide and mayhem. This is the gear of the trouble kids, the robbers and the baby gunmen. Who can blame Nick, the lanky center, who takes a ride home every day with the basketball coach, if he does not want to make it immediately apparent that he is unarmed and not disposed to violence and cruelty, that he is much closer to being a victim than a perpetrator? It is easy for Beck to ask the kids to dress like squares and bookworms. She will not have to pay the consequences.

When Beck leaves, the boys relax, but only a bit. Coach Moore is not to be taken lightly. He steps up on the raised lecture space and begins his policy statement in a sweet baritone voice. "Plain and simple. You must have an eighty percent attendance rate. You must go to class. You must come to the study period in Room 242–244 seventh period. If you don't come to the study period, you don't practice, and if you don't practice, you damn sure don't play in the games. I don't care who you are. An example is Nicky. I love him, but if he doesn't go to class, he will not be here. And about the hats. Don't wear hats in school. Homos wear hats in school." (Homophobia is standard fare in Brownsville and East New York. There are no openly gay students in the school.)

"You must learn not to react. Most teams are hostile to Jefferson. When we showed up at Fashion Institute for a game last year, the first thing the coach told me is 'We don't want any trouble.' I am the last coach to let my players fight. Let the other team woof. We want you on the team. We have a player here, as you all know, Ronnie, who is very talented. He is a man in a boy's body."

"A boy in a man's body," Cortez corrects, from his seat.

"But he will never play on this team," Moore continues, "because he doesn't go to class.

"We are a team. When things go wrong, we are a team. The crowd is gonna be yelling and going crazy, and you look up and down the bench and all you have to rely on is your team. And stop louding [constantly criticizing] each other. Don't laugh if a guy has short socks or a funny-colored hat." Like Beck, Moore is on tough ground here. Cortez, for one, has built his entire personality around the argumentum ad hominem of the streets. Already he has taken to calling starting point guard Ed Alcy "Head." When someone asks why, Cortez points: "Look at him."

"We are going to South Carolina to play in the tournament like we did last year," Moore announces proudly. "You get all you can eat, and believe me, last year Nick ate all they could offer. And when you get down there, be ready, because those country boys really get psyched when they come against you city boys."

"They got a mall," Nick announces to his teammates.

Carl is concerned. "Them country boys can really jump, right? But they don't bounce the ball 'cause they live on dirt?"

The same afternoon, upstairs on the fifth floor, Ms. King is entertaining her global history class. The back of the neat classroom is lined with ancient steel lockers covered by dozens of coats of thick paint, the last a pale blue. The lockers, used in the past for students' books, are now empty. The floor of the room is worn wood.

"Mussolini was a *dick*" — King waits like a borscht-belt comic for the word to sink in — "*tator*." She adds the final syllables with a wink. Things are going well in the class. King, prepared as always, has piles of typed handouts, even though today's lesson is drawn from the textbook. The atmosphere in the room is cheerful, not loose; the students are upbeat, not giddy.

A hard justice is dispensed to those who teach poor black and Hispanic kids in the city. A hard-working, talented teacher is often rewarded for his or her efforts, just as a bad one is punished. The reinforcement does not come from the administration, it comes from the students. If a teacher is lazy, afraid, incompetent, the students make his life hell. Disrespect mounts to mockery and outright abuse. The teacher retreats to fearful inactivity or bitter reprisal, jawing with students in the hallway, flouncing into the office with the big complaint. Not King. She is having a ball, and so are the kids. She is teaching about nationalism, aggression, and appeasement, about the sense of impending disaster throughout Europe before World War II.

Fifteen minutes into the lesson, Khalil Sumpter and his man Dupree stride in, late as usual. This rankles King. She was on a roll. Khalil sprawls in his seat with his head tossed back and to the side, his jaw slack with mock exhaustion. King walks over and positions a textbook on the desktop in front of him. She smiles tightly. He has been coming to class every day, but that is not enough for her.

One day a few weeks ago, in late September, she called him

into the hall and stared deep into his eyes. "What am I doing wrong?" she asked him.

From the refuge of his slouching, indifferent manner, Khalil thought for a moment. His standard school affect was not really working with King. His was not a flexible stance. His strategies were not designed to deal with the golden skin and sweet scent of a Ms. King. "Nah, 's not chu," he allowed softly. He didn't want to tell King about the fights with his nemesis, Tyrone Sinkler.

"Tell me what I'm doing wrong, Khalil, because I really want to do better." King pressed her advantage.

He just shrugged.

"If it's not me, then it must be you," King said kindly. "So I'm gonna assume that since you come to school, you want to learn. That you actually want an education. So I'm gonna make sure that you have your books and you keep them open. And that you write down the things that I'm saying."

Khalil nodded.

But of course it is not that easy. Khalil is coming to class and helping himself to the little kisses that King gives out, insisting that she give him his dead on the lips. He thinks he is conning her, getting over.

According to King, Khalil Sumpter is the smartest kid in class. "One time, I thought he was copying a paper from a girl. He had the girl's paper on the desk in front of him and he was writing for half an hour. I told him, 'No, you aren't slick, Khalil, you copied the paper of a girl who hasn't been in the class in a month. Now both of you can fail.'" Amazingly, Khalil's paper, while obviously done in haste, fulfilled the requirements of the assignment and didn't contain a single phrase in common with the girl's paper. According to King, he is brilliant, one of the smartest kids in the school. But he is quite simply "acting like an asshole."

King is back in the front of the room, selling global history for all she is worth, when Khalil flips his textbook shut and releases an audible groan. The soft-sell time is over. King's system has been working like a charm. She is handing out "chill bills," tickets to be turned in for small rewards, for students who are on the ball. The class is hooked. But Khalil is a dead weight.

King jams her World War II lesson to a halt and strides over to Khalil's desk by the back wall, next to Dupree's. "Open your notebook."

Khalil snickers. He mumbles something about a bitch and sits motionless, waiting for King to give it up and move on. But he underestimates the teacher. This classroom is her life, her world. This is what she cares about, what she does best. And right now it is all about World War II. Khalil Sumpter is not getting the best of Sharon King, not this time, not any time.

King puts her hand firmly on Khalil's shoulder and he shrugs it off. She reaches down and opens his book and he snaps it shut.

"What are you gonna do? Fight me?" King wants to know.

He mumbles menacingly.

She bends over and takes off her shoes. She is not from this world; like Beck, she has never lived in a neighborhood like Brownsville or East New York. But she knows that the only way to succeed here is to accept certain interpersonal truths: if you are not willing to get down, you cannot hang in the Ville, and Ms. King is in the Ville to stay. She is not about to summon any security guards or assistant principals.

She tosses her shoes aside and gets ready to rumble in Room 544. Her loyal students, the ones who love her, stand up, edge closer, and watch, ready to make a move. It is no easy business, this. A wrong move can bring dire consequences from Khalil and his friends.

"I can't hit you. You know that," he says, "'less you hit me first."

Smack. King lashes out with a locked elbow; her open hand slaps the side of his face. "Fair now?" she asks.

The teacher has crossed the line. She was born to cross the line. That is what all the kissing is about, what she is about. The slap is a stupid move for a teacher. But King is not just a teacher. She is something else.

The students jump back and huddle against the wall nearest the door. Theresa, the girl who is taking King's class for the second time, begins to weep. Khalil is stunned. Greg Harris, a six-four, 195-pound athlete who is a King aficionado, leaps forward and holds the two apart in a meticulously nonpartisan, nonconfrontational way. Sumpter and Harris eye each other, worried boys in the bodies of soldiers, trying to understand what kind of men they will be.

At last Khalil shrugs himself free and stalks out of the room. Ms. King is unfazed. This woman has bad days, never bad dreams.

"The Italians loved Benito Mussolini," she resumes, gesturing for the students to go back to their seats. She pauses for a moment as they sit. "Because Mussolini made the trains run on time."

GOING TO REPRESENT

Crossed signals. It is 4:30 in the afternoon on the last day of October and Ms. King is standing at the front of the auditorium in I.S. 55, a junior high school near Saratoga Avenue, some twenty blocks from Jefferson. This is the first meeting of the year of the Jefferson drama program, and understandably, King has big plans. But things are wrong from the start. For one, Sharron is not here to reclaim the spotlight. He didn't have the money to pay for his beeper charge this month, so King had to leave a message with his neighbor, Mrs. Dukes, and word never reached him.

There are worse problems. "Excuse me. I said, excuse me." There are seventy-five kids on hand, but few respond to King's request for quiet. They continue to chatter and giggle. "I'm not going to raise my voice. I don't *do* shouts," King says softly.

The fifteen veterans of last spring's play sit in the front two rows in a tight cluster, their faces raked with annoyance. They had looked forward to the start of the drama program with the enthusiasm of a gifted athlete looking forward to the sports season. They are ready for bigger and better things, ready to be stars again.

Finally, the beauteous, smoky-eyed comedienne Kenya, last spring's showstopper, who has traveled all the way from Sara J. Hale High School to be here, has had enough of the yapping. She raises herself slowly out of her seat, turns, and glowers at the witless bunch around her. "Shut up," she hollers in her stage-trained voice.

But it's no use. Almost all the other kids in the room are

junior high and elementary school students, from I.S. 55 and the surrounding neighborhood. King controls herself throughout the rest of the afternoon as the preteen rabble tries to focus on a fuzzy videotape replay of *Don't Give Up on Your Dreams* but ultimately succumbs to its members' rambunctious natures.

At six o'clock, King's outspoken regulars gather in the hall. The Jeff students have traveled to I.S. 55 by bus. Worse, they have had to come through unfamiliar neighborhoods. It is very important to these kids that they know an area. Even the most timid of them will express confidence that no one on their block or in their project will bother them because they "know everybody." It is hard enough for them to negotiate their way to and from regular school without doubling their vulnerability by having to travel to a second school for an extracurricular activity.

"I don't have car fare to be comin' over here every day," Sheryl complains.

Kenya rolls her eyes at the children scampering through the hallway. "This shit is just whack," she says.

"I don't know who was responsible for this, but we aren't going to have it," King says, and she quickly arranges for a protest meeting in Carol Beck's office the next day. She will stay out of the politics, let the students state their case and try to find out what the drama program is doing at I.S. 55.

For an educational initiative to be successful, it has to be active. The students have to have some feeling of power and be involved in problem solving. It is also crucial for the experience to have immediate application beyond the walls of the school. King's drama program last year, with its glorious week of performances in the spring, was just such an endeavor. Word got around Jefferson that the teachers in the drama program were "for real," that the school had spent serious money on the production. This was the kind of activity that could compete in the students' world with the cult of name-brand clothing and disrupt a hierarchy based on jewelry and violence. The Thomas Jefferson school play should have been used as a springboard to even bigger and better things; instead, it is headed for oblivion.

Somebody fouled up. Somehow, the Jackie Robinson Center got the impression that Carol Beck did not want its program back at Jeff. It may have been a matter of timing. A hands-on principal, one as accessible as Carol Beck, runs the risk of allowing organizational problems to develop. Usually Beck's loyal and fussy assistant, Ellen Greaves, rides herd on such details. This time something went wrong.

Mr. Ozelius Clement, the director of the Jackie Robinson Center, claims he waited as long as he could for Beck to commit. But Beck was having problems. She was juggling money from several sources and battling the centrifugal force of her freshmen Smurfs. The waning of the theater program, which King and her students will soon abandon completely, is a significant mistake, the kind that principals with much less command of the situation make regularly. The Jackie Robinson Center, with its layers of supervision and checks and balances and its emphasis on generous funding, was rated as one of the ten best such programs in the country by a federal commission. Nevertheless, Beck is unchastened. "I got along great before and I'll get along great after. If I want it back, I'll get it back. I know Jackie Robinson's widow."

"I know my son," Gloria Corley says, moving four steps through the living room into the doorway of the cramped kitchen. Plates of cold, half-eaten chicken sit on a counter next to the refrigerator. A plume of light backlights her carefully arranged, hennaed hair. "He doesn't even like house parties. It's ironic. He's the one who doesn't like them and he is the one who is going to get hurt."

It's early November; Indian summer is gone for good. This is clothing weather, profiling weather. Sharron is headed to a house party, and he's not listening to warnings from either Chantal or Gloria.

"I'm goin' to represent," he explains.

"Represent what?" Gloria scoffs as Chantal ducks her head behind her hand and giggles. Chantal has been tucking Andre under the goose-down vest Sharron boosted for her and carrying him over to the Corley apartment several nights a week. When she is not with Sharron in his room, she sits up with Gloria in the kitchen, playing with the baby and gossiping.

"He's gonna have your eyes, Chantal," Gloria decides after studying Andre's ruddy little face and glancing at Chantal. Gloria's full cheeks catch the light as she turns and smiles. The features of her face seem to have been created with a soft brush.

By contrast, Chantal, seated at the table with Andre sprawled in the crook of her arm, was drawn with a sharp quick pencil. She has black chevron eyebrows and cheekbones that jut against stark pale skin.

"I dunno. All babies got squint eyes," Chantal says. "You gotta wait 'fore you could say that."

Gloria chuckles. Her head rocks slowly. "Got a point, sweetie."

Chantal turns her attention to Andre. "Say, 'Don't play me.' Like your daddy says. Go ahead. 'Dooon't play me.'"

"Don't teach him that shit. Bad enough we got one fool around here," Gloria says, nodding toward the bathroom where Sharron is preening for his party. She laughs again. She is great company until she has had two or three drinks of vodka. Then she changes from a young mother to a vamp, a transition Sharron despises. Her hand rides her hip. Her voice gets husky, and she parades in front of the mirror, adjusting her hair this way and that, talking about ways and means to party.

Chantal has already asked Sharron to stay home, playing both sides of the fence. She wants to get closer to Gloria, whom she has taken to calling Mommy. But she knows full well that Sharron's decision to attend a party in Flatbush, at which both the LoLifes and the Steam Team will be present, has not been made lightly.

Gangs of the fifties used to fight; the Brownsville Jolly Stompers and Roman Lords called it rumbling or jitterbugging when they headed over the bridge to fight the gangs from "the East," East New York. But the LoLifes and Steam Team plan to go at each other tonight with designer clothing as the weapon of choice. They will sashay through the darkened party rooms, seeking pools of light, striking poses, "representing," comparing "ITs," name-brand items. The battle will rage between the Polo fall line, favored by the LoLifes, and the season's offerings of Guess, specialty of the Steam Team. Many of the garments will have a small tear somewhere in the fabric where the plastic antitheft alarm has been ripped away. Some of the kids are even glad when the tear is visible, proof that the IT was earned, not bought.

"It's about props," Sharron tells his mother when he emerges from the bathroom.

"What're props going to get you?" Sharron does not answer

the question, so Gloria responds herself. "They're going to get you killed."

"Yeah, but then my son will have them," Sharron answers back.

On cue, Chantal reaches for the cooing baby and slides her tiny finger over his glistening pink lips. She is keeping her mouth shut now, but she is already a grateful beneficiary of Sharron's props. Both Chantal and Shawanda are taken more seriously in the neighborhood because Sharron has maintained their modest wardrobes and kept his reputation in order.

Sharron was the star of the play. That was a bonus, a one-time payoff. The LoLifes are a steady gig. And respect is an everyday kind of thing.

"You may have the props," Chantal explains to Gloria after Sharron has left. "But you have to work to keep them. You have to represent."

Besides, the LoLifes are not about heavy beefs. These are not the Young Guns, or even the Howard Raiders. Nonetheless, Sharron is uneasy as he waits at the Franklin Avenue station for the #2 train to Flatbush. It is true that he does not like house parties. There is too much jealousy, especially in situations involving girls. But this is an exception. He knows many of the members of the Steam Team, and the party will be safer because it is outside the Ville.

Tonight, Shalo is sporting a gold jeans suit over a brown 450 Polo turtleneck sweater with a large horse head knitted on the chest. He has on high burgundy Timberland boots and his thick gold chain bracelet, a birthday gift from his mother. He has slipped gold caps onto two of his front teeth and topped the look off with a pair of yellow-tinted Nautica sunglasses. He even has an extra shirt under his arm in case he feels the need for a fashion change in mid-party.

Sharron arrives at the small Jamaican club on Flatbush Avenue shortly after eleven. The term "house party" refers not just to parties in private homes but to any small affair that is not hosted by an official organization. The spot is nothing but a dank two-room storefront social club. But there are plenty of girls here, the music is blasting a reggae song, "Me Me Me Na Na Na Wan Go Riker's Island," and the place is dark. Sharron pays no attention to the music; the dancing will come later.

Now he shifts through the crowd in full attitude, profiling. In the back room an earphoned DJ tucked behind a large table bobs to the music. Beside the disc jockey is an exit to a small back yard where people go to get fresh air. Sharron is drawn to the outside area because in his eagerness to represent, he has worn too many clothes for the weather. His extra shirt, awkward to carry, is on under his sweater by now.

After a few minutes in the night air, he takes the plunge back inside, slapping hands at waist level over and over again as he brushes by LoLifes he knows or has seen. He pivots and assumes a spot in the half-light near the disc jockey.

"Wha's up?" he responds again and again, jiggling his head just a bit to the music. Sharron does not want to converse too long with anyone now. He is a solo act for the time being, and he doesn't want the sight lines blocked. But the heat of the crowded room drives him again toward the doorway to the back yard, for a combination of cool air and light. There is someone behind him, and as he shifts his weight, he steps on the guy's foot. The guy taps Sharron's shoulder, and Sharron turns slowly. He can barely see the kid in front of him, but the kid can see Sharron because he's standing in the light.

"Yo, watch where the hell you steppin', mon." The island voice comes from the shadows.

"Yo, couldn't you have said that better?" As Sharron speaks, his face hardens to an ice grill and his hand slides to an inside pocket for his razor-edged Exacto knife. He has every intention of pulling it out, but the kid walks away into the party and Sharron eases up on the razor. It is not so much what the boy said as how he said it. There is no such thing as a minor insult in this setting.

When the boy is a few yards away, he turns and starts ragging. "What ya got der, boy?" he sneers. Sharron steps inside. The Jamaican turns to a small group of friends and utters a sentence or two out of the side of his mouth, keeping his eye on the advancing Sharron.

Sharron can't understand what the Steam Team boys are saying, so he moves closer and assumes a stylized prefight pose, back to back, cheek to cheek with his antagonist. The tension is so thick that Sharron decides he had better get some of his people, so he steps away. Just as he gets to the entrance to the next room, someone grabs his collar. He doesn't turn around, just lunges ahead, trying to free himself. He feels the hand lift from his collar. But before he can turn around, more hands grab the back of his jacket. Sharron fights to get to his razor, but the inside pocket of his jacket is blocked by the folds of the extra shirt.

By now the girls have spotted the fight and a tumult of shrieks drowns the music. Panicked teenagers scramble through the dark for the front door. Everybody wants to be out before the bullets fly. As Sharron lies pinned to the floor, an image materializes in his mind of a silver gun suspended in the darkness. Somebody shouts, "Where is he? Just hold him," as he wriggles on the floor. There are punches to the back of his head, three. Something tells Sharron not to turn over. Then a force lifts his assailant off him and heaves Sharron out the front door into the clear fall night.

Hysterical kids are bounding in all directions. Sharron still has guns on his mind, so he dashes around a corner, rolls onto a lot with high grass, and lies very still. No one has followed, so after ten minutes he rises on all fours and prepares to stand. As he does, he feels the back of his head where he was hit. When he draws his hand back, it is covered with warm, sticky blood.

He shuffles toward a streetlight and tries to hail a cab to St. John's Hospital. But when the empty gypsy cabs catch sight of him, they hurtle past. Then a police car appears.

"Yo," Sharron yells.

The NYPD cruiser slows to a halt. The driver's side window rolls down. "Yo? Did you say yo?"

"I had a accident. I think I should go to a hospital 'cause I'm bleedin'." Sharron extends his blood-webbed fingers toward the officer, who flinches.

"Is that how you call a policeman, yo?" Sharron is silent. The officer nods at Sharron's hand. "How did that happen?"

"I cut myself on a fence."

"*What* fence?"

Sharron breathes deeply.

"If you don't tell us how that happened and who did it, we can't help you," the officer says, lighting a cigarette and blowing the smoke from his first drag out the window at the starry sky.

Sharron sucks another breath and turns away. No disappointment, or anger.

He has to call an ambulance for himself. It takes him ten minutes to find a public telephone, another twenty-five for the ambulance to arrive. He sits on the curb with his right hand pressed to the wound, then his left, shivering. All the time he imagines himself bleeding to death. At Kings County Hospital, he receives twenty-five stitches.

When he arrives home it is 6:45 A.M. and he falls right to sleep. When he awakes at noon he walks out to the kitchen, where Gloria is doing the dishes. "I got cut," he says, wheeling to show the white dressing covering the back of his head.

"Yeah?" Gloria turns and stares blankly at her son. Maybe this is how she will lose him, she thinks, not all at once to a bullet but piece by piece to the knife. For a moment she sees him as a boy, wondrously bright, bounding out the door to play, then coming home weeping, telling her everything in his heart.

"I'm sorry, Mommy," Sharron says.

APARTMENT 5AB

visit to 295 Dumont Avenue by anyone other than a resident or a known crack customer sets off the vocal alarm. But the wily Nikia Vinson wants some publicity, so she has summoned a reporter. Recently released on bail because of her avowed willingness to testify, Nikki has refused an offer to enter the Federal Witness Protection Program. Instead, she has been promising people in the project she will double-cross Schulman on the witness stand.

It has been over a month since Born Son's federal bust. He and his boys are in the Metropolitan Correctional Center hard by the rushing traffic of FDR Drive in downtown Manhattan. Several times Nikki has bundled up Little Bit and taken him by gypsy cab to the jail, past the shotgun-toting guards stalking the sidewalk outside, to visit Bobby and assure him of her loyalty. Now she has another idea. She wants the press to know about Schulman's vendetta, and about the beating the Housing police administered to her lover a year ago, when they chased him into Apartment 5AB.

The walk up the short path to the front door of 295 is quiet. It is gray November in the projects. The last of the few leaves are gone. The only green left in the neighborhood is the surface of the all-weather basketball court, a state-of-the-art court complete with viewing stands, a block down Dumont. There is no one standing in front of the building, no one sitting on the bench there, but every step the stranger has taken has been watched from the dingy brick ramparts. The lookout on duty in the fifth-floor window picks up the intrusion. "Yo, hold up," he yells. The visitor waits. A report is made inside, the way cleared. "C'mon." The stairs to the fifth floor are still strewn with tiny red- and blue-tipped crack vials. There are no fortifications on the metal door, no double locks, no bullet holes.

Inside the apartment, the small living room is silent and hollow. Nikia and her square-faced cousin Renee sit beside each other in bright jogging suits on the edge of a damp and tattered brown couch. They are about the same age, but Nikki is in charge here. There are no curtains in the room, no lamps, no bulb in the overhead light fixture. There are no rugs, no stereos or televisions, no pictures on the wall. The apartment looks like a clubhouse inside an abandoned building, more a hideout than a home. The morning light seeps through the sooty window.

Through the hallway, past the kitchen, is another bleak living room, where two sheetless mattresses cover the floor. Between them lies a clutter of white Chinese restaurant takeout containers. In the bedroom beyond is a bunk bed sawed in half so the two pieces sit beside each other. The floor of a second bedroom is strewn with other mattresses and the overflow from the drawers of a missing dresser. A young man sits in his wheelchair in the shadows, listening to the sounds of a small radio. Renee's child toddles through the bedroom clutter, down the hall, and over to the couch. Renee keeps her eyes on her cousin as she hands the baby a box of dry cereal.

"They beat on Bobby with a radio," Nikia begins, referring to the time Schulman chased Born Son after the car stop. "He cu'n even walk. His eyes was close'. Mouth bleedin'. They still kept up tryin' to make him walk. We was asking what was the charge, and they kept sayin', 'Don't worry 'bout it. Y'all'll find out.'"

"Schulman put his gun in Grandma's face and called her a bitch," Renee adds.

In the fuzzy gloom of the apartment, Nikia continues her story. Another baby, this one in pink pajamas, waddles past as two tall, gaunt, scowling men in black full-length Los Angeles Raiders jackets enter the front door and stride through the room. These are the Worthy boys. They are in the apartment for thirty soundless seconds, then they leave. A stick-thin woman appears, picks her way through the living room, and goes back to the bedrooms at the rear of the apartment, all the while studying the floor like a nervous shorebird, muttering how pitiful it was to see the cops beat Born Son.

"They don' arrest nobody in all the projects," Nikia observes with a sweep of her arm. "They been sellin' around here for years." She squints and tosses her head toward the front door. "Still are," she says. "Schulman wanted one 'pecific person. That's who they wanted an' that's who they got, an' that's how they wanted it to be. Say Bobby came over here shootin'. Huh? How many times Born Son come over here? From Howard?"

"Once," Renee says. "That's it."

"Schulman killed a kid in Seth Low, you know?" Nikki thinks for another moment and adds, "He got 'Born Son Dies' wrote on his ammunition thing in white stuff," a reference to Schulman's speedloader. "Don't he?" Nikki looks at Renee, who nods.

Then Nikki attempts to humanize Bobby, to undo the myth that has grown too big. She starts with his name. "Born Son? His mother named him that 'cause she was in labor for a long time an' she was glad he was finally born. They say we made a *million* dollars. Say we was makin' eight hundred or nine hundred a day. Schulman watchin' too damn many movies. The person who's sellin's got to be paid. They got to be paid." She makes a gesture of disgust in the direction of the lookout on the fifth-floor landing. "We din't make nothing but seven hundred a day, all of us. You think if we was makin' crazy money Tanya'd be stealin' earrings and snatchin' dollar bills?"

Work is a funny word. Run ten miles around a track; that is play. Sell drugs morning, noon, and night, it's a crime. Federal Attorney Bob Fineberg, assigned to prosecute the Young Guns, and Bobby Schulman are certainly working hard on this case. Late at night in the basement of the federal building on Cadman Plaza, at the foot of the Brooklyn Bridge, they sit across from each other in Fineberg's tiny office and pore over the records of the case. There is a seized notebook, crack, drug paraphernalia, one gun, and jackets with "Young Guns" emblazoned on the back. There are months of surveillance records and videotapes. Much of the case, though, relies on Schulman's believability in front of a jury. Fineberg, in cowboy boots, suspenders, and a red bow tie, is behind an antique wood desk. Across the room is a cabinet holding his law books. Above the cabinet hangs a black-and-white picture of his father in an expensive suit, surrounded by distinguished-looking men. On another wall a movie poster celebrates the opening of *Die Hard.*

Fineberg is grilling the Housing cop on his testimony, checking anything a defense lawyer could shake him with: dates, angles of vision during surveillance, if and when he ever promised to get Born Son. Fineberg has a flat nasal accent, reassuring in its lack of passion.

"When I am cross-examining you, look right at me," he begins. "And don't let Bobby's lawyer make you nervous. The judge won't let him badger you." Schulman nods. He has been through this a hundred times in state court. This is Fineberg's first crack retail operation case, and it is he who is nervous. He has been shocked by the accounts of violence in Brownsville. Up until now he has prosecuted the kind of defendants who never make threats or carry them out. And he is more than a little wary of Born Son and the Young Guns. A week ago he asked Schulman for a bulletproof vest. Fineberg is also concerned that the defense will make Schulman out to be a gunslinger. The fatal shooting in the Seth Low Houses is sure to come up.

Fineberg has two identical pairs of glasses. He takes one pair off, replaces them with the other, and studies the Housing cop. Several years ago, Schulman was searching for a man wanted in a series of robberies. When he cornered the suspect in a project stairwell, the suspect pulled a replica of a gun and Schulman shot him dead. "Tell the truth about Seth Low. It's as simple as that. Don't at any point get aggressive. And don't volunteer any information. Just answer what is asked of you."

Schulman, wearing his bulletproof vest even in the stuffy office, runs his fingers along his handlebar mustache. "No problem," he assures the attorney.

Schulman's accent is pure Long Island, though he was raised in Florida and didn't move to the New York suburbs until he was fifteen. He is the real expert on this case. He has listened to hours of tapped telephone conversations. He knows which of the people he is locking up are stupid and which are deadly smart.

"I know what they're going to try to say," he continues. "I never said I was going to get Born Son. This was strictly business."

Fineberg nods his head. He is listening for the high pitch of the true believer, that plume of fanaticism that could ruin the case. But Schulman is level and straightforward. He will be just fine in front of a jury. In fact, Fineberg is starting to like Schulman quite a bit.

"Let Nikia talk all she wants," Schulman continues. "When it comes down to it, she knows she has to tell the truth on the stand or she's fucked."

When he and Fineberg finish for the night, it is after eleven. Schulman rises.

"Where to, Bob?" Fineberg wants to know.

"I gotta go back to the PSA."

"How're you getting there?"

"I'll take the A on Jay Street to Broadway Junction, switch to the L, and take that to Sutter. It's just five blocks to the PSA. I'll walk."

Fineberg, who has never been to Brownsville, is appalled. "You're not going to take the train out there this late?"

"Sure." Schulman laughs. "I have a gun and a vest and a radio. I'm set."

Still Fineberg is worried. He offers to give the cop money to take a taxi, and when Schulman refuses he hands him his home phone number. "Please call me when you get to the PSA," he insists. "I don't care how late it is."

"HE LOOKS LIKE A PERP"

A silver moon rides the barren black sky over the roof of a building in Van Dyke. Gary Lemite is looking for a body. A call came over the radio reporting that there were three young men with guns on a bench in front of a building and a shooting victim inside. The teenagers were there all right, two tall thin boys with large puppy feet and a stocky bow-legged friend, but no guns. A couple of bored 73rd guys arrived for backup and are holding the kids outside while Gary and his partner for the night, Jeff O'Donnel, search for a victim.

Of all his duties, Lemite dislikes the vertical search most. He and O'Donnel start with the roof. They play their flashlights over the graveled tarpaper in the space behind the brick elevator housing, where the pale moonlight doesn't shine. Nothing. They take a moment to lean over the railing and look down on Brownsville. Both cops are hatless in the sharp night breeze. O'Donnel rubs his eyes and gazes off toward Canarsie and Jamaica Bay, then turns toward the winking lights of the Manhattan skyline. Gary keeps his eyes on the streets and walkways. More than once he and J.R. spotted crimes from these roofs.

Then the cops turn and head for the stairway. With guns drawn, they work their way down the stairways at opposite ends of the building. On each of the sixteen floors they lean into the hall and nod to each other. Each time, Gary holds the door for a moment so it won't slam shut. On the twelfth floor, he waits a while for O'Donnel, who appears finally with a wave. On the tenth-floor landing, a cardboard box and pillow mark the spot where someone has been sleeping. Beside the makeshift bed lies a hypodermic needle. Gary steps lightly. If an officer is not looking for trouble, he bangs his stick on the cinderblock wall or turns up his radio so he won't surprise anyone. As he moves steadily down the bright yellow cinderblock stairwell, the only sound is the distant tinny notes of a stereo from somewhere above.

"You stick your head around every corner and you don't know," Gary says. "You see a little kid, a couple of teenagers making out, a mad guy, a bad guy." He keeps his finger off the trigger, straight along the barrel of the gun, to give him a fraction of a second of hesitation, so he doesn't shoot somebody if he's startled. Nothing. No victim.

As Gary and O'Donnel converge in the lobby, a handful of noisy kids are headed in. Another report comes over. Both cops freeze and tilt their heads to their radios. This time Central has the goods.

"9717," the dispatcher calls.

"17," Gary answers.

"Be advised, anonymous caller says the guns are in the mailbox."

The boys are standing thirty feet away, uncuffed, still guarded by the 73rd guys. After Gary and O'Donnel take the call, they hustle into the courtyard, but the boys have overheard the radio call on the backup cops' radios. The one named Errol stands his ground, but his two taller friends are of a different mind. They realize that the call will mean jail and simultaneously decide not to go without a chase. Like twin antelopes, they bound the two-foot fence and flee through the Van Dyke Houses. The 73rd officers stand rooted.

Officers from the 73rd and the 75th don't relish running into the project mazes, don't want to leap those fences or sprint along those walkways, where they are vulnerable from above. And God knows they want nothing to do with those stairways. Except for officers like Marino, NYPD cops give chase in the projects only if they have to.

But Lemite and O'Donnel take off after the kids, who run in different directions. O'Donnel bursts out onto Blake Avenue thirty feet behind one kid, who turns and bolts back into another cluster of buildings.

"Which way did he go?" the cop asks a handful of teenagers assembled around yet another bench.

"What I look like? A 911 tape?" comes the reply.

O'Donnel runs on, but only for a few feet. *Hut, hut, hut, hut;* it is a rounded, pneumatic sound, not as fractured as the noise of a firecracker. It is very close, probably from above.

"10-13, I'm fired on. Dumont, Gaston to Powell," O'Donnel screams into his radio as he backs out of the Complex. The kids on the bench scatter. In seconds an Emergency Service Unit truck skids up, along with three Housing sector cars, and a herd of cops charges back into the Complex with guns pointed up and eyes trained on the roofs. They scour the buildings facing the courtyard from top to bottom and find no one, no spent rounds on the roof. The two fleeing kids are gone for good. But Errol is under arrest. There are two guns in the bent and battered mailboxes, a .38 and an ancient four-fifth.

There are plenty of new TEC-9s, a weapon originally designed for South African security forces, and Berettas in the Ville. Incredibly, a good percentage of the new guns come in legally through Federal Express. But there are even more old used guns. Brownsville and East New York may be the used-gun capital of the country. Several times Mayor Dinkins has offered amnesty to the owners of illegal guns and a reward of $25, $50, or $75, depending on the type of gun surrendered. The gun has to be unloaded and wrapped in paper. But the response has been disappointing. "We got some inoperative guns, and a lot of people who we caught with guns trying to say that they were on their way to turn it in," a cop says.

As the police take Errol down the walkway toward the sector cars, a crowd gathers. Everybody is sticking up for him.

"He's a good guy, a funny guy. All he do is make jokes. When I was in jail, he was the only one who came to see me. I love Errol," a man in his twenties testifies. But somebody did not like Errol; somebody "dropped a dime," a street term that has been used since the price of a phone call was ten cents.

As Gary places his hand on top of Errol's head to guide him down and into the back seat of 9717, a stout woman on the sidewalk complains loudly. "It ain't the guy. Fuckin' cops always, always get the wrong person." Gary comments over the car to O'Donnel as he gets in the front seat, "It's the wrong guy again.

Did we ever get the right guy? These people got to decide whether they want to have guns around here or not."

"In this neighborhood, it is not aberrant behavior to have a gun for protection," Larry Phillips says. "The cops get all worked up about it, like it is a moral issue. Ask them how many guns each one of them has. We have an officer in the PSA who is in charge of keeping track of all the guns that the cops own. Some of them have ten guns. They live on Long Island and they have ten guns. Why?"

Just after 10 P.M., Gary is downstairs changing into his street clothes for the trip to Central Booking with Errol. He'll probably have to take the train home, and to avoid getting involved in an incident on the trip, he feels it is best to be out of uniform. O'Donnel is at the desk in the cell area, starting the paperwork for Gary, working slowly, doing his best not to make a mistake, when he hears that Errol's family is at the desk.

"Your mother and your sister are outside," he says over his shoulder toward the cell where Errol is standing. "Don't they have to get up early to go to work? I forgot, niggers don't work. Ha-ha." His voice is as relaxed and stress-free as if he were chatting it up at the Wall, far from Lonnie Hayes and Gary Lemite. His epithet is rare in the PSA, where blatant racial baiting is almost always replaced by code words.

"Suck my dick," Errol sputters back from his cell. These kids craft and reprise the most hilarious, embarrassing, devastating estimations of each other, but tonight Errol is frozen at the very moment he most needs his ability to hurt another with words. One cannot help but think that the same wall exists when it comes to deadly force. The kids will shoot each other with shockingly little consideration or remorse. They hesitate to shoot the white man — perhaps because killing a cop, or a reporter, will bring down more heat than they want to handle, but also because the white man is outside their system of initiatives and responses.

O'Donnel is having fun. "Let them out of the zoo, I guess," he says with a chuckle.

"Your fuckin' sister," says the voice behind the bars.

After a few minutes O'Donnel gets ready to fingerprint the kid. As he was taught in the academy, he secures his gun in a locker and calls for Gary to stand by. There must be two officers on hand, one to do the fingerprinting and one to provide security for the uncuffed prisoner. When Gary arrives, O'Donnel has nothing to say about race.

"Watch your back," O'Donnel says to an officer who has entered the room and whose gun is exposed, as he walks with Errol toward the fingerprinting area at the rear of the office.

Errol is not speaking, barely seems to breathe, his face a cloud of hate. For his part, O'Donnel appears to have forgotten his obscene words of just moments before. Maybe he believes that the shots fired in his direction were the real profanity; maybe he believes that the word "nigger" is not so bad because the black people use it themselves. Maybe he does not know about the history of that word and the dark country roads and the ropes on trees. He might not know much about history, but he does know procedure.

"Don't try to help me with the fingerprinting," he explains patiently, as if he is talking to his younger brother. "If you try to help and you move wrong, you'll smear the print."

Errol stares straight ahead as O'Donnel touches his fingers to the tray of black ink and presses his hand on the paper. In a moment, Errol, the funny guy, the kid everybody likes, is back in his cell.

"How much does a gun like that cost, Errol?" O'Donnel asks cheerily as Gary settles down at the desk to complete the forms.

At sunrise a van from the Manhattan Correctional Center transports Born Son and his boys over the Manhattan Bridge and up Tillary Street to the federal courthouse on Cadman Plaza. The shiny silver elevators are three times the size of the elevators in the Brownsville Houses. There are no bullet craters in their gleaming doors. In Judge Leo Glasser's courtroom on the fourth floor, there are no gang logos carved into the gallery benches as there are in the state courthouse on nearby Schermerhorn Street. The court officers here don't have to shout for silence. The room is as quiet as a church; the ceilings are thirty feet high, the floors spotless. The judge is far away and well elevated, high and mighty.

By afternoon Bobby is seated with his boys and their lawyers at a large glossy conference table behind the wooden barrier separating the participants from the spectators. He is well dressed in his green iridescent suit and flowered shirt, but unprepared. In the months since his arrest he has ignored entreaties from his lawyer to cooperate and restricted his strategy to trying to get Nikia to marry him from jail, presumably because he thinks she wouldn't be able to testify.

Nikki is not on hand today. Fineberg has told her that she will not have to testify until tomorrow at the earliest. Somebody has put in a call from Otisville Prison to her mother's house, threatening to have a bullet put through Nikki's head if she testifies. But Nikki is not one to be intimidated. She was raised on this kind of give-and-take. Her word to Bobby and the rest is that she will testify to avoid a long jail term that would take her away from her kids, but she will not agree to the quantity of crack the feds are insisting on. That way she will help herself by cooperating and help Born Son too, because federal sentencing guidelines are mandated by volume of drug sales. If she can shrink the weight, the sentence will go down considerably. It is a tricky plan. If she does not satisfy Fineberg, she won't get the letter of cooperation and request for a "downward departure" from him that the judge needs to sidestep the sentencing guidelines and let her off with light time.

After a droning morning of jury selection, Glasser starts the trial of Bobby James and the Young Guns. Tai Stick's mother and sister are on hand, as is Odums's father, in blue work clothes. Supreme's sister and mother sit stiffly in the back row. Born Son's mother is up front.

"Born Son James." Fineberg begins his opening statement. "This Born Son . . ." he continues in a wavering intonation thick with implication. The jury has to wonder. What kind of man is named Born Son? Neither Judge Glasser nor the jury understands the significance of the blizzard of nicknames in Brownsville, where the air is full of Boo and Smoke and Poppa. The new police computer lists thousands of nicknames, including a score of Justices, Blacks, and Kojaks.

Born Son's mother, Margaret, sitting in the third row, picks up the prejudicial drift. She is in a state of perpetual indignation. "How dare they say his baby name like it's proof that he committed crimes," she says out loud, cutting her eyes at Dan Murphy, Bobby's lawyer. "Why don't the lawyer protest?

That old drunk. How would the DA like it if we used his baby name?"

"How long have you been a police officer?" Fineberg asks Schulman, who is the first to take the stand.

"Ten years."

"And in what kind of areas have you done most of your work?"

"In public housing," Schulman says. "In the projects."

"What is life like in the projects?" Fineberg asks.

"The projects are low-income developments that house mostly people on welfare." There is a gasp and a howl of indignation from the relatives of the defendants who have taken the day off work to attend the trial.

"Objection," several of the defense lawyers interject. It is late in the afternoon. Glasser sustains the objection and adjourns the trial for the day.

The next morning, Nikia, in a burgundy and white running suit, Renee, and a full complement of shifty, slinky Worthy boys in their early teens are slouched on the polished wooden bench in the marble hallway outside the courtroom. Carlton, wearing balloon-legged jeans, scoffs at Schulman down the hall: "Tight-pants bastard." But the wisecracks are muted. The Worthys have seen plenty of rundown schools and grimy city agencies; they know all about Spofford Juvenile Center in the Bronx. But this is new. There is real money and power here. Only five miles away, but so far from Brownsville.

"I'll fight her, sure," Nikki pipes up, referring perhaps to one of Born Son's old girlfriends who is rumored to be coming to the trial.

"On federal property?" Renee wonders.

"Sure."

But there will be no fight. There won't even be a trial. Billy Odums is the one member of the group who is not intimidated by Born Son. He is simply too physically imposing, with great spreading muscles and sloping shoulders, to worry about anything. Besides, Odums came late to the group, never really had a chance to fall under Bobby's influence. Last night, spooked by Nikia's promised cooperation and offered a separate deal because he has the shortest involvement with the gang, Odums pleaded guilty. In return he got a promise of a letter of downward departure, which will probably spare him the prodigious sentences the others face. Maybe just five years, his lawyer guesses. When Odums rolls over, the remaining Young Guns plead guilty.

Only a day old, and the trial is over. Margaret James is down the hallway near those fancy elevators, smoking a cigarette during a delay in the proceedings, when Alan Polak, Chris Muncie's lawyer, steps out of the courtroom with the news. When Margaret hears the bitter words that her son has pleaded guilty, she screams, stumbles toward the courtroom, and falls. Only Bobby's lawyer, Murphy, is there to hold her off the floor. With his arms under hers, knees shaking with her two hundred pounds, he drags Margaret to where the Worthys sit, wide-eyed.

"My baby is dead," Margaret howls.

"You have two other children," Murphy manages. He may have dropped the ball for Born Son in court, but he is not about to drop Margaret James. In a state of extreme embarrassment and real fatigue, he pleads for someone to take the semiconscious woman from his arms. Nikia steps up and takes the burden. As soon as Margaret feels the whipcord arms of her son's woman, she stiffens and wipes her ink-black braids from her eyes. "Bring me Little Bit," she hisses.

Mid-November, and Gary's promotion to OSC, Operation Safe Community, has come through. Kammerdener has gone to the position he had his eye on all along, second in command at the citywide detective bureau. Jack Lenti is the new commanding officer. For him, the choice of Lemite for promotion to the OSC plainclothes detail was obvious. What could be better than a black officer, a collar machine who sweeps up guns like a magnet, one with no chip on his shoulder, who doesn't go crying to the Guardians every time he sees something he doesn't like?

Gary has been on the detail a week. He waits in line to pick up his radio in the front room of the PSA. Lonnie Hayes is twenty feet away, feet wide apart, chin on his chest, eyes alert, waiting for him. Both Hayes's and Lemite's partners are off, so the two will ride together tonight. Hayes is wearing a huge hooded parka and oversize sweatpants. There is no telling how many guns he's carrying. He smiles sweetly and strolls to the back of the room, where a young officer named Bauer is standing by himself. Bauer has been having all sorts of trouble on the street. He was hired under new department disability guidelines. His neck twitches and his eyes squeeze shut every thirty seconds. Most of the cops are avoiding him, calling him an EDP behind his back, and the locals around his solo footpost are eating him alive.

Bauer greets Hayes and launches into an account of a recent incident. Hayes nods, acting as if everything is going to be fine.

"He had like . . . four guys with him, talkin' shit. So I called the 85th," Bauer explains.

"Yeah." Hayes considers. "And they ride in and kick ass. But that doesn't do your props any good. Next time you're on solo footpost like that, you walk up to the guy in front of his friends, take out your radio, and call for a bus."

"A bus?"

"You say over the radio, 'Send me a bus, one male down,' and you give your location and a description of the guy in front of you. Look him in the eye, and you say, 'Hurry that up. He's bleeding profusely from a head wound.' Then you take out your stick."

"Really?" Bauer asks.

"Yeah. He'll walk away. He won't fuck with you anymore."

Twenty minutes later, Gary takes the wheel of the gray anticrime car and Lonnie settles beside him, quiet, peaceful. Neither officer quite knows what to make of the other. Unlike Gary, Lonnie was raised in Brownsville under much the same conditions he polices now. He's so streetwise that the ADAs sometimes enlist him to translate the slang in taped confessions. As a cop, he had a run as a heavy hitter in the collar department. But lately he has been looking at things in a new light.

The two cops cruise past the low-rise project buildings on Williams, by the Fat Albert building, which has a huge color mural of the cartoon character on the front wall. Then onto Sutter, up over the hill, and past the supermarket. The store is draped in corrugated steel gates, but there are no gates on the roof, and the place has been burglarized repeatedly in the past several months. Gary slows the cruiser down and glances at the front door of the store. It's seven o'clock; Rony and Zaid Shoman will be doing business until after eleven.

Gary turns right at the red light on busy Rockaway Avenue and goes past the Amoco gas station, where kids from Langston Hughes High School routinely rob motorists who stop for gas. The young highwaymen have escaped via the back door of 301 Sutter Avenue in the project so many times that the Housing Authority has welded the door shut, in violation of fire and safety codes. Gary turns on Belmont and picks up speed as he drives by the pacing, laser-eyed whores outside the factory on Belmont and Williams. Soon the two cops are riding by Fiorentino Plaza. Lonnie jerks his head toward Bradford Avenue. "That's where you were dodgin' all those bullets?"

Gary nods. Something about his reluctance to talk about the incident lights Lonnie up. He wants to tell Gary things.

"When I'm in pursuit," he begins, "I don't even chase the perp into the building anymore, 'cause I know somebody, not from the PSA but from the 73rd or the 75th, is going to mistake me for a perp. I almost got shot this week. I'm bending over getting ready to cuff this guy, and I see some idiot drawin' down on me. Then I look at him, and he moves the gun and says, 'I wasn't pointing my gun at you.'"

Gary says nothing, but his respect is palpable. "I'm getting a call that a guy is in trouble," Lonnie continues, "and I'm supposed to run up ten flights and fight for this guy's life, when he thinks deep down that I'm just another nigger? Stress. I'm a burnout. When cops start their bullshit, beatin' on motherfuckers, I make a wall in the air." Lonnie raises his huge hands to show how he separates himself from the white officers. "That's them. This is me. I tell the people."

Lonnie is rolling now; his words are not for entertainment. "One time I was bending over a guy who's shot. His people was cryin' and shit. I was gonna put somethin' under his head and then I stopped. I didn't do nothin', because in the reality of it, we're not healers. We're the Gestapo."

He settles deeper into his down jacket. He is only two years older than Gary, but he seems like a concerned big brother. He doesn't do much reading, but he does a great deal of thinking and listening. And he has heard the word on the street. The locals have asked him about Gary, complaining regularly about the "half-white motherfucker" they think is too heavy-handed. Lonnie himself is no stranger to violence. The story goes that a big-mouth threatened him once. In a blink, the guy's nose was broken. No one saw Lonnie's hands move. But he has come to grips with some things.

"I used to kick ass when they called me a Tom," he tells Gary. "Now I just hit them with a shot of cold truth: 'At least I ain't robbin' no grandmother.'"

Lonnie is "no joke," they say all over Brownsville. He's the strongest man in the PSA, with a black belt in karate. He is well liked by the white guys because of his friendly nature. But he stopped socializing with cops a while ago. He used to go drinking with his fellow officers at the Wall, but after a few beers, somebody would slip and say something about niggers, and after that he could never look at the guy the same way again. He advises Gary after a silence, "Don't be a fuckin' superman. It ain't worth it."

Gary steers down Mother Gaston Boulevard, past the library near the Brownsville Houses. The library used to have long lines of eager kids waiting to get inside. Now, at six o'clock on a fall evening, ten young men stand in an arc on the corner. They look as if they are waiting for something too. But their backs are to the locked doors of the library as they stare at the unmarked police car with midnight eyes.

"Project kids are different," Lonnie says. "They crew up early. They have to. When I was a kid we used to run in packs. We'd ride the subways and kick ass. We fought so much we trained. One guy would teach some karate, and another guy would teach boxing, and we'd get an older guy to show us jailhouse fighting moves." But as he talks about his youth in Brownsville, he never mentions guns.

Gary bumps the car up a curb and guides it carefully along the footpaths of the Complex. It's dinnertime, and windows glow up and down the five-story buildings. He slows the car to a stop as a pair of schoolgirls take their time stepping off the path.

"Thank you," Lonnie says to the girls, who cannot maintain their childish scowls in the face of his good cheer. An attractive woman entering a building stops at the door, turns, and bends slightly to get a look at him. She beams a winsome smile and waves. Lonnie waves back.

"Say you're walking down this street with your woman,"

Lonnie goes on, "and some guy around your building says, 'Hey, I want your lady to suck my dick,' and you just grin." Lonnie displays a lame smile. "Then the guys get together and they start talking. You know, 'Hey, I told that guy's woman to suck my dick and he didn't do nothin'.' Then they start getting the idea that they should rob you." Lonnie acts out the robbery, with the victim raising his hand in a feeble gesture of protest. Then he assumes the role of the tough guy. "'Put your hand down. I told you not to move your fuckin' hand.' The next thing you know, they have your old lady up on the roof and they really *are* makin' her suck their dicks.

"It's the same if some guy robs your mother on the way home from the subway. You get the name and the description and you go down by the train station and, 'Sure I know who it was. It was that guy Petee and his man.' Sure enough, there's Petee standing down in front of his building with his man. Then you hear, 'Be careful, Petee's crazy and he's got a gun.' Now, you know it won't do you any good to talk to the guy. He'll probably shoot you. You have to decide what to do. If you decide to take him out, you have to do it right, because if you fuck up, he'll kill you. You come up on him real fast with your head down and your hands in your pockets. Or you get your crew. That's why you need a crew. That's how you act when you live around here, and that is why so many brothers are in jail.

"There's only one answer." Lonnie twists his mouth into an unhappy smile and looks at Gary. "Take the guns away. Nobody wants to stab somebody. They figure they'll get hurt themselves."

But some of the kids have already begun protecting themselves against gunshots. The next night Bobby Schulman and Brian Lavin are staked out near the Cypress Houses, sitting in their car. Quani, the kid who shot Marcus McClain at the picnic on Labor Day, has been sighted. The scrip is over the air. He is wearing black jeans with a white handkerchief in the back pocket. Suddenly he darts by, his white handkerchief bobbing. Schulman takes off on foot and Lavin uses the car. The chase ends on Belmont. Lavin cuts the kid off and Schulman grabs him from behind. "I can't believe I got caught by an old man," Quani says in the car. He is wearing a bulletproof vest.

*

Two days later, November 14, 9 P.M. A crooked moon sits behind a scrim of purple clouds beyond the Pink Houses on Loring Avenue. Del Migliore and a couple of other Housing cops from PSA 2 crowd onto the elevator along with detectives Deutsch and McCabe. The group is headed to Apartment 7F in search of a kid alleged to have shot a guy in the head. McCabe knocks on the door.

"Yes?" says a woman on the other side.

"Housing police," McCabe begins, flashing his white shield near the peephole. "Detective McCabe. Mrs. Charles?"

"Yes," the woman answers slowly.

"We'd like to talk to your son. Will you open the door?"

"My son isn't home right now."

"You know why we're here. And we'd rather not yell in the hall. You don't want your neighbors to know your business. Do you?"

No answer.

"We'd like to come in, just ask a few questions, get something straightened out. Will you open the door?"

"He's not home right now."

McCabe turns and rolls his eyes toward Migliore and the other officers standing behind him in the hall. "I understand that. But we'd like to come inside, Mrs. Charles. We're not going to go away."

"My son isn't home now," the woman says in the same maddening tone.

"We will be back with a warrant," McCabe snaps. "He's in there," he growls to the others, and steps across the hall. He knocks on a door and asks the tenant to use the phone. He is going to call the PSA and ask for a lieutenant. Perhaps if a boss shows up at the door, he will be able to intimidate the woman into opening up.

Two officers stand in the hallway to watch the apartment door while Migliore and Detective Deutsch head outside. Migliore goes to his car to wait for instructions, and Deutsch walks over to advise a late-arriving sector car.

"Watch the windows," he says. "These fuckin' guys'll jump from anywhere."

But inside the apartment, the kid isn't thinking about jumping. He's on the phone to an accomplice in another apartment in the building, asking for a favor. The kid wants his friend to fire out the window to draw the cops in the hall outside so he can make his escape.

Migliore is out the front door, halfway to his patrol car, when half a dozen shots ring down from a top-floor window. He crouches and draws. Another shot hits him in the foot; his leg swings out and up as he topples to the pavement. He crawls off the sidewalk to the grass, rolls over once, and returns fire. Another sniper volley of seven shots blasts through the air, and a round catches Detective Deutsch in the calf. From a prone position, Migliore empties his gun at the window. An NYPD car roars to a stop, a cop drags Migliore and Deutsch inside, and the police car careens off to Brookdale Hospital. Alone on the street, an officer returns more fire at the window he believes the shots came from.

In minutes, scores of NYPD officers surround the wrong building. Gary Lemite and a group of Housing cops charge into the correct address, but Kammerdener orders them back outside. Massive searchlights play up and down the brick walls. The cops still aren't sure where the shots came from.

The members of an Emergency Service Unit team carry metal body shields into the Loring Avenue address and use a wedge to open the door of Apartment 7F, but the suspect is nowhere to be found. The NYPD canine unit is called in, and the animal finally sniffs the kid out. He is *in* a couch, not under it. The young fugitive somehow squeezed inside the mechanism of the convertible. No guns are found in the apartment.

"Smell a perp anywhere," an NYPD guy brags. When the kid is dragged out of the couch, the boss on hand suddenly has business in the hallway, turns his back and lights a cigarette, a tacit signal that some controlled ass-kicking is all right. No flashlights or head wounds this time, just body blows.

A search of the building does not turn up the sniper. Outside, the officers rub their hands together in the chill air and mill around the crime scene till after midnight, while detectives toy with laser guns to determine the origin of the shots. At 1 A.M., Chief Keeney of the Housing police department shows up. "These officers acquitted themselves well," he pronounces.

Some off-duty guys are waiting for Migliore to get out of Brookdale so they can go for ritual beers at the Wall or on the

Canarsie pier. Both Deutsch and Migliore will be all right. All Migliore has is a swollen foot; the bullet kicked off the side of his shoe. The damage to his feeling of invincibility will be much more lasting.

Gary, finished with his shift, arrives in his claptrap Dodge to join the vigil. He has a six-pack of Budweisers on the seat beside him for the wait and the toast. "What's the shooter look like?" he asks a cop, who doesn't quite understand the question.

The officer shrugs. "Wha'? He looks like a perp."

"TRAP OFF"

riday afternoon and a fight has broken out on the fourth floor at Thomas Jefferson High School. Gray-uniformed security guards thunder down the hallway, knocking students aside to get at the action. Walkie-talkies spit codes as students flood into the hallway to taste the chaos. Down the hall, a white male teacher and a black girl trade insults outside a classroom. The walls are free of graffiti, neatly decorated with black history displays featuring magazine photos of black heroes, but the air is crackling with trouble.

Last May, Dan Rather portrayed Jefferson on an evening news feature just the way Beck wanted. Television viewers across the country saw images from East New York that warmed the heart: gymnasts, a steel drum band, and young girls carrying five-pound "babies" made of flour as part of a program to teach them how difficult it is to be a mother. But now, six months later, things are not going well here.

On the first floor, the five members of a video team, commissioned through the board of education by Beck herself, set their equipment on the floor outside the gymnasium and rest for a few minutes before heading out to their van. They have been in the school all day, taping a promotion. They have been trying to highlight successful programs, such as the moot court team and the College Now program, in which students can earn college credits while still at Jefferson. They have not been looking for trouble, the way a regular news team might. The video is slated to be shown in East Brooklyn junior high schools so the better students will not opt to leave the area for other high schools, as they have done in the past. But the crew is shell-shocked. Given the run of the school, they have seen enough. Their words are sheer blasphemy.

"This is very rough," the director says.

"We've been to six high schools in Brooklyn already," a cameraman adds, "and this is one of the worst. The students tell us they just want to get out."

Can it be true? Are the Smurfs winning? "There's one teacher who's something to see, though," a young technician adds. "A woman, teaching global history. She's up there on the fifth floor doin' this rap lesson . . ."

Sharron is on his back in his bed on the night before Halloween, with Andre lying on his chest. The baby is fat-faced, with skin the color of rosy butterscotch, enormous black-marble eyes, and wicked little fists. Each time Sharron flexes his chest muscles, the baby bounces and squeals with pleasure. Chantal is sitting beside them, with her back against the wall and her thumb in her mouth.

"Mommy's takin' him next week so I can go to school for the new markin' period," she says absently.

"Whose mommy?"

"Mine."

"Mine's got school five days a week, Chantal."

"I know. I'm not sayin' nothin'."

Sharron places his finger in the palm of Andre's hand, and the baby squeezes tight.

"Little man's got serious grip action. Check it out. Look. Look at him tearin' it up. He's gonna be a guitar player. I'll be big-time by then. He can play backup." Sharron draws Andre closer and kisses him. "Baby got it like that."

"Where you was when I knocked two days ago, Sha? I know you was home."

"Who says?"

"Shawanda."

"I was at rehearsal."

"Yeah, right. Don't play me, Sha."

Halloween night passes, and still Sharron stays home with Chantal and Andre. It is more than a week since his tangle with the Steam Team. If it hadn't been for Little Earl, the kid who pushed him out the door, things could have been a lot worse. As it is, he has an inflamed and itchy row of stitches in the back of his head. Just as well, he thinks. There isn't a worse night for trouble than Halloween. Chantal lingers another night and then another, with the baby. Gloria is almost always happy to have visitors. She likes activity around her, and she has always liked to keep Sharron close, liked for him to do his thing with Chantal at the house. And Andre, of course, is a novelty. So quiet and good, bubbling, spitting, and waving his arms like a little fool. Chantal likes nothing better than to lie in the bedroom with Sharron while Gloria or Shawanda looks after Andre. But such an arrangement cannot go on forever. In the middle of the week, Chantal goes home and Sharron rallies himself back into the swing of things.

He calls his cousin Morris to arrange a practice session in Morris's studio. There is still a good chance that Sharron and Chris and Frank will get the opportunity to sing backup on a demo tape for a singer named Antoine. A couple of weeks ago, it seemed as if the gig was all but set. Antoine's agent said it was just a matter of scheduling. After that there was no word. When it comes to his singing, Sharron does not like to wait for opportunity to knock. So the Friday after Halloween, he calls Chris and Frank and arranges for a rehearsal at Morris's place the next morning. Morris's studio is only available until noon, and Sharron knows that neither of the others is reliable. But Sharron is all business when it comes to his performing career, so he sets himself the task of rounding up his partners.

The bright, cold November morning finds him on Chris's doorstep, staring up at the second-floor window. He has been knocking for fifteen minutes. Chris's mother, not happy with the commotion, has already waved him away from the door twice. Sharron retreats to the pavement and reaches for a handful of pebbles to toss against the window of his friend's bedroom. Then a white curtain moves and Chris's round face appears.

Frank is easier to rouse, but not easier to control at the rehearsal. He is the designated rapper of the trio.

"Frank, you gotta get into it," Sharron explains after one flat run-through of the half-rap, half-ballad he has written, "Nothing Can Go Wrong."

"I can't, Sha."

"Man, you got to ask questions about your life. You got to think about things that happened to you. This ain't just words. You can't just say the shit."

"I ain't into it," Frank insists.

Sharron looks at his watch. Morris is waiting upstairs. "Now let's do it. And don't fuck around."

Frank is not happy with Sharron's self-appointment as leader. It was easy for Sharron to direct the kids in the Jefferson school play. They were "just regular pupils," in Sharron's words. But Frank, like Sharron, has a reputation, props. His personality is wired to resist domination of any kind, even constructive leadership.

"Why you curse me, Shalo?"

"Niggers, we here to make *money*," Sharron insists. "I'll do what I got to do."

"Yeah, you better be ready to do what you got to do."

"You know, you stink, like you know . . . you smell bad?" Chris says to Frank, then falls to the floor, laughing.

"Shut the fuck up, chipmunk-eye motherfucker," Frank growls.

"That's it!" Sharron exclaims in Frank's face. "When you say the words in the song, you got to get mad like that."

Sharron manages to get an hour's good rehearsal from his undisciplined partners.

"This is business," he reminds them on the train on the way home. "Not some little-boy shit. You got to understand that."

Chris and Frank promise to concentrate better during next Saturday's rehearsal, when Antoine himself might appear. But it doesn't work that way. The next Tuesday, Morris gives Sharron the bad news. "Eddie, Antoine's manager?" he begins, as Sharron listens on the pay phone on his corner. "He's decided to go with just Chris and his brother as backup. They sing in the choir together and he likes their sound."

"Cool," Sharron answers, controlling his disappointment. He promises to call later in the week.

Life is not right. Not at all. Sharron skips school the next day and retreats to his room for the weekend.

On the following Monday, Frank and Sharron head down Saratoga Avenue to visit a friend, a fellow LoLife called Filo. Filo lives in a private home on Saratoga, past Livonia, a house cov-

217

ered with dozens of metal security bars painted white. The three boys share a forty of Power Master on Filo's stoop, tugging on the bottle till it's drained, looking up and down the avenue all the while for girls.

"Man, when you go to jail, you gonna feel right at home," Frank says, surveying the front of Filo's house. "You already behind bars."

"How the hell you gonna get out if there's a fire?" Sharron asks.

"We got a fuckin' fire alarm."

"You mean a smoke alarm," Frank corrects. "An' I know you disconnected that shit, 'cause your mother burns up the grits, aaah." He spots a pair of girls moving down the sidewalk and starts a low chant, matching the cadence with their steps: "She can't, she can't, she can't." As the girls pass by, he finishes with a flourish, "*Control that butt.*" The girls disappear, but Sharron is suddenly expansive.

"There was this guy in my school," he explains, jumping to his feet. "And we was fillin' applications for Job Search? And this dude writes in the spot where it says, 'Who do you contact in case of emergency,' he writes, 'The hospital.' Aaah."

Frank tumbles off the stoop with laughter, slaps Sharron's hand, and laughs some more. Then he and Sharron head back down Saratoga Avenue. They trot up the stairs to the subway platform so Frank can use the pay phone beside the token booth to call his girlfriend, Maxine. On the far side of the booth is a kid standing by himself in the grimy waiting room. Frank has seen the kid around the neighborhood. "Pussy," he says out the side of his mouth to Sharron, sliding his quarter into the phone and jerking his head toward the kid.

The young man, about Sharron's age, is wearing a burgundy wool Polo jacket with a blue crest like a police badge. It irritates Sharron to see a kid with a sucker's reputation wearing a jacket he would love to have. He himself is wearing his prize shearling on this chilly day. Frank has on a matching jacket. Both carry weapons in case someone tries to steal the coveted garments.

Sharron snorts in disgust and looks from the kid back to Frank. Frank is chatting with his girlfriend, but he's following Sharron's train of thought and nods sharply, affirmatively. A soft kid with a Polo jacket standing right in their faces: this is a call to action. Sharron's pulse lifts; his breath comes slower and deeper.

The youth is Sharron's height, maybe a bit heavier, but he is a punk, of that there is no question. There is no proud carriage to indicate that he's a martial artist, no street slouch or bulge in his clothes to signal a burner. He's just a vic, and Sharron will be damned if he's not going to take that Polo jacket for his collection. It will be just the thing to banish the blues about Antoine and put his head straight.

He walks straight across the small ticket lobby, catches the kid's eye, and speaks, not unpleasantly. "Let me try the jacket on."

The kid's hand moves to the zipper and stops. "It's kind of cold." The kid lobs the words softly, lest they offend.

Behind Sharron, Frank slaps the receiver onto its hook and skips down the stairs to the corner. This is a one-man sting. Sharron Corley, star of the school play, shining light of his family, and homecoming king of Jefferson High, fashions his features into a wicked "screw face," an ice grill, and opens his shearling to display the steel shank of the ice pick he has tucked into his waistband.

"Take the shit off," he orders.

When the kid's coat is over his arm, he twists toward the stairway, then turns back to the kid, who stands, jacketless and confused, rooted to his spot, just out of sight of the token collector.

"Are you gonna stand there?" Sharron growls. The kid takes off. Sharron hits the opposite stairway and hurries down Saratoga to his apartment building.

Done. No violence. "I wouldn't have stuck him anyway," Sharron tells himself. "Just perfect." He is delighted. He has passed the challenge, acted "on point," with courage and skill. His reward is his soaring heart, and the jacket. There is no way he would ever buy a jacket like this. No way he's going to give "them people," as he calls department stores, his money. There will be no problem with the cops, because the kid will never tell, and he is too much of a punk to grab a burner and come looking.

Sharron hangs the jacket in his closet, using the heavy wood hanger to make sure it doesn't lose its shape. He feels like a new person, and he has not even tried it on yet. "Clothes do make the man," he decides.

Gloria Corley has seen the expensive sweaters and coats. She has seen the shearling. She has warned her son about shoplifting again and again. Now she has let it drop. How can she deny her favorite child the only things he wants, things she cannot give him? Times are too hard to lose sleep over some penny-ante boosting. But the beautiful burgundy jacket in Sharron's closet has not been boosted. It has been stolen from another young man, with a weapon. There can be none of Sharron's rationalization about how it is all right to steal Polo merchandise because Ralph Lauren charges higher prices in the cities, where black folks live. This is simply the strong taking from the weak.

At 6 A.M. two days later, two Transit police detectives, Ricardo Perez and Dexter Blake, along with five members of the Transit police's warrant squad, arrive at 515 Saratoga Avenue. One officer stays outside to watch the windows in case any contraband sails out; two others head for the rear stairway. One cop positions himself on the roof. There are no battering rams, no machine guns. "We like to do these things at dawn," Perez explains about the warrants, "in the hours before the neighborhood is up, before the word can get around, before anybody is drinking."

The night before, Perez had the victim go through five hundred pictures of youthful subway robbers. "With that big scar and the high-top fade haircut, this kid Corley wasn't difficult to pick out," he says. When Sharron's picture was identified, Perez recognized it. "I had read something in the paper about this kid who lived in the area who was very talented, an actor in a play or something." There was something else distinct about Sharron Corley. "My teenage daughter still lives with her mother in the area," Perez explains, "and she told me that the kid with the fade, the one who was in the paper, had come up to her and her friend on the street around the way and had tried to pick up her friend. Nothing unusual. But it was the way he did it. He just walked up to her and started singing on the street corner."

Now Perez and Blake knock on the Corleys' door.

"Who?" Gloria wants to know.

"It's the police department."

The door swings open.

"I'm Detective Perez. This is my partner." Perez slurs the word "detective" and palms his gold shield quickly, trying to minimize his mission. "Sorry to disturb you. But we're here to talk to your son about an outstanding warrant he has for fare-beating a couple of months ago."

"*That's* what this is about?" Gloria questions, with equal measures of disgust for the police, the hour of the morning, and Sharron.

"Right."

Sharron steps into the living room, embarrassed but not worried. Jumping the turnstile is a way of life; getting a summons for it is just part of growing up, like breaking somebody's window with a baseball in suburbia.

"Nah, no handcuffs," Perez tells him cheerily. "But stay in the living room here. And don't touch anything." Perez glances at Shawanda, who had been sleeping on the couch and is now standing in the kitchen, rubbing her eyes. "Your sister?" Sharron nods. "Maybe your sister can go and get you your jacket and whatever else you need. This won't take long." Shawanda is dispatched to the bedroom to get Sharron's jacket for the trip to the Transit police headquarters. She comes out with the shearling.

"It's not that cold," Detective Blake comments, feigning concern for Sharron's comfort. Shawanda walks back to the bedroom, reaches into the closet, and grabs the burgundy Polo.

"I was looking all over the apartment for the jacket," Perez remembers. "When she came out with the burgundy, it was all we could do not to laugh."

"It won't take more than an hour," Blake tells Sharron.

Still, Sharron is not cuffed. If he were, it would not be the first time. He has been arrested half a dozen times. When he was fifteen, there was a fight between him and Frank and two neighborhood kids. A couple of plainclothes cops driving by thought it was a mugging and arrested Sharron and Frank after a scuffle. That was a misunderstanding. But there have been other arrests, one for robbery when he was sixteen, one for petty vandalism, one during rehearsals for the school play, when he was mistakenly identified for a robbery, and the turnstile-jumping thing.

As Sharron rides over to the Transit headquarters, he's convinced this is just a nuisance. The cops even stop off at "Mickey

D's" and buy him an Egg McMuffin. Nevertheless, he is frowning as he walks between the two detectives down the stairs at the Franklin Avenue subway stop and along the platform to the headquarters at the rear of the station. The frown is a choice, a selected demeanor to fit the circumstances. If the video cameras were rolling, as they almost always are in Sharron's head, this would be the right look. As he moves past the precinct cell area and into the small detective squad room, his scowl deepens.

Inside, Perez sits at his desk, leans back, and motions for Sharron to sit. The detective pats the four fingers of his right hand on the Formica top of his metal desk for a moment, then breaks the news.

"The real reason you're here is that you stole a kid's coat with an ice pick last night at the Saratoga station."

"No, I didn't," Sharron says, looking above the detective at a poster of a man wanted for homicide.

"The kid pulled your picture. He knew where you lived."

"Not me."

"Well, you can deny it, but you're gonna look pretty stupid when that kid walks in here and you're sitting there wearing his jacket."

Sharron confesses, even pens his own statement. "He was an easy kid," he writes. "When he knew we had him, he just gave it up. Me and my man, who is unimportant in this matter, saw a kid from around the way who in his point of view was a pussy. I approached him with the ice pick and willingly he came out of his coat and his beeper."

"Some of these guys stonewall the whole thing," Perez says. "He was no problem. But when we asked him why, he just sat there — no explanation whatsoever."

"The cops really played me," Sharron remembers.

The kid picks Sharron out of a lineup. All along, Sharron is worried but also offended. "You don't call the *police.* You just don't do that," he whines. It's confusing. The vic has simultaneously sunken to a new level of punkdom and shown some heart. Totally unpredictable.

The gates of Sharron's life are closing slowly. The deal is simple. Robbery two: plead guilty and get six months in Riker's Island, with five years' probation. Plead innocent and all kinds of bad things can happen. There is the matter of the ice pick, which the cops have found in Sharron's room. The charge then

Sharron Corley
(Charlena Berksteiner)

Sharron at age nine, with his sister,
Shawanda, eleven *(Courtesy of Sharron Corley)*

Sharron using "his" phone on Pitkin
Avenue *(Charlena Berksteiner)*

Brownsville circa
1910: the corner
of Thatford and
Belmont avenues
*(Courtesy of the
Brooklyn Historical
Society)*

Brownsville to-
day: on the border
with East New
York, overlooking
the Van Dyke
Houses
(Mitchell Zykofsky)

These "Rest in
Peace" murals
are now found
throughout the
Ville.
(Benny J. Stumbo)

Gary at age fourteen, with his grandmother *(Courtesy of Gary Lemite)*

Gary Lemite *(Mitchell Zykofsky)*

Gary with Lisa, Erica, and Zach *(Andrew French)*

This statue of Thomas Jefferson sits between Principal Carol Beck's office and the metal detectors at the school's entrance. *(© Eli Reed/Magnum Photos)*

Thomas Jefferson High School
(Charlena Berksteiner)

Sharon King *(Charlena Berksteiner)*

Carol Beck *(Courtesy of the Jackie Robinson Center)*

The Thomas Jefferson High School basketball team. *Left to right: front,* Willie Brown, Cortez Sutton, Carl Princivil, Marvin McLaurin; *kneeling,* Jude Princivil, Musbau (Nick) Ogunyemi; *back,* Greg Donaldson, Adrian Bradshaw, Kevin (Tumbo) John, Coach George Moore.
(Courtesy of George Moore)

Above left: Sharron and other members of the cast of *Don't Give Up on Your Dreams* practice outside.
(Courtesy of the Jackie Robinson Center)

Above: Student leader Bashim Inman at the side door of Thomas Jefferson
(Mitchell Zykofsky)

Left: Danny, played by Sharron, is warned by his mother and sister of the dangers of life on the streets.
(Courtesy of the Jackie Robinson Center)

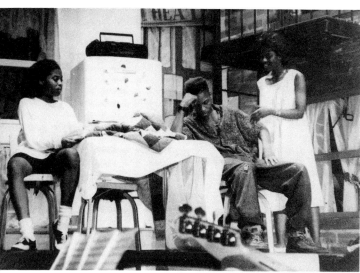

Left: The entrance to the PSA 2, on Sutter Avenue *(Benny J. Stumbo)*

Above: Cops on the four-to-twelve shift stand in line to pick up their radios. *(Mitchell Zykofsky)*

Left: John (J.R.) Reynolds and Gary Lemite on the job *(Mitchell Zykofsky)*

Officer Kevin Price, at left, helps carry the dying Tyrone Sinkler out the front door of Thomas Jefferson. *(Benny J. Stumbo)*

Sharon King comforts students after the second shooting at Jeff. *(© Eli Reed/ Magnum Photos)*

Students await the beginning of Carol Beck's cotillion. *(© Eli Reed/Magnum Photos)*

Sharron at work on homework, making his way toward completing high school
(Charlena Berksteiner)

Gary Lemite, wearing the medals that made him the most highly decorated New York Housing cop in 1992
(Andrew French)

would be robbery one — a couple of years if he blows the trial. The kids call the choice "trap off."

The very next day, the shoe is on the other foot. Sharron finds himself in the bullpen at the Schermerhorn Street courthouse, waiting for arraignment with three guys who know each other. One of the three flashes a jailhouse burner, the sharpened end of a twist of metal spring extracted from a bed, and Sharron's beloved burgundy Timberland boots are gone. They are not worth getting cut for. Sharron just gives them up, and squeezes his lips together tightly as he laces up a pair of dirty, sweat-softened, black-and-white Nike highcuts.

With the six-months deal done, it remains only for him to return for formal sentencing. Sharron has stepped from the winding and difficult path of accomplishment onto the beaten trail that leads the boys of Brownsville to the jailhouse. He boards the blue and white corrections bus for a trip to Queens and Riker's Island. The hatless Corrections Department driver grinds the gears down, and the dirty bus rattles to a stop on the corner of Tillary and Jay streets, near the Brooklyn Bridge. Sharron watches the rough young men around him, all gaping at the girls crossing the street, heading to classes at a local college.

"Yo, yo, light-skin," they scream through the mesh-sealed windows. "You got a man. Yo, check it out, light-skin?" The boys are frantic to get a reaction. But from the outside, viewed through the mesh, they are nothing more than shadows. "Stink bitch," one boy yells.

The bus rumbles onto the Brooklyn-Queens Expressway and over the Kosciusko Bridge, high above rolling acres of gravestones. The words of the reggae song that was playing at the Steam Team party come to Sharron as the bus picks up speed on the Grand Central Parkway and the boys around him fall quiet.

You never wan' go Riker's Island.
When de yout' first com' a New Yawk,
Da tell 'em learn a trade or go to school.
Don't skylark an' play yaself fa' a fool.

Incarceration. It is a rite in Brownsville. Sharron sighs. Shit, a lot of guys have done bids in Spofford or upstate. Most guys. Not those "pupils" maybe, the actors in King's play, the basketball players, but most of the LoLifes have been away, and that cock-diesel kid Bashim, who punched him in the mouth once over some "he say, she say" bullshit.

The bus shudders to a stop beside the checkpoint at the foot of the bridge to Riker's Island. There isn't a sound on the bus now.

Out of the window to Sharron's right are the runways of La Guardia Airport, jutting into the East River; ahead, the rocky shore of Riker's Island. Garbage bags, caught high in the razor-ribbon fence and weathered to a deathly gray by the wind from the river, flap like shrouds around the jail. Sharron's shoulders sag. Riker's is no place for the son of Gloria Corley, no spot for a sweet-tempered, talented kid like him. He's not hard-core. He is supposed to be going places. His mother loves him. Jail is supposed to be for the sons of mothers who do not care, kids who run the streets.

At the rear of the C-74 building, a corrections officer conducts the boys off the bus and through a reinforced steel door into the jailhouse. Sharron Corley has made it out of the Ville.

If the Housing Authority has its way, the Worthys will be leaving the Ville also. Judge Ira Harkavy is standing in his robes before the bench in his courtroom in the Housing court building at 141 Livingston Street in downtown Brooklyn. The eviction proceeding, *New York City Housing Authority* v. *Renee Asbury*, is about to begin, and the judge looks like a man who is enjoying his work.

"We've had ninety-five of the drug eviction cases so far," he reflects. "If I have the slightest inkling that those involved are users and not purveyors, I throw the case out. But we've had ninety-four evictions so far. It works."

Mike Pratt, a Legal Aid lawyer standing nearby in a blue suit and Italian tie, doesn't like Harkavy's self-satisfied tone of voice or his words. His clients, Renee and Kate, are sitting within earshot. This process is supposed to be about justice, not efficiency. What's more, Harkavy's figures are wrong. Pratt knows of at least three cases where public housing tenants turned back attempts to evict. But Pratt is upset for another reason. When the proceedings begin, he approaches the bench.

"Your Honor, we have done some background checking and we have found that the Legal Aid Society is representing someone else who may have contrary interests to the respondents here. We therefore cannot act as representatives for Renee Asbury, the legal tenant in this case. I'm sure you know that I cannot go into the details of our other representation."

Apparently Legal Aid is representing one of the Worthy boys arrested for selling drugs in the vicinity of the apartment. Just like that, Pratt is gone, and Renee and Kate don't have the slightest idea what to do. They shift on the bench in the second row of the small hearing room and look at each other. Kate snorts a puff of air through her nose and rocks her head back.

To open the hearing, the Housing Authority lawyer cites ninety-one criminal cases involving crack peddling around the premises of 295 Dumont. A building manager and half a dozen police officers testify about vials of crack dropped, bought, and sold by, and confiscated from the likes of Randolph, Lennie, Edward, Willie, and Jimmy Worthy and Blue Asbury. What they cannot do is place a single one of the sales within the apartment, or connect Renee, the lessee, with any of the sales. But the defense attorney is gone. The law says that Renee has no absolute right to a lawyer in this kind of case. There is no one to point out the weakness in the Housing Authority's case.

In a pathetic attempt to keep her apartment, Renee allows herself to be sworn in and takes the stand in front of Judge Harkavy. Without an attorney to guide her through her testimony, all she can do is mumble about how the Housing cops "beat on people."

"You are going to have to speak louder," the judge says softly.

"Tell how they busted in the door," Kate whispers from her seat.

"What?" Renee mouths the word. Kate shakes her head and draws the corners of her mouth down. She won't take the stand herself. Renee sits sullenly for a moment in the witness chair, then shrugs and joins her grandmother.

The hearing is over. The nineteen-member Worthy clan, including women, children, and the wheelchair-bound Philip, have just been evicted from their double apartment, 5AB, at 295 Dumont Avenue, under an archaic state statute known as the bawdy-house law.

"I don't know if I would call it a railroad, but it is a case of accelerated justice," a Legal Aid supervisor observes later about such evictions. The city has one judge to handle all the bawdy-house cases, and Legal Aid attorneys worry that hearing so many similar cases cuts down on Harkavy's ability to see each one on its merits. Even more dangerous, they believe, is the city's practice of building an eviction case by offering young offenders sentences of time served in exchange for guilty pleas in minor drug offenses, then using those pleas as evidence for eviction.

In the hallway, a burly white Housing police officer with a stiff brown brush cut can't suppress a snicker as Kate Worthy limps for the elevator. She hears the laugh and wheels. She spits a curse: "Motherfucker."

"At least I got somewhere to live, Kate," the cop says. He is right. When abuse fell on Robo and Schulman, it came down on a day or a night shift, on an eight-hour tour. When the bad news hits the Worthys, it is on their lives.

"IT HURTS, PRICE"

I t's Tuesday, November 26, 10 A.M. The door to Carol Beck's office is shut tight. The principal is taking no calls, no visitors, "no damn messages." She's poised, hands folded, leaning, straining to catch every syllable from Dorian, Kerrol, and Taji, a matched set of handsome, soft-voiced sophomores seated at the conference table. Two worn teddy bears and a Snoopy doll cling together at the center of the table.

These three boys are neither honor students nor troublemakers. They combine just the right measures of street bravado and restraint to make them popular in the school. When they walk the halls, they slap high, low, and middle fives all around. The girls study them, write their names on notebook covers. But they are more interested in having fun with their buddies than in following up on the girls. These are close friends, with special phrases and inside jokes. When one laughs, they all laugh, even when there is nothing to laugh at. All for one and one for all.

Dorian, an ocher-skinned, clear-eyed seventeen-year-old, is describing Jermaine Bentley, sometimes known as Joker, a friend who is not present. "Jermaine was like down with us, but he wasn't really down? He was always playin' around." Dorian pauses for a moment to find the words to describe Jermaine's status. "A wannabe," he says, and looks at Kerrol and Taji, who nod.

Jermaine was nervous and touchy. His playfulness had an air of desperation. He envied Dorian, Kerrol, and Taji their easy ways, wanted to hang out. He didn't have much to recommend him, just a passion to belong. And deep in Jermaine's heart there was something even stronger — ambition.

"He was like . . . a nobody. But he wanted to be the man," Dorian explains to Beck.

Jermaine wanted to set the styles, to be admired, imitated, and feared. Ambition can be the force that builds bridges, cures diseases, gets your name painted on the hallowed Jefferson honor board. Not this time.

"Jermaine was never a good fighter," Dorian continues. "He would take somebody's hat and then he would run behind me. I get around, but not in a violent way. After a while, it was known that he was with us. He tried to make it like if he got into something I would jump in with no questions, but it wasn't like that. I mean, I was like 'I'm chill with you, but I ain't ready to die for you.'"

There was another kid on the periphery of the group. His name was Jesse. At five-seven, he was no taller or heavier than Jermaine, but his face was etched with nicks from long-forgotten street fights, and his eyes were arctic cold. Jesse was always ready to raise the stakes.

"Jesse just don't care about nothin'," Taji says. "His man is Chubby and they always tight, they the same. They got brothers in jail and they used to shit, and they don't care if they get shot, if they die."

"When you have an older brother with a big reputation," Kerrol adds, "if you don't live up to the rep, you aren't nothin'. That's some heavy shit."

Ambition collides with pathological courage in a bleak world, and the process is born.

"Jermaine started all kinds of stuff," Dorian explains, "like arguments. Like he would even try with me. Then he would say like 'I didn't like what you said, so when you come around the way you gonna get jumped.' And then I would say to my people, 'You know, I got to do something about what he said.' But with me and Taji and Kerrol, we would come back, and he says like 'I didn't really mean what I said before, I was mad,' and you know. But with Jesse, he wasn't havin' all that."

Early in September, an everyday dis from Jesse led Jermaine Bentley to make the claim that he would be coming to school the next day with a gun. When he didn't bring the gun, he became a figure of scorn.

"Jermaine thought the gun would give him amp," Kerrol says, "but everybody was laughin' instead."

It wasn't over. In Brownsville, it's never over. There is no comfort zone where a young man or woman can relax, go for a stroll with a girlfriend or boyfriend, think about nothing but the other. There are borders, vendettas, trouble from long ago. Anything can be cause for a beef: if you look at someone or you don't look at him, talk to the wrong girl, step on somebody's new sneaker, take too long on a pay phone, accomplish something, make a joke.

Yesterday, a Monday morning, Jermaine and Jesse, the two wounded personalities, came face to face on the fourth floor. Those who knew their history understood the deadly possibilities. It is a rule of human behavior that people will do what they do best. Neither Jermaine nor Jesse cared much for school. They had fought on the street more often and more intensely than they had learned in class, practiced a musical instrument, or played a sport. Even though Jermaine was not much of a fighter, there was nothing he could do better.

Just before the fistfight started, a jubilant crowd gathered. On one level, the students at Jeff are delighted that their school has started to become functional under Carol Beck, has become a place where you can actually learn something. But a good fight is a welcome relief from the droning teachers. Forty students surrounded the spot where Jesse and Jermaine performed their scene obligatoire. The standing audience was five deep. Girls in the back of the crowd leapt up to get a glimpse of the action.

Dorian shouldered his way through the throng. "You got a gun?" he asked, reaching to pat Jermaine's midsection. Jermaine jumped away.

"Nah, my little man got it," Jermaine bragged. Dorian stepped away. He knew Jermaine didn't like to carry a burner. The reference to Jermaine's "little man" was lost on him in the swelling excitement.

First Jesse popped Jermaine, a quick jab to the neck, then staggered him with a chopping overhand. Dorian grappled with Jermaine's brother, fourteen-year-old Jason, to keep him from intervening. Jesse was pouring it on, blow after blow.

"Let me go. I won't do *nothin'*," Jason pleaded.

Dorian loosened his grip just enough for Jason to break free and land a punch on the back of Jesse's neck. Dorian and another boy pulled Jason back and the fight continued, with Jesse still in control. Jason seemed to sag in Dorian's arms, as if resigned to his brother's beating. Dorian eased his hold once more. The combatants were on the floor now, Jesse squeezing Jermaine in a headlock. Jason lunged again, this time with a bottle in his hand. He clubbed Jesse. The bottle skidded to the floor and broke.

"Fuck this. Fuck this. I don't need to do this with my hands. Gimme my bookbag. Gimme my bag," Jesse demanded, still pinning Jermaine to the floor. Dorian squeezed Jason.

"I won't do nothin', I swear," Jason begged.

"You already said that two times," Dorian answered.

The spectators assumed that Jesse's demand for his bookbag was a call for a weapon, but nobody left. For almost everyone in attendance, this was great stuff. One of the byproducts of television, coupled with lack of guidance and long-term goals, is a withered attention span. In everything the kids do, they go for the quick jolt, the instant payoff. This was "slammin'" drama. Did Jesse have a burner in the bookbag?

Jesse disentangled himself and began to step back into the crowd to get the bookbag. Jason wriggled free one last time. He would now do what he had to do. He reached into his backpack.

There are no metal detectors at Thomas Jefferson High School. It is Carol Beck's passionate belief that the obvious advantages are outweighed by the message their presence sends to students and society. Metal detectors greet youngsters every morning with the unequivocal statement that they are in a violent and dangerous place, that they themselves are dangerous. Beck also believes the devices will lull society at large into a false belief that something has been done about the problem of guns. "What good are metal detectors if the kids shoot each other on the street outside the school and in the playgrounds?" she argues.

What had happened so far on the fourth floor was not unusual here. This was still just a fistfight between a fool and a tough guy, or two fools. What happened next was madness.

Jason's hand came out of his backpack with a silver gun. He held the heavy piece away from his body at shoulder level, a lost look on his face. A girl's voice rang out from behind. "Do it. You gonna shoot it?"

Jason, the little brother, scant backup in a major throwdown, waved the pistol. It presented him with some major

problems. Any person, even a little brother, would be profoundly discredited if he had a burner and was afraid to light
it. Jason did not aim. He was standing alone now. The appearance of the gun had sent the audience scrambling. Jesse was
fifteen feet away, down the hall; Jermaine, on the floor. Now
was the time. Maybe Jesse was about to come up with his own
jammy, his own piece of adamancy. Jason turned his head away,
held the gun with one hand, out and up, with locked elbow,
and pulled the trigger three times. His arm flew up with each
shot as if he were holding on to the thrashing tail of a baby
alligator. *BAM . . . BAM, BAM.* There was a long hesitation
between the first and the second shot. The second and third
shots were close.

The sound of the gun in the crowded hall was like a cannon
blast, the noise stupendous, the chaos imaginable. In a shootout
in the street you can take cover, but everybody here knew that
a hallway means ricochets. The girls nearest the fight, so willing to see someone else get hurt, jumped for safety. In a reversal
of their usual inclination, the students fought desperately to get
into a classroom, any classroom. But the teachers and kids in
those rooms had heard the shots and slammed the doors, and
were holding them shut. All except the shop teacher, Robert
Anderson, who stepped into the hall in time to catch a bullet in
the neck. His hands flew to his throat and he pitched forward.

The concussion in the enclosed area of the hall threw Dorian
to the tiled floor. He landed next to Daryl Sharpe, a fellow
sophomore. "You O.K.?" he asked Daryl. "You shot? Check.
You shot?"

Dorian's hands ran down his own torso to his thighs and
stomach. He gazed blankly at his legs and arms. They seemed
to belong to someone else. He looked up to see Jesse running
down the hall straight at Jason, "like he didn't care if he lived
or died." But Jason fled in the chaos, sprinting down the hall to
the stairway.

Dorian still was not sure whether he or anyone else had
been shot.

"You got shot?" he asked Daryl again.

"I don't know." Daryl was on his back in the last moments of
his life, and he did not know whether he had been hit. "Get me
up," he said. "Get me up." The more he spoke, the softer his

voice became. "I can't feel my body," he whispered. "I can't feel nothin'."

"Where you got shot?" Dorian asked again.

Daryl pointed to his chest, but then he saw that he had blood on his collar. A lost, sad smile stuck on his lips.

"No. No!" Dorian screamed. Hands reached under his arms and lifted him up and away from Daryl.

Officer Kevin Price, the 75th precinct cop assigned to Jeff, was on his knees hovering over the wounded boy as the shooting call went out to sector cars in the area.

"It hurts, Price," Daryl whispered. "Price, it hurts."

In a minute the halls were filled with running policemen, their guns drawn. The shooter had not been found, and nobody knew if there were more guns. Beck, in white sneakers, was running too.

"I was afraid of a Wyatt Earp thing," she said later. "That blue brain trip. I was afraid someone would trip with their gun out and . . ." But in the next few moments, she was fluttering about, congratulating the officers on their control and restraint.

"Aren't you afraid to work in this place?" a young white cop asked Price as the EMS stretcher carrying Daryl Sharpe moved toward the elevator. Price, who is very close to the Jefferson kids, did not like the question.

"To tell you the truth," he spit over his shoulder, "if I got shot in here, I'd be more surprised than anything. I'd be more pissed than shot."

Dorian wandered around the upper floors of Jefferson stiff-legged, eyes cast far ahead. "I shoulda known, 'cause Jesse had all his people there and Jermaine didn't have nobody but his little brother," he rambled on to a girl he hardly knew. "I shoulda known he had a gun, 'cause Jermaine was acting with all kinds of heart." Dorian paused by a window overlooking the school parking lot on Dumont Avenue. He noticed ambulances streaming away from Jefferson down Pennsylvania toward Livonia, on their way to Brookdale Hospital. He had seen shootings before. He had seen people recover and return to the block. But now, out on the street below, kids were moving in slow motion. Two girls clung to each other, their bodies bucking with sobs. They stumbled against a fence and almost fell, but didn't let go of each other. Dorian knew then that Daryl Sharpe was dead.

Twenty minutes after the shooting, Beck got a call from Chancellor Joseph Fernandez of the New York City Board of Education, who suggested that she keep the students in school for the rest of the day. "That's too long," Beck told her assistant principal. "But we're not going to dismiss them right away, either. We have our next class. We don't do anything with a knee jerk." Thirty minutes later, she called the eighteen hundred students to the school auditorium to tell them that their classmate and a teacher had been shot. "It's your school, your community," she advised. "You don't have to talk to the television people. You have a right to your pain and your space." Later she would say, "These are not the Cosby kids; they'd know that they had the right not to talk. But our kids don't know what they are entitled to." "Don't whore your sorrow" is the way Ms. King put it.

Beck was everywhere. On Pennsylvania Avenue, a television reporter pressed too hard for an interview and she threatened to put her foot to the woman. A black cameraman came up. "I want to shake your hand for that," the man said. "I was proud of you."

Beck had to handle the students, the media, and the staff. She called the teachers in. "One of your own was shot. Robert Anderson will live, but I don't want to minimize it. You all are under stress," she told them. Then the United Federation of Teachers union drones showed up, talking about closing the school.

The next day, Thomas Jefferson High School is again swarming with officials and reporters. Beck holds a quick news conference. "I have retired teachers and Hy Smith, a guidance counselor, coming in to help in case other teachers don't show up. And do you know that the only teachers who haven't shown up are ones that were absent yesterday and were sick? When I saw the cars pull into the parking lot, I felt like kissing them all." Then Beck closes the school to the media.

She is determined to control things. She could not stop Jason, but by God, she will have something to do with how the press portrays this event. She speaks to the students and the staff again. She arranges for therapy workshops throughout the week for faculty and students, calling in crisis intervention experts to run sessions for the children. She roams the school, making sure that everything runs right. But of course, everything is not right.

In the library, a trauma counselor helps students express their feelings.

"Are you scared?" the trim, dark-haired man asks.

"No," a six-foot, baby-faced junior answers.

"What is Jefferson?"

"A name."

"A school," says a girl with a broad forehead and gold thread woven into her towering hair.

"A second home," a boy with glasses offers, looking around to see if he has said something foolish.

"I don't want to get shot in my second home," the baby-faced junior adds.

"Do you want to leave?" the counselor presses.

"Yes."

"How often do you see something violent? Something bad?"

"Once a day."

"More than once a day."

"Every half-hour," the boy with glasses blurts.

"It's according to where you live at."

The students are asked to form human sculptures of a table, a trash can, love. Shyly at first, then with enthusiasm and much laughter, they comply.

"Can you change your environment?"

"No."

"It's not the school that's bad, it's the students."

"Are the students bad?"

No answer.

"What are you learning in school?"

"Science. History. We learn that life is gonna be hard when we get out," the girl with the gilded hair says.

"Whatever you say. Whatever they say will go in one ear and out the other," a frowning girl leaning on a bookshelf by the wall insists.

"Do the teachers come to teach?"

"Most teachers are scared of us because of the way we are. They stay away from us," the baby-faced junior explains.

Upstairs, extra chairs have been crowded into a small lounge on the third floor. This is a quiet place where the teachers retreat from the torrent of adolescent energy in the classrooms and hallways. Today, ten teachers and teachers' aides are discussing the shooting.

"I think this is harder on us than it is on the students," a plump white man begins. "They're used to this kind of thing. I am traumatized."

Another white man is muttering and shaking his head. He has a confession to make. "I don't know if I'm a sociopath or what. I have seen shootings and I have seen stabbings here. I have seen heart attacks. I saw a Spanish teacher stabbed by a student. And when I saw this boy being taken out, all I could think about was . . . next period. When I heard that there were going to be memorials and grieving sessions after this shooting, I thought, why bother, what for? Let's just go on."

There is a long silence, and heads nod.

A white woman with excessive, nasal vowels pipes a lament that grows more frantic with each phrase. "I used to *think* I was safe here. I don't feel that way anymore. I don't know why I felt that way. I shouldn't feel that way. It wasn't healthy." More nodding.

All is not well here. A rotund teachers' aide launches a complaint about a certain teacher who has been treating him with lack of respect. It is not unusual to find an aide who would make a much better teacher than the certified instructor he or she assists. This aide's eyes dart accusingly. He may not have his degree, but he knows full well that he can do a better job than he has been witnessing at Jefferson.

The woman who used to feel safe attempts to pacify him, but the aide is having none of it.

"I was standing in the hall when the shots went off. I saw the fire come out of that gun. And I thought I was going to die. And I didn't see a *single* teacher come out to see what I was screaming for or to assist in any way. If you're talking about 'being together,' what the hell kind of thing is that?"

"It's a natural thing to stay inside when there is shooting in the hall," a slight, middle-aged black woman offers gently. "I, for one, was not going to come into that hall. You can understand that."

But the aide is making the most of the session, opening up wide. "How do you tell a mother that her son is dead? How do you form your lips to say that? How do we keep failing? Where do I turn . . . for a future?" The man stops for a moment. "I will never forget as long as I live standing there *by myself* in that hall. The boy turned and came toward me and I ran to the elevator. I was sure there were going to be more shots, and I banged on the elevator and the boy kept coming. Then those doors opened like the gates of heaven and I stepped on. And do you know that I have not gotten on that elevator since that day? And do you know why?" He waits a long moment before he gives the answer. "Because you do not ask the doors of heaven to open twice."

IF YOU MISS SCHOOL, YOU MISS OUT reads a bright red sign outside the Jefferson auditorium. Inside, both the balcony and the orchestra of the packed auditorium are bursting with anticipation. This is, several days after the shooting, a memorial for Daryl Sharpe. For the occasion, Carol Beck has invited rap singer Dougie Fresh.

The program starts on a low note. A board of education representative, a woman in a broad silk scarf and oversize tinted glasses, gives lugubrious condolences in a tone of involuntary, but nonetheless palpable, condescension: "We feel the pain, the pain of the mother who must bury her son. And just like you, we wonder what to do. But like you, we will find the strength." This lady is smart enough to know that platitudes will not suffice now. She determines that for once, she will appear without varnish. But she fails. She sounds as if she is talking to a crowd of infants. The assembled students are cold-eyed. They are uneducated in almost everything but the subject she is lecturing them about. These are graduate students of violent death.

They listen politely until a girl with a furrowed brow growls, "Fuck this," hurls down a notebook on the floor between her legs, and stomps to the back of the room. She tries to get out but is accosted by the ubiquitous Ms. King. "This is bullshit," the girl proclaims. "Ain't nobody gives a shit. Nobody cares. They just talking shit."

"Nobody?" Sharon King won't be included in the indictment. "Are you saying I don't care?"

The girl yanks King's hand off her. "Fuck this," she repeats, and pushes out the door.

Soon it is King's turn to be irate. The crowd gasps as the rap singer, Dougie Fresh, appears at the door and heads down the aisle toward the stage on a wave of energy, like a fighter heading toward the ring for a championship bout. With lustrous brown skin and even features, he has a delightful boyish glint to his eye. He wears his hair in a short fade. In the mid-eighties, he pioneered the rap genre with his music video "The Show." But he hasn't had a hit in years. In the world of rap music, he is old news. That doesn't matter to the kids now.

Fresh fondles the microphone. "Each of you has got to be strong enough to do your own thinkin'. It's got to change, and it's got to start with you." He mesmerizes the audience, but he has nothing new to say. At the end of his short, earnest presentation, he starts a gentle rap riff. The lyrics prepared for the occasion are appropriately grave, and the mood of solemnity holds for a while. But even the subdued hip-hop cadence of his words juices up the six student leaders seated behind him on the stage. One girl jumps up and snaps her skirt around her knees; several others rise and rock to the beat. Students in the audience leap to their feet, shouting and waving their arms.

Fresh ends his short song and bows. As he descends the steps at the side of the stage, the decorum breaks completely and two dozen students quit their seats and rush toward him. Nareida, the young actress who played Sharron's girlfriend in *Don't Give Up on Your Dreams*, clambers over her seat and charges down the row behind to get to his side. She tugs and pushes, turns sideways, and squeezes through the tight mass of screaming students toward the performer.

On the opposite side of the auditorium, Sharon King is horrified at this riotous development. She circles in front of the stage and does some pushing of her own till she gets close enough to grip Nareida by the shoulders and yank her back.

"What the hell are you doing? Are y'all crazy? This is a goddamn *memorial!*" she screams at the startled girl.

Despite King's protest, pandemonium breaks loose and more kids run up to Fresh. Much of the behavior of these young people is based on what they have seen on television. It's all theater, and as they mob Dougie Fresh, they are just reading from the wrong page of the script. The hysteria is macabre. Enraged, King wades into the crowd, tossing adolescents aside like sacks of flour. It's all she can do to refrain from throwing punches. It is five minutes before order is restored.

Most of it is an act anyway. Beck, King, and the counselors are trying to mark the death of Daryl Sharpe as a tragedy. But the teacher who said that the faculty was more traumatized than the students was right. The death is only shocking because it happened in the hallway of a school. These are the young of the Brownsville Houses, of Amboy Street and Cypress. They were close by when Officer McLean was killed at 340 Dumont and Tango, Boy, Powerful, and the rest lay dead in the Complex last summer. How much grieving can they do?

Later in the day, Carol Beck and a flushed Sharon King are seated in the principal's conference room. Beck is wearing a co-balt-blue blouse and her ever-present ivory Nefertiti brooch. "We are going to a new place as a school, as a community," Beck says, chortling. "They tell me not to talk to the press, but if I don't they start digging up and creating things. This way, they all get the same things and they go." She is subtly but relent-lessly self-congratulatory. The effect is entirely sympathetic. She seems to be building herself up for the benefit of the school. If she is wonderful, so is Jefferson, and so are the students, even though some of them may be shooting each other. She has seen negative images followed by violent behavior all her life, and she is determined to throw sticks in the spokes of that dreadful wheel.

The woman from the board of education walks into the prin-cipal's office and slumps into a chair, tired and upset. She has gold-tipped gray hair and carries a beige Vuitton bag.

"A child that can't be buried . . ." The woman sighs dramati-cally. King, across the table, rolls her prodigious hazel eyes. Beck cuts her a glance, warning her not to disrespect the board's representative.

"I'm not a politician. I'm a teacher. We get paid much less," King says, and walks out.

Beck is a politician and a teacher. After the board of educa-tion lady and King have left the office, she sits alone and ex-hausted at the huge table. Slowly, she unties the string around a box that turns out to hold a white and pink cake, a gift from several parents. "Cheer Up," says an inscription in blue icing. Beck thumbs through a pile of mail offering sympathy and best wishes for her and the school. Among the letters is one that reads, "Do what you gotta do. Keep the faith." Enclosed is a check for $500, made out to Thomas Jefferson High School. The letter has been sent from the Manhattan Correctional Center. It is signed "John Gotti."

The next day there is another sit-down with the media, this time with two members of Geraldo Rivera's *Now It Can Be Told* television show.

A young black producer with copper-colored hair blithely sets sail into Beck's waters. "We realize your dedication —" he begins.

"And I realize your need to follow up a story to get in the headlines," Beck interrupts, firing a cannon shot across his bow. "We're not about that. We are going to transcend sensationalism here. This is a different kind of energy. We are not going backwards. We are not about raising the Neilsen ratings, or selling newspapers."

"We believe this is a microcosm," the producer's smooth-faced sidekick says.

"We know all that," Beck fires back. "I'm not paranoid. I am racially secure. We know the problem. We want solutions."

The producer is intrepid. He graduated from Syracuse University with a degree in journalism, moved to Manhattan, and sailed to the top of his field like a weather balloon. He is barely thirty years old. East New York and Brownsville are the provinces to him, places important only for the story he has come to cover; Carol Beck is an insignificant drudge who just happened to be on the watch when something remarkable happened. He does not understand that in many ways this place, this school, is the most significant place of all, the place on which the future of the country will turn. And that Carol Beck is the important person, the kind of person he is so sure he is.

"What are those solutions?" he asks, with a cockiness that reveals how many things he has not felt.

Beck is calmer now. "We are trying to come to a different emotional and psychological place. You are constrained by time on television. You cannot get into the psyche of the black and Hispanic man. As a people, we are through with the talk show. I don't care about those people on Sutton Place. They are not here. They will never be here. Now is time to do some other things. I am not sure what they are, but I know that you are not going to get at them in forty minutes."

"I can see you're trying to do this yourself. We would like to talk to the parents," the producer says.

Beck calls across the room to an assistant, "Jerry, I'm not getting through to these people." Then her voice begins to trill with anger. It is now clear that she did not come to this discussion in good faith. She is using Geraldo's people to make herself feel better. "Why would you want to talk to the parents?" she demands.

"You don't have to raise your voice," the producer protests, wishing he had not made the trip.

"You want to show a picture that says, 'This is what the mother of a child who has been killed looks like.' I ain't about this anymore. Where is the benefit, the intellectual growth, that is going to come out of that? It's a type of prostitution. I'm not telling you about my pain anymore. It's tragic, yes. But do I need to share this with the white middle class? No, I am not exposing my wounds to Sally Sue in Kansas. If it has to stop with me, maybe other blacks and Latinos will also stop."

"We are not miracle workers," the producer's slim sidekick says.

"I didn't think you were," Beck snaps.

RIKER'S ISLAND

Front-page news for two days, the shootings at Jefferson are quickly forgotten. Today, sheets of rain assail a line of friends, relatives, defendants, and victims that stretches from the Brooklyn Criminal Court down Schermerhorn Street around the corner toward the looming Brooklyn House of Detention on Atlantic Avenue. In the middle of the line, a white woman with a bloated face and three grimy children straddles a puddle of rainwater. Her baby daughter drops a pacifier into the filmy water. The mother snatches up the rubber mouthpiece and dips it into her own mouth for cleaning before she hands it back to the toddler. A platoon of teenagers cut the line and wedge their way in toward the metal detectors beyond the revolving doors. No one complains. The courthouse where Sharron will be sentenced late this afternoon is an eight-story eyesore, a dingy, grimy contrast to the bleached stone and tinted glass of the federal court on Cadman Plaza a few blocks away, where the Young Guns pleaded guilty. The Schermerhorn building houses courtrooms, probation offices, record departments, and other offices.

The cops who have to testify here shuttle back and forth to the court from a building down the street they call ECAB, the Early Case Assessment Bureau. On the seventh floor there they sleep on filthy padded blue chairs with newspapers for blankets, waiting to be called for interviews with the ADAs, who will decide what kind of a case to make out of their collar. On a wall of ECAB's waiting room some misguided soul has written "The Killing Crew," with a short list of names of Housing officers from PSA 2 who have killed perps in Brownsville and East New York over the years. The list starts with the nickname Grahambo.

The cops are not allowed to use the clean semiprivate bathroom on the floor. Somebody scrawled "ADAs blow," "[ADA] Lynn Jaffee is a lesbian," and numerous references to "niggers" on the stalls, which upset the lawyers and minority complainants. The cops have been banished to a filthy toilet on the ninth floor.

In the courthouse, from his seat in the bullpen of Part V on the fourth floor, Sharron cannot see the rows of benches in the courtroom, where Chantal sits with Andre in her lap. The busy courtroom is half full of spectators and young men, who are here for any one of a score of reasons related to a criminal case pending against them.

"Didn't your lawyer advise you how to dress and conduct yourself when you come before this court?" a judge asks a flabby youth convicted of an infraction that is not serious enough to warrant incarceration. "This is the second time you have arrived here asking for a delay in the payment of your fine. Next time you are scheduled to appear, you bring some money with you. I don't care if it's a ten-dollar bill. Or you are going to jail. Do you understand?"

It is late afternoon by the time Sharron's name is called. He slouches out to meet the judge and hear the numbers he knows already.

"No reading," a court officer shouts at a man in the back.

Chantal and Andre are in the third row. Sharron nods. Though he is not cuffed, he does not wave. Chantal holds the kicking baby up to see his handsome father's face, but only for a moment. Sharron turns to face the judge. His plea has been accepted, the deal delivered, all in record time. Six months in jail and a hefty five-year probation. It is not about graduating from high school now. It is about doing the time without getting hurt. Maybe it was about that all along.

Sharron nods to Chantal and Andre again on the way out. He does not smile; his face is a jailhouse mask already. But Sharron Corley is a lucky man, or a lucky boy, as the case may be, because the judge has decided to put him in the adolescent house, even though he is eighteen and could have been assigned to the adult wing with the heavyweights. Sharron breathes a deep sigh when he finds he is going down with the boys.

At 5:30 on Sharron's first morning in Mod Six, the "newjack" barracks in the 4 Building at Riker's Island, a bank of lights flashes a stunning wakeup call in his eyes. He sits up and blinks, looking down the narrow room filled with thirty beds. Next to each bed is a waist-high steel locker.

"Walkin' to the mess hall," a corrections officer's voice booms. *"On the breakfast."*

Only four boys sit up. The rest roll over and cover their heads with blankets. Sharron does the same. Later in the morning, as he watches the boys around him dig into their stashes of cookies and potato chips from the commissary, he regrets his decision. Throughout the morning, he is alternately hungry and nauseous. The smells of disinfectant and boiled meat drift up from the mess hall and mix together in the room like a fresh insult. There is nothing to do but sit and stare until 12:30. The barracks and the TV room are filled with lean, staring boys, many of them coming through the system for the first time. Their eyes are open, their mouths closed.

"On the lunch."

This time Sharron lines up for the trip to the mess hall. *"On the gate,"* the corrections officer hollers and waits for each barred partition to be opened on the trip downstairs. In the bright green mess hall, the food is served through two narrow slits in an otherwise blank wall. There is a choice of halal, ritually slaughtered meat for Muslim inmates, or regular fare. Sharron's meal is three pieces of white bread, one bloated frankfurter, a fistful of cool mashed potatoes, an indistinct yellowish vegetable, and a container of milk. He gobbles the frankfurter, skirts the potatoes, which glow faintly green in the corner of his partitioned plastic plate, and swallows his milk in two gulps.

Back upstairs in the barracks, he cannot sleep anymore, so he stuffs his worn woolen blanket into his pillowcase for extra cushion, the way he has seen others do, and gazes dumbly at the low ceiling. Bursts of canned laughter drift from the television in the day room. He has heard that there is a school program; he has even been supplied with a notebook and a stubby pencil,

too short to be used as a weapon. But it will take time for the
school paperwork to go through. So for his first two days Sharron just sits glumly on his bed, staring across at veteran inmates
talking for as long as half an hour on the telephone in the hallway. He watches the phone, but does not make his move.

There is no middle ground in the adolescent areas of Riker's
Island. Either you are an exploiter or you are exploited. If you
are soft and have no connections, you will be forced to "go shopping" at the commissary for the more powerful guys and you
will get no time on the horn. If a guy wants to stay out of
trouble at all costs, his family may not hear from him for weeks
or months at a time, because the only thing that produces
phone time is juice, props. And juice is acquired mostly through
violence.

The Mod Six dormitory is small, now housing twenty-five
inmates, observed at all times by a corrections officer from a
window. But in the day room around the corner, where the television is, there is a spot visible from the CO's bubble only if the
officer takes his eyes off the security televisions, takes a step to
the right, and cranes his neck.

In Sharron's first week, a boy comes through Mod Six who
had trouble "out in the world" with a friend of one of the Hispanic leaders of the "4 Building gangsters." Even though Mod
Six is separated from the other housing areas in the 4 Building,
a pecking order flows through the walls, communicated
through meetings in the gym and mess hall and enforced by the
"gangsters." Sharron sees the system at work one afternoon and
records his observations in his notebook:

> We were all in the day room, and I felt the tension in the air, so
> I was on point. The next thing I know, this huge Spanish guy has
> the new guy in a sleeper hold and drags him to the blind spot. The
> new guy finally went to sleep, and the others walked out, so the
> corrections officer couldn't notice the event. Then, in the same or-
> der, they all came back into the day room and began carving up the
> guy's face something awful. Each slice sounded like a zipper being
> pulled up. Then they awoke him to a pool of blood.

Sharron spends the next few days in a flurry of concealment, his
indolent walk, bitter eyes, and scowl-twisted face a desperate
cover for his fear. In the world beyond Brownsville, his asset
sheet holds his good looks, charm, sensitivity, singing talent,

and quick mind. On the negative page are his obsession with image and his association with the LoLifes. In Riker's, the pages are switched.

After a little more than a week, Sharron is transferred to Four Main. As he enters the cell area, the inmates stand with their faces close to a Plexiglas window near the guards' station, watching his every move. Stepping through the sliding gate into their midst, Sharron knows that even a flicker of concern on his face will identify him as "new to this," as a sucker. Accordingly, he maintains a modified ice grill as he passes the cluster of boys, a pillowcase in his hand holding his belongings and boxes of cookies he has just purchased at the commissary. At the back of the group of staring boys stands Ralphlo, a Crown Heights LoLife. Ralph has two gold chains looped around his neck. It's clear at a glance that he is a person of some stature here. Sharron suppresses his delight at finding a LoLife with props in the bowels of Four Main and mumbles, "Wha's up, Ralph," as he steps past on his way to his cell. There is no response. Maybe Ralphlo is waiting to see how Sharron handles himself, waiting to see if he is a sucker, before he acknowledges their acquaintanceship. All eyes follow Sharron's dangling pillowcase as he moves toward his cell. The boys in Four Main have not had a trip to the commissary, have not been shopping, in two weeks. There isn't a cookie to be found in the housing area at any price, and now Sharron walks in like Santa Claus.

For Sharron, there are a number of quick decisions to be made. Should he secrete the cookies in his locker or should he toss them on his bed as a challenge to those who would steal them? In the spirit of Ralphlo's flaunted chains, he throws the three boxes onto the bare mattress for all to see. Before he can look up, a voice floats from over his shoulder and to his right, "Yo, Sha, wha's up."

Sharron keeps his head down and does not answer. The voice is familiar; Sharron caught a glimpse of the guy on his way in. It's a kid from around the way. Still, he doesn't respond. There's no telling if the boy is a sucker in here. Ralphlo is afraid Sharron is a sucker. Sharron is afraid this guy is a sucker. As Sharron lifts his head, he finds another kid before him, with a shaved head. This one certainly is not any kind of sucker. He looks like trouble. So soon.

"How 'bout a cookie, man?" the boy asks. Sharron watches

the kid's hands for signs of a burner. He has heard that guys in Four Main have melted pieces of razors onto the tips of their toothbrushes. How to answer? Should he shoot the request down pointblank? Should he respond matter-of-factly, or should he hand over a cookie? The kid with the gleaming head might be waiting for just such an excuse to slice him. But if he gives up the cookie, he might look soft.

"Take one, man," Sharron says flatly, then raises his voice for all in Four Main to hear. "But I got *no fuckin' food to be givin' away.*"

After tightly tying his prized cookies in the pillowcase and putting the bundle in his locker, he flops on his bed. He considers his situation. He has met Ralphlo only once before, on a meow, a shoplifting excursion, to Union Square in Manhattan, when a crew of LoLifes rushed a sporting goods store and made off with a rack of summer shirts. For Sharron, the connection is invaluable, but the introduction has to be done just right.

A couple of hours later, he approaches Ralphlo in the day room with the deference that a recent college graduate might use to introduce himself to a distant but influential relative.

"S'up?" he ventures.

"Do I know you?" There is not the slightest trace of warmth in Ralph's voice.

"Wow. Don't do me like that," Sharron answers. Both he and Ralph know the significance of the conversation. "We was down on a meow. Like, summer 'fore last."

Ralph pages through his memory. He wants to be fair. He runs three fingers down his cheek and looks hard at Sharron, who turns his head to display his scar. Ralphlo shakes his head.

"Nah," he says.

A few minutes later, back in his cell, a rebuffed and deeply concerned Sharron is on his bed, showing his photographs. He asked Gloria to send him a packet of photos for display. He is playing all his cards to impress the gangsters. One picture is a three-by-five color school portrait of Vanessa, the girl he met at the end-of-summer party; another is of a mighty fine Chantal. The Puerto Rican dudes Sharron is so wary of are "sweatin' Chantal big-time," studying the picture for minutes at a time, because she looks like a Puerto Rican sister. Another photo is of Sharron and his man Frank wearing Polo gear.

Ralph wanders over to the periphery of the small group checking out the shots. He leans in and gets a good look at Frank and Sharron in green Polo pullovers, and his face finally brightens, a blessed moment for Sharron.

"Yeah, downtown in Ma'ha'an," Ralphlo pronounces. "Bum shop. Got paid, son."

For many Americans, connections are a way of life. When a kid from Brownsville faces an interviewer for a job, there is never a familiar figure across the table, an uncle or a friend of the family somewhere behind the scene to shuffle his résumé to the top of the pile. These kids are not able to work off the books for a cousin's cousin in the summer, loading trucks or laying concrete, like the young guys in Canarsie. The trade unions are closed up tight. The only place these kids have connections that pay off is in jail. The only time the way is smoothed for them is when they get locked up. The LoLifes are Sharron's salvation.

"In Four Main I'm a gangster now," Sharron writes to Vanessa, "'cause I have props. I am hooked with Ralphlo, I now have no problem with the horn."

But he is lonely; he has no visitors. Gloria is pissed off, swears she will not come. Chantal is under age. Vanessa is busy going to school and working. Visiting day after visiting day, Sharron waits for his name to be called.

"Goddamn," he mutters, and slumps back on his bed as the line of boys heads out to the visiting area. "Down" two weeks now, and he still hasn't gotten a visit. He doesn't have sneakers or extra underwear. The photo bit will only impress the guys for so long without some pretty girls on the set. But he doesn't want to appear too disappointed, doesn't want to look like a loser. Though Four Main is a cell area instead of an open barracks, interaction is constant. Guys have tiny metal burners, what they call "guns," glued up under their beds with toothpaste or on portions of the bedframes they have managed to magnetize. Your things can get stolen, or you can get punched out or cut while you shower or watch television. Even though Sharron has important props, the pressure is still intense. He spends all his recreation time lifting weights. By the fourth week, his pectorals and triceps are straining against his gray uniform jumpsuit.

With his prized minutes on the horn, Sharron coos to Chantal or any of several other once and future girlfriends. There is no time limit on phone conversations. Each boy stays on as long as his props permit. As Sharron speaks, his housemates float closer and closer, like wolves to a flickering campfire, and brush him, or toss something in his direction, as he sits huddled, trying to create his own world out of a cupped hand and the black phone receiver.

"Yo, why you wanna do that, mister? No man, that ain't right," he complains when harassed. This is not going to be easy.

Then there is real trouble. Sharron has been keeping things together in Four Main; he got a job on "suicide watch," making sure nobody hangs himself and earning a couple of dollars to use in the commissary. He has even bragged to Chantal that he is a gangster with "mad props." Then one night in the day room, just after recreation, a fight breaks out. Two boys, then three, five. Soon a dozen boys are warring in the walkspace between the rows of cells. The beef has nothing to do with Sharron until he is passed a three-inch, razor-sharp burner with the understanding that he will back up Ralphlo and his people. A kid is carried out, his face wrapped in gauze, on his way to the infirmary for ninety-six stitches. One of Ralphlo's boys, who started the fight, gets ninety days in the bing. Sharron is scheduled for fifteen, and is transferred to East Mod. But somehow, with the move, the corrections officers lose track of his involvement in the incident, which could cost him his early release. There is still a chance that if he can stay out of trouble, he will get out in four months instead of the scheduled six.

"All of a sudden," Sharron writes in his diary, "I'm in East Mod and I'm nothin'. I just sit here and don't do nothin'. I'm with a lot of Puerto Ricans again."

A week later: "It's getting better, like I'm in the middle now, but when I first got here I was like chill. I wanted to get on the jack so bad I was ready to flip."

Sharron just cannot get comfortable. He catches some guy trying to steal his picture of Chantal. The attempted theft is a major transgression, but with his lack of status in East Mod, he doesn't really have the props to make any kind of a move. Ralphlo is on the other side now. Worse, Sharron's ally is in the bing again, this time for thirty days. By now Sharron has his own tiny metal burner, a twist from a clotheshanger which he keeps hidden under a carefully loosened floor tile in the bathroom. Burner or not, the sorry truth is that he is back where he started, looking longingly at the telephone, minding his own business, watching his back.

In Brownsville, Rony Shoman is hard at work, but he's watching his back too. *Pop pop pop.* Rony freezes for a moment, his hand suspended over the keys of the cash register in his supermarket. With eyes as blank as stone, he looks across at his brother, at the next register, and goes back to work.

The sweep team is right outside, cruising down Sutter over the bridge separating Brownsville and East New York, when the cops hear echoing shots and charge into the Van Dyke Houses courtyard. Gary Lemite swings out of his unmarked car, right behind. But the shots are coming from an upper window of 301 Sutter, in the Langston Hughes Houses, at the corner of Sutter and Rockaway, a block away.

"*Stupid!*" a woman yells, pointing her finger at the top floor of 301 Sutter. Quick little Willie Arroyo, a new sweep team member, knows when he is hearing the truth, spins, crosses the street, and sprints along Sutter. He turns onto Rockaway, trying to make it to the cover of the canopy over the pumps at the Amoco station at the corner. Gary is a few feet behind him, running sideways, presenting as small a target as possible, hugging the wall. The shots are cracking somewhere above. Arroyo figures if he can make it to the cover, he'll have a short run to the back of 301. From there he can slip around to the front door. But as he dashes around the corner, an ancient, sinewy arm reaches from a doorway and bony fingers tighten around his blue jacket. An old man pulls him to the safety of the doorway.

"*Está ciego?*" The old man asks the young cop if he is blind. Arroyo shrugs.

"*Gracias, señor,*" he whispers, turning and preparing to sprint across the street to the canopy.

Sergeant Toney and a couple of his anticrime boys have already made it to the floor below the sniper, and they can hear the sound of the shots throbbing through the walls. Across Sutter, Sergeant Bright, McMullen, and Galvin are heading for the

249

same cover, running with the deep conviction that no bullet is meant for them. But Del Migliore, like Arroyo newly promoted to sweep, has lost the faith, especially when it comes to snipers. He moves down Sutter in a deep crouch, with a stricken look on his strong face. He holds a fiberglass clipboard over his head as a pathetic defense against a bullet, which, ever since he was shot outside the Pink Houses, he knows can find him.

"Look out. Look out!" he shouts to Gary and the charging sweep team. "The job's not worth it!" he yells, his voice trailing off. A few minutes later, the snipers, two men in their early twenties who took time off from an apartment painting job to get drunk and try out a new gun, give up sheepishly.

That night, Gary walks into his apartment in Elmont and his family is there, the way they used to be. The way they should be. The kids are all over him before he steps down through the door, Zach hanging on one leg and Erica on the other as he places his guns high up on the living room cabinet. Then he hoists them up in the crook of each arm, their heads almost brushing the low ceiling, squeezes them together, and kisses both their laughing faces at once. Lisa stands off to the side in the doorway to the kitchen, beaming.

Gary is not surprised to find Lisa and the kids back. The Friday night counseling sessions with Merle, the pastor in Elmont, have grown less strained, the dinners and Sunday afternoon drives more and more enjoyable. In the past few weeks, when Lisa and Gary found themselves alone in the house, there was less arguing, more lovemaking. Anything Lisa wanted, she got. And Gary mapped out a plan for how long it will take him to get the family out of the basement apartment, to save the fifteen grand for the down payment on a house, including how much overtime he can expect to pull. Lisa was impressed, and she has never stopped wanting him. The kids have been missing their father too. And they have been raising too much hell at her sister's house.

Before the evening is over, Gary is dispensing discipline to Erica and trying to get little Zach to stick up for himself: "Erica, if you hit Zach again, no ice cream. Do you understand?" He tosses Zach up and down, calling him Bobo, trying to toughen him up. There is time to be made up.

The next day Gary drives Erica to her day-care center. On the steps of the school building, she points out a little boy named Paul. Later, as she says her prayers, she makes an addition. "Now I lay me down to sleep. Wish my soul for heaven to keep. I want God to bless Mommy and Daddy and Grandma . . . and Paul."

"What was that?" Gary asks.

Erica smiles mysteriously.

"Now don't forget to bless Aunt Melanie and Uncle Bill," Gary reminds.

"God bless Aunt Melanie and Uncle Bill . . . and Paul," Erica adds as she lays her head on the pillow.

Kate Worthy is thinking about lying down somewhere, anywhere. She stops at the foot of the subway steps, grips the handrail, stoops over, and breathes deeply. Her heart is acting up. "You all right, Grandma?" twelve-year-old Shantay wants to know.

"Yeah, I'm O.K. Just catchin' my breath."

Five Worthy kids between the ages of seven and thirteen shuffle and stare numbly while Kate wheezes herself into condition to mount the stairs. Just like the Housing cop said after the eviction hearing, the Worthys have nowhere to live. It is 5 P.M. and the family is at the end of a long trip on the #3 train to Abyssinian House, a Tier II shelter on 138th Street in Harlem. It took the Housing Authority over a month to evict the family from Apartment 5AB. When it did, many of the older ones found lodging in the projects in Brownsville. Renee, Wanda, and their kids found a spot with a cousin; Lennie, Randolph, and Blue, with friends. But the rest headed right to a Tier I shelter in Brooklyn, the kind of place where hundreds of cots are arranged in one large room.

After a sleepless night, Kate complained, and the Human Resources Administration assured her that if she took her passel of grandchildren and great-grandchildren up to 138th Street, they would have their own private lodgings, along with a range of social services.

It's six o'clock and dark when Kate walks into the front office of the five-floor shelter with her band of weary Brownsville refugees. When they are shown to their facilities, they are clean and indeed private. Just two people to a room, even a small kitchen.

"We don't have food, and no pots or nothin' even if we did," Kate points out to the shelter employee, an unsmiling Jamaican woman.

"Three blocks away from here we have a pantry, and we have pots and silverware."

Kate turns and smiles, touches Shantay's shoulder. A change in luck, she is thinking.

"Does Grandma got to go to the pantry? 'Cause she's tired," Shantay asks. "Can we get the food?"

"I'm sorry. There must always be an adult on hand," the attendant insists.

And that is the rub. Kate already has a small apartment in a senior citizens' building in Brooklyn. The only reason she has been trudging through the transit system, climbing those stairs, is that the kids need somebody to get them in the shelters. So Grandma Worthy and three of the kids head over to pick up some canned beans and vegetables, cereal and milk from the food outlet. For tonight, everything is all right. There is no giggling and no joking around. Everybody falls fast asleep.

But the next day finds the entire group — except for Kate, who heads to her apartment for some rest — back in Brownsville on the bench in front of 295. At dusk, Kate collects the brood and starts the trek to Abyssinian House. Evening after evening, she rides the trains with her ragamuffin band lined up on the subway seats beside and in front of her, from Brooklyn, through the throngs of well-dressed, home-bound commuters in Manhattan, up to Harlem.

In less than two weeks, all the kids are absorbed by one household or another. "Some left their clothes up there in Harlem," Kate says. "One day we just didn't go back. Left the food too, but that was free."

The sun is not up yet. Chantal is sitting in the kitchen of the Saratoga Street apartment, perfectly at home in this household, getting her hair unbraided by a neighbor in preparation to go visit Sharron at Riker's. Shawanda is busy looking for the package containing a plain pair of pants and some underwear, which her brother has been demanding for the last three weeks. Sharron has made it clear that he does not want any clothing desirable enough to be stolen.

Chantal has on a pair of black jeans and a black sweatshirt with the brand name Guess written in gold over her left breast. Her unbraided hair is oiled and pulled tightly back from her face, her ponytail cinched by a pair of red rubber bands. Shawanda, beside her, is not concerned with beautification. She is trying to gather the articles Sharron needs. Gloria is still asleep.

"I had the package. I had the thing last night."

Shawanda has a calm, authoritative air and miraculously small feet; her pink-and-white sneakers are almost as little as the shoes people hang on rearview mirrors. She has a fresh black eye, which she claims she got from her boyfriend, John, when he rolled over in his sleep. Since Sharron has been gone, Shawanda and John have taken up residence at the Saratoga apartment. They sleep in Sharron's room, in Sharron's bed.

Alleke glides into the kitchen like a dark ghost. His arms are wrapped around the package with Sharron's pants and a pair of unusual canvas sneakers, more like deck shoes, that Sharron tried to introduce as a style at Jefferson when he was riding high as the star of *Don't Give Up on Your Dreams*.

The girls leave the house at seven o'clock and join the march of working folks down Saratoga to the subway. A trip to Riker's Island is an all-day affair, a numbing exercise in shuffling, waiting, standing. On the #3 train, across the aisle from the hard-eyed day-shift people headed to Manhattan, Chantal suddenly turns to face Sharron's sister.

"Andre got ammonia," she blurts.

"What?"

"Ammonia, the doctor said it was."

"How the fuck the baby get pneumonia?" Shawanda grimaces.

"Maybe when we was at court when Sharron got sentence," Chantal answers. "That's the only time we was really out. Else maybe it was the window."

"What window?"

"The broke one in Mommy's room where Andre be sleep."

At Forty-second Street, the girls change for the #7 train to Queens. On the twenty-minute trip to the Queens Plaza stop, where they will catch the Q101 bus to Riker's Island, Shawanda recalls with some fondness how she once visited a boyfriend there.

"I'm sittin' in the place where you first come in and you get a number to go to the next room, and I see this bitch I knew he was messin' with sittin' there. I said to myself, 'Oooo, buddy, we gonna have some shit today.'" Chantal nods. This is her first such trip. But she knows that a confrontation with a rival at Riker's is not unusual for the eligible young ladies from Brownsville.

The bus from the train station heads from the commercial district of Queens through the neighborhoods of Astoria and past the neat row houses on Hazen Street, the homes of some of the New Yorkers who have jobs. The men here, washing their cars on this Saturday morning, do not look up.

Chantal and Shawanda chat about Sharron as the bus rolls over the narrow bridge spanning a stretch of oily water and shiny oozing mud. The smell of the East River at low tide is at once a salty notice that the city has been left behind and a sickening indication that a bad place lies ahead.

"Sharron called me when he was first there and he sounded all happy, like he was at a party," Chantal reports, as cheerful as a girl on her way to a dance. "And he said, 'Don't play me.' That's what Sha always says. 'Cept he says it different, like 'Dooon't play me.'"

At the reception center, the girls wait in a twisting line to sign in and receive a yellow registration card from an irritated corrections officer. He addresses the visitors as if they were second-graders. "Anyone with a Walkman or a radio of any kind, turn around and leave the island right now. *Pay attention.* I am giving you a card. Look at the sample on the wall. Put your last name first."

After they receive their cards, the girls will wait to be moved to the C-74 waiting room, another area of the reception building. After a lengthy wait there, they will ride a yellow school bus one hundred yards to a parking lot next to the C-74 building, where Sharron is housed. There they will be frisked for weapons and contraband, place their jackets, jewelry, and handbags in lockers, and wait again. When their names are called, they will be body-searched and moved upstairs to the last waiting room before they step into a visiting area the size of a basketball court.

Chantal and Shawanda sit side by side in the registration area, filling out their yellow cards and glancing up at a flickering television screen. In each waiting room along the trip to the visiting area, a television is bolted to the wall eight feet off the floor, so the army of toddlers cannot fool with the dials.

"Stop it, Reuben. I'm going to tear your butt up," a woman yells to her boy, who is running in circles like a windup toy. Shawanda and Chantal hand in their cards and return to their seats.

There are a thousand women here today, half of whom have children — kids visiting fathers who once visited *their* fathers here. In the crowd there is one flashy girl resplendent in fashionable fall plaid. But mostly this is a family affair. These are the plain girls, the ones who have a stake in their men. These are the reliables.

After Chantal and Shawanda spend thirty-five minutes in the registration area, a corrections officer arrives. "Seventy-five through one hundred," he announces. The girls step quickly down the hall to the C-74 waiting area. There, a woman with two bright-eyed children in tow squeals with delight at the sight of the rap duo Kid 'n Play prancing on the TV screen above. Information is exchanged about the state of Kid's towering fade. Kid — or is it Play? — cavorts around the stage in an imitation of the way the young men in the Ville walk and move, the way they slouch and gesture with the backs of their hands. Neither of the two performers onscreen is from Brownsville or anywhere like it. They are college kids from Queens. The homeboys from the ghetto have become big business. But the real homeboys are locked inside.

Every third or fourth woman in the waiting room has a scar on her cheek or neck. A husky-voiced Hispanic woman, Reuben's mother, has fresh marks on both sides of her neck. She holds a third child, an infant, while Reuben and Stuart, identical four-year-olds in impeccable matching winter jackets, stare at each other and wait to see if their most recent bit of mischief is enough to summon a smack. Later, during the visit, the twins will sit glumly by as their beefy, tattooed father fondles and coos with the baby and pays them little mind.

Someone knew what he was doing when he put televisions here. On weekdays, every set is tuned to the soap operas, and the seated women are mesmerized by the goings-on. An older

Hispanic woman says in a clear voice to her young friend, "The trick is to stay out of the system." The girls to her left and right don't even twitch their heads away from the televisions. There is no sense of regret in the women, no hint that they feel they have selected the wrong man to father their children. This experience, this day, is just a fact of life.

Numbers. They are calling number sixty-eight. Shawanda checks her card: ninety-four. It is almost one o'clock. A woman who has been here since eight-thirty in the morning, waiting for her son to be summoned from his housing area, starts to complain to the women around her, and then to the female corrections officer who stands surrounded by waiting women.

"Step back. Step back, *please,*" the officer shouts, flashing three silver teeth. "I want you to step back. Y'all are breathing down my neck. I can feel your *breath* on me." She shudders involuntarily.

A woman on a bench in the back, with skin the color of a damp brown paper bag, the face of a pretty clown, and the body of a girl gone slack with beer, yells out, "I'm gonna come over there and breathe on you in a minute." There is a tense moment as the group separates so the two women can get a look at each other. The heckler smiles. The scar that runs like a river across her plump right cheek squeezes. The smooth flat section on the bottom folds up to kiss the lumpy top part. The corrections officer laughs and waves at the woman, a regular.

Shawanda approaches the guard. "How long you think?" she asks sweetly.

"Dunno, they could be bringin' him from commissary or mess. What's his ID number?"

Shawanda stares blankly.

"I dunno how you got this far without no ID number."

Shawanda stays while Chantal leaves the C-74 waiting area and uses a phone in an adjacent building to get the number from prison information. While she waits for the operator to retrieve the number, a satin-skinned youth about Sharron's age and size strides up to the phone beside her. The boy is handsome, with a wisp of a charcoal mustache on his finely carved upper lip. A rakish effect is supplied by two slashes shaved in his right eyebrow. When Chantal spies him, she undergoes an extraordinary transformation. Her eyes enlarge to ovals, her shoulders drop, and her coral lips part. The hand that holds the telephone receiver drops to her side as she angles herself slowly into the boy's field of vision. She is entranced, available, brazen, all in an instant. The boy is unimpressed. He conducts his business on the phone privately, cocks his head at Chantal for just a moment, and walks away. Chantal Redding, fifteen-year-old mother, Sharron's "shorty," slowly returns the phone to her ear and listens for Sharron's ID number.

The ID does no good. The girls have arrived on the wrong day. Visiting hours at Riker's Island are scheduled on rotating days. One week, inmates with last names from A through L have visits on Thursday, those with names at the end of the alphabet on Saturday. The next week the days are switched. All inmates have a contact visit on Sunday. Shawanda leaves the package with the sneakers and the pants with a guard, and the girls head home.

Sharron is beside himself. He calls Ms. King. "I can't believe Chantal isn't here. I need things. I need some clothes. I know she is wearing my clothes. I know Shawanda is in my room, in my closet, wearing my clothes." He eases off, waxes diplomatic. "That's O.K. They need the clothes. I can't worry about my clothes. They're out there, and I'm in here.

"I don't want to lift too many weights," he tells King. "If I get too big, I won't fit my clothes." He lobbies for a sweatshirt and a pair of sweatpants, plain, black or gray. He now has a small black eye, something like the one his sister sports. "I wonder whether I should have somebody tell the people in Satellite that I'm in jail. I know a lot of people are disappointed in me. I can't believe my girl isn't here. I'm fed."

On his way back to his bunk, Sharron pauses outside a circle of boys talking about misdeeds.

"Dude hands the bis to his man an' points to this other dude an' he says, 'Do 'em.' An' his man wets him up, *bam bam*. Shit was cold. Like a motherfuckin' movie."

Sharron isn't in the mood to laugh, slap hands, and marvel. Instead, he continues on to his bed and digs out his diary.

"There are the drug people," he writes.

For them, guns are a necessity. They have to feel ruthless so they can pull the trigger. Then there's guys who are just part of the swing of things around the way, like some character in a story. Some characters play good and just want a gun for protection from the trigger-happy ones, who play the bad character. I'm more the good character.

I've been the stickup kid. If I had another chance to start all over in the same neighborhood, I don't think it would be different in most of my decisions. After all I've been through I like to think of myself as a determined and motivated guy, compliments of my mother, and people who've given me a hand and helped me positively. But there's times when I've had none but my mother and I couldn't see, or wouldn't see, her hand, due to my obsession with props and image and girls. In my earlier teens, I would stay in the streets of Brownsville doing mischief, or even take a ride with a friend or two to Manhattan on the Number 3 train to continue mischievous deeds to keep from having the misfortune of long meaningless days with empty pockets and minds full of ponder. I would always imagine some big-time producer knocking on my door saying, "C'mon, there's a whole world out there waiting for your talent." I'd suddenly be famous, known over most parts of the world, pursuing a career, taking care of my family. Then I'd wake up from my daydream with a tap from my friend, getting us ready for our meow. "Yo, Sha, check it."

Sharron has requested that his mother stay away, but Chantal has been begging her to go anyway, since she needs an adult to accompany her. Finally, just before Thanksgiving, Gloria relents and takes Chantal to Riker's.

Once again Chantal is bright and jovial, despite the fact that Andre has been in Kings County Hospital for a week for treatment of his lingering pneumonia. Gloria is silent. Chantal's mindless good cheer is putting her in a truly foul mood.

"I don't know nothing about Riker's Island," she growls. "I have never been there. I have never had any *reason* to go there." Gloria would like to make it clear to Chantal and the others around her on the rattling bus that she is not accepting her son's lawlessness or this trip as a part of her life, past, present, or future. "When he was under my supervision, there was none of this shit," she says.

In fact, Gloria would like to be traveling in exactly the opposite direction this weekday morning. Still young, intelligent, and well-spoken, she would like to be on her way to a good job in Manhattan. By a directive from the welfare department, she is enrolled in a program that requires her attendance on 14th Street in Manhattan each weekday, where she learns to write a résumé and represent herself well in job interviews. She mutters to friends that her time would be much better spent in actually looking for work, and complains that the program is really a punishment for being unemployed. She is most interested in construction work, a job she once did, because it pays the best.

"How's the baby?" Gloria asks, changing the subject.

"The doctor said he's gonna be all right," Chantal reports, adjusting the angle of her ponytail by shifting the rubber bands. "Mommy, do you know that the window in the room where his crib is at has a broken window?" she asks. "My mommy called the people but they didn't call or come. She said that she is going to sue 'cause the baby got sick."

"Sue the landlord," Gloria suggests. Chantal hesitates. She does not know what the word "landlord" means.

"Where is Andre at?"

"Kings County."

"What are they givin' him?"

"They din' say. They said he turned blue for a while. Now he's gettin' better, they said."

"Blue," Gloria repeats. "Mmmmmm," she laments softly, and goes silent for a full five minutes while Chantal stares out the window.

"Sharron told me that he didn't want me to come," Gloria says finally. "He told me I should go to school. Some mothers, when their sons go to jail, it's just like a hotel. They sit up on the phone and get everything brought to them. Not me." Gloria looks over at Chantal, who is trying to catch her reflection in the bus window.

Gloria's grumpy demeanor changes later in the day, when Sharron steps through the doorway into the visiting room. She draws a long, deep breath, closes her eyes, and shakes her head. When she opens her eyes, they are glistening. She is smiling. "My baby," she says, even before Sharron is close enough to hear.

Sharron slinks across the room like a jaguar, his eyes scanning the terrain, his face twitching from the effort to control his smile. Gloria pushes her chair back and rises to embrace her son. She presses her cheek to his. Their identical cinnamon complexions blend as they hug. Sharron looks over his mother's shoulder and puckers his lips at Chantal, who jumps to kiss them but misses. In a moment he is giving her a righteous kiss as he holds his mother's hand. When the three sit down to talk, he notices a girl he knows from Brownsville eyeing him from across the room. A flutter of delight passes through him at the possibility that Chantal will see the girl's flirtation and argue with her on the way out.

Sharron leans across the small table that separates prisoners from their visitors, whispering and kissing Chantal. He turns to Gloria with feigned annoyance.

"I told you not to come," he says like a worried father. "I told you you should be goin' to school, not comin' all out here. Stay in school," he says sternly. The phrase reveals his inability to tolerate a real picture of Gloria. "Stay in school" — as if she were plugging away on a college campus like Gita Malave.

"Sha? How you got a black eye?" Chantal asks.

Sharron shrugs, squints, and squeezes Gloria's hand. There is no sense lying about how tough it is inside.

"You got to be careful, Sha, don't be fightin' over the phone. I don't care we don't speak till you get out," Chantal says wisely.

Several days later, Sharron is on the phone to Ms. King again. "Everything is smooth," he tells her. "Just got to keep it smooth for three more months. I got eight pictures of girls, only four fit on my locker, so I got the best four." He tells her about Gloria's visit. "Moms was tryin' to act all mad an' shit, but she's cool." He mentions that he has spoken to Chantal about the baby's condition. "Chantal says the doctor says that Andre got pneumonia, the worst kind. He even turned blue, but now he's gettin' better."

As Sharron talks, a harsh voice cuts through the jailhouse din. He reacts. "Hey man, why you got to curse when I'm on the phone? 'Five minutes'? Who the hell can I call in five minutes? No, sir, you don't be cursing when I'm on the phone. No, sir, you heard that."

WINTER

"HE'S GONE"

A smoky weekday November evening, and Gary Lemite is starting his tour. "Let's go look for DeeSo," he says, getting into the passenger seat of the new OSC Chevrolet Caprice. His partner nods tolerantly. Everybody on the squad says Gary has a hard-on for DeeSo.

No sooner did Gary get the assignment to the plainclothes detail than he set his sights on this reputed middle-level drug dealer, whom he and J.R. once arrested, months ago. DeeSo, who likes to write his name Dee$o, is a clean-cut twenty-four-year-old who wheels a blue Acura Legend around Tapscott Street and the Unity Houses. He is not big, maybe five-ten, with wide shoulders and narrow hips. His muscle is supplied by a roughneck from Unity named Tiz. His brother, Ra Ra, handles the business. With his casual clothing and spectacles, DeeSo looks more like a college student than a drug dealer. And he likes to be known for his good manners. When Gary and J.R. gave him a summons for public drinking, he was not guzzling a forty-ounce malt liquor; he was standing at the arched iron entrance to the Unity Houses with a bottle of Moët White Star in his hand. "Never buy champagne cold," he advised the officers. "Keep it in a refrigerator too long, stuff gets burnt out. Check it out."

DeeSo took the "toss," the arrest, with grace, even offered the cops his version of his life story, told Gary he was just out of jail for attempted murder. He did not try to hide the fact that he had taken over the crack commerce in Unity. He never said as much, but he issued no bogus denials either. "Can't talk to you now," he said at the time. "If you catch me dirty, we'll talk. But you won't catch me like that, 'cause I don't touch shit. I show respect," he told Gary. "You will find that I always show respect." Gary was not charmed.

Jack Lenti, the new commanding officer of PSA 2, is giving the troops more freedom, and they love it. There were eight arrests under Kammerdener on the last two Housing Days, targeted dates when the Housing cops sweep the projects for quality-of-life infractions. Forty-two bodies are snatched on each of the first two Housing Days under Lenti. But the people in the community may not like this style. Surely, the politicians will not be as happy as they were when Kammerdener was in charge. When City Councilwoman Priscilla Wooten wanted something done, Kammerdener jumped. If there was going to be a meeting in a project, he sent his people in days in advance to make sure there would be no unsightly drug dealing to embarrass anyone on the appointed day. Lenti is not like that. He's a cop's cop. If someone in the community has an unjustified complaint, Jack Lenti will tell them what time it is. However, he is not a stupid man. When the representative of the Guardians, the black cops' association, showed up at his office one day, demanding to be moved to NEU, a borough-wide narcotics specialty unit, Lenti threw him out for blatant influence-peddling. Somehow, he was sent to NEU anyway. Lenti claimed it was because he didn't want him in his command anymore.

But Lenti does want Lemite in his command. Gary is leading the PSA in arrests. He's leading in overtime, and he's setting records with his gun collars. Lenti has requested that he be awarded the Combat Cross for bravery in the Fiorentino shoot-out.

Gary makes a right turn off Sutter Avenue and wheels up Tapscott Street, looking for DeeSo. Instead he finds the drug dealer's brother. He and his partner cruise slowly up beside Ra Ra's white Infiniti, parked on a side street. In the car are four guys Gary has never seen; piles of green bills are in plain view on the dashboard. In the back seat are boxes that once contained glassine envelopes, and rubber bands, technically drug paraphernalia. On the strength of the federal "zero tolerance" law, Gary confiscates the car. He is looking for some respect of his own.

For his efforts, he garners a quick civilian complaint.

"What you got against my brother?" a young man over on Tapscott wants to know a week later.

"I don't have nothin' against him, 'cept the fact that he's a drug dealer," Gary says out the window of his unmarked car. He is loving this. He often gets out of his vehicle now, just to talk to DeeSo or his associates, harvesting the respect he earned when he snatched the Infiniti. DeeSo won't give Gary the satisfaction of getting angry about the car. He has already written it off. "Business loss, Lemite," he tells the officer one day.

But Gary is gathering more information, watching for drop-off spots and potential informants, testing the air for slingers with grudges against DeeSo. Unfortunately, he soon finds himself under investigation for the charge that he stole several thousand dollars from DeeSo on the day he took the car. But DeeSo makes a major mistake. His boys neglected to count the money before it was confiscated. The complaint alleges that $2,000 was in the car. Internal Affairs verifies that Gary vouchered $3,900. The case is closed.

It is dusk on a clean and windy fifty-degree Thanksgiving Day in Brownsville. There is an immense mauve sky with plumes of frail gray clouds. Gary is home in Elmont, getting ready to eat dinner upstairs in his mother's dining room. But second-year officers Kenneth Finn and Gene Madden are starting their shift. They are headed out, but they can hardly wait to make it back to the PSA for a meal.

"We've got fifty pounds of turkey," Finn bubbles, "a case of broccoli, mashed potatoes."

"Don't tell me any more," Madden protests. "I'm getting a hard-on."

"Peas," Finn continues.

"But I can't eat peas. I had some peas and I farted so much I had to turn off the electricity."

It will be Madden's twenty-fifth birthday tomorrow. "I just want to enjoy myself now," he muses. "In twenty years they'll be takin' my asshole out."

Somebody makes a gobble-gobble sound over the portable. A call comes over for an aided case, some sort of health condition. A woman is having trouble breathing in the relatively peaceful Kingsborough Houses. Finn and Madden drive across Brownsville and pull up in front of the project.

"Happy Thanksgiving," a woman towing a small child says as she crosses their path. But bad feelings radiate from a line of young men hanging outside the food mart on the corner. "Housing pussies," somebody yells.

"Don't be here when we come out," Finn tosses over his shoulder to the layabouts.

The retort is well-chosen, symbolic, mock confrontational, but ill-timed. Veteran cops know never to make threats on the way inside, only on the way out. A few minutes later, after the bus has arrived for the stricken woman, as Finn and Madden are exiting into the fresh night, there is a loud crash. To their left, a figure sprints down the street. Finn and Madden jolt into a run. As they charge, another youth in their path starts to run. The first kid is long gone, but the second stops after a few strides. He probably could have gotten away, but he stops, perhaps in the belief that he should not have started running in the first place. It did not take two people to shatter the driver's side window of the RMP with a rock.

Finn and Madden corner the gangly kid. They chest up to him on both sides and scream at the top of their lungs dead in his face. They want the first kid who ran.

"Where does he live? Where does he live?" they bellow. Spit from their mouths spatters the youth's cheeks. The kid is shaken. "Take us to him. Take us to him."

The "holler" method, apparently one that Finn and Madden have practiced, is working. The kid is sputtering, starting to talk. He's about to give the rock-thrower up. But windows are flying open above, and a pack of women jog through the shadows to the spot where Finn and Madden are working their shouting game. One woman is the boy's mother.

"What the hell is going on?"

The officers don't want to break the control they have over the kid. They continue to glower in his face.

"I asked you what you think you're doin'," the woman demands.

"His friend broke the patrol car window," Finn says out of the corner of his mouth.

"What do you mean, his *friend* broke the window. What are you doin' to my son? Are you people insane?"

Finn faces the woman now. "We were answering a call for a woman who's having a heart attack. That coulda been your mother."

266

The woman is profoundly unimpressed. She is not buying the public servant angle. She looks as if she wants to throw up. "White motherfuckers" is her answer.

An object flies out a window and lands nearby. Finn and Madden step away from the youth and walk backward for a few paces, looking up at the stone ramparts. There have been times when community reaction here has forced officers to give up their prisoners. Once during a summer riot, a crowd swelled out of the projects and surrounded a young officer and his hand-cuffed prisoner. The cop fled, leaving his prisoner and his cuffs behind. The boss wanted to know what happened. "I don't know, Sarge," the cop replied. "I guess you could say he called a perp 85."

When Finn and Madden get back to the patrol car, there are shards of glass over the front seat. Madden brushes off the seat with a rolled-up newspaper as Finn locks eyes with the glaring locals. The cleanup operation takes two or three minutes. When the officers finally settle into the car, Madden balls up the newspaper and hurls it out the window in a gesture of disgust with the neighborhood.

"I got to talk to Flanagan. He's the PCO here, and he let the fucking place get out of hand. I told him that he has to control his mutts," Finn complains.

"Yeah, this is the kind of shit that leads to guns and shit. I have no desire to come home with a hole in my body that the good Lord didn't put there," Madden says. "This shit would never happen if he had the place under control."

Back at the PSA on Sutter, Finn is not thinking of turkey or broccoli anymore. He buzzes around, organizing an assault team to go back to Kingsborough Houses to restore order and respect for the Housing police. Sam Tilly, Marlene Pemberton, and others on their meal hour are ready to back his play. In twenty minutes, a caravan of three RMPs, a van, and eight cops is poised on a small hill overlooking the Kingsborough Houses.

There are radio calls coming in; Central is growing impatient. "I'm holding Housing jobs," Central insists. "9717. I have an EDP armed with a stick at Mother Gaston and East New York." But Finn is adamant. He is waiting for one more car, to make a real show of force. In the back seat of his RMP he has the "daisy chain," a metal rope equipped with a string of handcuffs. His strategy is to swoop down on the food mart, snatch up everyone who is standing outside, and take them back to the PSA, where they will be given dis con summonses.

Finally, the platoon moves down toward the delinquent project. But no one is lounging by the whitewashed front wall of the food mart. "We'll be back tomorrow," Finn screams out the window to no one.

A huge red sphere rises out of the east on a December dawn. The familiar sulfur stink of the river lifts from the mudlands as the Riker's Island bus passes over the bridge to the jail. The numbing lines are already in place at 7:15 A.M. — endless mothers and children and the occasional pretty girl in a leopard-skin miniskirt, here to impress a man who was once a prize and is now a project.

Shawanda awakened in the pitch dark to ready herself for this trip to see her baby brother, her look-alike. Gloria has always declared that Shawanda has her looks and Sharron her ways, but both children look like her, and each other.

"I only met my father twice," Shawanda says from her place near the end of the line in the registration area. "He called me once when I was sixteen and said he wanted to see me. He called from the train station at Saratoga. But he never did come over. The two times I saw him was when I was a little girl. He's little and light-skinned, like me. He has bowlegs and a mole right in the middle of his face. My mother won't talk about him to me. She tells Sharron about him. But not me.

"Sharron was so shy when he was little," Shawanda remembers, "he was like a little girl. I would bring my girlfriends over and he would run into the other room. Then he would come to me later and say, 'Ooo, she's cute.' Then I would tell him to tell her, and he would get all embarrassed and say, 'Oooo, nooo.' Then all of a sudden, when he was fourteen, he started up. I would look in the room and Sharron would be singing to them." She shuffles her tiny feet, barely visible under the folds of her droopy jeans, and thinks about Sharron's present predicament. "Now, when he's goin' out and I ask him why he's doin' shit, he says for reputation. Sharron is my brother, and I'll tell anybody he is not a leader. He is a follower."

Shawanda prides herself on her good sense, her knowledge of

city geography and the transit system. Right now, she shakes her head, as if to clear her thoughts, and sets her gaze grimly ahead. It isn't the hour of the day that is bothering her, nor the place. The jailhouse is no big thing to her. She has another burden. Shawanda's mission today is to tell her brother that Andre has died of pneumonia.

The boys in Sharron's barracks have been denied access to the phone for several days as punishment for a fight, and Shawanda has determined that Sharron cannot possibly be given the message by a stranger.

"He has to be told *something*," she mutters as she fidgets in line and readies her identification papers.

There is raucous laughter from several women within earshot. A righteous woman is explaining how she will lay down the law to her man, who has been using his phone calls to pluck the strings of an old romance, using his visits for the same purpose. No one nearby can guess that Shawanda carries a message of the death of a baby boy, the child of a fifteen-year-old girl with fetching eyes and a father who believes in nothing so much as Polo by Ralph Lauren.

When Sharron arrives in the noisy green visiting room, hours later, he wears floppy white terry-cloth slippers and his gray jumpsuit with DOC, Department of Correction, stenciled on the back. His jumpsuit is open down his chest to reveal his carved pectorals. He walks with a dip and a slide, shooting glances around the room, and embraces his sister. He is unable to suppress a smile. He is bigger, much bigger than he was just weeks ago. His shoulder muscles bunch up, and the cheap cloth of his uniform grips his swollen biceps.

"I was gonna beat you up when you got home," Shawanda jokes. "But when I saw how big you got, I changed my mind."

Sharron reviews his short history in Riker's for his sister. "We got burners and bangers. Burners are for slicin' and bangers are for stickin'." He tells Shawanda the story of Ralphlo, about how he had no time on the horn, and then he did, and then he did not. About the Puerto Ricans. About Love, the new house honcho. The fact is that after almost five weeks in East Mod, Sharron is still in a transition stage. He is not in the miserable state he was in when he first arrived, but the drama is not over. There is one cock-diesel newcomer, named Jersey, who has been lurking closer and closer to Sharron, mumbling, threatening to "get in my area," Sharron reports.

As he talks he gestures with his wrists, jailhouse style. His hands seem thicker. When he is not talking, his hands hang over his knees like indolent, corrupted bullies, slow to work, quick to violence. In jail, men's hands seem to grow because of the loose way they are carried. The inmates hold their hands so as to emphasize mass. Fingers are never raised or pointed. Hands lift slowly to accompany weighty pronouncements and are never waved about indecisively or used for punctuation or other light duty. In jail, men's hands are their only allies.

After fifteen minutes, Shawanda wets her fingertips with her lips and rubs the moisture into her eyelids. She leans across the table and reaches for her brother's hands. "Did anybody tell you anything?" she asks softly.

A wave of pain crosses Sharron's face and he bows his head. The reaction is reminiscent of a moment in his portrayal of Danny in *Don't Give Up on Your Dreams*. He raises his head and speaks flatly of how he had a notion, even before Chantal gave him the news on the phone.

"Yeah, Chantal called. And she was all nice and happy. And we was talkin', and she got all quiet and she said, 'Sharron, I don't know how to tell you this.' I said, 'No, don't tell me that.'" Sharron describes how he let the phone dangle for a moment before he picked it back up and submitted to the words, "He's gone, Sha."

It has been three days since Chantal's call, four since Andre died, after a month in the pediatric intensive care unit. "Don't worry, we can make another one," Chantal had insisted on the phone.

There was something about her tone that set Sharron off. "I told Chantal that I wasn't about that. I don't know. I don't know. I told Chantal that I wasn't gonna be with her no more. She ain't actin' right. She's in Ms. King's class and I heard she ain't been goin' to school. I mean, she looks good, but she's going down the wrong path."

Sharron's disappointment over Chantal's immaturity appears more genuine than his reaction to Andre's death. When Gloria found out Andre had succumbed to pneumonia, she was beside herself. For two days her rage leaped like a hungry beast from the attending doctors to the landlord to the hospital to Chantal and her mother. Mrs. Redding, Chantal's mother, was racked by similar anguish. "You know I got a goddamn baby here with pneumonia," she blurted to a stranger on the phone a month before Andre died. When she learned he had died, she put her hand through a windowpane, an act of desperate grief.

"Chantal's mother's eyes were all red and puffed out," Shawanda tells Sharron. "But Chantal was gettin' ready to go out. And she was laughin'. And I told her, what was the deal, and she said that she deal with her pain in her own way."

"She was laughin'?" Sharron questions. "I'm gonna leave her. She's not what I thought she was. She's not actin' right."

He stays quiet for some time, then resumes the description of his discussion with Chantal the night she told him the baby was dead. "I was like ready to flip. The guys in East Mod have been thinkin' that I was gettin' ready to flip for jack time anyway. Some guys remember when I first came, before I was down with Ralphlo, how I used to just sit there and stare at the horn, and some of them think that I'm still like that. After I got off the phone, I walked over to where the sinks are at, and tears was just like comin' down." Sharron makes a motion with his hand down his face with his fingers spread. "Then Jersey came over. Cock diesel, and he's got this look on his face . . . don't *nobody* mess with him. For two weeks the man has been fuckin' with me. And like he walks over to where I'm at, and he thinks I'm messed up about the phone. For once, he come out nice and says, 'Why you don't ask Love for some time on the horn?'"

Sharron is building his story to his moment of triumph in East Mod, the moment that set him up for the rest of his bid. He knew that he was ready to explode as a result of the dreadful news he had received. But he also understood that he could use his impending loss of control to make a move that would make his days easier, and might even save his life. He explains how he turned to Jersey, the mad agent of East Mod, ready for war. "'I just got off the *fucking* phone,' I said." As he continues his story, he rises from his seat, reliving the full flush of his triumph. "I threw that shit right in his face, and Jersey just like walked away. I knew what I had to do. I was flip. Went with it. Motherfuckers all around was like 'Wow, I don't believe he did that shit.'"

Sharron sits for a moment, thinking. He reveals no more remorse over using the news of his son's death to get props in East Mod than Sir Laurence Olivier would have felt over using personal tragedy to bring a character alive.

Sharron has managed to do something to the pockets of his prison jumpsuit that makes them bulge in a way that pleases him, and he takes a moment to describe the technique to his sister. "I really miss my gray Nikes," he says wistfully. Shawanda promises that she will try to bring him the sneakers, but Sharron interrupts. "No, I want a guy to bring the sneakers." It's only right, apparently, that Frank or another LoLife show respect by bringing him his prize gear.

"Mommy went out for her thirty-sixth birthday and didn't come home till Friday," Shawanda says. "She was partyin'. Stayed at Auntie's house."

Shawanda sits for a few moments, then swings into the second phase of her agenda for this visit. The responsibility of telling Sharron about Andre was unpleasant in the extreme. The opportunity to tell on Chantal is the reward. Not only did Chantal perform badly in her reaction to the baby's death; apparently she has another boyfriend. According to Shawanda, Chantal has had another man for some time.

"When Mommy and me came up to Chantal house, Mommy wanted to know who this guy was. Chantal tried to front and say it wasn't nothin', an' this was just a friend of hers from around the way. But he was in the house by the bathroom. He was in the room, Chantal's. We went to the house twice after the baby died, 'cause Mommy was upset 'cause she wanted Andre to have a funeral, and Mrs. Redding just wanted to cremate the baby. I mean, Mommy was crying, and so was I, and even John had a tear, but not Chantal."

Out of the pile of words Shawanda tosses on the table, Sharron grabs the dope, the part about the other man; the rest is cut, filler. He snaps to attention. "Tell me that again. Run it again." Shawanda tells the story of the other man in Chantal's life in more detail. It seems as if Sharron's big sister has been doing some investigation. The guy in the house is a seventeen-year-old small-time drug slinger. Shawanda's theory is that the boy is not an interloper at all but has been Chantal's man all along.

"*He* is her man," Shawanda insists, explaining that that is why Sharron never visited Chantal's house or had a proper meeting with her mother.

Sharron shakes his head to clear his thoughts. "Again." Like a young Othello, he demands a review of the evidence.

Shawanda is worried. Perhaps she has gone too far. The stress of jail and the death of Andre, and now this. As she talks, she maneuvers the meeting with the other boyfriend out of the house onto the stoop and alters the dialogue to include some harmless neighborhood boys who "always hang on the stoop." But Sharron is not fooled. He is not prone to free-floating mistrust or anger. Now he does not wallow in regrets. He is the very picture of wounded strength. And he has a plan.

"Get my clothes." He flies through an inventory of exactly what Chantal has that belongs to him. "I want my sweaters. I want that scarf with the flag on it."

As he runs down the list, Shawanda nods. Sister is up to the task. Seemingly, she is unafraid of the mayhem the retrieval mission will surely provoke. Sharron picks up her resolve and tempers his charge.

"I don't want you to strip the clothes off her. I want you to pack the stuff up and take it out." He describes some jewelry, then goes back over the list. "She won't have no clothes," he concludes, allowing himself a moment of bitter contemplation of Chantal's sorry state once the mission has been accomplished.

Shawanda mumbles something about the hospital. Sharron is picking up all messages now. "The dude was with her when she went to the hospital? He was with her?" Shawanda backs off once again. Sharron expands his list of items to be repatriated. There is a pair of sneakers and a jacket, the goose-down vest. But mention of the vest triggers something in him, a grace. In a moment, it is clear why it is easy to love Sharron Corley, despite his unseemly craving for approval and adulation, despite his ice pick and his burner. He has a heart. He considers the Nautica vest he boosted just for Chantal. A stricken look crosses his soft face. "She won't have no coat. Don't take the goose."

"CHRISTMAS IS FOR WHITE PEOPLE"

The next day, on the fifth floor at Jefferson, Ms. King is collecting her books following her one o'clock class. Khalil Sumpter and his man Dupree are deep in conversation a few feet from her desk. After the confrontation two months ago, Khalil has been in class every day.

"I'm gonna have to ice the dude," he tells Dupree, loud enough for King to hear.

Black men threatening to harm, trying to intimidate other black men — King has had enough of that. She takes one step away from her desk and smacks Khalil with her palm, hard, on the back of his head, for his threat against a fellow man.

"Oh shit, Ms. King, you smacked the shit out of me. Oh shit, I can't believe it." Khalil is not really shocked.

"Believe it. What I can't believe is what you just said. I don't ever want to hear anything stupid like that again. Do you understand?"

Khalil backs up to the door with his hands up, giggling. "Did you see what she did?" he says to Dupree.

Two hours later, Carol Beck is downstairs in her office sorting things out, talking with her guidance counselor, Ms. Marion Brown. It is almost four o'clock, the time when most of the staff is headed home to Long Island or already there. The dedicated teachers are still here, because this is the best time to do their job, the time of day to see the kids whose lives are falling apart. There are children here in Jeff who are homeless, and after four o'clock in the afternoon they are easy to identify because they don't go home.

Over in the gymnasium, the basketball team has gotten some

bad news. They will not be going to the Christmas tournament in South Carolina after all.

"Christmas? Christmas is for white people to make money," Michael Washington says, bouncing a ball.

In previous years, Burke High School, the host of the Modie Risher Tournament in Charleston, helped defray the costs of the trip for visiting schools by feeding the players with meals cooked by their booster club. This year money is too tight, and no home-cooked food can be provided. No trip. The kids are stoic. Cortez Sutton just turns his head to the side and snorts, even though these would have been the only games he would be permitted to play all season. Once the regular season starts, his superintendent's suspension will kick in. Michael makes a crack about how those country boys are "too black to play night games anyway."

These kids insist on designer logos on their clothing as charms to ward off just such disappointment, to convince themselves and advertise to the world that they are not unconsidered, the ones left out and left behind. They dress to cover the hurt from the time their father did not show up to take them on a promised trip or their mother could not produce the present they craved for their birthday. These are not kids who break when something goes wrong. In fact, they are quietly surprised when something does not go wrong. Not one player complains when the trip is canceled, and no one on the team celebrates a week later, when it is put back on the schedule.

Several days after the cancelation, an article in the *New York Times* sports section explains that the Jefferson basketball players, rocked by a killing in their school, will have to undergo another setback by having their Christmas trip canceled. The unwelcome celebrity that Jefferson gained when Daryl Sharpe fell dead and Robert Anderson was toppled by a bullet in his neck could be used to some advantage, as Carol Beck, who has been busy seeking funding for a dormitory for Jefferson kids living in "transient and stressful" conditions, understood early on. The *Times* article solicits contributions to send the Jefferson High School basketball team to Charleston for Christmas. A Manhattan investment banker, an ex–Ivy League college basketball player, responds quickly with a check for $2,500. A Brooklyn doctor matches the sum. There are other checks. Small donations come in from as near as Canarsie, where the less affluent of the Jefferson alumni moved following the influx of blacks, and as far away as southern California.

It's the Christmas season, but Gita Malave is not thinking about the holiday. At six-thirty on a forbidding December morning, she is leaving her eighth-floor apartment carrying two heavy shoulder bags. One is her pocketbook; the other holds her schoolbooks, a thick text for the remedial math course she has to pass and a tome for her documents course in legal studies. She pushes the elevator button and checks her watch. One minute, two. Dammit. She leans forward and peers into the crack between the elevator door and the wall to see if the mechanism is moving, lays her ear against the door to listen for sliding cables. Nothing. She sucks a deep breath and starts down the staircase. The strap from the bookbag is already digging into her flesh, and she shifts the weight out on her shoulder. Gita is no stranger to this stairway. The only people out early in the morning are the crack smokers and the working people, and those pipeheads know whoever is leaving has some money, she reminds herself. As she moves past the fifth-floor landing, she tenses slightly. It is precisely at this spot she was robbed of her pocketbook three months ago.

After she makes it safely down the stairs, the rest of the trip to the Brooklyn Medical Supply Company is easy. Here Gita answers the phone for eight hours: "Medical, how do you do?" She puts buyers through to the proper department. Five calls often light up the board in front of her. "The math is kickin' my ass," she tells Marietta, the operator by her side, the woman who suggested that she start college.

"You can do it," Marietta answers. "You're the smartest person I know." There is little time to talk; the calls are jumping.

After work, Gita hustles over for a short visit with her sister, who is in Long Island College Hospital, dying of tuberculosis. Gita visits three times a week. In these times, when the fresh hell of the gun comes on after the scourge of crack, family bonds do not hold people together so much as they pull good people under. Born Son's mother is so sick at heart that she can barely make it to work anymore. Her younger son has dropped out of college and sits in her spotless, spartan apartment watching television and brooding over his brother's fate.

Gita shakes off the gloom from the hospital visit and strides through the Fulton Mall to New York City Technical College. Five minutes late for her six o'clock class, she faces the packed elevator. It doesn't matter a whit now to her that she's a grandmother and her classmates are less than half her age, or that her daughter-in-law is walking the same college hallways. "Sorry, that's the way it has to be," she says, and pushes her way onto the elevator. "Push seven for me, please."

Gita cannot afford to miss a minute of the lecture on polynomials. If she fails this course, things are going to get rough. Her state grant money for tuition is running out. Next semester a new college policy that limits the number of times a student can take a remedial course will go into effect. If she does pass, she will have just one required course left for the spring semester, and she will be the first in her family to graduate with a two-year college degree.

She powers her way through to nine o'clock, her energy fading fast as her documents class comes to an end. But she has a good memory, a feel for the law. This is the course she really likes.

She usually gets a good half-hour of studying done on the train. She shifts her bags to the seat beside her and opens her math book. But the numbers dance and blend together tonight. What Gita needs is a little rest. She lays the book on the seat and rocks her head. There is a quick pang of guilt at the missed opportunity to review the math lesson, then a flood of relaxation. This will be her half-hour, her vacation. It's 9:50 by the time she gets off the #3 at the Rockaway Avenue stop.

As she enters her building, she nods a greeting to a boy blocking the door, and he shifts to let her past. Inside, she steps past the kids hanging by the mailboxes in the lobby. Gita has made it her business to know every small-time drug dealer and mugger on her side of the Complex. She glances at the empty, stalled elevator. The corrugated metal of the half-open door is pocked with dents from forgotten gunshots. An elderly woman stands off to the side, wondering how she will get upstairs. Gita plunges up the staircase. She is in much too evil a mood to be frightened. *Just somebody fuck with me now*, she thinks, shifting her bags to keep her hands free.

Upstairs, her children have already fed themselves, but her

son Kendall has been in not one but two fights in school, and her daughter Tashana is complaining of a cold. Gita does not raise her voice as she faces Kendall in the kitchen.

"If I have to lose a day's pay to go up to that school, I am gonna be beyond upset. This is final exam time for me. Don't pick now to act like an idiot." She lays her hand on her sniffling daughter's head. "You don't have a fever. You took the Tylenol?" Tashana nods. A blood-curdling scream rises from the parking lot below. The children hustle to the window. Gita picks up her developmental math book. "As long as blood doesn't come under that door," she says, "I don't care what madness is going on outside."

Victories do not come in clusters in Brownsville. There is no clear line of progress, no inspiring line of development. Everyone, it seems, is fighting alone. Gita is going to graduate with an associate's degree in legal studies if the effort kills her. Then she will hope to find a better job. But her children are not galvanized by her feats of faith and endurance. They will not surpass her and head off to four-year colleges, to the Ivy League. The pressures are too great for that kind of momentum to build. Instead, the victories are like sparks in a meadow; they flash and burn out. Nevertheless, her family is intact, there is no gunman stalking her son, no police officers are pounding on her door. She is not complaining.

Christmas Eve. It is just after midnight at roll call at the PSA. Gary Lemite checks out his radio and wanders over to the front desk. He is ready to hit the streets. But his partner for the night, Jay Kern, is still downstairs. Off to the left, the massive-armed Jeff Desimone has run out of patience with the stooped, narrow-shouldered night tour lieutenant. The lieutenant has long greasy hair and wears his seedy trousers four inches too short, dangling over dingy white socks. He is not a leader of men. Determined not to make a mistake, he will sit mute for hours at a time, steadfastly refusing to make a decision of any kind.

Desimone is staring at the lieutenant. "Sooner or later, Lieutenant," he says, "you're gonna have to reach into your ballbag and make a decision."

"Hey, Gary," the desk sergeant calls, "what ya doin' working Christmas Eve? I thought you had connections."

"All I got is bills."

"You see that fuck we had in the squad room Sunday?"

Gary shrugs.

"Somethin' wrong with the guy's baby," the sergeant begins, determined to tell the story even without encouragement. "Can you believe we didn't know that the baby had been abused till the guy that did it had been taken to Gold Street? Didn't get the chance to tune the fuck up. I really feel bad about that."

Jim Priore, standing ten feet away, thumbing through his memo book, has more congenial things on his mind. He looks up at the scowling duty sergeant. "On this job I have been pissed off maybe two times in ten years for ten minutes at a time, that's it." He wheels and heads back down the hallway opposite the front desk into the sergeants' locker room. There he pours himself a cup of coffee and sits for a moment. The radio is quiet. It is hard to get to the bottom of Sergeant Priore's exorbitant good will.

"I don't talk to my wife about what goes on out here. When I get home, I always hope that she'll be asleep," he explains. "I got a medal last month and she didn't even know what it was for until they announced it up on the podium."

It had been a gunmetal gray winter day in East New York. Priore was assigned to a plainclothes anticrime unit cruising around the Cypress Houses. Before his partners pulled around the corner, he stepped out of the van and walked into the International Stationery Store on Sutter Avenue. The moment he was inside he knew something was wrong. Even before he saw, he heard. Silence. At the counter, Eddie Vargas, a pistolero, was scooping up handfuls of bills with his right hand. In his left hand, he jiggled a gun. Vargas bolted straight for the only door. Priore pulled his own gun. Vargas tried to throw a juke move on the cop and blast past to the street. Priore grabbed at his weapon in an attempt to jam the slide bolt and make the gun inoperable. Vargas grabbed Priore's right wrist and shook it until his police revolver fell to the linoleum floor with a thud. Priore concentrated on the slide bolt while Vargas smacked him in the face with the extra-long barrel of the weapon. "It all took so long, so long," Priore recalls. "I kept thinking, 'Where are the guys in the van?' I was sure his gun was going to go off in my face."

Vargas pried himself loose, stumbled, and fled toward Pitkin Avenue as Priore grabbed his gun off the floor and charged after him. In front of 2763 Pitkin, Priore grabbed him, spun him around, and threw him up against a parked car. In Vargas's waistband Priore found a black leather holster and a six-and-a-half-inch Tanfoglio Titan II pistol, blue metal, with a black grip.

Some officers would have given Vargas the slow ride, taken him the long way back to the station house, used the freebie to pound him to a pulp. But on the ride, Priore was experiencing an unfamiliar emotion. "I don't know what it was. I felt this release, and a wave of feeling. Then I realized it was gratitude. I turned around to the perp and said, 'Thanks for not shooting me.' He looks up and says, 'Thanks for not shooting me.'"

That night, after he had the paperwork finished, Priore went out to get some dinner for the guy. "It wasn't any takeout shit from Brownsville," the sergeant remembers. "I went over to Canarsie and bought him an Italian dinner."

Priore got the Exceptional Merit Medal for the incident, worth about one tenth of a point added to a passing score on the civil service test for lieutenant he's planning to take.

"I'll start studying eight hours a day after New Year's. I love this job," he muses. "They'll have to carry me off it." He checks his watch; he will have some serious bicycle assemblage to deal with when he gets off his tour. "This is the first Christmas I have worked in ten years," he says. "My wife was rippin'."

Outside, it is a clear, crisp twenty-nine degrees. A fat yellow moon, a hunter's moon, hangs over the gossamer cables of the Brooklyn Bridge, and the glow carries all the way out to Brownsville. Even on this holiday evening, Gary Lemite is looking for DeeSo. Kern is driving the unmarked van.

An hour into the tour, Gary thinks he spots one of DeeSo's dealers and asks Kern to follow at a distance. "Silent Night, Holy Night" wafts softly from the radio as the two plainclothes cops cruise half a block behind DeeSo's four-door sedan. There are very few cars on the street. Lee Brown, the police commissioner, begins a speech over the portable. He's talking about working on Christmas Eve. The troops are not having it.

"Asshole," a cop says, cutting through Brown's voice with a dry whisper.

"Be nice," Central says, "be nice."

"We want the Glock," another anonymous caller interjects.

The Glock is the controversial semiautomatic weapon the cops feel is their only hope against the multitude of weapons they face on the street.

Gary hasn't seen DeeSo himself, but he continues to watch the blue Legend, now parked outside a bodega on Legion and Dumont. Every inch of the windows of the store he is watching is covered with posters to deter surveillance. Around the corner is a barber shop named the Barbers of the Ville.

"Fucking Christmas Eve and the radio is going off," Kern says as more calls come over the portable. These are jobs for the uniforms. Lemite and Kern, in a specialty unit, are released from the radio, free to gather information on DeeSo's operation.

After half an hour, a man walks out of the bodega and gets into the Legend. This time it is no minion. It is DeeSo himself. He's drunk, and he knows he's being followed. He signals ostentatiously at every corner, makes expansive turns, and pulls over on Georgia Avenue. The door of his car swings open and DeeSo staggers to the pavement. Lemite and his partner watch as he hands money to several men who stand half in the shadows, their shoulders hunched against the cold. Kern rolls the Dodge slowly up the block and Lemite gets out.

"What are you doin'?" he asks DeeSo pleasantly, nodding at the handful of bills the clean-cut drug dealer holds loosely at his side. DeeSo is usually much too careful to be approached holding a fistful of money on the street by anyone, cop, perp, or citizen. But this is Christmas; the champagne has padded his reflexes, but not his mind.

DeeSo nods at his shivering slingers. "I thought they were homeless," he tells Gary. "The holidays, you know."

Gary turns back to Kern, watching from the driver's seat. "Smooth bastard," he says softly, and gets back in the car.

Christmas Eve, East Mod. Here is Gloria Corley's best boy on his bunk, staring straight up into the dark, thinking about rhymes. "New to this, due to this . . ." It has been a strange night. No horn. The CO canceled the phone after the fight on Friday. Guys have just been sitting up on each other's beds talking, arms around each other. Nostalgic. It has been so quiet, not a shout since maybe eight o'clock. Like somebody has died. Sharron is thinking, *I don't belong here. I'm not like these guys.* But what to do? Get a job packing bags? There has to be something more than scraping by in life, he thinks. People with regular jobs in Brownsville don't even know where Bloomingdale's is, he tells himself. There has to be something more. Has to be. The lottery? Sharron sees himself, a millionaire, in a billowing silk shirt in a white car. The music will do it, if he can get a break. The advertising world. Executive, creative. He will have to wear suits, but then he will be older, so the suits will be cool.

The dream fades away quickly, and he is alone on his bunk again in the gloomy barracks. A yellow glow comes from the corrections officer's window down the corridor. Something is slipping away from him, and Sharron feels big tumbling tears. Good thing it's dark. On both sides, he hears spasms, muffled sounds. All over East Mod, the trouble kids, the quick-punch, fast-feet boys with their burners tucked away in cracks between the bathroom floor tiles and behind the toilets, are crying. Sharron listens hard at the bunk directly behind, where Love "lives." Same sound. *Damn,* he marvels. *Even the meanest niggers is broke down.*

COUNTRY BOYS

At three o'clock on Christmas morning, the Thomas Jefferson basketball players begin arriving in front of the school on Pennsylvania Avenue. Brothers Jude and Carl show up with their watchful parents. Diminutive Michael Washington pulls up in a cab with his mother. The big Grenadian center, nicknamed Tumbo after the seven-foot Nigerian NBA rookie shot-blocking sensation Dikembe Mutombo, walks down from the #3 train. Cortez arrives by car service from the Linden projects, down the street. A gunshot rings out a block away.

Mickey Mundell stands in the middle of Pennsylvania Avenue, trying to figure out how to get five dollars for a vial of crack. "Anybody got a quarter, or a candy bar with teethmarks in it?" he quips to the players and parents standing next to the humming charter bus. Mickey's family moved from North Carolina when he was a baby. He was a church boy. Now he does not sleep, stands outside at all hours, a ghost of himself, with protruding cheekbones. "Smokin' lovely," they say. Somehow he stays alive as he haunts the Brownsville streets, using his skills as a mechanic to rip off a bumper or an alternator on special order here and there.

"I almost didn't make it," one player says. "I'm recovering from the flu."

"I'd a flew you," Coach Moore says.

The players are thrilled to be going, but it takes only a minute for them to start entertaining themselves by criticizing each other.

"Let's start a fund. Everybody puts in one dollar, and the guy who gets the most pussy . . ."

"I predict none for nobody," Michael Washington yells in a prescient moment.

"You ain't seen me pushin' up strong, son. I'm gonna be gettin' busy," Cortez counters. He's the best student on the team, and the slickest mouth.

"Shut up, Cortez, when they see you down South you ain't gettin' no pussy. They gonna say you're too black," Ed Alcy cracks.

Cortez loves this. "Man, look at your head. They ought to use your head instead of that ball they drop on New Year's Eve."

"Shut up, muck-mouth," Michael snaps.

On a more serious note, another player floats an attractive idea. "When they find out we're from New York, the girls're gonna be sweatin' us."

Cortez is back on his happy offensive. "Tumbo. You took the train here at three A.M.? Ain't you never heard of cars?"

"We are livin' in luxury," somebody says and sighs. Indeed, the bus is well appointed, with reclining seats and a bathroom and television monitors.

"I'm gonna sit on this side," Michael, who has driven down South before, says. "That side gonna be crazy boring. All you gonna see is cars."

"Shut up, you black beetle."

As the bus driver guns the engine and slips into gear to pull away, Mickey Mundell heads across Pennsylvania Avenue, absorbed, thinking, watching, figuring a way to make a couple of bucks to ride a wisp of white smoke. His hands are thrust deep in the ripped-out pockets of his grease-smeared ski jacket. His fingers sort through the four Zippo lighters there, and the short pipe with the tinfoil-covered bowl. For him, there is no such thing as comfort or satisfaction at a task well done, just the dizzying jump between the worlds of bare survival and chilling happiness. The big purple and white bus pulls past him down Pennsylvania Avenue, under the elevated #3 and out toward Linden Boulevard.

Throughout the trip, Coach Moore admonishes the players for calling each other names. He points out that obsessive name-calling undermines togetherness and team play. The players are happy and truly like one another. Still, they continue to relate to each other by sometimes hilarious and often hurtful name-calling.

Many of the players — Marvin, Michael, Donnel, and others — were born down South; some even spent part of their youth in North or South Carolina. They are going back to their roots, but the thought does not cross their minds. They do approach the trip with some wonder, though.

"When we cross the border, your ass is mine," Nick tells Michael.

"They got too many niggers down there."

"I'm starvin'."

Broad-shouldered, sweet-tempered Tumbo swivels to answer the latest insult directed his way.

"Just turn your ass around," Michael warns.

"When I get in the room," Tumbo promises, "I'm gonna beat your ass all night."

"Why don't you shut up, you hungry elf," Cortez says to Michael.

The bus has been on the road for only an hour, but Moore has had it. He travels the length of the aisle to put an end to the nonsense. He gives his third lecture of the trip when the bus reaches the New Jersey Turnpike. The kids just can't stay quiet.

"I feel so good I could run down South," a player says as the bus rolls on.

The driver puts a movie starring tough guy Roy Scheider on the television monitors, positioned at every third row. The players may have left East New York and Brownsville behind, but they will not be without the sound of gunfire. The film is not five minutes old before a machine gun starts its own chatter. Halfway into New Jersey, and suddenly almost everybody is asleep. From somewhere ahead a young man's voice claims, "This is the life."

The sun comes up on the bus as it rolls through the pine forests of Virginia. "We will stop," Coach Moore announces. "My first wife left me because I wouldn't stop."

The team stops for a breakfast of grits and pancakes, while the bus driver coos to a middle-aged woman in a wig and gold-rimmed glasses, who is all ears. Back on the road, a skunk smell fills the bus full of city kids.

"Tumbo, how could you?" Michael wails. "Move your African ass to another seat."

Tumbo has had it with the foolishness. He's weary of mock threats. He enjoys silence, does not crave hilarity. He did not grow up like this, insulting his friends for fun. He sits and glowers out the window, adjusts his Walkman, and stares.

The only player who pays the slightest attention to the Carolina landscape, the black creeks and the cypress swamps, the tufts of moss on bone-gray ruins of trees, is Cortez Sutton. Cortez is from the Linden Houses, near Jamaica Bay, and is an amateur naturalist, a member of the Audubon Society, a bird watcher. He bounces from one side of the bus to the other. "A falcon, you can tell by the way they circle," he tells nobody. "A a great white heron," he announces. "A sparrow hawk . . . back is sky blue, face is like striped." He sees an osprey. "The only thing I haven't seen is a bald eagle," he brags. The rest of his teammates study the spitting, crackling TV monitor as yet another movie about mayhem, this time a karate movie, *Little Tokyo*, shows.

It's mid-afternoon when the bus pulls past the great old houses of Charleston, the worn Colonials and the gleaming gabled homes with sweeping porches. The kids pay no attention. They are looking for their motel.

The team is booked into an old Ramada Inn near Burke High School, a few miles out of town, with a view of a McDonald's on one side and the brown Charleston River on the other. There is no water in the perfunctory swimming pool, just some dark, damp leaves. The players are ecstatic.

The Burke High School gym is large, with sweeping bleachers, but the floor is not wood but brown pasteboard, worn pale around the three second lanes. The Burke High mascot is a bulldog, and there are blue pawprints down the middle of the court. At the shoot-around the next day, a few hours before their first game, the Jefferson team looks like a bunch of dead-end kids. They have no practice uniforms; Michael looks like a fifthgrader.

"Yo, give me your money," he says with an ice grill to a sixfoot-six player from Wilmington, Delaware, who chases a ball down to the Jeff end of the court. The Jeff players stare at the team warming up at the far end of the floor, exaggerate their bigcity slouches, and whisper among themselves. Ed Alcy wears his wool cap as he pops long jump shots. The team lines up for a lay-up drill. Of all the players, Jude, at six-three, with long arms, looks the most like a ballplayer and has the most potential.

When the team manager, Adrian, appears with the camcorder Moore has brought to film the games, Cortez lights up. "I got it," he shouts, scampering off the lay-up line. "Adrian, interview me."

He reclines in the first row of the wooden bleachers as Adrian turns on the machine and delivers questions from off-camera. "What does it feel like to be in Charleston, South Carolina?"

Cortez deepens his voice. "First, I'd like to say hello to my fans down here. Thank them for all the letters."

The team gathers round. There are more interviews. Moore appears, grim-faced, in the doorway of the gym. The players pop back onto the court.

Later in the afternoon, the boys file into Moore's bright motel room. Some pile onto the beds, others sit on the windowsill. Moore is wearing an orange and blue African print Kente cloth cap. He is scowling. It is not clear why he is so perturbed; there has been no real trouble from the boys.

"I'm a little pissed off," he begins. "As crazy as Ronnie was last year, he knew how to conduct himself adequately. There is just too much bickering, too much bull. I know in the neighborhood you have to wear your hats to the side so the knuckleheads won't bother you. But you're not hoodlums and you're not bums, and I don't want you to act that way." Cortez nudges a slat from the vertical blinds and takes a peek out toward the Charleston River, but quickly refocuses his attention when Moore raises his voice. "And the stuff with you, Michael, calling Cortez black. We're all black. I don't understand that. I don't care if you're light, or yellow, or Chinese, you have to treat each other with respect. I will cancel the season," he warns. "It will be my way or the highway."

What sounds like the usual empty threats by an irritated coach has special resonance. All the players have to do is look around the room at the team's personnel to know that the best ballplayers in Brownsville are not here; not even the best players in Thomas Jefferson are here. These are the kids who can play a little ball and keep their grades above a seventy average. Carol Beck was serious when she said that she was not about to make compromises to have a good basketball team. Nick, a skinny guy with a fair jump shot, has a passive, tentative game. Willie, the clean-cut captain, is a rugged six-one and has hops, but he's not the type to lead a team. Cortez is sneaky, quick, and ever eager, but for all his self-promotion, he is very inexperienced, as is Jude's brother, Carl. Michael is in way over his head. The other subs are Marvin, who is called Face because he's so handsome, Donnel, and Lashawn, just nice kids.

At the end of Moore's speech, instead of letting the words sink in and take effect, Adrian cracks wise. Observing the coach's flashy cap, he moans, "Uh-oh. Mr. Moore has the same hat he had on when we got whacked by fifty." Everybody laughs. Moore shakes his head, then he laughs too.

In their orange-and-blue uniforms, they lose the first game big. Michael complains from the bench about the "fat pork-sausage ref." Though the Jeff team does not play badly, it is sorely outmatched. Alcy is not a natural point guard. Moore rides him so hard he has lost his confidence, and the team is lucky it can get the ball over half-court much of the time. Tumbo is a fine physical specimen, but he grew up playing soccer, and it shows. He is the bowling champion of Thomas Jefferson, one of the top bowlers in Brooklyn high schools, of all things, and the captain of the handball team. Those skills are of little use here. He does not box his opponents away from the backboard, cannot put the ball on the floor to drive to the basket. Most of Jeff's baskets come on solo slashes to the basket by Willie and Jude.

After the contest, the host team, Burke, puts out a spread of deviled eggs, salad, and cold cuts on folding tables in the courtesy room. The homemade food is for the coaches and other adults. Pizza is ordered for the kids. The gray-haired, septuagenarian Modie Risher, Burke High's basketball legend and retired master coach, after whom the tournament is named, pads across the bare utility room with the unmistakable pigeon-toed walk of a former athlete. He samples the hors d'oeuvres, twirls a toothpick deftly in his fingers, and holds court. He's not talking about basketball.

The Jefferson boys are all the way down South now, but the talk is still of killing. "We've had a killing every day here in Charleston for the past fifteen days," Risher says "The record was forty-eight. We've already got fifty-two. And the year is not over. But you know, I don't like to complain. 'Cause when people see you comin', they say, 'Let me go, 'cause here comes Modie Risher.'"

The next day, Jefferson is down 18–0 near the end of the first quarter to a local Catholic school, St. John's. The trip looks like a fiasco, the team like badly outclassed urchins from a city that does not give a damn whether its young black men live or die, flourish or waste away. They came a thousand miles to get their skinny butts whipped by the children of the very place their parents fled for a better life. It looks as if neither trip was worth the effort.

Michael, squirming on the bench, has stopped cheering his teammates and is trying somehow not to be associated with their ineptitude. Incredibly, Jeff bangs back into the game. Nick hits a few turnaround jump shots. Tumbo muscles for the ball, works inside. Michael is informed by a fan behind the bench — a man who moved to Charleston from Brooklyn and has bragged incessantly to his friends that Brooklyn basketball is state of the art — that the ref is an alumnus of St. John's. Michael tells the stocky bus driver, who launches a diatribe against the referee that is beyond the pale for the genteel Charlestonians. The ref halts the game and warns the driver to stop his cursing.

A few moments later, on a questionable call against Jeff, the driver does go crazy. "You reffed yesterday. You're not supposed to ref twice in forty-eight hours. You cheatin', blind bastard!" he howls.

The ref blows his whistle and summons a police officer from the sidelines. The driver from Brownsville is escorted from the gym, yelling insults over his shoulder. "Don't show your sorry ass in Brooklyn!"

The fan who told Michael about the ref's ties to St. John's beams to his friends. This is the spirit he has been telling them about. The crowd is too mellow to boo the driver as he lingers in the doorway, hurling still more insults.

At halftime, Moore is in an inexplicable rage. Jefferson is executing well on offense, but he thinks they are playing soft defense. "You are not in East New York, gentlemen. Nobody is going to shoot you if you put a body on him. Nobody is going to grab a gun and kill you if you knock him down. This is Charleston, South Carolina. I want to see some bodies fly."

The second half starts with a couple of quick hoops by the Jeff captain, Willie, and soon it is too late to stop the orange wave. Released from their paralyzing fear of humiliation, the Jeff players gambol about, snatching lucky long rebounds, stealing passes. Everybody on the bench begins to believe that tonight is Jeff's night. Jude gets loose on a fast break and scores. Cortez sprints into the game. His defender plays his right hand and Cortez skirts the defense to the left for a baseline lay-up. As he backpedals on defense, dreams of stardom are etched on his face. The score is 58–57 Jeff, with two seconds to go, when a player from St. John's tries a desperation three-pointer. He misses.

Cortez is a fountain of revisionism in the locker room, describing the moves he made in his limited time on the floor. "I *left* the man. I *used* him. Did you see that move? Did you see his eyes? The man was frozen. Ha-ha. Did you see the way I charged the shooter at the end, bothered the shot? Did you see it? I saved the game." Cortez is hell-bent for recognition. He has an eighty-seven average in school, a good left hand. So what if he is banned for the regular season for that incident over at Lafayette? This is his day. He is determined to be a star.

Cortez's buddy over at the Linden Houses is E-lo, Ian Moore. The two are so close that Cortez calls Moore his godbrother. Lately E-lo has been hanging around more with Tyrone Sinkler, the big kid who has the beef with Khalil Sumpter. But E-lo has listened often to Cortez's descriptions of what it will be like when he, E-lo, sees Cortez on national TV. Cortez has already figured out what reactions will be going through E-lo's mind. "At first you'll be jealous: 'I can't believe Cortez is famous.' Then you'll be happy, 'cause when I got all those props, you'll have them too. 'That's my homeboy,' you'll yell. And you'll be happy. You can come and visit me and shit."

Post-game, George Moore is the prototype of a grumpy coach. He seems no happier in victory than he was in defeat yesterday. He takes it all out on the bubbly Cortez. "I told you not to jump at the three-point shooter in that situation. You'll give the man three foul shots and we'll lose. Did you think of that? Stop trying to make yourself a hero."

Then, with exquisitely poor timing, Adrian reports, "Coach, we ran out of videotape before the game was over."

Moore looks at Cortez, back at Adrian, and mutters, "I'll bet we got plenty of interviews, though."

The next day, several players, including Nick, Michael, and Cortez, take a cab to an upscale mall. There are several blocks of expensive shops and fancy restaurants by the water. The wharf area is a tourist attraction. But there is not a brown face to be seen in the throngs of pastel-shirted yuppies. The boys stand transfixed by a white model who has been hired to pose motionless as a promotion for a new line of clothing. With features as delicate as china, the girl seems neither to move nor to breathe.

In the Polo shop, the boys check out the gear. "Did you see the guard? He was clockin' us all the time. He like jumped when we walked in the door."

"Yeah." Michael smirks. "But it looked like it was easy. I should've stashed something."

The Jefferson team does not win the tournament. The next day, they lose the third game, 63–57. After the contest, the players climb high into the stands to watch Burke High School in the championship contest. The game pits Burke against a cross-town rival. The gym is rocking with the sounds of the Geechees and their high-country neighbors. These black Charlestonians speak a creole language called Geechee or Gullah. It is based on English and influenced by several West African languages. To the untrained ear, the Geechees have the same lilting speech tones as the Caribbeans back in Brooklyn. "What're all these Jamaicans doin' here?" the Jeff players want to know.

Burke High has a real star on its team, a major college prospect, and there is no hero like a hometown hero. Melvin Watson, six-foot-two, 190 pounds, pops warm-up shots with a delicate touch. The stares of hundreds of eyes reflect off his beautiful body. He retrieves bouncing balls and generously passes them off to teammates, benchwarmers who won't see a moment of action. The fans nod and point. Melvin is "the man" in Charleston. The locals whisper his name and legend to one another, for the edification of the Jeff players. The Brooklynites are experts. They have seen the best. Maybe even Born Son James was as good a player as this Melvin Watson. They settle back to find out.

Heads turn as Modie Risher enters the gym, waves, and takes his place in the stands. In Charleston, there is history, the kind of history that has the locals talking about the games Modie Risher played and has fathers watching their sons try to match the memory of those old feats. Here, store proprietors gush when they see the high school team's big gun walk by. In Brooklyn, it does not work that way. Even the kids who are headed through schools like Jefferson to the pros don't experience this kind of enveloping warmth. They ride the subways anonymously, gangly kids with gym bags. Maybe the bad guys cut them some slack around the way because of their basketball reputation, but the status ends there. The Jefferson kids sit in the stands and watch what it would have been like if their families had stayed down South.

But before the Burke game starts, some players on the Jefferson team draw some attention of their own. Ed Alcy and handsome Marvin are seated in the first row of the stands. Ed wears his wool hat with earflaps, the kind that a mother would put on a baby on a chilly day — a style that, along with pacifiers, has become the rage in Brownsville. Both boys also sport burgundy Timberland boots and ultra-baggy jeans riding halfway down their butts. These are the New York guys, and everybody is eager to catch a whiff of the latest craze. It's a sure bet that the baby hats will make an appearance on the streets of Charleston before long. What is more, the girls are showing a lively interest, and it is not long before the ubiquitous Cortez, Donnel, and Ed are all "kickin' it" to some country girls.

Once the game begins, the gym is a caldron of noise. The Jeff players who are not engaged in flirting are transfixed by the spectacle. Jefferson plays its home games in virtual silence; almost all fans are banned from the gym because of the threat of trouble. When a white teacher, an eighteen-year veteran at Jeff, did show up at a game early in the season, he whispered behind a cupped hand to a cheering colleague, "Don't waste your breath. They don't have the intellectual ability to understand the game."

The opposing team is playing a pressure man-to-man defense against Burke, double-teaming Melvin Watson whenever he makes a move to the basket. But he turns sideways, slips through the traps, and pulls up for short, fluid jump shots or dishes off to his teammates. On one play, he sails into the air to cuff a defensive rebound and shrinks to a cannonball as he bursts by two defenders who try to pin him to the sideline. Like a running back, he dips and weaves, and finally throws a look-away pass to a Burke player, who misses the lay-up.

Even more remarkable than his high-level game is Watson's on-court personality. He is a man among boys. You can see it on his face. When Burke is ahead in the first half, he passes the ball to his teammates, blends into the fabric of the game. He works and works some more, never complains and never shows off. But his teammates are having a bad night, and Burke is down by ten points with just three minutes left in the contest. Then Melvin Watson starts to rumble. He is burdened with four personal fouls. He's dog-tired, grabbing at the hem of his shorts as he stoops over, foraging for air during time-outs and foul shots. But the handicaps just make things more exciting for the fans.

Everybody in the gym knows Melvin is coming. He pops off a pick and scores. His team is down five. He takes the ball the length of the court and scores; three. He steals the ball; one. The hometown crowd is raising thunder, stomping on the boards of the bleachers. This is going to be one of those games they talk about for years.

Ah, Melvin, handsome, strong, willing, and able. The other teams loses the ball. Melvin rockets upcourt. He spins away from one defender and then another. His body is more than the sum of its parts. No time for passing the ball to his fledgling teammates now. No time for anything but Melvin Watson and the scoreboard. The rival team is banging him. They want to stop his roll, but they can't catch up to him. In the pande-monium, no one can hear the refs' whistles anyway. With two defenders hounding him, Melvin nails the winning basket, with no time left on the clock. According to the script, the crowd pours down onto the court to pay homage. The Charleston faithful edge close to Melvin Watson as he stands under the bas-ket, holding his small son in his arms.

After the game, the Jefferson boys walk back to the motel with no fewer than five girls. As the group moves through the parking lot of the McDonald's, they pass two cars with a heavy bass beat coming from behind dark-tinted windows.

"Country boys make too much noise," somebody among the five or six Jefferson players cracks. As they reach the exit of the parking lot, one of the cars backs up and pulls past them. The driver accelerates onto the main drag, and there is a loud report. *Bang.*

Donnel takes two long strides and dives into the tall weeds. Ed pops up and dashes off like a flushed rabbit. The rest of the team scatters for cover. The girls stand there, confused. When the boys realize the sound was the backfiring exhaust of the car and not a blast from a sawed-off shotgun, Donnel crawls out, brushing marsh grass from his clothes, and the rest sidle back up to the girls without a word of explanation. All except for Ed, who doesn't stop running till he is at the motel. He takes the elevator up to his fourth-floor room and waits for news.

Cortez was meant to be happy. He cannot believe his luck. "We got four girls in our room!" he brays up and down the hall. His group is trying to make the best of the situation with the girls; others are in Tumbo's room. Tumbo has signed up for the pay-per-view pornography channel and is charging admission to watch. There is much milling in the hallway.

The next morning, spirits are high over the girls' visit, despite Michael Washington's charge that "they just ate your pizza and drank your soda and booked."

"That's 'cause you scared them away, you black elf," Cortez mocks. Rumor has it that Donnel, the benchwarmer, has managed to have some kind of sexual contact with one of the visitors. "This nigger here was gettin' busy, doin' *work*," Cortez attests, content this one time to perform the role of witness.

Coach Moore is listening and intervenes. "I don't want to hear the *n* word," he admonishes, perhaps because there are white people close by. "It is not appropriate. You are not kids anymore." The coopting of the most hurtful of racial epithets is a complicated psychological maneuver, but Moore chooses to see it as a sloppy habit. He is also concerned about his team's seemingly thoughtless attitude toward sex. He addresses Cortez. "What would you do if you played in the NBA and girls followed you around all the time?"

"Well, I'd just get busy, that's all. I'd be pushin' up strong."

"Then you'd end up like Magic Johnson," Moore counters.

"I'd rather die gettin' skins than any other way," Cortez rebuts.

Tumbo is not present at yet another "big man special" break-fast of pancakes and eggs in the motel. Cortez is ready with an imitation of the big guy's protestations about the food. "I want some yams," he mimics, opening his mouth wide for the vow-els, "and some good dumplings. And I want to go home and get a purge. Ha-ha."

"Who wants to go home?" Michael says. "I don't want to go. Do you? Who wants to go home?"

Nobody.

Cortez is the self-appointed historian of the trip, hard at work on the way home, rearranging the facts of the games and the previous night to suit himself. "I was pushin' up strong on those girls at the game . . ." He knows that before long his version of events will prevail.

As the bus rumbles through Richmond, Virginia, Lashawn, the only substitute who did not play a single minute, points out the window. "My brother's locked up there," he says glumly. "He got seven years for robbery. I was supposed to go visit him. But I came on the trip instead."

Into the dusk, there is a dead-serious discussion in the shad-ows at the back of the bus. The team members are gathered around, listening, thinking, and asking questions. Marvin, the pretty boy of the team, is telling a story about some kind of a knuckle-up between two students at Jeff. So far on the trip he has been quiet, because he has not been in his element. Marvin is truly no ballplayer. But when the conversation turns to may-hem, it's apparent that he may be the most streetwise of all. He lowers his voice and starts to talk very quickly, his language drenched with the most current slang for trouble in all its forms. These kids are their own newspapers, their own town criers. The problem is that unlike African griots, they feature only cur-rent events. Not one of them ever mentions where he is from, or where his parents are from, or what they do now or once did. The present commands every bit of their attention.

Marvin turns a quick phrase, and the level of attentiveness rises even higher. This is not gossip. The boys on the periphery fall silent, lean toward the speaker, and cock their heads.

"The one with the brown and gold jeans jacket, in the office."

Cortez looks down for a moment, thinking. "The guy with the fronts in his mouth?"

"No," Marvin says.

Cortez reconsiders. "The guy who just got the fronts in his mouth."

Marvin reflects. "Nah. This dude always be with Dupree, with the eight-ball jacket." He means a popular style of red leather jacket with a large eight ball stitched on the back. "He's Dupree's man," he emphasizes. "Remember, we seen him outside Ms. King's class on the fifth floor. He was talkin' about 'Who want it? Who want it?'"

The group is mesmerized. There is something critical about the information they are receiving. They are gathering data, putting together a scouting report on the tendencies of a new tough guy in their school.

"I know who you mean," Cortez says finally. "I know the guy. Brown jeans jacket. He think he's bad. Front'n. He just wants props." Cortez decides that the guy who hangs with Dupree, despite his threats, is not a mad agent.

The boys will spend five minutes trying to ascertain the identity and proclivities of any character in a story about a fight or an argument in the school or neighborhood, especially one in which weapons or death threats are involved. They want to be prepared. There are so many "front artists," they want to know as much about people as they can. The conversation goes on.

"Moe? Light-skinned Moe from Amboy? Who used to play ball?"

The level of danger in the neighborhood is apparent when the players, the boys in the school kept on the team not because they are basketball stars but because they are straight arrows, discuss their own security precautions. "I had the little .25 that time," one player says. "It seems that whenever you have something, don't nothin' happen."

Jude and Nick discuss the proper way to deal with a potentially hostile crew on the street. "I just sort of drop my head a little," Nick says, "and if I know somebody I say, 'What's up?' If the dude says, 'What's up?' you're O.K. Sometimes the guy you know don't really wanna say, 'What's up?' He wanna say, 'Nothin's up,' but he can't, 'cause he *do* know you. School I used to go to, there be mad Decepticons rollin' up after school." The Decepticons are a citywide gang with a fading but fearsome reputation. "If I don't know the people, I don't say nothin'. I don't act like I'm scared, even though I am. I just dip my head."

"You can tell when somethin's up," Jude says. "Then you run. Sometime your only chance is if the gun jams."

As the bus slows to a crawl in traffic near the Maryland-Delaware border, there is talk about how the JV team was approached last year by a group of guys with guns and Michael got beat up. More talk of guns in hushed tones. "I think the four-fifth jammed," Jude says.

Later, as the charter rumbles over the Delaware River into New Jersey, Willie and Cortez are talking about girls.

"Willie, you never had your heart broken? You ain't in the club?"

"Sure. I cut her off."

"You cut her off for who?"

"I cut her off for a bitch, and then she cut me off. I was crying, cryin'. I bought her teddies. I took her to Footlocker and bought her new kicks. When I think of what I did to get her back, I could kick myself."

"Right, Jim." Cortez acknowledges Willie's mistake with the wisdom of the ages about him.

It is after midnight when the bus pulls up in front of Jefferson High School, but Jude and Carl Princivil's parents are waiting on the sidewalk, standing in the cold.

"Home sweet home," Michael says. "Back in the jungle."

Several other parents are also waiting, sitting in cars and cabs. Thomas Jefferson High looms above like a great dark castle. One by one the cars nose into traffic and slip off; the bus growls a last time and is gone. As the last of the team fades away, Carl, Jude, and their parents are still standing on Pennsylvania Avenue, looking for a gypsy cab.

"LET THE DOGS LOOSE"

Damn snitch house," Sharron writes in his diary on New Year's Eve. "Somebody told the CO about where the burners were, under the sink, and now there's no TV. Guys crying again, all over the place. Talking about their problems. Girl gone, Mom's in the hospital. Everybody been in jail two or three times before. In here, with all the talents I have and I'm not using them. Usually the lights go out at eleven, but another CO let us into the day room to watch the ball come down, controlled the TV from the bubble. It's like a party, only no music and no girls. Guys jumping around, acting all wild. Banging on the windows. Just like a party. But in jail."

To the delight of his neighbors in Howard Beach, John Gotti flouts local authorities with a lavish display of illegal fireworks every July Fourth. The same raucous spirit of celebration inspires the youngbloods from East New York and the Ville, who are getting ready to make some noise of their own. In recent years, a tradition has developed that on New Year's Eve young men come out and fire their guns off the roofs, out the windows, or even from the walkways, up to the patches of night sky between the project buildings. The impulse undoubtedly owes something to the high spirits of the holiday, but also to the fact that there is no better time to try out a new bis than when the shots are camouflaged by the heavy booms of M-80 firecrackers and the cluster pops of slightly more reasonable types of fireworks.

But this year the Housing police are going to do their best to ruin the Brownsville party. Somebody above Lenti in the hierarchy of the department has made the decision that this year Brownsville and East New York will not crackle with the reports of TEC-9s and four-fifths, jammies, burners, and all kinds of Ravens. "In the past, we used to head over near the drag strip on Fountain Avenue, have a few cold ones, and maybe pop a bottle of champagne," a Housing cop says. "After things had cooled down, we would come back out and clean up the mess. That way, everybody would get home safe. But they didn't want to do that this year." The new idea is that if it is business as usual with the local gun wielders, the full contingent of PSA 2 officers will be on hand to snatch up the collars. It is a bad idea. Scores of cops are heading out to confront hundreds of young men bent on firing their guns, and it looks as if somebody is going to get hurt.

Sam Tilly is riding with a guy named John Montemauro; Gary Lemite is driving Sergeant Billy Bright; Hammil is with O'Donnel. For Gary, this night is unusual. Most nights he spends his time watching for subtle signs — the bulge, the quickened step, the infinitesimal list from the weight of a big gun, a heavy jacket on a muggy night. This is different.

A few brave souls who will clearly fight for their right to party are standing on street corners outside the Cypress Houses. Three hopeful girls in party dresses stand on the corner of Fountain and Sutter, waiting for transportation. A cruising gypsy cab gathers them up like wildflowers.

Eddie Hammil, seated down the street in his RMP, watches Smokey Thompson, who is not so lucky. A block away, he's pacing up and down, also hoping for a cab to come by. After several minutes he goes inside and calls one. "That fucking Smokey," he mutters. Thompson is the guy who fired a volley of shots at him several months ago. There were witnesses and recovered rounds, the whole deal. There was an indictment, but the DA refused to prosecute. Hammil remains more than a little peeved. Thompson pops out the front door of 315 Fountain Avenue, then draws back in. The moment he goes inside, the cab he called pulls up in the frosty air. Hammil sees his opportunity and pulls up next to it.

"You get a call from 315 Fountain?"

"Yes, sir," the driver answers obsequiously, his eyes sliding sideways toward Hammil. Gypsy cabs are illegal, allowed to operate only because the licensed yellow cabs will not enter the neighborhood.

"The guy who called the cab canceled. You can go," Hammil says, and Smokey Thompson's ride pulls away. Hammil chuckles.

The cops are having fun. There are numerous strange sounds coming over the radio, including an underwater howl that sounds like a whale call, made by putting the radio outside the window as the car is moving. A few blocks away, over by the Pink Houses, close to where Del Migliore was shot in the foot, Montemauro and Tilly sit with their lights off. Tilly shakes his head and laughs at the antics of his fellow officers on the radio. He is the kind of young man you cannot help but like. He has a soft stutter and a sturdy body. He plays in the fife-and-drum corps for the Emerald Society, the Irish police organization, and ever since he took a bullet in the arm in Manhattan he has been wedded to the department in deep ways.

When Tilly and his partner approached a cab in Queens several years ago, they were pretty sure two robbery suspects were inside. But Tilly let his guard down for just a moment. "When I think about it, I should have shot the guy when he rolled out of the cab," he says now. But who could think that fast? Who could be ready to shoot a man before he was sure the man meant to shoot him? Tilly waited a second. That was all the time it took for the gunman to put a bullet in his arm. As Tilly went down, his partner opened up on the guys in the cab, killing one and wounding the other.

Tilly used to think about the shooting all the time. But as the years go by, the aspect of the incident that sticks in his craw, the thing he emphasizes when he talks about the morning he got shot, is the fact that his partner got the top honor of the department, the Medal of Honor, usually given posthumously, and he got the penultimate one, the Combat Cross. He implies that black officers receive favoritism in the department. "I mean, I'm the one who got shot. Isn't that fucked up? I'm white and he's black." Then the stutter: "I g-get sh-sh-shot and he gets the Medal of Honor."

Tilly is a nice man, a good cop. "I have s-s-seen a lot of things out here that I don't agree with. I have seen people do wrong on both sides. I don't understand what motivates these kids. But I also don't b-b-believe in smacking a guy around when he is in cuffs. That is something I would never do."

In the minutes before midnight, there are dozens of calls over the radio for shots fired. "A number of shots fired at that location," Central announces calmly. It's easy for the dispatcher to say. She's sitting in a booth on the ninth floor at One Police Plaza in Manhattan, not on the outskirts of Brooklyn, on the streets of the Ville on New Year's Eve.

Montemauro and Tilly take a call at 265 Livonia, Gita Malave's building. A bullet has sailed through a window on the floor below her apartment. This time no child is shot in the neck, no aspiring musician is killed, nobody's loved one is maimed. Tilly is directed to a back room, where a large poster of rapper L.L. Cool J is taped to the bedroom wall. L.L. wears a red hat and a huge gold chain. Where his gold teeth used to be, there is a fresh bullet hole.

At 12:05 Central reports, "Shots fired, *of course.*" Soon Central is holding sixty-one jobs. All over Brownsville, young lions are roaring at the sky. Tilly and Montemauro ride over to Cypress, sit and wait again. Soon they hear the snake-thin voice of a .22 close by. The officers stiffen and look over their shoulders. There is no way to ascertain where the shots are coming from. It is time to go. Another officer, somewhere else in Brownsville, has the same idea. "Let's get the fuck out of here," a voice says.

Then a 10-13 comes over the radio like a bugle call. Tilly jacks the RMP backward, stands on the accelerator, and hurtles toward Georgia Avenue. To hell with the TV commercials; Tilly is glad there are no antilock brakes on this vehicle. He plays the skids like an old song, sliding the RMP into the turn, pumping the brakes, jamming the gas before the skid is over.

Montemauro checks cross traffic. "Good on the right. Good on the right. Good. Good. Go."

"*Slow it down,* slow it down to Georgia," Central pleads, calling the 10-13 off. Tilly eases up, but just for a second. There is another 10-13. Then there are three at one time. Each time, after Tilly, Montemauro, and half a dozen other police cars charge across Brownsville and East New York, the shooters are gone. The Housing cops are getting angry.

But over in the Unity Houses, Gary has another one of his

plans. Shots were fired from a spot in front of the building. The shooters let a few rounds go and ran inside. The scheme is to hide at the side of the building in the shadows, so when the kids fire again, Gary and the rangy, quick Sergeant Bright can pounce on them. But the officers' approach to the hiding spot leaves them in the open at the stroke of midnight. First one shot rings out, then another. There are shots coming from above, and then somebody starts blasting from a nearby parking lot. Bullets are kicking up dust around them as they skip double dutch in the dark.

To some of the cops, this is just Brownsville fireworks, but Sergeant Bright is not amused. Somebody tried to "bust a cap" on him, and the red-faced cop is stomping mad. So are the rest of the troops. Somebody is going to get hurt tonight.

As Tilly and Montemauro pull up in front of the PSA, Anti-crime is taking a skinny kid out of the car. He is in cuffs. He was not arrested with a gun, just snatched up running with a shooter, who got away. The plainclothes guy walks the kid briskly to the front door of the PSA and bangs the kid's head into the glass. "Oh, sorry. I thought the door was open," he says.

As Tilly walks past, he turns and pops the kid in the side of his head with his fist, moving at half speed. "Baby punch," he whispers sweetly. The look on his face says, "I couldn't help it."

On a Tuesday morning two weeks later, eight cars and a van assemble on Belmont Avenue for the ride through Brownsville to the site where one of Gary Lemite's warrants will be executed. The team, comprised of the borough-wide NEU SWAT-style entry team and most of the special detail officers of the PSA, will raid a small drug operation in the Breukelen Houses, a relatively quiet complex of four-story buildings in Canarsie. Commanding officer Jack Lenti rides in the third car, behind the blue NEU van with the battering ram and the automatic weapons, and the car with the roof team. "One good thing about this caravan," Lenti jokes, "is that every fucking Rasta from here to Hinsdale is gonna shit in his pants when we drive by."

Lenti is full of jokes, and his troops are ready to laugh. As the caravan moves through the "lawless" area around Riverdale and New Lots, past vacant lots and hungry dogs, smoky fires in garbage cans and piles of worn tires, a handful of frisky black kids throw sticks at an open dumpster. "Practicing their spear throwing," Lenti cracks. His remark draws guffaws and appreciative nods from his dark-haired, blue-eyed Irish driver.

For Captain Lenti, soon to be Deputy Inspector Lenti, nothing is sacred. He bemoans the "curse of the Irish," which, according to legend, leaves the sons of Hibernia with small penises. He labors to spread the blasphemy evenly. But such things just won't come out even.

Lenti's openness makes him wildly popular with almost all the men, and charms Gary Lemite, who readily forgives him his remarks. "He does it to everybody. I really don't think he means anything by it. Lenti will tell you to your face if you are full of shit." He can do that because Jack Lenti himself is not full of shit. He is proud of that. But he has no respect for explanations of crime that cite the effects of poverty, prejudice, and isolation on people of color in Brownsville. Like virtually every other cop in the PSA 2, he refuses to apply any standard but his own narrow observation and emotion-scarred afterthought to the question of the violence and debilitating anger here.

As the assault team arrives in front of the Breukelen Houses, police officers bound from the cars and sprint across the cement approach to the buildings. Women to the left and right sweep their children off their feet and flee into the lobbies to avoid the charge. A twelve-year-old girl puts both arms straight up and freezes at the sight of the rushing officers, then runs inside, with her hands still in the air.

The location is right, the timing wrong. The only occupant of the third-floor apartment, an eighteen-year-old male, is arrested and handcuffed near an open window in a rear bedroom. Four officers, including Gary and Sergeant Toney, search the premises. Gary starts in the back bedroom, where the CI said the drugs would be. The room is full of boxes and black plastic garbage bags stuffed with clothes. Gary feels carefully through the folds of each musty garment before tossing it onto a pile, which is soon chest high. He taps the legs of a small table, examines an aerosol can. His heart is sinking. There is nothing here but a few empty crack vials on the dressertop. In the kitchen, Toney is searching the refrigerator, reaching into the recesses of the freezer. The sergeant opens the stove, squats to look inside. Lenti lounges on the landing outside the apartment.

Then there is a shout from below. A beaming cop strides up the stairs toward Lenti, holding a TEC-9 machine pistol he found in the grass outside the open window. Gary, relieved, steps from the ransacked apartment and fondles the gun.

Lenti is pleased enough. "It's a good thing they found the jammy, Lemite, 'cause you woulda been walkin' for at least a month," he deadpans.

Sharron's haircut is not crisp anymore. The brown roots have flourished; the gold tips are almost gone. "I haven't had too many visitors," he says glumly. "I was tellin' people I didn't want them to come." He keeps looking down at his right hand, swollen from a recent fight. He has been in jail for two and a half months, and his speech patterns are jailhouse jumpy, counterarticulate. He rattles on, trying to confirm with every phrase that he belongs in this noisy, nasty, indoor world.

Sharron is in another barracks-style module in the C-76 building now. "I got it comfortable. I just worry 'cause I'm short," he says, referring to the fact that he is soon to be released. "And I don't want nothin' to go wrong. Know what I'm sayin'? Know what I'm sayin'? I saw the guy that took my boots. He came through. And I got my boots back. You know what I'm sayin'? I just spoke to my man on the other side when I saw him. I got the boots. My people duffed him up. You know what I'm sayin'? Like in here you know it's all about who you with. You know what I'm sayin'? My man Ralphlo, you know what I'm sayin'? Dude who hooked me up when I first got here, ran into a shamble with this guy in the bing, and then he sent word when the guy got out that we should duff him up. You know what I'm sayin'? Get in his area."

As he talks, Sharron hums with satisfaction at his successful metamorphosis to a jail-seasoned hardrock. This is yet another triumph for the actor. He has not only survived, he is back to his old tricks, building up props, grabbing some attention.

"I got soldiers in here. You know, when you got to do something, you just let the dogs loose, and the guy gets his ass all out. This guy owed me two boxes of cookies and I told him, 'After one week it's four, and after that your ass is out.' You know what I'm sayin'?"

He breaks character for a moment and offers an aside: "Livin' with fifty niggers ain't easy. I like my personality. I like the heart I have and my sensitivity. But you can't show none of that in here. It's a different world. You know what I'm sayin'? You show that, and guys look at you like . . ." Sharron makes a twisted face indicating that the one who shows sympathy will be the next one to be exploited. "They moved me and my boys. There are eight of us from Four Main. We brought our burners and our bangers with us. I got a guy shoppin' for me. I tell him to get this and if he don't have the money I tell him to call home and get it. That's the way it is." Sharron considers the possibility that he might be considered a leader and shivers at the idea. "I ain't a leader. There ain't any leaders."

Then he looks into the future. He has heard that Shawanda and her boyfriend have moved into his room. He has been doing a lot of thinking about sex, and he is going to need his room. "I just hope . . . when I get out, I'm just gonna stay in the house for a while. All I know is that Shawanda better get out of that room 'cause I'm gonna be doin' my thing, bangin' an rockin' those walls, you know what I'm sayin'?

"When I get out, I'm not even gonna go to Chantal's house. I'm gonna meet her at the train station and take her to the crib and do my thing. You know what I'm sayin'? That's it. I got to do that." He rises half out of his seat. "Vanessa wrote me a letter sayin' she wants to give herself to me. That's who I'm gonna be with."

Sharron tilts his head toward the floor as an attractive female corrections officer, assigned to keep the time for visits, passes by and points to her watch. A couple of months ago he would have smiled; now he scowls and rubs the back of his swollen hand under his left eye, over the faint scars from the time a cousin melted a toy soldier and flipped the scalding plastic bits at him.

From 7 A.M. to 1 P.M. Sharron has been attending math and English classes in a high school program. And he has decided that he might want to get his GED (high school equivalency diploma) when he gets out, instead of spending the rest of this year and probably half of the next one earning his regular high school diploma. In a GED predictor test given in the jail, he got 240, a good score. As he dreams of what it will be like when he gets out, the images foremost in his mind are girls, a job, and finding a way to get into Ms. King's school play, if she ever has another.

The only aspect of that dream that will be easy is the girls. It will be no simple task for Sharron to find even part-time employment. In fact, he does not know many people who have a job. Neither his mother nor Alleke nor Shawanda has one. John, Shawanda's boyfriend, has a job as a security guard for a building in Queens, but he makes so little money that he and Shawanda have had to move in with Gloria.

A week later, Sharron is lying on his bed, nursing a bruised shoulder, when he gets the word that he has a visitor. Things have gotten tougher for him. He has been transferred yet again, this time to South Main, which, according to Sharron, is another snitch house, a police house. When he and his boys around the way were growing up, they played a game called knockout, in which they would sit on a bench and take turns trying to knock out with a single punch the first adult man who walked by. But the guards in South Main do not fit the victim profile. "These COs are cock diesels," Sharron moans, "too big to be hittin' on kids. They be *destroyin'* guys." Here, the COs don't write people up, they kick ass. That policy actually has some advantages for Sharron. If he can avoid being brought up on charges for an incident in the barracks, he is due for release on March 7. At this point, he would rather take a beating than a loss of good time that would delay his release. Still, the beatings are no joke.

Sharron walks with a sly roll toward Sharon King, who wears tight jeans decorated with black panels on the front and white panels on the back. Teacher and student, coach and talented performer, visionary and vision meet. Their reunion should be taking place in an airport waiting room after Sharron's first successful semester in drama school, or in a midtown Manhattan café following his debut in an off-Broadway play. These two are not supposed to meet in a jail, and King knows it more than anyone. As Sharron approaches, she jumps off her seat, takes two quick steps, reaches back, and punches him in the chest with a thud that can be heard across the noisy room. Sharron spins away, more embarrassed than hurt, watching out of the corner of his eye to see who has seen the punch, calculating his response to meet the expectations of the witnesses. Apparently, no serious reaction is mandated.

"Ms. King . . ." he whines, crumpling in mock collapse to his chair.

But King is not finished. She remains standing, her finger pointed. "You robbed another black brother. You threatened and used a weapon to rob a brother, Sharron. And I am hurt." Her anger depleted, she sits, reaches across the table with both hands, and squeezes Sharron's face for a long moment.

At the end of the visit, King tells Sharron, who is delighted at the attention the sexy teacher is drawing from inmates and guards alike, "You bring your ass on home to me. You know what I mean. I don't care whether I'm in the school or at home or whatever. You'll be all right." Later, outside the jail, she insists, "Sharron *will* be all right. He will adapt to his environment. We just have to make sure he has a good environment. Clothes? Well, when it comes to clothes you might as well say, 'He's gotta have it.' But I'm not worried about Sharron."

DISCONTENT

February in Brownsville. An icy dawn eats into the night as working people hunch against the swift wind on their way to the #3 train on Livonia. The gusts are lashing around the corners of the Unity and Tilden Houses. Miraculously, five young men are still outside in front of 312 Osborne. "Homeboy" is only half accurate. These are young men, not boys, but they do stay close to home. Maybe they will never leave. The wind howls through the bullet holes in the lobby windows behind them. They rock back and forth and hug themselves, blowing hoary puffs into the grizzled dawn. How bad must it be inside if they are out here? Some are working, slinging, waiting for customers; others are fed up, homeless, unwanted, or locked out — boyfriends or sons no longer welcome.

Sergeant Priore and his driver step carefully to avoid patches of ice as they move past the shivering sentinels into the lobby of 312 Osborne. There are no bitter words or stares. The morning says all that. Priore removes a glove and pushes the elevator button. This is a domestic dispute. The rookie who answered the job has called for a boss.

On the twelfth floor, a muscular old man is standing in the hallway in his long underwear. "I'm gonna kill him," he promises. "Today's the day."

The rookie looks at Sergeant Priore and explains, "Kid's a crackhead, boss. Been harassing his father here, and the mother." Then the young cop whispers in Priore's ear, "Mother's a soft touch, gives the kid money."

"*Today.* Goddamn him," the man blusters, jiggling the handle of an ax at his side. This seventy-year-old strongman is used to settling disputes with his hands. All his life he has battled. He marched down the years fighting thugs, robbers, and the guys who disrespected his wife. In the last year he has grappled with his youngest son, and he will soon fight him again. But the man is old. The hand that holds the weapon shakes.

"You'll need an order of protection," Priore begins.

The man snarls. He hates his son. He has had a hard life, but he has lived it decently and has made it through with his wife at his side. Now his days are haunted by the grasping fingers of a ghoul with his face and name. The man cannot sit on the bench in front of his building with old friends without the whining, threatening shadow of his last-born to block the sun. No meal at home, no afternoon or nighttime sleep, is safe from the son's hateful visage. He is sucking the blood out of his elderly parents like a vampire. As Priore talks about court orders, William T. Loomis continues to curse and shake his stick at his son, who has materialized down the hall, near the elevator. Priore asks Mr. Loomis to put away his stick, but the father is enraged.

"I'll kill him now," he swears.

The cops turn to the lynx-eyed son who stands half in the elevator, half out of it. He doesn't challenge his father physically now, though it would be an epic struggle, the longshoreman against the street bum — strength on youth, hatred on need. No blows are struck tonight.

"You'll *never* be rid of me, William T. Loomis!" the son yells as the elevator doors close behind him.

It is a day later, the heart of the midnight tour. Priore's RMP picks its way past the debris on Van Sinderen Avenue, a one-lane alley between Dumont and Sutter avenues, running below the tracks that carry the L train. This is a place where huge mounds of tires, as high as a house, appear mysteriously in the dead of night, where a five-thousand-pound, six-foot-tall safe arrives one night and is gone two days later. "Jesus, what the hell happened to that?" Priore says. "You'd need a fucking winch to move that thing."

Ahead of the car, to the left, a spitting, smoking fire in an empty oil drum keeps a semicircle of wretched men warm. Priore's car makes a right-hand turn. Three men with filth-caked clothing are headed up Blake Avenue at four o'clock in the morning, slipping and staggering under the weight of a large door.

"Fuckin' mongos," Priore's driver mutters.

The men the cops call mongos are metal strippers. Often they are covered with grime from head to toe. Some are white, others Hispanic, but the dirt renders their ethnicity obscure. To the cops and everyone else, they are all just mongos. Like vultures, they perform a function. Nothing of any value lies around in Brownsville. The mongos will snap it up. More often than not, though, they take things that are not discarded, just unattended.

Priore and his driver pull over beside Hammil and his partner, who have already spotted the men. The metal door the men are transporting is painted Housing Authority green. It comes from a project; in fact, it is a front door. The mongos claim that there was a fire and that firemen told them they could take the door — a plausible story. They look more miserable than evil. But to be a police officer is to disbelieve. The cops search the men and find the tools of their breakdown trade — hammers, picks, and screwdrivers galore. Hammil is hurt.

"Didn't I let you sleep in there when it was very cold?" he asks. "Didn't I give you a break? And then you chump me off, play me like a sucker, and come back and take the door. You *steal* the door."

A police van arrives, and the door is lashed to the roof. A rookie takes the collar. Standard Housing police wisdom says that such a collar will bring a medal; "Catch someone stealing some property and you get a commendation," the officers insist. "Actually recover some Housing Authority property and you'll probably get a medal."

A few days later, at about the same time of night, on the same spot, Sergeant Priore spots a Dickensian mongo pushing a shopping cart filled with narrow strips of copper that look as if they may have come from the flashing on the roof of a project building. He steps out of his car and gestures for the mongo to stop. He speaks softly into his radio: "9510, Housing sergeant, Central. Have 9712 85 me, nonemergency. At Blake and Williams."

Priore wants Horan and Galvin, in car 9712, to check the roofs of two nearby buildings. He waits with the man in the street as a light snow tosses a slippery skim of ice on the black pavement of Blake Avenue. Galvin and Horan take the shuddering elevator to the roof. The copper flashing is intact. The same holds for the adjacent building. Horan drives up to where the boss and the mongo are standing. Priore is smiling through the snow.

There is something amazing, even annoying, about Priore's ability to maintain his good spirits in all conditions, as if he is mocking everyone around with his easy air and jaunty walk. You might even think he is a fool. That is, until you see how he treats less-than-able cops and frightened, tear-stained complainants. He does the right thing, always.

"Nothing, Sarge," Horan reports. "No flashing missing from either building. We checked. It's all there."

The mongo has at least three layers of clothing rotting off his frame, at different states of decomposition in different areas. His knees are down to the last level. His chest and hips bear their full complement of three outfits still. He is as filthy as a chimney sweep. No one has asked for his ID. Even to the regulation-oriented Priore, a mongo's name seems beside the point.

Priore is perhaps about to ask Horan to check a third building on the block. After all, the man got the copper flashing somewhere. Before he can speak, the man interrupts. "May I go now?" The voice is smooth and cultured. Better not to have spoken at all. The words bespeak good schools, parents, a home, and a dreadful fall. Worse, the words show that the man has landed in this awful spot fully conscious. It would have been much better to believe he had come from a family of mongos, maybe even a race of mongos, who liked their wretched midnight world of scraps. Better if he had been a groveling coward, a blubbering madman. As it is, he is just a man, and the truth is disconcerting, even to the unflappable Priore.

"What's your hurry? You got an appointment?" the sergeant snaps. Then, regaining his renowned composure, he laughs, waves the matter off, and heads back to his cruiser.

Riding with the sergeant is like riding up and down the strip with your father at the wheel. You see the same things as the guys in the hot cars and the convertibles, but you know you are going to miss the fun. Some cops who drive sergeants like the regularity, the lack of surprises, the proximity to the decision-making process. If you drive Priore, you have to like the stories.

He tells about the gangster Jose, the toughest guy in Brownsville. "I get the call. I'm the first on the scene and I run into the store he owned. 'Jimmy, they shot me,' Jose says. There was a hole so big in his chest you could see his spine." Priore makes a fist to signify the size of the shotgun wound. "I put him in the car. Fuckin' guy stayed alive all the way to the hospital, walked under his own power up the ramp to the emergency room at Brookdale. 'Jose, you're my hero,' I told him just before he collapsed and died."

A week later, on a Saturday in the final week of February, Priore has rotated onto the four-to-twelve shift. Jimmy Galvin is his driver for the tour. The two cops are in East New York near Cypress in the fading daylight when a call comes over for a 75th precinct sector car.

"75 Eddie. 10-10," Central begins, using a general code. "Male standing on the corner of Belmont and Euclid, possibly with a gun. Caller says he's wanted for a homicide."

Priore's car is just a block away from the spot. Even though the location is off-project, Priore picks up the radio.

"Housing sergeant. Be advised I'm 84. I'll check and advise. No further needed at this point."

When Priore and Galvin pull up, the homicide suspect is no more than a boy. "Kid was just in a fight on Sutter. Dude who got his ass kicked probably dropped the dime," explains a man on the sidewalk in a flame-red suit, with a vest and hat to match.

A police officer needs many skills. One of the most important is the ability to tell when he is getting good information. It does not matter that this man looks as if he has been airlifted from the 1970s, that he looks like a jester; Priore knows what he says is true. Maybe it is the kid's torn trousers, or the flush of childish concern on the boy's face.

The sergeant goes through the perfunctory toss, with the kid bent over the orange and blue sector car; he reaches between the kid's legs and up and down his torso. "You had a problem?" Priore chats soothingly. "Somebody pissed at you." He feels the kid's armpits and inside the waist of his beltless pants.

Suddenly a white chariot of a Jeep appears, and Chris Moore gets out. His 180-pound body is stuffed into tight blue jeans and a white shirt. His waxy brown skin sags a bit today. He wears no jacket and sports half a dozen gold chains around his thick neck. Moore takes a few wincing steps in his pointy-toed cowboy boots and stops ten feet from Priore. Somehow, this afternoon the drug dealer appears way past his prime and at the apex of his life at the very same moment. He looks smart, evil.

Without looking up, Priore greets him as sweetly as he would greet his neighbors in Belmore, Long Island.

"How ya doin', Chris?"

"Hi, Jim. Wha's up?" Moore answers with similar equanimity.

"Nothin'." Priore won't extend himself to explain the trivial nature of the operation. Jim Priore, who likes to tell stories, has also mastered silence.

Moore made his early money selling marijuana. He survived the A Team and the police. He bought buildings and businesses like the lingerie shop on the corner. But in recent years he has ventured into the crack trade. "Too legit to quit," he likes to say.

The guy in the red costume, eager to do something to impress Moore, shuffles and reshuffles his mental deck and comes up with a stupid idea.

"You want me to call somebody? Chris?" The man reaches inside his polyester jacket and repeats the question. Moore does not react.

There is no need to call anyone, certainly no need to emphasize to the police officers that this ragamuffin in new sneakers is a Chris Moore operative, worth a phone call to a lawyer. It is time to be quiet and still. The man in red is neither. He thrusts his hand in his jacket pocket again, as if to reach for a quarter.

Galvin is a funny guy, but he is in a bad mood. He does not have Priore's appreciation of the picaresque, does not like the way the red-suited dude is digging in his jacket. *Who keeps quarters in the inside pocket of his suit jacket?* Galvin is thinking as he moves his hand slowly to his .38.

"I don't know about you, Jimmy," he says, as the cops drive off a moment later. "If anybody was going to make a call, it was going to be to the morgue, 'cause if fucking Superfly stuck his hand in his pocket one more time, I was gonna cap him." Priore chuckles.

A woman in a third-floor apartment in the Tilden Houses is not laughing. It's another midnight tour later in the week.

"This is my castle," she says to Hammil and his partner, "my welfare hotel. I want him out." The cops mill around the apartment. "He's crazy anyway. Held a gun on me. He has a fatal attraction, and I want him arrested."

The boyfriend stands in the hallway, glaring dangerously. The cops refuse to arrest him. Instead, they escort him from the building. Once again it is icy in Brownsville. Tilden, Langston Hughes, Unity, Howard, and Pink are quiet and warm. Above, some windows are open. Public housing has its nightmares, but the city sends up the heat; you can count on it, and little else. The cops watch as the expelled boyfriend stalks down the wind-swept street.

"He'll be back," Hammil's partner predicts.

It's too early in the shift for a collar like this to bring any overtime. When the man comes back later in the night, he will leave in cuffs. "Just like Paul Masson says," Hammil comments as the two move toward the warmth of their RMP, "make no arrest before its time."

But Gary is always looking for a collar. An hour later, half a mile away, he spots what looks like a mongo crouched near the rolled-down gate of Rony and Zaid Shoman's ramshackle supermarket, hard by the Van Dyke Houses.

Gary pulls over. The young man, a mongo with a green plastic bag full of garbage, is caked with grime. Gary orders him to put his hands up on a fence and dumps the contents of the bag on the street. Isn't it hard enough to be filthy and cold and homeless, with no apartment and no suitcase, without being rousted by a grumpy, collar-crazed cop?

"What's in the bag?"

"Stuff I got from the garbage."

Lo, there is a shotgun in the bag and an armful of boxes of drugstore remedies, cough suppressants and aspirin. "You *found* the shotgun in the garbage?" Gary exclaims. "You found these drugs in the garbage?" The man is silent. "Where do you live?"

"I live right up there." He points to a window high above, in the Van Dyke Houses.

Gary cuffs the man up and puts him in the car, lifting his own nose out the window into the stiff cold as the sickening pungent smell of an unwashed human being fills the car.

Back in the cell area behind the front desk, where the grimy man is locked, Gary goes about recording the inventory of the recovered goods. The medications are perishable, so they cannot be vouchered. They must be photographed and returned to the owner, so Gary arranges the boxes of cold remedies in an elaborate display before he snaps a Polaroid of them. His partner is on the phone to the Palestinian store owners.

"Mr. Shoman? This is the Housing police on Sutter Avenue. Sorry to wake you. Our records show you're the owner of the food store on Powell and Sutter. There's been a burglary, and we'd like you to come down to identify some property we believe was stolen from your place."

Sleepy-eyed and disheveled, Rony and Zaid arrive quickly from their home in nearby Bensonhurst. Rony, thirty-four, the shorter and fuller-faced of the two, is missing two teeth. Nevertheless, he sports a wry smile. He waves off questions about the shotgun.

"Yes, you keep. Just keep."

The brothers sit on the plastic chairs in the front room and wait to get a chance to talk to the burglar. They pay $3,000 a month rent for their store, which has been robbed six times in the past two months, and they are determined to get to the bottom of the break-ins.

"Three times they come in the gate. We fix. Three times they come in the roof," Rony says. "They don't have guts to come in the day."

"Their mother teach them steal," thirty-one-year-old Zaid says.

"No." Rony won't have it. He waves the comment off. Rony's life is invested in the people of Brownsville. The Shoman brothers had a store in San Francisco. Then they moved to New York and bought a store on Ralph Avenue, in Bedford-Stuyvesant. Later they expanded to the small supermarket on Powell and Sutter. Their families live together in a two-family house.

"Six years, don't buy house. Still rent," Rony says. "Work. Don't care if eight days, twelve hours a day. Month to month." He considers for a moment the people from Van Dyke who frequent his store. "If good customer's funeral? We can't go? So send flowers. Baby? Pampers? Fifteen dollars? Take it." Rony tosses his hand to emphasize that money is not the most important thing to him. "Need money, two dollars to go to work, give."

"Six, seven steal." Zaid flattens his hand out in front of him at the height of a small child.

Rony understands more. "First six months, we fight every day. They talk from far away. They will 'kill' us, 'shoot' us. If steal a bag of chips, we fight. We no afraid. We chase in apartment and fight. Karate. A big guy, he steal meat. I catch him in parking and give him karate. But now . . ." He opens both hands and spreads his arms. "We see them more than family. They *are* our family."

Business has been bad. Besides the break-ins, there is the recession and the crack epidemic. "Some week we don't take penny out of store. We used to have five or six customers, spend three or four hundred dollars a month. Now, one hundred dollars. Things change since crack."

Their store sits at the foot of the small bridge that separates Brownsville from East New York. On the other side of the bridge is a grim flight of stairs that look as if they lead to a gallows. Actually, the steps lead to a green wooden enclosure that houses the token booth for the poorly lit, ultra-dangerous Sutter Avenue stop on the L line. Next door to the supermarket is a check-cashing place and a greasy auto body shop.

Gary, preoccupied with the arrangement and inventory of the stolen property, does not notice as Rony receives a nod from an absentminded officer at the front desk and slides into the inner sanctum of the processing and holding cell area. Rony inches closer and closer to the cell where the sleeping figure of the man who robbed his store lies. He peers into the tiny cell and inspects the ragged man. His eyes glow.

"Frank, it's you," he hisses in triumph. "Frank, you bastard, you." The man stirs, blinks, looks up at Rony, but does not speak. Rony has not sneaked into the off-limits cell area just to curse the man who broke into his store. "Frank. Who took the scale?" In one recent break-in, thieves took the cash register. Now the Shoman brothers hide the remaining cash register and the meat slicer when they close the place at night. In another raid, somebody made off with the meat scale. Rony wants that scale back.

"Who took the scale, Frank?" he whispers again. "*Who* took the scale? I know your mother, Frank. I charge your mother. I don't have to charge you. I *clean* you good, Frank. I *clean* you. I fix you up. I break you hands."

Rony's strange threats hit home. Frank lifts his head and whispers, "The guy who owns the meat store on Belmont has it."

Rony snorts, steps away to think for a moment, and stalks out of the room to the bench, where he confers with Zaid over strategy to recover the scale.

The next day, Rony and Zaid are hard at work in the store. Rony banters with the customers. "Wha's happen?" He nods at a young mother holding twin five-year-old girls by the hand. The girls are gleeful on this trip to the store. They dance as much as they can, cackling about ice cream and candy. A few minutes later, as they are led from the store, they are a study in sadness. Each head droops in response to a judgment against which there is no appeal. Their mother pushes no shopping cart heaped with essentials and treats. In fact, none of the people who have been in the store this morning have walked out with large grocery bags. The rail-thin mother carries only a plastic bag, the cutout grip of which is wrapped around her wrist as she tugs her daughters home. Visible through the milky white plastic of the bag is a green pack of cigarettes and a brown forty-ounce bottle of malt liquor.

"TWO TEARS IN A BUCKET"

February 26 is a special day at Thomas Jefferson High School. There have been a lot of special days at Jeff in the last few years, since Beck took over, and nothing less than celebrity status since the Daryl Sharpe killing in November. This week, as a public relations maneuver, Mayor David Dinkins and his administration have chosen to set up shop at Borough Hall in downtown Brooklyn, and this morning the mayor is on his way down Atlantic Avenue to visit Jefferson and address the students. At 8:30 A.M. there are twenty police officers waiting for His Honor outside the school, and many more inside. Blue uniforms are everywhere. The regular unarmed Jefferson security staff has been augmented to twenty-three for the day. At the front door there is a metal detector, manned by six specially trained security guards sent over by the board of education.

Things have been looking up at Jeff in the past few weeks. Beck's relentless sweeps have been paying off. But the principal herself has been having health problems. Early in the month she felt sharp chest pains. After a stay in the hospital and innumerable tests, the doctors proclaimed her ailment harmless angina. She hurried back to East New York. She did not want to lose momentum.

Ironically, the shooting has opened up some funding sources, given Beck a pulpit from which to pitch her dream of building a dormitory for her students. She has more security now. Even on regular days there are security guards all over the school, and a bank of TV monitors in the second-floor security office covers

318

every hallway. And as a result of the shooting, Beck has been permitted by the board of education to banish even more Smurfs. She understood the posses. "Their mothers aren't glad to see them. Their teachers aren't glad they came to school. The only smile they see all day is the one they get from their gangster friends." But she also knew what she could not handle; they had to go.

Over on Sutter Avenue, Gary Lemite is sucking down a large bottle of tea-flavored Snapple, getting ready to hit the streets for an eight-to-four shift. Khalil Sumpter is already awake, donning his brown jeans jacket, when his mother comes into his room to wake him up for school. In an unprecedented display of filial concern, he prepares to walk his mother to the train station on her way to work. Tucked in the waist of his pants is a six-shot, stainless steel Smith and Wesson Model 64MP .38 revolver. The thirty-four-ounce gun has been modified to include a thumb spur for rapid firing. It is exactly like the weapon Gary has in his black holster. In fact, Gary is carrying two such guns on his waist, minus the thumb spurs, which are against police regulations. As Khalil kisses his mother on the cheek at the train station and heads up Pennsylvania Avenue, Gary finishes his drink, tosses it in the back of the unmarked gray car, and rolls onto the streets of Brownsville.

Khalil is carrying the gun, and has walked his mother to the train, because of the running feud he has been having with a couple of guys from the Linden Houses, Tyrone Sinkler and his slim buddy, LoLife Ian Moore, E-lo. Sinkler still believes that Khalil was responsible for the year he spent in Spofford. There have been threats and fights. Khalil is not as big as the 220-pound Sinkler, and has not fared well in the bouts. Two days ago somebody pegged a volley of shots at him outside the Linden Houses, and he is sure it was Sinkler and Moore. Worse, he has heard that Sinkler is threatening to shoot his mother.

Wired and worried, Khalil Sumpter, with his brown "baby fade" and matching jeans jacket, approaches Jefferson High School, checks the mob of police at the front door, and circles around to an unguarded side entrance. At 8:40 A.M. he meets his friend Dupree, climbs quickly to the second floor, and stands at the head of the stairs. Five minutes before the end of homeroom, the corridor is full of latecomers. At the opposite end of the hall are his two enemies and two of their friends. Indeed, the crew had been scouring the school for twenty minutes, looking for Khalil. The two sides eye each other, and Khalil strides forward.

Khalil Sumpter. This is the kid Marvin described in the back of the basketball team bus. *This* is "Dupree's man," the one who asked, "Who wants it?"

This time, Khalil makes no threats. He draws, fires two shots. The first blasts Tyrone Sinkler in the head, the second tears through Ian Moore's chest. Khalil pivots and bounds down the stairs. He flees the school, but two blocks away an unarmed school security guy throws him against a car. He does not fight back.

Cortez Sutton is studying a history book in an empty room on the fifth floor. He looks up to see people sprinting in the hall. Sharon King is in the guidance center on the first floor, using nail polish to fix a run in her stockings, when a student runs by screaming about shots on the second floor. She starts grabbing kids and shoving them toward the open door of the auditorium, because she thinks that whoever is shooting might be coming down to the first floor.

Gary Lemite is on Blake, just a block away, when he gets the call: "Shots fired in Thomas Jefferson High School." He sweeps around the corner, jams his Grand Fury at an angle to the curb on busy Pennsylvania Avenue, bursts in the front door, and takes the side stairs two at a time. There are two bodies on the floor. Officer Price is giving mouth-to-mouth to Sinkler. Ms. Kim Pierre, a teacher, is asking over and over again, "You need relief? You need relief?" Price, possessed, never looks up from his task. Five compressions, a breath. Five compressions, another breath.

A few feet away, a Housing detective named Romanelli is performing mouth-to-mouth resuscitation on Ian Moore. Gary Lemite, who would run at a gun spitting red flames a foot and a half out of the barrel, charge straight at bullets promising paralysis and death, stands aside. He is not called on to do anything valorous here. If he were, he would hesitate. There is blood everywhere. Gary says later, "I don't know . . . I don't think I was ready to do that mouth-to-mouth. Maybe in another environment. These are hard kids . . . you never know."

Price and the Emergency Medical Service technicians sprint out the front door beside Sinkler's stretcher. Sinkler's neck is swathed in bandages; a green bookbag is strapped across his thighs. Moore's stretcher is right behind.

Kids lean far out the windows of the upper floors as the bodies are trundled out the front door. Cortez, who stands in the crowd of students peering out the second-floor window, sees the orange jacket on the second gurney and suspects that his friend has been shot.

Mayor Dinkins goes onstage anyway. He steps up to the microphone in a windbreaker instead of a suit jacket, as if to send the message that he is a man of action. Above him, hanging on the wall of the Jefferson auditorium, is a banner bearing the likeness of Martin Luther King, Jr., and the inscription THE CHOICE TODAY IS NOT BETWEEN VIOLENCE AND NONVIO- LENCE. IT IS BETWEEN VIOLENCE OR NONEXISTENCE. To Dink- ins's left is a large potted plant; behind him on metal folding chairs sit School Chancellor Joseph Fernandez and Carol Beck.

"If someone steps on your foot or disrespects you in some fashion," Dinkins pleads, "and you feel compelled to show your manhood or your womanhood, think again. I don't know what anger broke out in this young person to cause him to fire point- blank at two people, knowing that it would take lives. What I do know is that there is a better way. If you don't have a gun, you're not going to use a gun." Then the mayor asks the stu- dents to do something braver than he understands. He suggests that whenever they see or hear of anyone with a gun, they turn that person in to the authorities. Before hurrying over to his temporary headquarters in Borough Hall, the well-meaning mayor delivers a line straight out of *Mad* magazine: he advises the students to try counting to 10 or 110 the next time they get angry.

"I play a high-risk game," Carol Beck is fond of saying. The task of telling an auditorium full of students that two more of their number have been shot dead is daunting. But Beck is a descendant of a line of women accustomed to facing such mo- ments on this country's soil. When she makes the announce- ment, there is a whoosh of breath, a groan, and silence. Some students cry. Others appear unmoved. They have been watching bodies pile up since they were old enough to see out the windows of their homes. Seventy-five Jefferson students have died violently in the past four years. In the same period, many more have been injured on the school grounds. These are children who have grown to adolescence watching guns go off on their TV screens and in their hallways. The demented siren of the sector cars and the EMS buses has been their lullaby. Who can expect them to cry now?

The next day, Beck finds herself once again busy at damage control. Sandra Feldman, the president of the teachers' union, has been demanding that Jefferson be closed. Parents have lined up to transfer their kids. Like a weary fighter, Beck is stuck in a corner, taking punches. It seems as if she has lost the battle for Thomas Jefferson High School. Just as she feared all along, the Smurfs did her in. Jason Bentley, the shooter in the Daryl Sharpe killing, was fourteen years old. Sumpter, Moore, and Sinkler were all freshmen or sophomores.

The press outside is thirty strong, looking for sound bites. News trucks with their transmitters erect to the sky are lined up on Pennsylvania Avenue. But why put the killing in Thomas Jefferson on the front page when kids are killed every day here? Last night a fourteen-year-old was murdered in the Pink Houses by some Cypress guys, probably members of the new A Team. But the press is here to trumpet the degradation of Thomas Jefferson High School. There won't be a word written about how none of this would have happened if Ms. King had been able to send Khalil Sumpter someplace where he would have gotten help, maybe even a real future.

On the front steps of the school, Sharon King turns her back on the reporters, hugs a student, and says of Khalil, "I knew, I knew, but I just thought I had more time."

Inside, Beck is back onstage, talking to the faculty and students. She is wearing a blue suit, with a gold African Kente scarf draped over her shoulders, and her sneakers. The chest pains are gone for now. She is getting good at this kind of oratory.

"If you have heard the drums," she thunders, "I have heard the drums. They are talking of closing this school, of closing *your* school. But this school will stay open. I want to say to you that you have it in your power to stop this. Just like you can make something happen, you can make it not happen. *You* made gold earrings and gold chains happen. You did it. And now they are doing it all over the world. You can do it. We have to set the rules. Can we do it?" But the center cannot hold. Carol Beck is standing alone on the stage of the overflowing auditorium.

King, in black-and-white bell-bottom pants and a 1970s-style puffed cap, is now drifting up and down the aisles. Despite the gravity of Beck's message, the auditorium is buzzing, not with dismay or even news but with the trivialities of youth. Giggles, urgent nothings, are flung across the rows. Now Beck is trying to explain the revised schedule for the day, but she is losing her audience. The principal is under tremendous pressure. Since 7 A.M. she has been bolstering her sagging staff and cajoling parents to leave their children in Jefferson. (Ultimately, only three parents insist on the transfer.) The United Federation of Teachers is nipping at her heels; a delegation is wandering the hallways at this very moment. They are not saying as much, but the UFT representatives cannot figure Jeff out. There is no graffiti; the place does not look at all like a hellhole. But a hellhole it must be, they figure, so they keep snooping, looking for cracks.

Beck is besieged, and at this moment she is not getting what every teacher needs from her students — quiet. To speak in the students' defense, Beck has made a rare tactical error. It is unreasonable to think that anyone, even a wired Carol Beck, can hold the rapt attention of eighteen hundred teenagers with logistics, scheduling. What do they care if there is a little chaos? Beck's message simply is not urgent enough; she does not slip it in fast enough. The principal stands contemplating the disturbing haze of chatter. Then a fountain of laughter bursts from the mouth of the student body.

"I won't embarrass you. I would never embarrass you. But you are embarrassing *me*. You are embarrassing me!" Beck shouts. Like all good teachers, she rarely raises her voice. There is quiet. Then she makes another mistake. After playing her volume card to win silence, she sends a horde of young girls to their lockers, a necessary but unfortunate maneuver. More noise. More loud laughter. "We have visitors," Beck says. The students do not give a damn what the visitors see or believe. The visitors are Beck's problem.

There is a commotion down at the left. Cortez Sutton has

been reading a newspaper about the shooting of his buddy. In front of him, a guy he does not know asks to look at the paper.

"No," Cortez says flatly. He is not in the mood for the curious protocols that mark interpersonal relations among young men in Brownsville. He gives no deferential dip of the head, excuse, or softening lingo.

"Yo, money, your paper ain't all that. They gonna be readin' about you tomorrow," the other kid says, maybe looking for a little rep on this day of big reps.

Cortez has been controlling himself all term, letting all kinds of possible trouble slip by. Not today. Ian Moore was his real friend. The two teenagers lunge at each other. Across the room, Jude, slim as a bullwhip, his hood pulled up and his dark glasses clamped on, spots the action and bounds to Cortez's defense.

In a minute, a horde of security guards has broken up the fight. Order is restored. More security guards drift down the aisles, watching.

Beck goes berserk. "I am not a lion tamer," she rails. "I am an educator. Talk about *disrespect*. You don't know what disrespect is. Real disrespect is so subtle that when you see it you won't even know what it is. The people with the power will do it to you with a smile."

She is wailing for a generation of African American children whose lives are going grotesquely wrong. She knows what they know and what they do not know, how they think. Their minds are full of dreams their country has given them little chance to fulfill. Their hearts are beating for designer clothing. Their nervous systems are programmed for daily jolts of excitement and cheap respect. They are at once victims, dangerous fools, and glorious possibilities. Beck is raging for their souls.

"Power. You think a mean face brings you power? I'm black — I know all about that. That's not power. The guy who pulled the bullets, I mean the guy who pulled the trigger, that wasn't about power. The people who really have power do it with a smile." Then Beck gets personal. It is always personal with her, the students know. They have known that since the day she showed up.

"I refuse to be defined by you. I don't give you the permission to define me. I refuse to let you define our community. You haven't got the right to have rage. You haven't earned the right. All over the country, they are thinking of you as out of control."

Beck is breathing hard. The worn, venerable auditorium, with its Corinthian columns and neoclassical details, once home to Danny Kaye and Shelley Winters, is silent, save for the crackle and hiss of security walkie-talkies. A small-boned white woman teacher with black hair whispers to a colleague, "Somebody better get her off that stage before she collapses." But Beck goes on. Her children are lost, and she wants them back.

"You aren't entertainers, you are students, and you are supposed to look bright-eyed and bushy-tailed, with pens and pencils and bookbags. Education is your last hope. And whether you know it or not, this woman standing on this stage may be your last hope. When I throw up my hands and walk away, you're finished. But I am not going to do that. The teachers and community leaders and clergymen — we are not going to allow this to happen."

Beck is on the stage by herself, but she isn't playing this hand alone. She calls Bashim Inman, who strides up on the stage.

"What are you thinking?" he asks the student body. "What are you going to do? What are you going to do?" He asks over and over again, to titters and shouts. He keeps up his challenge. "What are you going to do? I'm askin' you. You know what I'm sayin', 'cause I'm scared. You know what I'm sayin'? 'Cause that could have been me on the ground on the second floor. You know what I'm sayin'? You know what I'm sayin'?"

"You know what I'm sayin'" is the mumbled catchphrase of the Ville. It is meant to indicate that the speaker is not a person who considers things carefully or takes care to explain, that he is too primed for immediate action for the intricacies of communication.

As big as a kodiak bear, Bashim is the perfect spokesman. He glows with intelligence, promise, and Brownsville rough. He never does get to the rest of his speech. He just keeps asking what the students intend to do. He leaves the stage with the words, "This, this here, has *got* to stop. You know what I'm sayin'?"

And then Sonny Carson steps up. Opportunist, activist, convicted kidnapper, and one-time gang leader, he wears a black fez with golden studs, like some kind of wizard, and carries a walking stick. Beck has taken some chances calling in both Carson and the band of bow-tied Muslims who are sitting downstage right. But Carson keeps the antiwhite rhetoric down and holds the interest of the students.

"The brothers got to stick together, 'cause you don't understand. It's all about getting rid of you." Carson calls the school's young men up on the stage. The boys flow forward and pack themselves tightly on the wide expanse. Then Carson tells the girls to applaud the boys. When the boys sit down, he refers to the people outside, the press, "who don't want us to succeed." He says all the right things this day. He calls for a "black parents' night" in support of the school. Beck quickly steps up and reminds everyone that there are Hispanic and Asian students and that the night should best be called "parents' night."

Beck is nervous. One antiwhite or anti-Semitic word and the heat will go higher than even she can stand. She is gambling, just like she did five months ago when she brought in the Reverend Al Sharpton and the Reverend Herbert Daughtry after the Sharpe shooting. She can get away with such maneuvers because both her black and her white faculty trust her deeply. But she also knows that she needs every bit of community support to turn back the efforts of the teachers' union to shut Jefferson down.

Conrad Muhammad, a Nation of Islam minister, is up next. He is flanked by meticulously attired aides, who assume their traditional secret service agent stance, staring off into space. "Salaam aleikum," he begins. The students repeat the phrase; they are getting some kind of civic education this morning. One cannot help but wonder how things would be if this level of urgency were achieved every day at school, if the people in the country, the city, cared as much and did as much for the students.

"The Honorable Louis Farrakhan greets you and sends his best wishes in this difficult time. He understands who you are, even though you don't. There are people outside," Muhammad says, referring to the press, "not the *brother* man but the *other* man. You are not naughty by nature," a play on the name of the popular rap group. "You are divine by nature. But the *other* man keeps taking away your history. You are playing into the hands of the man who would like to see every brother in this room dead. You have *no reason* to kill each other, because you are allies in the struggle."

*

Ian Moore, E-lo, is laid out in a shirt by Polo, eulogized by a community leader, the Reverend Johnny Ray Youngblood, from St. Paul Community Baptist Church in East New York. Bill Cosby comes to the funeral and embraces Carol Beck. The national spotlight plays off the brick walls of Jefferson. James Brown arrives, declaring himself the "godfather of Thomas Jefferson High School." Even the campaigning Bill Clinton appears for a photo opportunity on the front steps of Jefferson. The students are quiet and confused, their self-image flipping like the picture on an MTV video. Are they blessed or cursed, celebrities or throwaways?

"I grew up in St. Louis, and when I lived there as a young girl a long time ago I had a friend." Beck is addressing the modest turnout of seventy-five parents and visitors at Parents' Night. "When this friend saw me on the news, he thought I needed help, and so he packed his bags and headed out here to watch my back. I'd like you to meet my friend." From the rear of the auditorium, a lanky gray-haired gentleman unfolds and gestures shyly. "Everybody has got to help in this," Beck says, "because I'm tired."

There is more talk from a succession of speakers about stopping the proliferation of guns and violence. The kind of kids on hand, like Tumbo and Nick, lingering near the back door of the auditorium, don't need to hear this. Nick is on hand because he rides home with Beck and she has been here since school ended at three o'clock. Tumbo just likes to spend time around the high school.

Afterward, in the lobby, Beck is surrounded by a group of well-wishers, "My bodyguards," she gushes. The immaculate Muslims proselytize discreetly, handing out fliers in the lobby to the earnest parents, who linger with their teenagers and toddlers.

"They have to make guns unacceptable, the way they used to be," a man with a transit worker's patch argues. "They spent the last thirty years glamorizing guns, and now it's their responsibility to turn it around. You think they can't do it, but they can. The media put its mind to it and they drove cigarette smoking right out of style. If they want to, they can do the same with guns."

Soon the meeting breaks up. It is a warm night with a peaceful mist of rain. As the parents drift back to Unity, Linden, and Brownsville Houses, with their teenagers and toddlers, Gary Lemite is out on Blake Avenue again, sitting in his car while his partner, Willie Arroyo, is on the street writing a ticket for a double-parked car.

"These guys are wearing their pants so low that they actually have to hold them up. Look at that." Gary points to a fifteen-year-old with baggy trousers halfway down his plaid boxer shorts, clinging precariously to his buttocks. The boy holds his pants with his right hand and an umbrella with his left.

An exotic sports car zips by, and Gary straightens up in his seat. Then comes a red Range Rover. "You know how much that car costs? Thirty thousand." Gary pushes a puff of air through his front teeth. Arroyo, back in the vehicle now, repeats the noise. Conventional police wisdom says that many people are manipulating the system while police officers are working hard for everything they get. The officers wear American flag pins on their uniforms, but they cannot seem to make up their minds whether America is the greatest country in the world or one big rip-off.

"It isn't the first warm night like this that gets bad," Arroyo observes. "It's the second warm night. I noticed that."

The radio refutes his theory. Twenty minutes after the parents' meeting is over, someone is sporting a sawed-off shotgun on Mother Gaston Avenue.

"Can I get a scrip on that man with a shotgun, Central?" Gary asks.

"That is one male black, heavyset, about seventeen years of age, with a striped, hooded sweatshirt, in possession of a sawed-off shotgun."

Arroyo aims the car toward Mother Gaston and Blake. Gary is checking cross streets, computing routes of escape. As they pull in in front of the Unity Houses, a sector car with Madden and Finn in it noses to a stop in front of them, and the two second-year guys leap out. Standing there on the sidewalk is a stocky young man with a telltale striped, hooded sweatshirt.

The kid is guilty of at least three big mistakes, not counting carrying a shotgun with a banana clip through the projects on Gary's tour. First, he has showed the gun to somebody who just doesn't like him or made somebody angry enough to call the police. Second, when he starts to run, he heads straight across the area known as "the circle," a hundred-yard open space between the project buildings, instead of fleeing inside, where he might find an open door or what the cops call a "bad Samaritan" to let him in. Third, and probably most damning, he is obese. As every Housing cop knows, the fat guys are the ones who get caught, because they run slowly. Madden gains on the youth, with Finn right behind, and Lemite, who got a bad jump out of the van, is behind him. The speedy Arroyo had the worst start of all, but he won the medal for most athletic in his police academy graduating class, and he is coming like a shot on the left. Three of the four cops have their guns drawn. Lemite keeps his holstered. A cluster of people stand blithely on the walkway entrance as the pistols come their way.

"Get down. Get down!" Gary screams.

On the service road that leads to the circle are two rows of parked cars. A woman with a baby wrapped in blue blankets ducks low behind a car. On the grass close to the brick buildings, shadowy figures run with the officers to watch the spectacle. Above, words are flung from windows. "He dropped it. He dropped it!" The woman shouting from above is not assisting the police in their recovery of the gun. She is trying to keep them from shooting the fleeing boy.

Almost through the circle, just before the road beyond, the fat kid falls, and Madden runs up to him. Afraid that the kid is about to roll and fire the shotgun, he has his finger on his trigger. But the kid pops the gun off his hip where he carried it under his sweatshirt, lets it drop, scrambles to his feet, and lunges away, with Madden a stride behind. The kid leans too far, gets ahead of himself, and falls again, this time flat on his face a foot from the wheels of a speeding white Buick. Madden kneels on his back and cuffs him.

Twenty feet away, Finn scoops up a curved banana clip from the ground with some twenty rounds in it. A 75th car squeals to a stop, and a six-foot-four black cop leaps to the asphalt, runs up, and kicks the cuffed kid hard in the ribs. Then he promenades back to his police car with his chest puffed out, gets in, and his partner pulls away.

The small crowd on hand is incensed. A Hispanic woman who may be the boy's mother screams, "Stop! We aren't violent people. Don't hurt him."

Finn can't take the contradictions. "Not violent? What's

this?" He holds up the banana clip. "What's this?" he demands again.

"Don't hurt him," the woman wails. An ancient grandmother, her wizened face wrapped in a dark scarf, is now by the woman's side, screaming at the police. "Don't you touch him. I beg to you. Don't."

A 75 cop with an eerie golden glow to his cheeks, as if he just stepped out of a tanning salon, is also on hand, and in no mood for dialogue or community unrest. He advances with his nightstick on the growing crowd of project residents, who have seen too many ass kickings to obey the orders to disperse. The people back up slowly and curse.

"Fuck the police. You think you all the cavalry, but the Indians was right," a man says. "I'm twenty-three years old. Don't start shit. You know how *we* get."

The prisoner is cuffed and taken off to the precinct. Arroyo circles back to get the shotgun. Just in time — a neighborhood kid is bending over to pick it up when Arroyo points his pistol.

"Don't even *think* about it. Step off," he commands. The kid walks backward into the shadows, his eyes riveted on the officer's .38 as Arroyo grabs the rifle.

"I LIKE THE WAY I AM"

A guy on the other side of the 6 Building just got banged on the head by some of Sharron's boys, but Sharron is lying in his bunk reading. He is weeks from his release and he is praying not to be drawn into the action now. Ms. King brought him some books and he has read *The Autobiography of Malcolm X, Manchild in the Promised Land,* and *A Streetcar Named Desire.* It is becoming more and more evident to the others in the building that despite Sharron's ability to act like one of the guys, he is different. When he uses a term they haven't heard or a word with a couple of extra syllables, they stiffen, as if the language is a slap at them. "C'mon, Sha, why don't you say it without all that?"

Sharron feels sorry for the guys around him. Most of them quit school in the tenth grade and have been in jail most of the time since. There is one other guy, Earl, who is thoughtful, "slick on the cap." In the school sessions, as five out of the ten guys in the class lay their heads on the desk and sleep, Earl comes up with answers quicker than Sharron. The two find furtive moments to exchange thoughts that would not be appreciated by the others.

Sharron has been thinking about his future. Lying on his bunk for hours, just thinking. But his thoughts are disordered. He sees himself getting out and taking Vanessa to his bedroom. Vanessa is definitely the one. She goes to school, has a job, and she has sworn to give herself to him. Sharron is sure of nothing more than that he will do his thing on his gray day bed next to the sign saying, "What are your suggestions? We'd like to know."

Sharron still follows the exhortation "Don't give up on your dreams," but the truth is, he does not know what the dreams are anymore. And he has no real plan to make any part of his future turn out right. Instead, he muses about writing songs and singing, and doing the right thing when he gets out of jail, which means heading off to school and not being arrested. There is nothing whatsoever in his thoughts that involves giving up his minimum standards of dress to insure that he will never get in trouble again. He does not regret boosting, and believes in his heart that he will once again reap a harvest from the Manhattan department stores.

The guys in the mod are onto Sharron big-time. "You don't belong in here, Sha," they say right out. Even the cock-diesel guards know that something is up with him. They rarely see anyone reading a book or writing. Sharron has penned scores of letters to Vanessa and a handful of notes to other girls he has met in the borough of Brooklyn. He knows full well the trouble that can come from being different in jail, but he has not been able to subdue his personality. "I like the way I am," he writes to Vanessa. Of course, he has been singing. That and the picture of a bare-chested Marlon Brando on the cover of *A Streetcar Named Desire* have raised some questions among the gangsters about Sharron's masculinity. It's a good thing his time is short. Real short.

Unlike Sharron these days, Gary is not interested in blending into the crowd. He looks like exactly what he is, a plainclothes police officer. He laces up his black workboots, puts his two-inch .38 Ruger five-shot backup gun inside his waistband, and pulls on his black-and-white PSA 2 T-shirt. He tucks the badge he keeps on a chain around his neck inside his shirt, and pulls on his black hooded sweatshirt. He checks himself in the mirror. The transition to the Brownsville look would not be hard to achieve: a pair of Timberland boots instead of the glossy military looking footgear he wears and a Triple Fat Goose down coat would have worked just fine. The gaudy eight-ball jackets are already out, in favor of toggle coats, canvas car coats with corduroy collars. It would be easy to look like a local, and by extension logical to the police, a perp. By way of disguise, Gary sometimes dons a short brown jacket he borrows from his brother-in-law, a parcel post driver. But for the most part he wants to look like a cop, because despite the protestations of the police that they are the endangered and embattled minority, the cop look is one of the safest styles of all in the Ville.

"If I walk up on a set, the spot where they're sellin' crack or whatever, and I look like just another guy, who knows what could happen," Gary says. "The dealers I'm walking up on could think that I am there to rip them off, so they start shooting. Or they could be down to rip me off because they figure I'm new in the area." The police look cuts down on the element of surprise, but there are more important things, even to Gary Lemite, than the element of surprise.

Tony Logan is Gary's new partner; it is the first time Gary has had a black partner. Logan is a huge man with a big regard for himself. At six-four and 235 muscled pounds, he gets automatic props from some perps. Despite the respect he has been garnering, though, he is raw when it comes to the street. And the street is where he and Gary are headed.

It is dusk in the "lawless" section over near Riverdale and New Lots. From the Howard Houses on the western end of Brownsville to the sprawling Cypress Hills complex on the eastern border of East New York, the brick project complexes simply do not look bad. But this corner of East New York, just east of the ravine that separates Brownsville and East New York, fenced by the intersecting elevated #3 and L lines, looks exactly as bad as it is.

As the sun dips below the roofs of the Brownsville Houses in the distance, the rusting iron stanchions of the train tracks look like prison camp watchtowers, throwing melancholy shadows over the lots of garbage and bullet-scarred derelict cars. On a nearby street, a gauntlet of dreadlocked men lean toward passing cars, whispering about "blunts," joints of marijuana, and "sens," or sensamilla, the potent form of the drug. Sometimes the 75, responsible for the area, throws a couple of blank-faced rookies onto a corner in the area, and they try their best to mind their own business. But mostly NYPD stays out of here.

Gary and his hulking new partner are in the unmarked van on their way to dinner at Mr. W's, on Flatlands Avenue in Canarsie. Gary looks at the lawless area and licks his lips, but he has to stay away. This is off-project.

333

Just then, Logan pulls the van to a slow stop. "I think I just saw two guys with guns," he says.

Sure enough, just forty feet behind the van is an amazing sight. In a scene from the dusty streets of frontier towns 120 years ago, two armed men stand in the street ten feet apart, staring into each other's eyes. The ruby sun is almost gone for the day, but it is high noon in East New York. Each man palms his pistol in his right hand, arm straight down at his side. Incredibly, a third man has positioned himself just out of the line of fire; he appears to be a referee. At an even safer distance on the sidewalk are thirty spectators.

Logan backs the van slowly toward the men, but the high-pitched warning tone that sounds when the vehicle is rolling backward draws all eyes toward the two policemen. Gary is first out of the van as one of the men runs north, the other south. Logan is a step slower out of the driver's side. Gary gains on the guy running north. He is almost close enough to grab the fleeing youth when the stocky kid leaps onto a garbage can, steps up on a six-foot spiked wrought-iron fence, turns, and fires a shot. A tongue of orange licks from his gun, but the shot misses as Gary slams against the wall of the building. The shooter leaps down on the far side of the fence and flees along the side of the gutted brick structure. Gary hears two quick shots from behind and to his right as he scrambles to his feet and charges around the outside of the fence through a garbage-heaped lot. When he steps around the corner, the kid is on the other side of a flimsy fence, tugging on a door. The kid sees Gary and throws his gun over the fence, then continues his struggle to open the door.

"Hands up or I'll fucking shoot you." The kid's hands move slowly upward, and he leans wearily, forehead to the wall.

Doctors say an adrenaline rush dilates the pupils for better vision, widens the capillaries for strength, produces galvanic skin responses. "All I know," Gary says, "is that I had never been near that building before, and I knew exactly where to go to catch the kid — exactly." Something else was strange to him. Something new. "If he didn't put his hands up, I was going to shoot him right there. I heard it in my voice. He heard it too."

When the chase began, the guy who fled south also ran to a locked door, at basement level in a building across the street. When he jumped back out on the street, he spotted Logan behind Gary. The man squatted in a combat stance and pointed his weapon at Logan, but did not fire. Logan did, squeezing off two rounds at the guy, who quickly abandoned the shooting posture for some pure perp flight. Logan's shots popped holes in the windshield of a red Toyota abandoned on the dirt beside the building. The perp sailed around the corner and out of sight.

When Jim Priore and a score of backups arrive on the scene, Gary climbs the fence and cuffs up the kid who tried to kill him.

"Why don't you head back over to the hospital and relax?" Priore suggests.

But Gary is adamant. "I'm not going anywhere until they find that gun." As he stands in the chill dusk, he tells a Housing cop at his side, "I was shot at. It's legit, but it's gonna look fugazy if they don't find the evidence. I want that gun."

An Emergency Service Unit truck lurches into the back lot where the chase ended. Then a 73 car with a cage in the back seat arrives, and an NYPD cop unloads a German shepherd named Rambo, who hits the dirt in a full crouch and slithers over the area with his nose an inch from the ground. But the dog can't find the gun. Gary's frown deepens, but he doesn't utter a word. Lights are played off the lot and the search goes on. An hour passes. Then a 10-13 comes over the radio, and the Emergency Service Unit truck rumbles out of the lot to answer the call. In five minutes, the dog's yelp leads the cops to the spot where the vehicle was parked. Embedded in the soft dirt where one of the truck's tires was is a Chinese-made nine-millimeter semiautomatic.

Priore has had enough. Last night the detective squad received a call from a resident on Riverdale who said that someone was hiding in his basement. The squad hustled over and grabbed the guy who had pointed his gun at Logan. Half an hour later, some uniforms arrived to transport the prisoner. They gave him the long ride, and when the man arrived at the PSA he was badly beaten.

At this morning's roll call Priore tells the thirty assembled officers how things will be. "The next time somebody tunes up a perp in cuffs, that guy is going to be headed down to Gold Street in cuffs. Because I am going to write it up for IAB just the way it happened. Everybody got that?"

Priore's promise to tell the Internal Affairs Bureau the truth about the next beating has the troops muttering as they step into the Brownsville air and head to their sector cars. "Who the fuck does Priore think he is?"

But Priore does not care what the cops are saying. "When the squad got over there," he explains, "they had the guy, and he was talking, and all that good stuff. Then these knuckleheads show up and they tune the guy up good, right in front of the detectives. The detectives come to me and want to know what the fuck is going on, and I agree with them. This guy is cuffed and cooperating, and he comes in with a broken ankle. One of the guys who did it is the same guy who is on restricted duty because of a similar incident last week."

The crux of the matter is that the police believe that the criminal justice system is either unable or unwilling to mete out punishment that will deter attacks upon their persons. So they do it themselves. It is difficult to convince a person not to pursue a course of action that he thinks may save his life. J.R.'s words to Gary resonate for the grumbling rank-and-file: "If somebody tries to hurt a cop, he isn't going to the lockup. He is going to Brookdale."

HOMECOMING

March 6. It is three o'clock in the morning of a moon-less wind-lashed night. Sharron is riding on a grim blue and white bus with thick wire covering the windows, over the bridge heading out of Riker's Island. The cop at the wheel has already warned the fifty young men behind him that if they "smoke and act wild," he is going to turn the bus around and head back to the jail. Just as with a blustering elementary school teacher, it is unlikely that he will carry out his threat and redeposit his charges inside. But Sharron is not taking any chances. The last few weeks inside were excruciating for him. Now that he is on the bus, he is not going to allow any stupidity, even uncontrolled good spirits, to set him back.

This one time, Sharron becomes a leader. He stands at his seat and yells, "Chill the fuck out." A moment later he tells the kids on his right and behind him, "No reason to celebrate. We in jail till they let us out at the subway."

When the bus pulls up at the Queensborough stop, the wind is whipping hard enough to rattle the metal bus stop sign out-side the Lucky Pizza Restaurant. Wearing the gold jeans and sneakers that Shawanda dropped off two weeks earlier, Sharron is without a coat in the chill. He left his recovered Timberland boots back in the mod, for his boys to wear when they pose for photographs with their girlfriends on visiting days.

Some of the releasees head into the all-night Twin Donut Shop for hamburgers; others, like Sharron, just climb up to the ele-vated platform to wait for the train that will take them home.

Sharron gets to 830 Saratoga Avenue at 6 A.M., just about the time the Transit detectives showed up at his house in November. It's great to be back, but already he can see problems. John and Shawanda are asleep in his room on his bed. His black jeans and shearling jacket are tossed on a chair in the living room; someone, probably Alleke, has been wearing them. A quick look in his closet tells him that his clothes, the cornerstone of his identity, are in very bad shape. "Dammit," he mutters in the morning shadows.

It takes Sharron two days to work out the logistics of getting John and Shawanda out of his room for a couple of hours and Vanessa in. The young couple make love for the first time. It is quiet and sweet. Vanessa has been a loyal friend as well as a level-headed adviser.

But as they lie on the day bed, it is not long before Sharron starts to worry. Shawanda has another black eye. "Don't be fooled by John's smooth exterior," Sharron tells Vanessa. "He's hardrock." Just days out of Riker's, and Sharron, on probation or not, is already in a situation where he might have to do something that the authorities might not understand well: he may have to get into it with John.

"You be careful, Sharron. I don't want you back in jail. That's their problem," Vanessa says.

"I worry about Shawanda," Sharron muses. "She don't have no drive to do anything for herself. She had all these applications to college, and she doesn't do anything with them. She just wants someone to take care of her. At least Mommy got her GED and is in the training school."

The next day Sharron heads over to Chantal's house with Franklo. The visit is a near disaster. Chantal is full of seductive hugs and wet kisses. But Sharron is stiff and aloof, turns his cheek to her lips. All he wants now is a sweater and the white hooded sweatshirt Shawanda failed to recover. If the two were alone in his mother's apartment on Saratoga, he would not turn down the sexual advances. But here, with Mrs. Redding on the couch in the living room and his friend waiting outside, there is no way he is going to get into it with her. Still, back in Chantal's room, a drop of sweat rolls down his spine and the skin on his chest tingles as she hangs on his neck, nibbling at him, breathing promises in his ear. But through the glossy toss of her hair, he can see cardboard-framed photographs of her with the boyfriend that Shawanda told him about. Sharron wrenches free.

"I ain't down for that. Just get me the turtleneck and the hoody, Chantal."

"Sha, c'mon."

"Tell that shit to him," Sharron snaps, his eyes flicking to the pictures on the wall.

"*Sharron.*" Chantal is angry and insistent, standing in front of the closet, blocking access to the clothes. Sharron is tempted to smack her, but he controls himself.

"What the fuck you *doin'*?" she whines. "There's no boy-friend." Sharron looks at her and scowls, summoning his ice grill.

At last Chantal steps aside and allows him to get to the clothing. "You're lucky he's not here to kick your punk ass," she warns as Sharron walks out the bedroom door with his hoody and his sweater. He freezes in the doorway, then shakes his head, deciding to say nothing in response. He lets the threat slide and heads out the door with the armful of clothes.

The principal is in the front hallway of Thomas Jefferson today, just a few feet from the new Vortex metal detectors, eye to eye with two junior varsity basketball players. Flanking her at the impromptu conference are Mr. Singler, a roly-poly teacher who also coaches the JV basketball team, and Ms. Letteri, the frowning, nitpicking athletic director. The two teachers are hard-working members of the faculty, but they are adversaries in this proceeding. Letteri wants the players kicked off the team for their actions during a showdown game yesterday with the squad from the elite Brooklyn Tech, which is leading their league.

Just one referee showed up to work at the game. The fact that the other referee was not in attendance was not surprising to the Jeff players or their coach. Since the Daryl Sharpe shooting, there has been a rash of cancellations and no-shows for Jeff games.

After a bad call, a sophomore playmaker blew up. He stared menacingly at the referee, then sprinted to the sideline where his gym bag sat. In light of recent incidents at the high school, this was interpreted by the referee and some others as a threat.

"He just wanted to get out of the gym. He was really pissed," the cherubic Singler says, standing up for his player. "He lost his temper."

The other player in trouble was in a short fight near the end of the game. Letteri's report to Beck requests that both players be suspended for the rest of the season. Another principal might listen to the charges and rule that a serious breach of discipline occurred and the miscreants must be punished. What are the junior varsity basketball careers of two kids compared with the image of Thomas Jefferson High School? But Beck listens carefully, with a million other things flying through her mind — a trip to Albany planned for tomorrow, a segment on the *Today* show scheduled to air tomorrow morning, a cover story in *Newsweek* featuring a photo of Tyrone Sinkler's body being carried out the front door of the high school.

"I am going to take your side against my own athletic director," she tells the shuffling boys. "Do you know what that means? It means that if I ever hear of you being in the slightest way disrespectful or troublesome, I will kick your ass personally. It means that you will never play for another team at this high school. Never."

It is the contention of one senior administrator for the board of education that Carol Beck's personal approach is part of the problem at Jefferson, that her family style debilitates young men and women, weakens them in the face of the demands of a world that will not lay a warm hand on their shoulders. That complaint seems far off the mark when you see Beck doing her best to save these two young men, who may be hanging on to school by the thread of the JV basketball team, the way Sharron Corley held on to the thread of the school play.

A moment later she is on the phone, assuring the newsman Gabe Pressman that she will be available to speak on his interview show. "Don't you worry. Call me at home at any hour. I am one of God's children."

Next she takes a seat in her conference room, with Ellen Greaves, her assistant in charge of administration, by her side. There is little indication in Beck's appearance of the kind of person she is; she could be a burned-out teacher of elementary students, a weary secretary counting the last few years before retirement. Today she wears a gold-plated pin showing Sojourner Truth on her lapel. "When it gets rough, I put on Sojourner, so I can remember what the mission was." She is weary, snappish. "I have to get home and get some sleep. I'm getting evil."

Beck is copying and collating copies of the ten-page itinerary for the Albany trip sent by Assemblyman Saul Weprin, a Jefferson alumnus, so the eight students accompanying her will have their own packets. Someone is banging at the side door. There stands a mother and her towering son, who have arrived for a meeting of the Future Engineers Club, a group of some of the most talented kids in the school. The petite mother looks to be of college age; her son has a blue bandanna wrapped around his head, droopy jeans, and a shimmering gold cap on his right front tooth. He looks like a gangster, a street tough. He might be a future engineer.

The faculty member in charge of the meeting has not shown up. Some teachers have assumed that such frills have been suspended during these times of trouble. The mother can't disguise her delight at the apparent cancellation. Like the youthful Gloria Corley, she has things to do, a life to live. She cannot possibly be thirty years old. She makes a move to leave. "I understand. I told him," she says, gesturing at her frowning son, "that the meeting would probably be called off."

But Beck asks the two, along with another parent and student who have arrived, to wait in the library. She will conduct the meeting herself. She makes a disapproving face at the youth's bandanna. "What is that?"

"L.A. style," he whispers.

By eight o'clock, Nick and Yolanda, one of the best girl basketball players in New York City and a B student to boot, are talking about vocabulary as they wait for Beck to drive them home.

"Extemporaneous, what does that mean?"

"I would never use a long word like that," Nick says. "Why not use a lot of short words?" His face lights with an insight. "If you have to do a two-hundred-and-fifty-word essay, you don't want to use one word when you can use a whole lot. I am good with the the's and who's — I can work them good."

It is after nine o'clock when Beck drags out of her office with Nick and Yolanda in tow. On the otherwise clean yellow wall opposite the office and on the window of the vestibule by the side door are chalk letters: E-lo. Beck has left the graffiti there in honor of Ian Moore, LoLife. She nods at the letters and mutters, "Shit."

*

The following afternoon, Sharon King boards the IRT for the hour-long trip to the Bronx to visit Khalil Sumpter in Spofford. She sits alone as the #4 flies out of Brooklyn and races under the East Side of Manhattan, beneath the Harlem River, and up to the Bronx. It is another disappointing March day in a moody spring. She hustles up the walk to the front door of the Spofford Juvenile Center. The outside walls are as white as bone, stained in places by streaks of rust from the roof gutters. The building brings back memories for King. When she was fifteen, she was kicked out of her home for insubordination. When her mother couldn't locate her after a month, she filed a PINS, shorthand for person in need of supervision. When Sharon was found, she was detained in this very facility for a week.

In the visiting room there are two long rows of chairs facing each other. The adolescent prisoners sit on one side and the visitors on the other. King peers up and down the rows, but she cannot make Khalil out. Nothing but a column of gray-clad manchildren facing a long line of girlfriends and mothers. An arm reaches out from the far end of the line of chairs and beckons. It is Mrs. Sumpter. King stops in her tracks. She has wondered what she will say and do at this moment. Her anger at Khalil for his stupidity, his murderous shortsightedness, gives way, and she hurries toward the mother and son.

Khalil's mother is given to tough talk and quick tears. "What are we gonna do? What are we gonna do?" she asked King earlier on the phone.

"Ms. King," she says now, standing to face the teacher. "Oh, thank you. I'm glad you could come." Khalil rises and steps forward shyly. The three wrap their arms around each other. King and Mrs. Sumpter sob softly. Khalil squeezes them tight, glancing about the room over their heads. Then he buries his head between their faces and cries along with them. The three stand huddled until a guard pries them gently apart. Khalil sits down quickly, eyes lowered to the floor.

"What do people think of me?" Khalil whispers as King takes a seat beside his mother.

"They think you're an animal," King answers, with a sidelong glance at Mrs. Sumpter.

Khalil thinks for a few moments. "I saw you on TV," he says, referring to the news pieces on the Moore funeral. Somehow, he shares the sadness of it all. But his reaction to the deaths of his schoolmates is like that of a distant relative or a close neighbor, not the murderer himself.

"What do *you* think of me?" he asks King.

"You know what I think. I'm here." She leans forward and touches the back of her hand gently to his cheek.

"Why you dress all *Soul Train*?" Khalil asks. King is wearing black ankle-high boots with heels and sleek black slacks with a cropped jacket.

"That's the style, Khalil."

In a short time the visit is over. One of the male guards whispers a comment about King as she exits. Khalil glowers. "Don't be sayin' shit about my aunt, hear that?" he warns.

"Khalil is hard-headed," King tells her class a few days later. "William Kunstler is going to be his lawyer. Khalil won't stop insisting that he just did what he had to do."

On Sunday, Vanessa's mother allows Sharron to spend the night on the living room couch. The next morning he heads off to Satellite. He has heard through Frank that the academy is ready to take him back for the semester that starts in March. Neil, his counselor, is said to be waiting for his return.

Satellite is set up for students like Sharron. The rapid credit system allows them to make the most of the time they spend in school, with the understanding that personal problems may draw them away. A New York City high school student needs forty credits to graduate. Sharron has twenty-two, after four years. The four credits that he was taking in the fall were lost when he got locked up. Now, even if he passes all his courses in the spring, he will need to take a course in summer school to have enough credits to qualify as a senior. It is tough going. If he is not careful and lucky, it won't be long before he is just another coarsened man with dreams as shapeless as clouds of sewer steam lit by neon, a strong young man at the beginning of his life and the end of his promise, with no skills but how to use a burner and a banger, how to "get paid" without working, how to hurt someone without losing sleep.

He signs up for six courses. The science mini-course about the human brain meets in the morning, right after his strat, or counseling session, for which there is no credit. Next is a class

called "Novels." Neil conducts the fourth-period human science class; the topic for this marking period is the ever-popular
human reproduction. In the afternoon, Sharron has a course on
ideas, followed by an African American history class. He wraps
up his day with a writing course. All the units are conducted in
classes with no more than fifteen students. Sharron is happy to
be back, glad his life is not grist for the gossip mill over at Jeff,
which he now calls a "rumor school."

SPRING AND SUMMER

"I CAN'T WALK"

It is drizzling. Gary is waiting in his gray Grand Fury around the corner from the PSA, nibbling on sunflower seeds, which he coaxes from the plastic package just a few at a time. The light rain picks up as Michael T. happens past.

"Yo, Michael T.," Gary says.

Michael, who goes by the street name of Miz, looks over his shoulder with exaggerated irritation. "I told you, man, don't be callin' me by my government name." He stands staring at Gary for a moment. "That your car?" He gestures across the street at the beat-up old Dodge.

Gary nods.

"What a piece of shit," Michael T. scoffs. "I bet that car wouldn't even make it down South."

Greg Harris, the tall, good-looking boy who helped break up Ms. King's classroom confrontation with Khalil, wanders up.

"Watch out for this jake," Michael tells him, nodding at Gary. "He's smooth. Slide up on your ass."

Gary laughs.

"Hey, lemme sit in there." Michael nods at the empty front seat of the police car. "It's rainin' an' shit."

Gary starts to move some papers and a clipboard off the passenger seat to make room for the kid. Over the past few months, he and Michael T. have developed a curious relationship, waving tentatively at each other on empty streets, teasing each other. Anytime a kid in the neighborhood, especially one as close to the action as Michael T., is in a talkative mood, Gary is ready to chat. Tiny pieces of seemingly useless information are valuable as lubricants in conversations with those who have real stories to tell.

"Nah," Michael decides. "People see me, think I'm talkin' to you."

Hanging out with Michael T., Gary thinks, and chuckles as the big kid moves off.

Sharon King has a gaggle of girls in her after-school guidance cubicle on the first floor. She dominates the conversation with a mixture of shock talk about her personal life and keen analysis of the four girls.

"What's with your hair, Tanaya?" she exclaims to a large, awkward girl who stands in the doorway. "Get it done. I'll pay for it. Please, get it done." The four girls inside eye Tanaya's botched coiffeur and nod.

King turns her attention to a girl slumped on an office chair in the corner. "Roxanne is angry. She isn't a dizball. She is messing up her life on purpose, because she's mad at her mother."

Roxanne, a pretty sophomore with the classic Brooklyn look — baggy jeans, large earrings, and T-shirt — is as cool as the spring rain that's been falling for a week. She nods in agreement with King's assessment, but adds, "I don't like school. I'm a hangout girl."

"How did you fail gym?" King wants to know.

"Gym is for white girls. I get so bored sometimes, I just want to fall asleep."

King decides to place a call on a speakerphone to Milton Lowers, who was shot, along with his friend Rodney James, a week ago. They made the mistake of visiting the Linden Houses. As they left 570 Stanley Avenue with a girlfriend, they were followed and shot by a young man named Randolph, an acquaintance of Sinkler and Moore's. Randolph knows Lowers to be a friend of Dupree's, and Dupree is known as Khalil's man. That is all it took — the wrong friend, the wrong project. Lowers was hit in the left thigh, his femur shattered; James received one bullet in the stomach. A dozen more .45 shells blasted the trunk and back window of a faded green Cadillac that sat by the curb. James will recover fully. Lowers will wear a brace on his leg for a long time, maybe forever. At Jefferson, attention is paid to shooting victims the way it used to be lavished on classmates who had the measles or were getting ready to move to another town.

"You want us to bring you something?" King asks over the phone.

"No," Lowers answers.

The girls speak up. "You don't want anything?"

Lowers mumbles something.

"What? What did you say?" Tanaya raises her voice from the doorway.

"I think he said skins," Roxanne replies. "Is that what you said, Milton?"

This time the word is clear: "Skins." Followed by a nervous laugh.

"You want me to come and give you some skins?" Roxanne teases.

"Yeah." There is a flutter to Lowers's voice; he is embarrassed.

"You want me to come and give you some *infected* skins?" The girls howl at Roxanne's joke.

"When you comin' back to school?"

"I ain't comin' back."

"Why? You scared?"

"I can't walk," Lowers blurts.

Roxanne leans to the speakerphone and asks a question that lands like a blunt instrument. "You *ever* gonna be able to walk?"

There is no answer on the other end of the phone. A frowning King takes over, promises a visit, and says goodbye with a kiss. Each girl kisses the air once for Milton Lowers, who sits alone in an apartment with a flickering television, waiting for his mother to come home from work, wondering if he will walk again.

After the students have left, King talks to one of the guidance counselors. "What would I have done differently with Khalil Sumpter? If I had the money, or the situation was right, I would've turned him on to a strong black male in the school, who could take him under his wing. Humans are the most valuable resource there is. Somebody who could have showed him that there are other ways of dealing with pressure."

King insists that Khalil is no sociopath. "If I believed he was crazy, I'd throw the whole thing out now. It isn't them that are far-fetched and outrageous, it is their environment. Look what they grow up with. These kids like Khalil are good Americans. They want something, they figure out a strategy to get it. They take risks, just like they were taught to do. I just wish I was there when Khalil came in. I'd have stepped in and I wouldn't have moved out of the way. I told Khalil that, and he just shook his head, but I pressed him. 'What would you do, shoot right through me?' And then after a while he had to admit that he would not have shot me. He's not crazy."

Two Housing detectives, Gerry Fitzpatrick and his partner, Artie Norman, are following leads in the Lowers-James shooting. Tall and fair-haired, Fitzpatrick looks like a young college basketball coach. Today he wears a purple-and-black-striped sweater under his blazer. Norman's eyeglasses are tinted a sinister yellow; he looks like a bookie. The detectives are looking for a guy named Bibo, a six-foot-seven Linden local with large eyes. The word is that he is a witness to the shooting. The detectives head straight to Apartment 8D in 570 Stanley. The apartment belongs to Charles, a forty-year-old man who looks as if he is seventy.

"Charles just gave up," Fitzpatrick says. "He lets the home-boys use his place to deal drugs and have gangbangs, and he lets us in too."

Inside the dark, filthy apartment sits Mark, a fresh-faced fifteen-year-old with skin as smooth as golden glass.

"What's goin' on?" Norman wants to know.

"Nothin'," Mark returns flatly.

"Where's Charles?"

"He went out."

"Where?" Norman presses as Fitzpatrick heads into the back room.

"He went to the second floor," Mark answers, his eyes following Fitzpatrick, "and then he said he was gonna go to the store and then he was comin' back."

"Who's he visitin' on the second floor?"

"I don't know." Mark shrugs.

"What are you doin' up here?"

"Just come up to talk to Charles."

"It doesn't look like Charles does much talkin'," the detective comments, removing his glasses and rubbing the bridge of his nose.

"He talks."

"What do you do up here?"

"I watch TV."

"There is a TV on in the bedroom. Why is that?"

"Charles leaves it on."

Norman is looking for some contradiction to crystallize the absurdity of Charles's apartment, to reveal the implausibility of Mark's story. To him, it is obvious that no clean-cut fifteen-year-old boy spends his days and nights in a dank hole with a man wasting away from crack addiction, just a few feet from a pair of blood-stained pants that belonged to another young man, who was murdered in the apartment a few weeks before. Mark's story is absurd, but Arnie Norman is not succeeding in making it seem funny.

"You seen that guy we're looking for?"

"Bibo?" Mark questions.

"Yeah. I thought you said you didn't know him."

"I don't."

"Then how's you remember his name like that?"

"Easy. Bibo, bimbo. It's not hard," the young man reasons.

"Where do you go to school?"

"I go to Linden Prep for my GED downstairs."

GEDs are designed for people who dropped out of school and want to return. They are not supposed to replace the socialization process that school is meant to provide. Mark's socialization is now being taken care of in Apartment 8D.

When Charles comes back, Fitzpatrick takes him into the bedroom for a talk. Charles is emaciated; his eyes are wide with permanent surprise. His face appears frozen in the moment after a bad decision. He weighs 120 pounds. He will soon be evicted. He will soon be dead.

When Fitzpatrick and Charles return to the living room, Fitzpatrick's light touch inspires some biography from Mark. "Charles used to hang around with my father. My father's dead now. He died of HIV in '89. He gave it to my mother. She died in January. I live with my older sister." Mark has not moved an inch. His glance slides sideways and he flashes eye signals to Clarence when he thinks the detectives are not looking.

Finally, the cops realize they are not going to get the answers they are looking for today. "We'll be back, Charles," Fitzpatrick promises. "I want you to get a little more into the housework. Be careful, Mark."

"Clean-cut lookin' kid," Norman explains on the elevator, "but he's dealin'. Every time we go up there, he's inside. Would you hang out in there?"

The detectives want Bibo badly. They continue their search for hours, cruising around the Linden Houses, looking for his car. "These guys do this revenge shit not because they liked the guy who was shot, or even to protect the honor of the neighborhood. They do it because they feel like it. It's the new thing. It gives them a rush and it helps build them a reputation," Fitzpatrick remarks to his partner, who shakes his head.

They drive around and around the block, looking, checking cars, ignoring the hard stares of the young men who stand in bunches on the street corners. The officers are disliked; years of sneering guys in blue coats have guaranteed that. But the hostility is laced with some confusion. These cops are not here to stop theft from a commercial area; there is no business here to speak of, just a few understocked gunsmoke bodegas. They are not on a mission to head off an insurrection — not yet, anyway. They are sent by the city to stop the residents here from killing each other.

Fitzpatrick and Norman have no luck on this case. But a few weeks later the detectives find the alleged shooter himself, Randolph, hiding on Riker's Island. He turned himself in on an old warrant because he knew the police were looking for him in the double shooting. He is charged with gunning down Lowers and James.

"I AM THE VILLE"

There is only half a day of school today, so Frank and Sharron head back to the Ville. Frank convinces Sharron to accompany him to the cleaners while he picks up a sweater. On the way, the two decide to visit Terrance, the third of the Brownsville musketeers, who is back in Brooklyn for a visit. Terrance, a droopy-eyed LoLife, was a big part of Frank and Sharron's lives until his mother sent him to Dallas to get him away from the troubles in Brooklyn. But he found similar trouble in Texas. He heard it was worse in Houston. It is the same all over — south central Los Angeles, Detroit, Roxbury in Boston. God help a black teen in Washington, D.C., or Miami, East St. Louis, or Milwaukee. What about Flint, Michigan, or Charleston?

For families like Sharron's, there is no getting away from Brownsville unless you get rich. You could even get a little money and not escape the danger. Scratch up a down payment on a house in Canarsie or in Queens and some racist cracker might throw a Molotov cocktail in your front window. Try to live in Island Park and Al D'Amato might show up with a bulldozer.

Sharron has not seen Terrance, or Tee, since he got back, and their reunion is heartfelt.

"Yo, money, wha's up?" Sharron gushes.

"Back in the *Ville* ready to *ill*," Tee rhymes. He steps forward and stoops slightly as he and Sharron hug like brothers. Sharron holds tight, squeezes Tee for a full twenty seconds, while Frank looks on. The moment is almost perfect.

As he embraces his friend, Sharron holds back a small, painful thought. While he was in Four Main on Riker's, during one of the endless sessions in the cell corridor when the young rogues told their fantastic stories, Terrance's name came up, and Frank's. Terrance had a more extensive citywide reputation than either Frank or Sharron. But there was another side to all that. The story that someone told that night in Riker's was about how Terrance had bragged that he had gone to Sharron's house once a year earlier, when Sharron was not home, and taken two sweaters. The sweaters were described accurately. The story was not the product of somebody's imagination, not just a mean-spirited attempt to break up friends. Sharron didn't want to hear it, but it was too late. The words yanked something away forever. Just now, Sharron feels the loss again. He doesn't say anything, but the fullness of the reunion is gutted.

Sharron and Terrance and Frank, acting like everything is just the way it always was, head over to pick up Terrance's LoWife, Dada. With her in tow, the three friends walk over to the cleaners to retrieve Frank's sweater. To get there they cut through the Marcus Garvey Houses, where a contingent of LoLifes lives. Beside a bench at the foot of the main building stand Stevelo, Skilo (who was in Riker's with Sharron), Ronlo, Beklo, and another kid, who is unfamiliar to Sharron and his friends. The spot where the boys stand, backed by the stone geometry of the building, evokes a stage in ancient Greece; so does the dramatic tension, and the ritual.

Sharron approaches first and gives a chest-level high five to all except the kid he does not know.

Then Frank says "What's up" to Ronlo and Stevelo. When he gets to Beklo, Beklo smiles and tosses his head to indicate that he is disinclined to slap hands.

Skilo follows up the slight and starts woofing. He snickers to Beklo, "So what. Fuck the kid. Fuck a Frank. You ain't got to say nothin' to that nigger."

When he and his boys approached the group, Sharron noticed that Skilo and Beklo were playing in a similar manner with each other, exchanging mock disrespect. Now he studies their faces, looking for a sign that this is more such play. It is hard to tell. Sharron decides it is a joke. Frank is not so sure.

"Ain't I good for a five?" he wants to know.

Beklo sits tight, inscrutable. It is a test of nerves, one of a thousand little contests that are won or lost in a day in Brownsville.

Frank does not want to overreact. "I don't need you to be my man, son," he says.

"Son," a complex appellation, is used by the kids at different times for endearment or disrespect. Frank uses it as a subtle diminution of Beklo. The term also calls into the mix a reminder that few of these kids have fathers who stayed around long after they were born.

The air is getting hot, so Sharron steps up and slaps some more fives around. "We out," he says.

Frank backs off across the street, muttering to himself, while Tee, oblivious, is off to the side, holding a conversation with Stevelo about Texas. Sharron moves away with Frank, as a gesture of solidarity, and flashes a sign to Tee that he is going. Tee and Dada start across the plaza toward Frank and Sharron. In the stylized, courtly manner of the Ville, Tee nods to each of the seated LoLifes, offering a "chill" with each movement of his head. The group nods back, except for Beklo, who whispers a dreamy, "Bye, Dada," and turns his head away. Tee, unaware of the previous friction, misses the tone, the move, the dis. He has already pivoted and is heading blithely out of the plaza. But Sharron and Frank see the gesture clearly, and they burn. Frank is now sure that he did not overreact, and Sharron is alerted to the possibility that he was just a shade too conciliatory.

Frank talks to himself as the foursome head around the corner to the cleaners. "Bek is the last motherfucker to be playin' me like that."

It is all information stored for later. Small tests, smaller slights that indicate power shifts, the dreaded devaluation of one's reputation from respect to disdain — it can happen in a minute, and it can ruin everything. There is not much to look forward to in the narrow world of a Brownsville teenager, but to live the life of a punk, with guys laughing at you, making open plays for your woman, or disrespecting your family, is a world of hell. Even though the loss of reputation might only last for a year or two in real time, until the peer group is dispersed by jail sentences, shootings, and relocation, Sharron and his friends truly believe it is a kind of death.

*

Gary has already had a few beers. "Get yourself a pitcher," he advises a late arrival. "The food is in the back room. They got everything. And don't lose your raffle ticket, you fuckin' ball-bag." This is a 10-13 party, held by the Housing police as a bene-fit to raise money for the medical bills of Charlie Devine, a well-liked officer at PSA 2. Devine used to have a thick brown mustache. Now he has cancer.

The party is held at the Castle Casino in the Bronx. The name is a double flight of fancy. The place is no casino and cer-tainly no castle. It is a hall somewhere near the foot of the Throgs Neck Bridge. The PSA 2 cops would never even think of having their party in Brownsville. There are several hundred Housing officers from all over the city here. As you look around the room, you can spot old and new faces. Platt has brought some Fire Department buddies from his Marine Corps days. Schulman is in the middle of the room in cowboy boots, trim black jeans, and a tailored shirt, sober as a judge. But Maritza, the impatient proprietor of the bodega across the street from the PSA, is already drinking hard, waiting for the music to start. Lenti is here. He can be trusted. He's getting drunk. Kammer-dener, in a sharper, crisper blue suit, is on duty. He doesn't drink and leaves halfway through the affair, with a plastic smile. The word is that the K-Master will be a "full bird" (inspector) within the week. There are just half a dozen policewomen on hand, the same number of black officers. Lonnie Hayes is not in the house.

J.R. stands off to the side, smirking, talking to Sergeant Bright. J.R. has been a detective for only a few months, but he looks as if he were born to dress like one. "It's the suits. The perps see the suits and they just put out their hands to be cuffed. They don't think about fightin'. Not a day goes by where I don't miss the Ville," he admits. "In the Bronx and Queens, compared to Brownsville, the perps are soft. I mean, in the Ville you got stone-cold perps, guys whose sole purpose in life is to be perps."

There are pitchers of beer aplenty. Devine mixes in the crowd, the picture of good cheer in a gray wool suit and wrinkled white shirt. The Housing police bagpipe contingent stands by in kilts and black shirts. There are about fifteen of them, including Tilly and Finn, and one woman from another PSA.

"About ten-thirty we'll do our thing," Tilly assures Gary.

Eddie Hammil floats past, a glint in his eye that says he is determined to have a good time.

"Hey," Gary lofts in his direction. "I thought you were on Fire Island. I thought you went with Paddy." Paddy Gleason appears and scuttles toward Lemite.

"Yeah, we did go and we came back and lemme tell you why. Listen to this," Gleason chortles. "We meet two girls. One of them is all over me like I can't believe."

"Yeah, tell us how chicks dig you," Hammil scoffs.

Gleason is determined to finish his tale. Lemite leans in to catch the words. "It's only four o'clock on a Friday afternoon. I can't believe how hot she is. But her friend doesn't like Hammil. We go back to the house. There are like five girls in the place. They share it for a season. I'm in the living room and the chick is sittin' on my lap, and the other one goes upstairs and her two friends are like goin' in and out. Then this other roommate comes in and asks like, 'Where is everybody?' Hammil is sittin' there and he says, 'Your friend Carol is upstairs in the bathroom. Linda went out five minutes ago, and the blonde, I think her name was Darlene, left with a guy about six feet with black hair.' All of a sudden the chick on my lap looks up at Hammil and says, 'What, are you a cop?' Then she looks at me and 'What, are you *both* cops?' That was it. They musta had marijuana or somethin' an' everybody was whisperin' an' shit. Ruined the weekend, ruined every fuckin' thing. We left."

Hammil heads off through the crowd, Gleason dogging his footsteps, the tale of the lost weekend at the ready.

A three-year veteran cop named Magee walks up to Gary. The live band at the rear of the hall has just started to wail a Beach Boys song, "Surfin' Safari." Magee raises his voice and explains his way of looking at things. "I know there are a lot of assholes on this job. They come on with some kind of a problem. Not me. I came on when I was twenty-eight years old. I knew who I was." Gary listens and nods vigorously. It was the same with him.

"If somebody is going to threaten my safety," Magee says with a shrug, a plastic glass in one hand and a pitcher of dark beer in the other, "then I will react. I have to react. If somebody calls me a white motherfucker, I think to myself, 'O.K. I am going home to my nice apartment and my nice neighborhood, where the worst possible thing that could ever happen is an argument over a parking space,' and I keep on walking. I have no problem. But sometimes they keep it up. They call you a pussy, and you get the feeling that they really believe you are a pussy." Magee reflects for a moment, watching Maritza, who dances slinkily nearby. He is thinking, trying to reconcile what he said before with what he is about to say. "They call you a pussy and sometimes you have to react, because nobody can survive being called a pussy."

Gary dips his glass into a passing pitcher of beer and toasts Devine. In January 1991, when Devine was diagnosed with lymphatic cancer, his life became a litany of treatments. But at one time he was the PCO in the Brownsville Houses. Once he pursued Randolph Worthy up the stairs and stumbled into the apartment at 5AB. Devine, an ex-Marine, doesn't enjoy speaking about the incident. In any group, there are those who dramatize and those who don't. The two types need each other. The storytellers, such as J. R. and Priore, don't make things up. They have seen so much, they don't have to. But they need guys like Devine to chasten their reenactments, just as the Devines need the storytellers to make things live again.

"It wasn't anything." Devine struggles more with the notoriety of the event than with the facts. "As I remember, I was chasing the kid, one of the young ones. We tumbled into the apartment and we were like struggling in the dark. It was a dance. That's what I always say. I was dancing in the Worthys' apartment. It was only for a minute. I wasn't attacked by anybody. Everybody was screaming. And then the troops showed up. That was about it."

When the pipers march single file to the center of the hall and issue forth their din, conversations about guns and women die out. The primitive clamor of the bagpipes and the sight of the kilts send shudders through the room. At first Gary is not impressed by the sound, as the spellbound Irishmen around him are. "I heard they don't wear drawers under those kilts. I wonder about the broad," he whispers soggily, before he too succumbs to the spectacle.

The pipes screech and howl to the ceiling and to the four walls, a relentless din, too energetic for a wail, too high-pitched for a dirge, a fantastical knell issuing forth in great spasms. The kilted cops circle in the center of the room, forming an ellipse, like a ring of Saturn. Instinct or custom draws Devine into the center of the group, where he stands with a huge furry black hat on his bald head. In his right hand he holds a dark wooden staff with a gold tip, which he bangs in ceremonial cadence on the linoleum floor. The pipe noises leap over each other like hounds on the chase. Devine pounds the floor harder and harder. The moment is steeped in measures of ancient courage and fear. The leader of the pipes, a stout Irishman, lifts the black furry cap from Devine's head, revealing the symbol of the officer's illness. He rubs the head for good luck and replaces the ceremonial hat. Then the pipers turn and file from the room.

Around the room, the troops are getting drunk, but there is not a fall-down guy in the crowd. Detective Eddie Davison, Gita Malave's favorite cop because he caught the guy who robbed her on the staircase, is very drunk. All the kids in Brownsville know him. "He never changes his clothes. He sleeps in his car," they say. "Don't let Davison get you."

"I am the Ville," the sagging Davison proclaims with reverence.

How could a white man claim to be the embodiment of Brownsville? How could he presume to represent anything but a restraining order against the lives of the people there?

"Because I love it. I love it," he says again. "The people know it. They know there are two Davisons. I got people off drugs. If somebody is right, I treat 'em right, and if they aren't, they deal with Dave. Ask around. I *know*. I go out, and I find out." Alone in the crowd and slush-eyed drunk, he is talking more about the people of Brownsville, their courage, their identity, than he is about himself. "You ask Born Son. You ask any of them. I am the Ville."

Hammil is handing out last drinks from his pitcher with the warning "I just stuck my dick in this." Nobody turns down his offer.

The party is over. No brawls. "What a nice bunch of young men," the tiny red-haired old woman in the coatroom says softly.

Spirits are soaring as the crowd spills out into the chilly spring night. There is the distinctive sound of a pistol shot, then another. Heads turn; trained eyes scan for an image from

Brownsville, black kids running. But there are no perps down the street where the shots came from, just several cops standing by a car, laughing.

Another Saturday evening. Vanessa and Sharron tramp over to the Kentucky Fried Chicken place on Belmont Avenue. The meal is to be Vanessa's treat. The little money that Sharron does have is at his apartment. He is spending a lot of time at Vanessa's house, keeping out of the Shawanda and John mess and staying off the block.

Apparently, there is something about having Vanessa control the purse strings that bothers Sharron. When the order is placed on the counter, he strides over to a booth and sits down.

"I'm payin' for the stuff," Vanessa says, raising her voice. "Least you can do is help carry it." Sharron does not budge. When Vanessa takes the food over, he will not eat.

"Pride. You can spell that with a capital P," Vanessa says. "So stupid."

By the time the two reach Vanessa's house, Sharron has returned the $95 gold neck chain Vanessa gave him.

That night, he goes back to her place to continue the argument. Vanessa produces the photo album they have started, the teddy bear, and the sweatshirt; she insists that they return the gifts they have given each other. "But the necklace is different," she says. "I want you to keep the chain." She extends her hand, the gold rope dangling. Sharron steadfastly refuses to accept.

"I want you to have it. It was a gift. Jewelry is different." The argument continues out in front of Vanessa's building. Sharron stands on the sidewalk, his arms full of tokens of his affection, Vanessa on the middle step of the entrance, fingering the graceful necklace. "Take it." She extends the piece yet again, her voice as soft as a kiss.

But Vanessa's mother has been listening from the front window. She shouts, "He does not want the chain. Why are you trying to make him take it?" Vanessa's mother did not want her usually level-headed daughter to buy the chain for Sharron in the first place. He was a nice boy, but buying gifts for him was a bad precedent, she believed, and the thing did cost $95. Now Vanessa has it back and wants to give it away again?

"I'm sorry I raised a fool. Will you let that boy leave with his things? And you keep what belongs to you. You are making me sick. You *idiot.*"

"Stop!" Sharron yells at her.

"Who are you speaking to, young man? If you know what's good for your skinny behind, you'll head on down the road."

Vanessa explodes in tears. The delicate coalition between boyfriend and mother, so crucial to her happiness, has been blasted to bits. But the clash between Sharron and her mother draws her back to Sharron almost immediately. The very next day, they are cooing on the phone, estimating how long it should be before Sharron reappears. But matters get worse.

Vanessa's mother is a churchwoman. She does not force religion on her children, but the Baptist church has done wonders for her, helped her through the breakup with her hyper-entrepreneurial Caribbean husband, through the raising of her three kids with the knowledge that their father was raising another family under more comfortable circumstances in East Flatbush. Her only son is a loss, God help him and those who trust him. But Vanessa is pure promise.

Vanessa has been complaining about excessively painful cramps during her period. Her mother has tried everything — painkillers, home remedies, soothing words; still Vanessa cries for the better part of a day every month. Something has to be done about it. What is the city employee health plan worth if you do not use it? So on a Tuesday, mother and daughter head downtown and sit next to each other facing a doctor.

"Are you having sex?" the physician asks early on, pencil at the ready.

Vanessa is trapped but self-possessed. "Yes," she answers bravely. The word does not sound so bad, she decides.

The news does not have a negative effect on the doctor, who crisply checks a box and looks up. But Vanessa's mother's head snaps toward her daughter. She moans, then leaps to her feet and flees from the room.

"I'm very sorry," the doctor sputters.

Mother and daughter do not speak for a month; they communicate via notes on the refrigerator. Sharron remains banished. Vanessa insists on the right to visit him at his home. But he remains persona non grata at her house for the next six weeks.

*

The students of Thomas Jefferson High School are having a ball. In satin gowns of white and ivory, the girls face a line of boys in tuxedos. The music commences. A pudgy, splay-footed boy at the end of the line embarks alone across the sixty feet of floor with a pained expression and a curious mincing gait. This step is something he has practiced for a long time, but perhaps not long enough. Left, right, hitch, shuffle, step, right, left. Parents and teachers seated at tables around the dance floor watch the performance with suspended breath. The boy's fearless aunt records the feat with a video camera; his mother grips the tablecloth. Like a tightrope walker on his way over Niagara Falls, he is halfway there, almost across, then . . . home. The clumsy boy, transformed by his accomplishment, bows rakishly to his waiting partner, gathers her in his arms to a burst of applause, and fairly sweeps across the floor to the exuberant music. The next boy follows, and the next. Soon the dance floor is filled with gliding, twirling couples.

This is not a school dance; this is Carol Beck's "cotillion." The lobby of the fancy hall in downtown Brooklyn where the event is held is decorated with gilded mirrors and a great glittering chandelier, according to Beck's "channel changer" philosophy. She does not want to hear about basketball and rap music. She wants gymnastic teams and waltzes.

"I'm not going," Nick grumbled earlier in the week. "Thirty-five dollars, for what? There ain't no pretty girls gonna be there." But there are plenty of pretty girls for this Saturday evening affair. They flutter back and forth from their parents to their friends, flouncing by the mumbling boys. Mostly they just smile. Later in the evening, each participating student bows to his or her mother or guardian in appreciation of the support and love he or she has received. The mothers, many very young, and the grandmothers beam with pride. The evening is the height of videotaped gentility. And of course Beck has invited the press. A magazine photographer trails her around the room.

But Bashim and Michael T. are not here. Neither are Sharron, Sheryl, or any of the basketball players. Nearly every one of the thirty-five students at the cotillion is of Caribbean descent, a first-generation American. The road to this kind of optimistic aspiration at Thomas Jefferson, it seems, does not run through North and South Carolina. Teenagers from those places are the most disillusioned. Or are they just forewarned? They already know about Jim Crow and de facto segregation. There is not one white child among the eighteen hundred students at Jefferson. In Brownsville, blacks don't drop out of school at appreciably higher rates than other urban ethnic groups, but they sense there is not much of an opening at the end of the academic pipeline. So, according to laws of physics that anyone can understand, they back up, collect at the source, and stagnate.

The same reluctance is evident when it comes to taking just any job. Unlike many of the Caribbean students, young men like Sharron do not see menial work as a beginning; they see it for the miserable trap it was for their ancestors. Once, as Sharron walked by a young East Indian man pumping gas in a filling station off Atlantic Avenue at midnight, he shook his head. "Times must be hard for that dude," he muttered. "I would never do that."

TWENTY-FOUR SEVEN

A Saturday afternoon in April, and Sharron is in an unusual position, sitting alone in his room looking at an anatomy book, studying for a test. A pool of afternoon sunlight rests on the dusty floor in the hall outside his room. He shuts his door to the beckoning spring day and lies back on his bed, holding the science book aloft. "Ovary: typically paired essential female reproductive organ that produces eggs in vertebrates."

Produces eggs in vertebrates? Sharron asks himself. *What are "vertebrates"?* He scrutinizes the color diagram of an ovary on the next page and sees no mention of vertebrates there, so he thumbs to the glossary. "Vertebrate," he reads. "Having a spinal column." But the spinal column is part of the skeletal system, he remembers. Damn. He hunches up against the wall and writes "Vertebrates — ovaries?" in his notebook. Then he checks the definition again, walks across the room, avoiding the mirror, and repeats the words to himself.

Music floats through the apartment, and for a moment his concentration wavers. He imagines himself and Frank and Chris onstage. Their group, Public Figure, has been getting together again; Morris has offered more studio space so they can complete their demo tape. "Ovary, female reproductive organ that produces eggs," Sharron says out loud, snapping back to his task. "That's good enough." Then he returns to his bed. "Placenta . . ."

Since his release, Sharron has spent a lot of time with Vanessa. The last several Saturday afternoons, they traveled to the Brooklyn Public Library on Eastern Parkway to study, but today he is punishing her, not answering her calls on the beeper, because she got drunk on Wednesday and smoked a cigarette. He is convinced the whole thing was really Shawanda's fault. She's the one who bought the beer. Vanessa drank one forty-ounce, then part of another. She was fine until she got upstairs. Then she threw up and passed out. Sharron took off her clothes and cleaned her up. He collected the soiled sheets and soaked them. But he was not happy about it. Sharron does not like women who drink.

Another five pages of studying, he decides, and he will go downstairs to call Vanessa back. But a loud knocking comes at the front door and he raises himself. A neighborhood kid named Fonzo stands outside, breathing hard.

"Dude be smackin' shit out Shawanda. Beat her down." As Sharron races out the door, Fonzo adds softly, "Think it's her boyfriend, Sha."

Right there by the garbage cans, a few feet from the parked cars, John is standing next to Shawanda, who is holding her hand over her right cheek and weeping. A crowd of neighborhood onlookers stands in a semicircle at a respectful distance.

"Shit's gonna stop," Sharron says.

John wheels. His forehead is wet; his eyes are filled with menace. "Or what?" he wants to know.

Sharron feigns amusement. "Or what? Or what?" He chuckles. This is a man who is sleeping in his bed while he spends nights on the couch. He could have made a big deal out of it when he got home from Riker's. He could have insisted that Shawanda and John be out by the time he got home. His mother would have taken his side. Gloria always puts him first. But Sharron did not say a word, stayed cool, let the situation slide, and now this security guard was fronting for the people in the neighborhood.

Two youngbloods, Dee Whiz and Fitty-Sen, stand in the street studying Sharron. They have been watching him for years. They know all about his Polo signature, the LoLifes, his girlfriends, and his recent bid in Riker's. They haven't been seeing him in the street much lately, and the one time they did see him, he was carrying a book. Strange. Sharron hasn't fashioned his reputation, his props, for half a decade to let himself be disrespected in front of these people by a girlfriend-beating chump. This is Shawanda's fault, he thinks. This is how people get hurt. This is how people die.

"Whatever. Step to it," he tells John.

John is not a real hardrock. But he's not a punk either. "Whatever," he says. He wheels and heads upstairs.

Dee Whiz and Fitty-Sen assume that Sharron has a burner in his waistband, hidden by the drape of his shirt. But in order to stay out of trouble, Sharron has gotten rid of the gun. He gave it away to a LoLife in East New York a week after he got out of Riker's. Everybody knows that John has an Uzi upstairs. Guns are just like money in the bank. No matter how you dress, your neighbors usually know if you have money. It is the same with a gun. With a machine gun, it is almost impossible for people not to know.

Sharron stands his ground. This is his home. This sidewalk is where he grew up. He delivers an aside to Dee Whiz and Fitty-Sen: "Dude be doin' mad foul deeds. I ain't jumpin' in no jet-stream, 'cause he *owns* a oowop. See him get busy with it."

The audience is captured by Sharron's presence as he steps forward and guides Fonzo's gaping six-year-old sister away from the lobby door, out of the line of fire. The fan of spectators opens outward, creating an alley for the bullets. A streetwise driver, spotting the no man's land, slows and stops his car in the street for a moment, then presses the accelerator and drives quickly through. It is the first balmy day of the year. But the soft breeze doesn't mean peace. The pressure goes on day in and day out. Two women walking on the sidewalk feel the tension, spy the crowd of rubberneckers and the young protagonist.

"Not again," one says.

"Twenty-four seven," her friend replies.

Sharron does not fidget or pace. He rubs the back of his hand under his nose, measures a dive and a roll behind a row of garbage cans along the side of the building, and stands his ground. He waits a full five minutes before he walks over to the phone to call Vanessa. John never does come back downstairs.

"Big front," Fitty-Sen scoffs, disappointed there has been no gunplay. Dee Whiz nods. The two teens turn and stroll down Saratoga Avenue.

The fighting continues. A week after the sidewalk beef, Sharron opens up the apartment door in time to see John flatten Shawanda with a right cross on the fourth-floor landing. The truth is, this is how Shawanda relates to John. She makes him as jealous as she can, teases him and plays him to the limit, and then he explodes. Then they make up. Neither Shawanda nor John seems to care what people think.

Sharron ducks back into the apartment, reaches into the pocket of a coat, and brings a box cutter with him into the hallway. John backs into the shadows under the stairs to the fifth floor as Shawanda storms into the apartment. The two young men measure each other in the half-light. Sharron is shorter and lighter than John but quicker with his hands. John may kick his ass here on the marble floor, but he is going to get cut doing it. Hands up, John takes a step back. Sharron does not move forward.

"This mess is over. Are you hearing me, goddammit? Over." Gloria's voice from inside the apartment is shrill with anger. She is finally telling some kind of truth.

Shawanda is not having it. "Fuck all you all! Fuck all you all!" she screams. She throws some belongings into a plastic bag and bolts out of the apartment. John slides out of his corner and the two head out of the building. Sharron can hear John questioning Shawanda as they hurry downstairs.

"What you doin'?"

The following Monday, during the first class of the day for Sharron, strat, he is not there. He is late again. He does not appear for his A-slot class either, the half-credit unit on the brain. The trip from his door on Saratoga Avenue to the #3 train and from there to the Chambers Street stop near the school takes about forty minutes. Sharron shows up at nine-fifty, dressed with care in a white Polo sweatshirt with an American flag design on the front, black-and white pump Reebok sneakers, his favorite gold chain draped outside his sweatshirt, and gold-tinted Polo nonprescription glasses for effect. He carries no book into his B-slot class, which is a course in novels. The teacher does not comment on his tardiness.

The book under discussion is *Lord of the Flies*, William Golding's fable about a group of boys abandoned on an uninhabited tropical island without adult supervision. Things go terribly wrong in the children's society as sanity is overwhelmed by moral anarchy, violence, and death. The surviving children are ultimately rescued by a naval officer in a crisp white uniform.

It seems that many of the students have not read the book.

They are polite but uninspired by the lesson, which begins with students reading aloud from the text. The first excerpt is a dialogue in which one of the boys is trying to talk sense to another. The reading drones on. Sharron is asked to read. At first he demurs, then he doffs his vanity glasses and reads competently to the class.

"What about a time when *you* tried to talk sense to someone?" the teacher interjects. "Have you ever tried to change the course of events through that kind of leadership?"

The question is a good one. The students in this class have been abandoned on their own urban islands, fashioned their own tyranny, perhaps mutely witnessed the death of their fellow children. What measure of responsibility is theirs? There is no immediate response to the question.

The teacher remains unfazed. He rephrases the question. "Did you ever try to save someone from harm?"

Satellite teachers have been selected because of their easygoing ways with the students. There is absolutely no threatening or name-calling by the teachers or students in the Satellite Academy.

"Talk sense to someone? I have no sense," says a large girl with a shock of extensions twisted into her hair. There is a flutter of laughter from the class. Then she changes her tone and tells how she tries desperately to keep her wild younger brother out of trouble. "I see him gettin' into stupid shit, and I ask him why. An' he don't have an answer. It's like he's deaf. He just looks, he just keeps on. I don't want to see him get killed over some little kid shit. But tell you the truth, what I say don't make a difference."

Often the kids in Jefferson and in schools like Satellite Academy are burdened by the responsibility of caring for siblings and even parents. Sometimes, in order to succeed in school and move on to meaningful employment, they have to abandon those responsibilities — in effect, cut their loved ones loose.

Following up on the question, a lanky girl explains, "I don't say nothin' to nobody. I let them do what they want to do. You have to mind your own business around my way."

As the discussion continues, Sharron engages in a tête-à-tête with an Indian girl with long wavy black hair and an asymmetrical face. He springs to attention when the teacher calls his name. He is facile enough to perform several tasks at once.

"I care for my sister much," he begins. He knows what words to say to make him look sympathetic in the video that is running in his mind. "But my words of advice don't have much penetration. It is the same with me. My friends told me, 'Don't hang out. Don't hang out. Don't hang out.' But I used to hang out anyway." Heads nod. It's hard enough to control yourself, the class is saying, without trying to be a leader.

As the students file out, the teacher balances a paperback copy of the novel in his hand and purses his lips. There is no rescue party coming for these kids anytime soon, he may be thinking.

The next slot is the full-credit course on reproduction taught by Sharron's adviser, Neil. A sign over the door outside the classroom reads, "Showing up is ninety percent of life." Neil has the ideal temperament for a teacher. He is seasoned, compassionate, organized, and tough. He is also fascinated by the subjects he teaches. The room is darkened for a masterfully produced educational film that uses microphotography to show the path human sperm take to fertilize an egg. As the film rolls, Sharron is once again in close contact with the raven-haired Indian girl. Seated next to each other at a small desk, their shoulders and legs brush.

A voice-over explains the images that appear on the film. Bouncy traveling music plays as the sperm swim out of the testicles. A heavy drumbeat knells as a swoosh of fluid blasts out of the prostate gland, then there is a crash of symphonic exultation as the sperm are catapulted into the woman's vagina. Sharron straightens up in his seat at the sight; the Indian girl edges a few inches away. There is rapt attention throughout the room as the sperm stampede through the reproductive canal. The class erupts in laughter as the flailing, witless sperm lose their way and one tries to fertilize the first round object it encounters, a regular body cell. "Of the two hundred million sperm," the narrator announces, "only fifty reach the egg."

"The anatomy test is tomorrow," Neil reminds his students as the lights come on and they reach for their books. Later he explains, "Sharron is doing reasonably well — when he is here, which is not all the time. He will probably pass my course with a P, although he is doing the minimum it takes to get by. He is not applying himself." Neil takes out a homework worksheet with questions like "What happens in the placenta? Why is it important?" and "Why is amniotic fluid critical to the fetus's development?" Sharron's responses are perfunctory. He wrote, "It keeps the fetus from drying out."

"True, but there is so much more to it." Neil sighs and shows the papers of more motivated students, who have listed the multiple functions of the amniotic fluid.

Sharron is coming to school most days. He is carrying books. He is far more motivated than he was in the classrooms of Jeff, but he's still not convinced of the absolute necessity of education. Many of the successful African Americans he sees on television have made it without an academic education. The black teachers, lawyers, and judges he has seen represent a compromise of identity and style that is distasteful to him. As tough as things are for him, he likes himself the way he is.

But he has another problem. "There have been a couple of incidents," Neil explains with a rueful shake of his head, "where Sharron got into confrontations when he didn't have to." It seems guys arrived from another school and got into a disagreement with a girl from Satellite. "Sharron was right in front of the school, going face to face with them. Unnecessary. To some degree, he's recreating Brownsville here."

On the last Friday in April, Sharron manages to pass his anatomy test with a 75. Also, an article he has written about his time in Riker's has been published in the school newspaper. Proudly, he carries both documents to Vanessa's house.

Across Brownsville in East New York, Gary is not in nearly as good a mood. He has been looking for a collar all night. Nothing. Now his partner has some paperwork to fill out, so Gary jumps in the sweep van, just like old times.

There are a handful of young men standing outside a doorway in Cypress. "Just roll up on them, I got a feeling," Gary instructs. As the van pulls up, Nephtali steps lightly away, then grabs his side and runs. Gary is out of the vehicle with a bound, and Nephtali runs into the building, with Gary right behind. There is a clatter. Nephtali is under arrest. "He tossed the jammy in the compactor," Gary announces. Sensing trouble, he calls for a boss. Good thing — Nephtali's mother and sister are on hand in seconds, beating their chests. The mother has dark hair; the sister is fair. When the sergeant shows up, he calls for an Emergency Service Unit to come over and take off the lock to the basement door so the gun can be recovered.

"He din' haf no gun," Nephtali's mother whistles through a broken front tooth. "I was walking with him. I don' never walk with 'im if he haf a gun."

"What d'ya do, frisk him when you leave the house?" Galvin quips.

ESU has trouble with the heavy lock to the basement. When it finally pops, they head inside and sift through the compactor. There are a dozen cops on hand now, as a crowd gathers on the sidewalk and the grass beside the ramp down to the basement door. Fifteen minutes. No gun.

The cops upstairs on the steps into the lobby exchange knowing looks. *It's about time Lemite came up wrong,* some of them are thinking. They have been around too many times when the cocksure Lemite wanted to turn left on a pursuit, they wanted to go right, and he turned out to be correct — too many times when his plans and hunches came out just the way he said they would.

The ESU is finished, getting ready to call the whole thing a mistake. "Lock and door probably cost a grand to fix," a Housing cop cracks. But Gary is not finished. He reaches into the compactor with his hands. There is a half-eaten sandwich, an elementary school penmanship assignment on wrinkled composition paper, a birthday card, the stuffing of an old pillow. And there is a goddamn gun.

"Got it," he yells to the doubting officers about to head out the door. On the way back to the van, he winks at Nephtali's mother.

JUDGMENT

It is ten o'clock on the morning of Thursday, April 30, the day after the first Rodney King verdict. Five OSC officers are lounging in the roll call room downstairs, waiting for the moody Sergeant Toney to arrive and give the assignments. There hasn't been much for Gary to do lately. He's had to lay off DeeSo because his squad has been restricted to the Complex.

"I can't fucking believe it," Gary says to the cop beside him. "I was drivin' home when I heard 'not guilty' on the radio and I was like, 'Holy shit.'" There isn't a trace of anger in his voice, just surprise, as if a benchwarmer had hit a home run to win the World Series. All over the PSA, the troops are talking about the trial in L.A.

"I tell you, the LAPD gets more respect than we do," a stick-figured cop expounds in the hallway just outside the roll call room. "They're a professional police force. Look at their uniforms. They wear black for the fear factor. We wear powder-blue shirts like a fuckin' buncha pussies. What color are our new RMPs? White, so the community won't be 'intimidated.' Don't they know that police work is about intimidation?"

Lonnie Hayes steps out of the weight room, where he has been spending a great deal of time lately. He is wearing a leather girdle over his sweatpants. He eyes the bony shoulders and scowling face of the complaining white man. "You couldn't intimidate nobody if you was wearin' . . ." His voice trails off. The TV room is open behind him. On the screen, south central Los Angeles is burning to a cinder. "Ah, fuck it," Hayes mumbles. "Just shut up, man," he says sweetly, and goes back to heaving plates of iron.

372

Finally Toney arrives, twirling the corners of his mustache with one hand, holding a clipboard with the other. He positions himself behind the plywood lectern with the blue Police Department crest on the front. Toney has eighteen years on the job. His mother lives in the Complex.

"It's Healy and Lemite in 9602, Omar and Seton in 9510. There's been four robberies around 265 Livonia in the last two weeks, from four in the afternoon till eight at night. Apparently, people are being watched in the check-cashing place on Rockaway and followed into the Complex. The perp is tall and thin, about twenty-five to thirty, and he keeps his hand in his pocket, simulating a gun."

Then Toney lays the clipboard down on the lectern and looks out across the room with an uncharacteristic knit to his brow.

"After L.A., Omar wants to remind Gary that we're not going to be aggressive making arrests today."

Gary flinches but remains silent. He stares straight ahead and fumes. Just weeks ago, he was riding with Omar to deliver some paperwork to another precinct when a gust of wind blew a man's coat open, revealing a gun. "He's probably on the job," Omar said as he stepped on the accelerator. "Besides, we got things to do."

As Gary and Jerry Healy approach the Complex, Gary can't contain his anger. "What's this 'Omar wants Gary to know' shit? He's a cop and I'm a cop. What right does he have to tell me what to do? We get dressed in the same locker room. That is just bullshit. I don't care what Omar thinks. If I see an arrest is justified, I am going to make an arrest."

Later in the shift, there is a disturbance in front of a bodega at Christopher and Powell. Four cars and eight cops are on hand, including Gary and Omar. A handful of drunk teenagers are mouthing off, and one spits at the officers as they walk away. Gary pivots, reaching for his cuffs, ready to bring the kid in and write him a summons for disorderly conduct, when Omar steps forward.

"It didn't happen," he says.

Gary backs off. "You're a fuckin' empty suit," he tosses at Omar.

The same afternoon, Sharron Corley is looking for a job as a busboy in a restaurant not far from his school, on Chambers

Street. There is a surreal quality to Manhattan today as rumors of an impending race riot flash across town, up and down the gleaming skyscrapers. Fear abounds. Black looters are headed out of the boroughs, bent for the stores of Manhattan; the windows of Macy's have already been smashed, the story goes. An all-news radio station declares that a city bus has already been overturned. The crush to escape Manhattan begins as frightened office workers are dismissed from their jobs in the early afternoon. Penn Station is quickly jammed with panicky white commuters, who totter at the edge of the platform and peer down the tracks for the next train to whisk them away from the revenge of the black mob.

No such attack occurs. But a platoon of angry black protesters, some thirty strong, is stomping its way up through lower Manhattan, and it passes the restaurant window where Sharron sits, filling out his job application.

"No justice, no peace," the protesters chant.

"Get away from the windows, away from the windows!" the manager of the restaurant shrieks. "Lock the front door, no more customers. We're closing. We're closed."

Sharron shifts smoothly from one seat to another, listens to the chants, and considers the prospect of black-on-white violence. A look of dismay floods his face. He is truly saddened. "That's not right. Not right," he says to himself.

At five o'clock, Sharon King is alone on the subway, headed home from her job at Jeff. There wasn't any trouble in the high school about the L.A. verdict. The kids seemed barely to notice. King was once roughed up herself in Queens for protesting police violence and nothing ever came of her civilian complaint, so the 'not guilty' decision was nothing more than a confirmation for her.

At the Junius Street stop, three rowdy boys in their early teens pile onto the subway car. Ignoring King, they open and re-open the sliding door between cars, spit, and curse through the open windows at people on the platforms. Most adults would move to the next car to avoid them. King crosses the aisle and sits next to one, a boy of fourteen.

"What if your mother heard you talking like that?" she says sternly.

"My mother don't give a fuck about me," the boy answers.

King continues to talk with the suddenly well-behaved trio until she reaches her transfer at Franklin Avenue. When she leaves the train, she waves. Timidly, the boys wave back. But King is not in good spirits today. For the first time since she was a teenager, she is feeling left out. Carol Beck, a dozen of her staff members, and 150 or so students have gone for several days on a retreat to a resort called Falls View, two hours outside New York. The money came from City Councilwoman Priscilla Wooten's office. The idea is to promote bonding, build leadership in the student body for the coming year, and give the shell-shocked students a treat. There are to be three outings in all. King has simply been passed over for the trips. Word has circulated from the retreat organizers through the faculty that she is not wanted, that she is too "frisky" with the students.

Several days later, the early May sun reflects off the front of the glass and marble federal courthouse in front of the small park in Cadman Plaza. A racially mixed group of two dozen high school students from St. Ann's, an elite private school in Brooklyn Heights, plays an earnest game of soccer on the grass-fringed dirt field. It is sentencing day for Born Son and the Young Guns. Upstairs, Dan Murphy, Born Son's lawyer, sits on a bench in the deserted fourth-floor hallway. The courtroom of Judge Leo Glasser has been the scene of jury selection in the John Gotti racketeering trial all week. For several days, headlines have flown over the proceedings like flags. The so-called Teflon Don has even broken his characteristic silence, berating the federal prosecutor for being preoccupied with him. "Guy probably turns over in bed at night and calls his wife Gotti," he quips.

To hear Margaret James tell it, Bobby Schulman was no less obsessed with Bobby James. "Bobby used to come to me and tell me how scared he was. 'Schulman is out to kill me,' he would say. There were days he wouldn't want to come out of the house." Certainly the press and the public care less about Born Son. There is a not a single news reporter on hand for the proceedings. Counselor Murphy looks damp and bloated. "I feel sorry for Bobby," he says in the hallway an hour before the sentencing. "I just feel terrible. Nikia and Edward, the Worthys, knew how to play the game. Bobby didn't."

As it is, Born Son could not be in a worse position. He is the admitted manager of the operation. Under the mandatory federal sentencing guidelines, he faces decades in prison. All the possible mitigating factors that might allow the judge to lighten the sentence have been nullified in the presentencing report.

"I feel sorry for Margaret James," Murphy continues lugubriously. "She has a son on a basketball scholarship at UNLV and a daughter who is supposedly in medical school down South. She got two out of three out. She saved two out of three." The story about the basketball scholarship is not quite accurate; neither is the one about medical school. Margaret James's other children are not in trouble, but they are not world-beaters either. "I even feel sorry for Schulman," Murphy goes on. "I saw him at the library and he was wearing a bulletproof vest. What kind of life is that? Pray for Bobby James," Murphy says as he rises from his wooden bench and heads for the courtroom with a limp.

Judge Glasser is weary. It is four-thirty. There are just ten people inside the large and stately courtroom. Five are the friends and relatives of Born Son's associates, Chris Muncie and Carlton Smith. Bobby Schulman shows up in a cotton sweater; the dour, pockmarked Mathew DeJong, in a rugby-style pullover. Schulman has been working long hours on a federal case against Chris Moore, which is about to bear fruit. But there is more to the ballfield attire of the police officers than their work schedule. They wore suits to the previous courtroom dates of Born Son's trial because they had to. Now they have the chance to show what they really think of the most important day in Born Son's life.

Margaret James shows up late, slips into a seat two rows behind Schulman, and narrows her tiny eyes to glittering pinholes.

Licking his lips, Bobby James steps into the courtroom wearing the same green pants and flowered shirt that he wore in court almost a year ago — the same iridescent outfit that a court officer handed over to his mother after he changed into his prison togs following the proceeding. But now he has no suit jacket with him. Perhaps the jacket has been forgotten; perhaps the omission is an attempt to give the impression that he did not profit as much from the proceeds of the sale of crack as federal attorney Robert Fineberg says he has.

If such is Bobby's intent, he has a point. No one has been able to account for most of the money. Schulman, Fineberg, Glasser, and DeJong, for all their surveillance and investigation, could never find the money that would have been the result of such a bustling trade in crack. "People have a way of spending money," Fineberg says carefully, perhaps in a veiled reference to drug use. Surely the Worthys did use some drugs. Bobby tested positive for cocaine when he was arrested, but no one inside the crew or the police ever claimed that he and his boys were crackheads. "They were just a bunch of stupid kids," Margaret always said. Surely money had been wasted. But where were the millions?

The Worthys' large apartment at 295 Dumont Avenue was virtually without furniture — no lamps, rugs, toys, bicycles, or stereo equipment. Born Son spent much of his last year of freedom with his mother in her spare Bedford-Stuyvesant basement apartment. "I had to give these penny-ante kids five dollars for milk and Pampers," Margaret attests. Bobby had the Jeep, but Margaret insists that it was hers, bought with money paid on an insurance policy. Chris Muncie had a Honda. But there were no bank accounts, no savings, no homes, and no businesses. Margaret James has an answer for everything. She should have been a lawyer. But she is not, she is a mother, and this is going to be the hardest day of her life.

"My wife told me," Murphy begins, "that the sad part of this whole thing is that Bobby James had a chance to get out of Brownsville. He was a gifted basketball player. He went to Laurinburg Prep School in Virginia for a month. But he came back. And when he came back, he got involved in the kind of thing that goes on in his neighborhood. He has brains and physical talent." Murphy pauses, looking up at Glasser. "I ask you to depart downward," the lawyer says, importuning for a breach of the mandatory sentencing guidelines. His voice cracks with sympathy. He ends his short plea with a request for a ten-year sentence.

"Is he crazy?" Margaret James whispers.

But Leo Glasser is not buying the Brownsville defense. "I feel sorry for you, Mr. Murphy, and I was moved by your impassioned plea for your client. But I don't accept your attempt to suggest that the neighborhood was at fault. To do that is to condemn everyone in these communities. There are thousands of young men in Bedford-Stuyvesant and East New York who don't sell drugs, who struggle to go to work every day."

Visions of the 4 A.M. A train from East New York to Manhattan and the 6 P.M. elevated #3 from Pennsylvania Avenue float through the courtroom like pale smoke. But Glasser has probably never seen those trains. If he had, he would know that though they are packed with working people, there are precious few young men like Bobby James aboard. Government labor experts report that only about 17 percent of youths in New York City between the ages of sixteen and nineteen, the age at which Born Son entered the drug business, are employed. The employment rate in Brownsville is estimated at half the citywide figure, less than 10 percent.

"Those people are working every day," Glasser continues, "while Mr. James and others like him are bursting into people's apartments, carrying guns, poisoning those communities by selling poison to the people there." He turns from Murphy to the fidgeting Born Son. "You had a mother who cared about you, and relatives — a hard-working mother. But I guess there was just too much excitement, too many guns, and too much money. You must be some kind of Jekyll and Hyde character, Mr. James. When I read the letters that were sent by your relatives, I didn't read about the Bobby James that I have come to know throughout these proceedings."

Glasser removes his glasses, rubs his eyes, and stares above the heads of Murphy and James. "Do you have anything at all to say for yourself?" he asks after a pause. "Can you give me any reason why I should not impose the guidelines for the crimes to which you have pleaded guilty?"

By all accounts, Bobby James is a gifted talker, a monologuist of the streets. He could always make the layabouts laugh with imitations of Jamaicans, jokes, cracks, woofs. He could get all kinds of respect with his words. But he knows he cannot talk to Glasser. It's not just because of his deeds. Young men like Bobby have built their own language, and they change it frantically, precisely to exclude Glasser and what he stands for, because they understand instinctively that whoever sculpts their speech will take whatever freedom they have left. Leo Glasser does not understand how far away he is from the young man in front of him. When given a chance to speak, Bobby James mumbles something about "being fair."

Born Son is not a good guy, to be sure. But what of his decisions, his life? Sheltered by a doting mother, he was out to prove something every day on the streets. He fought because he had to, then because he wanted to. He impressed the people he meant to impress. In his own way, he tried to do the right thing. But it wasn't the right thing according to the Leo Glassers of the world. They had the schools, the jobs, cars, houses, bank accounts, and clothes. And in the end, somehow they even had justice on their side.

Glasser would be the first to admit how hard life is in Brownsville and East New York. He is a fair man, and this was a fair trial. But where were the fair men when the Brownsville schools fell into disrepair and disrepute? Where were the judges when Margaret James was paid just about enough for her car fare to and from work in job after job? Where were the fair-minded men of influence when the white people ran from Brownsville and took the teachers, businesses, and means of credit with them? Where was the justice then? The only truth and justice in the Howard Houses in those days was Hank Walters and Officer J.R. Reynolds, and God knows those men had their hands full.

"Bobby James, you never did take responsibility for your actions." Glasser lays out Born Son's criminal record: an attempt to bribe a policeman, forgery, resisting arrest, criminal impersonation. "In the end, the money and the cars and the clothes were just too easy. The money was just too good," Glasser repeats lamely. His voice suddenly slips to a whisper. He says something that ends with the words "five years' supervision."

How could Glasser know what this was all about? To understand, all he had to do was think of himself. How did he become a lawyer and a judge? He did it, no doubt, by following a path he saw before him, by determining early that he wanted to be an important man, and by persevering. Born Son is not so different. It is by no means easy to do what Bobby James did. It is ambitious and dangerous beyond imagination.

It is also cruel. Young men are still dying every day on the streets that Born Son will no longer walk. People in other cultures live on next to nothing without the murderous activities found in Brownsville. But they have a system of beliefs that gives them respect and solace. The mad American marketing machine that trumpets, "Get things, get money and don't settle for second best" makes ambition a religion, while the social system denies access to the legitimate hierarchy. The result is predictable. The kids create their own shadow system and fight each other to reach the top. Born Son, standing before the judge in his green iridescent slacks, with his bulging jailhouse muscles and shaved head, is the living record of those crazed messages. They drowned out the voice of his mother. But nothing will drown out her voice now.

"What did he do? What did he give my baby?" Margaret James demands. With a heave, she is up and out of her seat. She approaches the sheepish Murphy, who has returned to his chair by the wooden railing at the front of the courtroom. "What happened?"

"Thirty years," the lawyer announces.

Margaret James shouts, "No!," takes three steps down the center aisle, and throws herself to the marble floor. "They took my baby. They killed my baby. The stupid lawyer. Those bastards. They lied. They lied. They lied."

"Baptist flop," a handsome, middle-aged court officer sneers as he and the other federal officers bend to their duty. It is difficult to lift Margaret James. Displaying little sympathy, the white men drag her along the floor and out of the courtroom. But she is far from finished.

In the hall, the surly officers cajole and threaten. "You won't be able to visit your son if you keep this up." But she continues to howl and remains flat on her back, legs splayed on the glistening floor. The men try to drag her to a bench as a young black woman protests the treatment. In the end, there is no respect for Bobby or Margaret James. Not even for motherhood. "Leave her on the floor — that way she can't fall down" is the expert advice of one of the court officers.

Margaret's face is drenched with tears. Her wails mount. "He didn't even turn around. I didn't see his beautiful face. They took my baby." She curses Schulman, who has taken the back door out of the courtroom. "He hates my baby. They lied. They lied. The racist bastards live in their mansions and they took my baby."

Back inside the courtroom, under the cloud of a mother's curses, Glasser shows good sense and postpones Chris Muncie's sentencing. Murphy, DeJong, Schulman, Glasser, and the rest are gone now, as the EMS people arrive with an oxygen mask and an arm wrap to take Margaret's blood pressure.

"I can't do anything," she cries. "I can't even raise my child."

"BIG DAYS"

On a fresh day in June, a camouflage-colored army vehicle that military people call a deuce-and-a-half sits with its engine idling in front of the PSA. The truck, on loan to the Housing police from the National Guard, takes up three parking spaces and creates a stir in the neighborhood. Boys on bicycles and curious men sidle up and squint, step closer, and run their fingers along the steel-plated doors. What is an army vehicle, an instrument of war, doing in Brownsville?

"I seen that in the movies," a boy says.

"Shit has some big-ass tires," his friend comments. "They bulletproof."

"You stupid, ain't no bulletproof tires," the first boy scoffs. Then the two fall quiet, imagining what it would be like to be a soldier.

The deuce-and-a-half is here today to be used in the execution of a warrant at 666 Dumont Avenue, the crack house across the street from Thomas Jefferson High School. An hour before the afternoon raid, twenty-five cops are downstairs in the roll call room, waiting for instructions. Gary's OSC unit is here, as is the Housing police NEU team, a SWAT-style group with ballistic shields and battering rams. Seven agents from the Bureau of Alcohol, Tobacco, and Firearms (ATF) are on hand as well, dressed in black, carrying machine guns. Ten uniformed officers will handle backup support and traffic and crowd control.

"We're gonna hit the two doors in 666 and one down the street, all simultaneously," the lieutenant begins, producing a sheet of paper. "Hammil, you're on the roof. Lemite, the third-floor search team. Hayes, exterior."

"They reinforced the front door," a scowling officer explains to an ATF agent at his side. "Every time we break it down, they put up a stronger one. Let's see what the fuck they do now."

"You know that Puerto Rican flag they got?" Eddie Hammil whispers to Gary. "We're gonna put up the American flag so high they can't take it down. I called the firehouse over on Sheffield. They're gonna come by with the ladder."

A spit-shined National Guard officer with a crew cut steps to the lectern and faces the agents and officers. His delivery is practiced. This is not the first time a military show of force has been employed in a Brooklyn project. "Listen," he instructs, "when you come out of the truck, don't try to be Rambo and jump. It's too high. Drop your butt to the floor of the truck and slide off. Every time we do this, we have a guy falling. You've got automatic weapons, and even if you don't mind breaking your leg, it's dangerous to trip and stumble all over the street. I'm saying it one more time. Don't jump."

The briefing is short. This will be a standard warrant execution, with an entry team, a roof unit, a squad to watch the windows, recording officers to inventory contraband, and backup people to escort prisoners. The difference is that this time the troops will roll through the streets, past the projects, and up to 666 Dumont in a caravan led by the lumbering deuce-and-a-half. For once, the cops are thinking, this will look like the war it really is.

As they mill around the front room of the PSA waiting to saddle up, the officers are excited at the prospect of a full-scale assault on a crack house. So are the people from the neighborhood, who continue to gape at the war wagon in the street. The only one who remains unenthusiastic about the operation is an old cop who watches the eager invasion force from his usual position, leaning on the front desk. He is big, six-foot-three, a mountain of ruined flesh, with a little head, and the slenderest of ankles visible beneath his abbreviated pants. His gun holster, shifted to the front like a codpiece, hangs loose and low. Observing the busy preparation, he grumbles, "What happened to the good old days when nobody gave a fuck?"

Outside on the sidewalk, an NEU officer is telling one of the Housing cops about a recent warrant that went wrong. "We took the door and right away my heart hits my knees. The place is immaculate. And get this, there's a college diploma on the wall. Right away we knew, wrong fucking place. You can imagine the shit that hit the fan after that. It was in the papers, for cryin' out loud."

"Wish I could be a punk when I grow up," a boy speeding by on a bicycle shouts to the crowd of officers.

"You'll never grow up," Sergeant Toney answers from the sidewalk.

The paramilitary operation is attracting attention all around the Sutter Avenue station. As the vehicles get ready to move out, a man standing near the tailgate of the deuce-and-a-half suddenly becomes excited by police work. "I sure wish I was goin' along," he says wistfully, looking as if he would vault into the personnel carrier with the slightest encouragement. Then the big green truck shudders and pulls out, preceded by a marked car and followed by five more police cars and two ambulances. The convoy proceeds slowly down Williams Avenue to Blake and over to Pennsylvania and Dumont. The commerce of daily life is suspended as folks on the sidewalk gape, then wave and cheer. Inside the vehicle, the air reeks of stale bodies. But that doesn't bother the cops, who cradle their weapons and peek out the opening at the rear of the truck, soaking up the attention as if they were General Bradley's Fourth Infantry Division riding into Paris.

The landing party arrives. With a jolt and a holler, the officers clamber out of the deuce-and-a-half and charge toward 666 Dumont. At the corner, Mickey Mundell hops quickly onto Pennsylvania Avenue and waltzes through the speeding traffic until he is safely on the other side of the street.

"On the wall!" the cops scream at the startled people standing near the entrance to 666. "Get on the wall. Feet back. *Feet back.*" One by one, the people are searched and ordered to kneel by the side of the building with their hands behind their heads.

Upstairs, Gary Lemite and a handful of other officers are ransacking the targeted apartments, searching for drugs and guns. Lonnie Hayes and his unit stand outside, watching for tossed contraband. The day is hot, and the search drags on. A gun and a small amount of drugs are found. More drugs and crack-cooking paraphernalia are discovered in an apartment around the corner. The uniformed officers cordon off a wide area with crime scene tape and warn the growing throng of curious people to stay back. Lenti and Borough Commander Kempf stand in their shirt-sleeves in the middle of the street and chat. Forty-five minutes pass, and still the detainees — fifteen men, women, and children — kneel in the sun along the Dumont Avenue side of the building, beneath the ruby-red R.I.P. mural for a girl named Lyty. Ten more minutes, and an officer appears with a handful of garbage bags so the women won't have to kneel on the dirt or the pavement. The search drags on.

Lonnie Hayes mutters, "This is fucked up. You don't leave people outside like this. You either arrest them or you don't. You go down the line and you say, 'This is a keeper, this isn't.' "

Some cops are having a good time. "I can't wait till the Fire Department gets here and we can put up the flag," Hammil says with a chortle.

A jolly crowd gathers beside the army truck parked on a side street. "Like a fuckin' Rambo movie, bro," a shirtless Hispanic man offers. "All *riiight!*" another man yells. But this movie goes on too long. The people behind the crime scene tape slowly lose their taste for the spectacle of their neighbors kneeling with their hands over their heads like prisoners of war. Gradually the cheering section grows mute, then uneasy, as symbols of national pride give way to personal truth and the thrill of watching a gung-ho invasion becomes anger at the realization that they are the enemy. A bottle sails from the crowd and crashes near Commander Kempf. The uniformed officers wade in and push the crowd back. Another bottle thuds against the side of a patrol car.

A distraught woman arrives. Her handsome young son is among the detainees. She cries and begs for his release, studying the officers with the fierce and frightened eyes of a mother who believes her child is in danger.

"He's a *niño*," she wails.

Lenti and Kempf continue to chat and watch the front door of 666. They don't want any mistakes here. Internal Affairs is on hand, stirred to vigilance by the recent highly publicized arrest of a clique of crack-selling cops, dubbed the Losers' Club, several of whom worked at the 75th precinct.

Five young women, alleged associates of the operators of the crack operation at 666, are escorted from the building in handcuffs and seated in a waiting van. Two of the women are weeping. One, a frantic blonde, babbles the names and addresses of people she insists are the real culprits, trying to convince the officers to set her free.

Finally, a decision is made to release the people kneeling by the wall. The mother charges across the street and hugs her son as if he has been rescued from Huns. "The kid is standing in front of a building where there is a homicide every week, and she's scared we're gonna hurt him?" a female Housing cop grumbles. "Denial. The whole area is in a state of denial."

Before the officers pull away with the five women in custody, Hammil walks over to the streetlight on the corner of Dumont and Pennsylvania where the Puerto Rican flag hangs limply, midway up the pole. He hoists himself up and takes the flag down. Then he climbs back up and secures an American flag to the pole.

"The Fire Department had a call; they couldn't make it," he explains as he gets in the passenger seat of an unmarked car.

When Judge Glasser reconvenes for Chris Muncie's sentencing, there are even fewer people in the courtroom than there were for Born Son. The wavy-haired court officer who directed the removal of Margaret James the previous Friday asks, "Is she here? As long as *she* isn't here." "She was upset," another officer jokes. "She lost her source of income." The court officers chuckle with the ease of people who are among their own kind, who share stores of unspoken, forbidden beliefs.

Alan Polak, Muncie's lawyer, is much more persuasive than Born Son's attorney was. He strikes to the heart of the matter, as Muncie stands at his side. There is no talk of basketball scholarships. "If this case were handled in the state courts, it would be a class B felony, with a maximum sentence of eight and a third years actual time served." Polak pauses for a long moment, gathering his thoughts. Behind him to the right, Mathew DeJong casts a smile at an attractive female assistant arriving with a sheaf of papers.

Polak moves to another point. "There is no implication that this was a bad-faith prosecution," he allows, "but there is some reason to believe that the lead investigator had a personal vendetta, an antagonism, against Mr. Muncie's codefendant and this has had a fallout effect on Mr. Muncie."

Polak then asks Glasser to consider that the harsh sentences against crack dealers are discriminatory to inner-city black youths. "Under Title 21, section 8-41, Colombian nationals who supply cocaine would have to import more than four hundred kilos, which would net them $8 million, to get the sentence that my client faces." Schulman twists a bit in his seat. Polak points out that Asian drug gangs would have to sell seventy kilos of heroin, which would bring in about the same, $8 to $8.5 million, to get the sentence mandated for Muncie by the federal sentencing guidelines. "The effect is discriminatory," he concludes, "and I posit the court never fathomed the true effect."

Glasser covers his face with his long fingers. It looks as if he is getting ready to cry. Then his hands fall away and he bellows at the lawyer, "I didn't write the guidelines. I didn't write the law, Congress did. You are asking me to give a state sentence in a federal court. You are asking me to do something lawless. Do you think this comes easy? You think this is something I enjoy?"

Schulman and DeJong exchange a quick glance. Glasser switches gears. "These young men dealt thirty-three kilograms of crack. When the police broke into their operation, there was a veritable arsenal of guns and hundreds of rounds of bullets. There were random shootings, shootings at rival drug dealers. They broke into an apartment and pistol-whipped a young woman to force her to let them use her apartment." Glasser wearily offers some advice. "March on Washington, Mr. Polak. Let them know the horrors they have created with this law." Then, in a thready voice, the judge gives Chris Muncie, who has never been arrested before, 324 months — twenty-seven years — in jail.

Muncie says something about being sorry. Then he turns to his mother and his sister, who is wearing a white turban. Both are the color of light toast, much fairer than Chris; both are crying. He points at his mother and mouths the words, "If you're all right, I'm all right." Then he blows a kiss.

Near the elevator Muncie's sister says, "This court system is not for us. Not for us at all."

It is graduation day at Jefferson. Carol Beck spins her magic to the end. Yesterday she was at the school till midnight, making preparations for the ceremony. "I'm going to get fired because of all the reports I have not done," she says, "but I have prioritized."

You can tell something important has happened here. Not by the trumpets of pink and white gladioli that flank the podium, the wreaths, or the smiling, proud faces of the 120 graduating seniors in their blue ceremonial robes draped with orange Kente scarves. You can tell by the number of dignitaries seated on the stage in front of the graduates. There are no fewer than nineteen big shots here, including H. Carl McCall, president of the board of education, and Sandra Feldman, the UFT president.

The graduates are arranged in two groups at the rear of the stage, boys on one side and girls on the other. Every time a speaker approaches the podium, the entire graduating class rises crisply to its feet. In the audience, Ms. King slouches delinquently in her seat, sucking on a dripping mango and scoffing audibly at the self-serving pronouncements of the speakers, drawn like flies to this school, which has become oddly popular since the killings in its halls. But when the elegant McCall leans toward the microphone, King is suddenly attentive. He talks of achievement in the face of tragedy and of the responsibility of adults for the state of the world.

"This year was a test of the spirit," he declares, comparing the graduates to the biblical Job. "So hold fast to your faith, and your hope. Go out and make this world a better place. Fix the things we have broken . . . mend the wound we have inflicted . . . and scale the heights we have not imagined. You can make it happen. My brothers and sisters, you are the finest people in our city and our nation."

King is all ears. "That is a good man. He understands. He cares," she testifies to anyone within earshot. "Let the kids speak," she shouts when McCall finishes.

Thomas Jefferson High School receives an award for excellence in education from the National Educational Honor Society. The woman who presents the award recounts the recent history of the school, reminding her listeners how in the early eighties Jefferson had the highest dropout rate of any school in New York City. Now its students are competing for Regents scholarships and Westinghouse Science Awards for the first time. "There are over *sixty* new programs," she proclaims, citing a moot court, a civil service exam preparation program, a

P.M. school, and a College Now program in which students can gain college credits. "And," she concludes triumphantly, "there are two graduates going to Vassar College."

Satellite Academy held its ceremony yesterday, but Sharron Corley was not among the graduates. He passed all his courses, even earned an A in his great ideas class. But his stint in Riker's set him back too far. He will have to go back to school in September if he wants to get a high school diploma. The prospect of attending high school at nineteen does not bother him. "I'll be back," he says with an accent like Arnold Schwarzenegger and a hearty laugh.

Gita Malave didn't make it either. The day before her final exam in the troublesome math course, her sister succumbed to tuberculosis. Gita stared blankly at the equations she had studied so hard, and failed. For the first time since she started college, her resolve faltered, and she decided to pass up summer school.

The woman from the honor society yields the stage to the salutatorian, a wisp of a girl who has managed to graduate in three years. "Don't give up. You can do anything you want to do," she exhorts, quivering on the stage like an arrow of hope. She speaks without notes; her clipped words tumble and collide as her mind races faster than her tongue. She is not just a survivor, she is a prodigy. Her parents beam, and the attending faculty members nod approvingly.

In the center of the auditorium, Hank Walters, the youth leader from the Howard Houses, takes a deep, satisfied breath and leans back in his chair. This is a proud day for him too; his daughter is at the back of the stage, draped in blue, preparing to receive her diploma. Carol Beck, seated to the side of the podium, watches with a frozen smile. She will give no speech today. "I told the graduates what they had to know yesterday, during the rehearsal," she explains later.

The valedictorian steps up next. He is a mahogany lad, of East Indian heritage, from Guyana, and who spent a year and a half on a science project that helped him win a scholarship to Brooklyn's Polytechnic University. His address begins promisingly, with "It was the best of times. It was the worst of times." But the boy is more scientist than orator, and there isn't much originality in his speech, though a touch of faith rises from his closing words. "I don't know why I came to Jefferson," he says with a shrug. "But I am glad that I did."

Then each student crosses the stage, is handed a rolled-up piece of paper by Carol Beck, and pauses to have his or her picture taken with the beloved principal. Bashim Inman, the Howard House Raider, buddy of Born Son and perhaps future community leader, receives the loudest reaction, cheers mixed with some anonymous boos and hisses.

Only Officer Kevin Price is glum. Yesterday he attended the sentencing of Jason Bentley, who shot Daryl Sharpe in November. Jason got three to nine years for manslaughter one; his case was plea-bargained down from the murder charge. The sentence is not what is bothering Price.

"There wasn't a mention of Daryl," he says as the graduates file out into the sunshine to have their pictures taken by family and friends. "It was like his fifteen years on this earth never existed. He might have been something. He was treated like he was nothing. All Jason's father wanted to know was 'Is this everything? Are you taking care of all the charges at once?' Nobody even said a word to the Sharpe family, or even made mention of them."

On the wall of Beck's office is a sign proclaiming that over $4 million has been given in scholarship money to the graduates of the class of '92. The list of colleges exhibited includes Vassar, which is credited with giving $200,000 in the form of full scholarships to two girls. Both overcame incredible odds. One spent part of her senior year with her mother and sister in a shelter for battered women.

Their teacher, Audrey Lee Jacobs, a graduate of Vassar, engineered the admissions, advising both girls to write their application essays about the Moore and Sinkler shootings. Both have very high grades but combined math and verbal SAT scores of only about 750. The Vassar standard is about 1250. The 750 score is significant. It is not just low, it is very low. It does not tarnish the achievements or the unlimited potential of the girls; it speaks of the war zone conditions they come from. The way things are now, the best and the brightest of Jefferson can barely qualify for a good private college, and will only be noticed under the glare of a nationally publicized tragedy.

The graduation was a glorious ceremony, a celebration of significant deeds in spite of community conditions that are a national disgrace. It signaled that now there is order and hope at Thomas Jefferson High School. It is a place where better things can happen, where good teachers have a chance to weave patterns, compete for space in their students' minds with television. But it is still by no means a good school.

Beck, the image-maker, knew she needed a triumph today. The school needed it. The community needed it. Each graduate is a victory, a tribute to family and teachers and fortitude. But the happy ending Beck scripted onstage was in some sense a fiction. Of the 120 "graduates," a significant number did not really graduate. As many as one third, including Bashim, who has been in the school for six years, are "candidates" for graduation; that is, they will have to go to summer school to earn several more credits in order to get their diploma. If the "candidates" had been removed from the graduating class, there would have been only about seventy-five students on the stage.

"Some parents are mumbling, 'This ain't a real graduation. They ain't gettin' no diploma,'" Beck says candidly. "But I know that those students, ninety-nine percent of them, will get their diplomas at the end of the summer. They will come to summer school right here in this building. They won't like it. But they will come. I trust them."

There is another significant truth about the graduates of Thomas Jefferson, class of '92. Beck estimates that 60 percent of the students on the stage are immigrants from Haiti, the Dominican Republic, Guyana, Jamaica, Trinidad, and Barbados. "They even like to keep their accents," she says later, "because then they let people know that they are not American blacks. I tell them, 'Keep the accent, but try to become bilingual.'" The sad fact remains that at Thomas Jefferson High School, which has a heavily African American population, there may be as few as twenty-five African American graduates.

"These are not the Cosby kids," Beck says, referring to her students. "They are darker-skinned and bolder-featured. And they intimidate people, especially when they are seen in groups." The fact may be that despite Beck's heroics, the kind of contribution that cannot be expected to continue with the next principal, these African Americans, who have been passed by immigrant group after immigrant group, are being passed again. This time they are being eclipsed by an almost invisible contingent, one that looks like them but has come from a number of very different cultures, cultures that were not exposed to such high levels of racism. "We just didn't have so many white folks around growing up," the Jamaican Sharon King says. "We made decisions on our own."

Hanging over the day is the memory of the previous graduation. Beck played that ceremony like a sweet harp as well. She had students and parents and educators eating out of her hand then too. In September, the board of education sent her five hundred freshmen, many of them from social work caseloads. "They're comin' again in September," Officer Price says, "the kids that have to be stopped."

And soon Carol Beck will no longer be at Jefferson. After the ceremony she is exhausted. She tells King, "I'm going to retire after next year. People keep saying I won't, but I want them all to get together and put up some money, 'cause I'm going to be toes up in front of the television, watching *As the World Turns*. I'm trying to wean Jeff away from me now, trying to teach people how to pull the right strings and get things done. This Jefferson thing isn't based on me. Who the hell is me?"

BROWNSVILLE

It is high summer again in Brownsville, but a gray rain has cut the heat, and it is blessedly cool in the vestibule of the Brownsville Community Baptist Church. Gary Lemite has just finished up a twelve-to-eight day tour, and he is driving over to Cheap Charlie's to grab a few beers. From where he sits at the red light on the corner of Mother Gaston Avenue, he can see the people filing into the yellow brick church. They are coming to see *Lord, Why Can't They Hear?*, a play written by Shirley Benning, a member of the congregation.

As the arrivals enter the church, they pass double glass doors to the chapel, where two wide pews covered with royal blue material sit empty before the muted brilliance of two twelve-foot stained glass windows. This Friday evening, the buzzing church members are headed downstairs to the broad basement, which the two-thousand-member congregation calls the Fellowship Hall. There are already one hundred people inside, seated around large round tables, nibbling chicken wings and homemade crabmeat salad.

Soon there is a furious tapping of microphones from behind a yellow scrim, a fussing and shuffling. Like *Don't Give Up on Your Dreams*, the play to be performed is more than mere entertainment. It is about the loss of young lives, and the actors, who range in age from six to twenty-nine, are the models for the characters they portray. Some of the youngest performers have come to this very church seeking sanctuary from the violence in the Complex across the street. "Some who show up every day have parents who have never set foot in the church," Benning says before the performance. "But they find family here."

393

In five lively acts, the play delivers the message that church members should stop worrying about how good they look in their newest clothes, about their own dreams, flirtations, and pride, and start reaching out to their dying community. The first act introduces a single mother with two teenage girls who are headed in different directions: one to the church, the other to crack. "Friday night?" the mother scoffs at her churchgoing daughter's invitation to a choir performance. "Friday night, girl, is *my* night."

The second act brings on the burly Mr. Wannabe, an upwardly mobile entrepreneur with a son at Harvard Medical School, who despairs at his younger son's lack of success. The second son believes he has been called to preach the word of God. But like the self-absorbed mother in act one, Mr. Wannabe mocks the idea. "All the money I spent on piano lessons! If you think pickin' up that Bible is gonna get me to spend more money on you, you better call the prayer hotline and get the saints to put in a prayer for you."

At a church business meeting in act three, Mr. Wannabe is equally unenthusiastic about the idea of reaching out to those in the community who are less fortunate. "Knock on doors? I really don't think so. I might donate money, but I don't see myself knocking on doors."

"What would we *wear* to a community self-help group?" a well-coiffed woman at the meeting wonders aloud as she examines her face in a hand mirror. But a mysterious new member, a tall, clear-eyed woman, rises slowly and addresses the gathering with a most tranquil voice and the deepest conviction. "I will knock on one thousand doors," she says, "if I can save one soul."

There are many hilarious goings-on in the fourth act — a grandmother wants the preacher to perjure himself so she can win a lawsuit for a bogus injury — and assorted jealous or libidinous members of the congregation. Mr. Wannabe's ne'er-do-well son begins to preach the word of God despite his father's discouragement. "I want to preach when they want to hear and when they don't want to hear," he announces. "I want to preach in season and out of season."

A woman in the audience rises half out of her seat in appreciation. Then, catching herself, she explains to the woman next to her, whispering, "This is good. You know, I don't come out in the street for nothin'."

The language rolls and rumbles. "Let me. Let me. Let me. Let me explain myself to you." Mr. Wannabe's son has the message, and he wants to tell it. "It's not all about 'Let me do it my way.' Because your way is not the right way. It says here in Webster's Dictionary that to hear is to comprehend by the ear. I want you to hear. I want you to form your lives around the word of God. So you can *live* right. So you can *walk* right. So you can *talk* right. So you can *be* right."

In the final act, the beautiful young crackhead is saved from suicide by the charismatic young Mr. Wannabe, the malingering granny throws away her cane and wiggles her ample behind to the howls of the audience, and the burly elder Wannabe hugs his son so hard the collision rings out like an open field tackle in a pro football game. Then the choir dances down the aisle in purple robes, their faces gleaming. The young preacher leaps in the air.

"Why can't you hear?" the choir harmonizes. They are in a basement half a block from where Officer McLean was murdered in a stairway across the street from 295 Dumont Avenue, where Born Son and his Young Guns shot it out with the Tilden boys, where Powerful was killed, and where Randolph Worthy is now building his own modest crack business. The tumult of voices rises, falls, and lifts again, like the howling bagpipes at the Housing police 10-13 party. They are meant to quicken the heart, summon the spirit to battle.

Another July. This afternoon Gary is on Loring Avenue, outside the Pink Houses, sitting behind the wheel of a late-model Thunderbird. The car is an ATF undercover surveillance vehicle, and Gary is waiting for Sergeant Bright, Tony Logan, and an ATF agent to talk to the mother of a guy wanted for conspiracy to traffic drugs. The lightly tinted windows of the car are open only a few inches, despite the heat, because a confidential informant, the man who supplied the address of the fugitive's mother, is in the back seat. Gary says little to the man, just sprawls lazily in the front seat, drawing on his bottle of Snapple.

Gary is wearing his black polo-neck shirt and his black jeans. Both his guns are on his waist, and he shifts around in his seat a bit so they don't dig into his stomach. He is going to have to lose a little weight, lay off the beer, if he's going to have a good softball season in the church league. Maybe Merle shouldn't be the coach this year, he muses. The team did better when he left town for a while last season. Imagine, a pastor who wants to hit a home run every time up instead of just going for the base hit. Gary chuckles at the thought.

"*Up!*" The shout comes from outside the car, and there is a jolt to the left side of Gary's head. A robbery? A perp? Fucking Michael T.? "*Freeze.*" The voice comes from near the driver's side window. Gary holds stock still. Out of the corner of his eye, he can see a man leveling a short gun at him through the opening in the passenger side window.

"Police officers, don't move. Show the hands. Put 'em on the dashboard." The voice shifts toward the man in the back seat. "*You*, you put both hands out the window and keep them there."

"I'm a —" Gary begins.

"Shut up. Don't say a fucking word."

Gary moves his hands up ever so slowly, evenly, and lays them palms down on the dashboard. A long moment; nothing. Gary speaks, his voice as light as air, his carefully chosen words pure police argot.

"I'm on the job. Housing. My portable's between my legs. My tin is in my front left pocket, my ID in my back left, my service and off-duty in my waist, right side." A white hand moves slowly to Gary's pants pocket and pulls the badge into sight. The hand turns the badge over, flips it onto the dashboard.

It will be over now, Gary thinks. But neither the gun at his left temple nor the one aimed at him through the passenger's side window moves or wavers. Seconds stutter by. Gary's heart lifts in his chest. *What the hell is going on?* he thinks. Silence. More time.

"That's the Anticrime van in front of us. My team is in that house." Gary nods faintly toward the row of houses on the street.

"Where's your precinct?"

"PSA 2. On Sutter."

"Who are you?" the cop closest to Gary asks the man in the back seat. "Get out of the car."

Gary can see the blue fabric now. The guns are still pointed at him. The prodding fear. This is the same thing he has done a hundred times to perps. The extra touch, the intimidation that makes the mutts remember him, makes them hesitate to point an index finger in his direction and pull an imaginary trigger when he drives by, maybe hesitate to shoot him if that time should ever come. Intimidation. These guys are doing it to him. And they know he is a cop.

"Out of the car, I said."

"No," Gary snaps. Gary Lemite may be singularly without rancor at the behavior of the white men who are aiming guns at him, but he is not about to let them blow a case, allow them to put the informant's life in danger by forcing him to show his face on Loring Avenue. "That man is a registered federal inform-ant," he says, his voice trilling with anger and fear. "I will get out and follow all directions. But he's not getting out." Slowly the guns are withdrawn, sheathed. The cops pivot and saunter back to their car.

"We had a scrip that fit you," the 75 sergeant tosses over his shoulder. That's all. They are gone.

Gary sits still for a long time in the front seat of the car. He's not scared now, not even angry, just vacant. From the back seat, the informant is gazing serenely at Gary's silver badge, which glitters foolishly on the dashboard. When Bright and Logan pile their big bodies into the car, Gary barely hears their chatter.

"What's up? You okay, Gary?" Bright is asking.

"Yeah, sure," he says. Bright and Logan are in the mood for some pizza. But Gary shakes them off.

"Drop me off at the house," he says. "Pick me up after you eat."

With his eyes locked straight ahead, he walks across the front room of the PSA. For the next few minutes he doesn't want to see another blue uniform. He has been in mortal danger a dozen times, but this emptiness is worse. At the top of the stairs, he realizes where he's headed and quickens his step. Maybe Lonnie Hayes is down in the weight room, pushing some steel. The 75 sergeant took something from Gary. Lonnie knows what it is; maybe he even knows how to replace it.

Three weeks into the summer, in the middle of July, Sharron is doing the same job he did last summer. He is downstairs at

Brooklyn Youth Outreach, ready to head out for his site visits.

"Sharron!" Aubrey yells his name. The director isn't a funny man today. He is livid. Somebody has fouled up.

The city came up with a windfall of federal money two weeks ago, and there was a mass hiring of kids, an influx of new workers in the system. Sharron's program alone hired three hundred new youth workers. Reorganization became necessary. Juanita, Sharron's immediate supervisor, told him that he would no longer be responsible for picking up time cards from the Long Island College Hospital site, but she neglected to reassign the site. The time cards were never picked up.

"I'm gonna have people coming in here lookin' for their paychecks and there won't *be* any checks," Aubrey growls. "You know what that means?" Sharron lifts his head to answer, but Aubrey cuts him off. "It means that this is a fuckin' mess. And this is what I *don't* need."

"I was reassigned. That wasn't my site no more," Sharron protests gently. For him, confrontation is something that takes place on the street, or in a holding cell, or on a stairway. When it comes to sticking up for himself in a situation like this, he is passive, fatalistic.

"There will be parents coming down here, raising all kinds of hell," Aubrey rants, "wanting to know who's responsible for this mess." He walks around his desk and faces the window, with his back to Sharron. Then he turns slowly. "It's either going to be you or Juanita," he says. "I'll talk to you in a couple of minutes. Wait outside, please."

After a short talk with Juanita, Aubrey emerges from his office with a hard smile.

"No hard feelings, Sharron," he promises. "You're terminated, but nothing negative will be put in your record."

The only consideration Sharron requests is a letter for his probation officer. As he walks away from the program headquarters, he opens the envelope and reads the letter. It states that he has been fired for "nonperformance." He hurries back to the office. The letter will stand, Aubrey explains, but the employment records upstairs will contain no reference to nonperformance.

Sharron frowns and heads back to Brownsville.

Backup. Sharron once had Gloria and Ms. King in his corner,

but he doesn't have anybody now — no incensed father to storm down to the Youth Employment Office and straighten out the bad deal he has just gotten, talk to somebody who knows somebody to put it right. He just heads back to Brownsville on the #3 and walks up Saratoga toward home.

Sharron's gold chain, bouncing in the noon sun, catches the eye of a pretty girl, who tosses her head as she passes. For once, Sharron does not turn around. He is not in the mood. He is thinking about Aubrey. *Damn. Always got along good with Aubrey. Used to slap me on the shoulder every day, almost.*

There are a couple of young guys — Dee Whiz and Fitty-Sen, the partners from around the way — on his heels as he walks into the cool shade of his building and turns up the stairs. Dee Whiz passes. him. Young kid, maybe fifteen. Sharron's head is down. *Ain't this a bitch*, he thinks. *No more $320 every two weeks. No more job to go to.* On the second-floor landing, Fitty-Sen leaps up from behind, yokes Sharron, and tries to drag him to the floor. From above, Dee Whiz dives for the gold chain.

Sharron coils, flips Fitty-Sen off his neck, and elbows Dee Whiz across the bridge of his nose. Then he flies up the stairs three at a time and shoulders his way through his apartment door, which stands half open for extra breeze. "Narrow-ass punks. Little bubble-gum bastards." He sprints into his room and leans into his closet. His hand gropes the top shelf for the Raven. The gun is gone. Sharron remembers. Handing the gun away was a difficult decision. Sharron dreams of going places, but he is still in Brownsville, and without the burner he is at a fatal disadvantage.

"Nah, nah, nah," he mutters, as he throws on his jeans jacket and hurries back outside. "It ain't gonna be like that. Fucking kids? Nah, nah."

It is white-hot on the street; the sun aims like a laser at Sharron's face. His left hand moves up to shield his scar from the stinging light; his right hand slides inside his jacket and dips down toward his waist. Fronting, acting, for the people on the street, gripping a gun he no longer has, Sharron moves slowly down Saratoga, looking for the boys who tried to steal his chain.

EPILOGUE: LATER

Born Son is serving his thirty-year sentence in a federal penitentiary in Texas. Nikia is in an Indiana prison. She will be released in two years. Margaret James talks regularly to both of them and spends her time worrying and searching for a lawyer to handle her son's appeal. Randolph Worthy now runs the retail crack trade in the Complex.

Bobby Schulman was promoted to detective. He was seated at his desk in the small squad room in the Marcy Houses in Brooklyn when a teenager tossed an M-80 firecracker through the window, which blew Schulman off his seat. "The cops always mess with me, so I messed with them," the kid stated at the time of his arrest. Schulman's hearing is permanently damaged, but he is back on the job, working on the Chris Moore case.

Jim Priore, still a sergeant at PSA 2, has his eye on a position with a proposed Housing police Emergency Service Unit or a promotion to lieutenant. Danny Horan purchased a home in Suffolk County and is high on the list for promotion to sergeant. J.R. Reynolds is a detective in the borough of Queens.

Carol Beck has retired. During her last year at Thomas Jefferson, she held a second cotillion and conducted numerous retreats, which by year's end had enabled most of the student body to spend time outside Brownsville and East New York. Her dream of building a dormitory for Jeff students took shape when state funding was allocated for planning.

Sharon King still teaches social studies at Thomas Jefferson High School, and coaches the cheerleading squad. She directed

401

another school play, which was performed in a Manhattan performance space.

Bashim Inman graduated and is a youth worker in Brownsville, waiting for his college admission to be processed.

In his senior year, Cortez Sutton starred on the Jefferson basketball team, which made the playoffs for the first time in over a decade, and was elected president of the student body. He plans to attend Savannah State College in Georgia.

Gita Malave arranged to sit in on a math class and retake the final exam she failed. But that very day, her son Kendall was shot in the stomach in a jewelry store in the Fulton Mall while shopping for rhinestones to decorate his collection of baseball caps. Kendall is expected to live. Gita is seeking trauma counseling for herself and her son when he gets out of the hospital.

Gary Lemite was promoted to the NEU, the borough-wide narcotics unit. He received two Combat Crosses at a ceremony on the steps of City Hall, prompting Mayor Dinkins to quip that if he gets any more medals, "He'll need somebody to help him carry them home." Gary is working in a group again, and his overtime is severely restricted. The last two people he spotted on the street with guns turned out to be out-of-town police officers. At a recent meeting of his unit with the chief of the Housing police, he raised his hand. "When are they going to give these people in the projects some jobs?" he demanded, to groans from his fellow officers for his heresy. He and his wife, Lisa, have had a third child, Jasmine. They still live in their basement apartment in Elmont.

Sharron Corley was arrested for shoplifting at Bloomingdale's. When no one came forward to pay his $500 bail, he served sixteen days in jail, pleaded guilty, and was sentenced to community service and time served. He went back to Satellite Academy. Since his return, he has passed all his courses and dreams of attending college. He got a job in a clothing store to earn spending money. His singing group, Public Figure, signed a management contract with Warner Brothers Reprise records. He has auditioned for several movies and worked as an extra in a video. To stay out of trouble, Sharron spends most of his time in the house with Vanessa or writing songs.

EPILOGUE: 1994

In the year following the publication of *The Ville* stunning changes occurred in the lives of Gary Lemite and Sharron Corley.

Gary's promotion to the borough-wide narcotics unit proved frustrating. Against all counsel, he forsook the detective career path and requested a transfer back to his anticrime unit at PSA 2. Soon he was on the streets of Brownsville again, developing drug cases, watching for guns, working for a down payment on a house on Long Island. But there were only so many times Gary could pursue armed men down half-lit streets, only so many times he could stand alone in a stone staircase, face-to-face with a man with a gun, before someone would die.

The orders for Gary and his anticrime boys on New Year's Eve were ambiguous: "Get in the bag [wear your uniforms]. Lay low and back up patrol." The stroke of midnight brought the traditional fusillade from rooftop, window, street, and doorway. A building in the Tilden Houses was particularly hot. Backing up a sector car on one of scores of calls for shots fired, some of Gary's unit sprinted into the building and herded a group of boisterous youths outside. As the Housing cops moved, their backs were exposed to the back door. Alone for a moment in the lobby, Gary instinctively flattened himself against a wall and watched the rear entrance. Almost immediately, two men entered. When they spotted Gary in his blue uniform, one bolted outside and the other, wearing a beige jacket, headed for the stairs, a black automatic in his hand. Gary could have stepped back. He was already half-concealed behind a door. Instead, he stepped out and gave chase. At the top of the second landing the man with the gun wheeled around, his weapon leveled at Gary, a flight below. Gary fired one shot. In the stunning explosion the man turned and disappeared. Gary dashed after him, taking two stairs at a time, expecting the noise to draw his unit in support. His radio remained in his back pocket. He knew he couldn't run up stairs with both hands occupied, and he chose the gun. It was five minutes after twelve and the radio was useless anyway, bursting with static and calls for shots fired.

On the third floor he turned back. A pursuit around so many blind turns was just too perilous. On each landing the man could duck into the hallway and slip back into the stairwell from his rear. No backup was coming.

"I think I just shot a guy," Gary stuttered to his anticrime team, whose members now filled the lobby. But they were distracted in the chaos. What did it matter if Gary "thought" he shot a guy? There were bullets blasting down from the roof and up from the street. Gary was shaken, and for several moments his report was ignored. As the unit began a hasty vertical search, a man cried his name. "Lemite. My cousin's shot on the seventh floor. You gotta help me."

Gary peered through the throng of Housing cops and tenants that clogged the seventh-floor hallway. When he spotted the man on the floor he shuddered. He was about thirty years old, dark-skinned; it looked like the guy he'd shot at. The beige jacket was gone. It would be retrieved a few days later from the family. But there would be no gun recovered, no bullet casings anywhere. The lab would find no fragments in the hallway or in the body of the wounded man.

"Don't worry. You can't kill these guys," Lenti assured Gary.

"The guy from the book did it," said a voice from the crowd as the body was trundled toward the elevator. Two days later the man died in Brookdale Hospital. A Manhattan resident on parole for armed robbery, he had been visiting relatives for New Year's Eve.

In the following days, rumors flew through Brownsville and the ranks of the Housing police. Gary had not reported the shooting, the story went; the shooting was "shaky." But without witnesses and ballistics, only Gary's own words linked him to the dead man. Once more, Gary found himself at home, nauseated and afraid. He had Lisa with him this time, but over and over his racing thoughts met a stone wall. He had taken a life. No gun recovered. As the investigation continued, he was transferred to a PSA in Coney Island. Lenti was afraid Gary's high profile would make him a target. He wanted Gary off the streets for a while, wanted him to slow down. Ultimately, the medical examiner's report supported Gary's story, and his account prevailed. In three months he was cleared and requested a move back to Brownsville. There were reasons—overtime, commuting expenses from his new Long Island

404

home—but the truth was, Gary didn't want to get run out of Brownsville.

In December, on a short trip to promote *The Ville,* Sharron walked on a treadmill in a deserted hotel gym. As he padded slowly, he stared at himself in the mirrored walls first from one angle, then another. A soft sound floated from his lips. The voice was plaintive and distant.

"*Bonjour,* Sha."

"*Buenos días,* Sha."

In Sharron's vision, he was a superstar strolling a broad avenue lined by fans desperate for his attention. "Sha," they wailed. Sharron remained aloof as he deigned to smile and wave to the fans. However outlandish, Sharron's thoroughly wrought daydream was more than a fantasy. It was destiny.

When *The Ville* was published, Sharron's picture was featured in newspapers and on the cover of *The Village Voice,* which carried an excerpt from the book. The sweeping searchlight of the national media settled on Sharron Corley's face. For a week, phone calls pursued him like hounds. One call came from a casting director for a film by Universal produced by Spike Lee and directed by a hot new filmmaker. The $6 million movie was about carjacking. In his moment of fame, Sharron was neither unnerved nor intimidated. His emergence had been scripted in his mind a hundred times. Accordingly, he rose to the challenge like a veteran and in a series of auditions snatched the film's lead role. The lofty William Morris Agency caught word of his talent and won the right to represent Sharron Corley.

The following spring, Sharron was again on the streets of Brooklyn. Once more, there were hard words, tough looks, and guns pointed his way. But this time it was all make-believe. Production assistants held back the onlookers as the cameras rolled and young men paced the restraining barriers, squinting at Sharron, wondering what life would hold for them.

EPILOGUE: 2015

It is August 2014 in Brownsville. Little seems changed. There are no scars on the landscape, no burnt-out apartments, no boarded-up windows. Instead, the lawns and grounds of the New York City Housing Authority buildings lie broad, green, and inviting. A bouncing ball, the heartbeat of Brownsville, thumps at the basketball court off Mother Gaston Boulevard and Sutter Avenue.

But there are signs of trouble. Half a block from the basketball court, a three-story, white-metal scaffold fitted with a small booth on top sits on the street outside the Van Dyke Houses. It is an NYPD observation post. There are several more such structures looming over the entrances to city housing developments throughout the neighborhood. Called Skywatch, the mostly unmanned towers have been towed in to discourage crime on and around city property.

As the day unfolds, platoons of young police officers congregate on street corners and around the benches of the Langston Hughes Apartments. These officers are members of the Impact Zone initiative, where recent graduates of the police academy are assigned to a precinct en masse, not so much to solve crimes or patrol but to stand in place and act as human warning signs. With no experience or special training in high-crime areas—and explicit orders not to get involved with drug activity or conduct investigations—the clusters of young cops are nearly as impotent as the unmanned Skywatch towers.

In the past twenty years, crime in New York City dropped so fast and so far under so many different police commissioners and in so many different types of neighborhoods as to defy explanation. From 1993 to 2013 in New York City, homicides—the category of crime least susceptible to arbitrary downgrading—plummeted from 1,927 a year to 335.

In Brownsville in the same period, murders fell from 74 to 31. Still, by the beginning of June 2014 there had been more shootings in the less-than-two-square-mile area of Brownsville than in the entire borough of Manhattan.

It is not that the police haven't tried in Brownsville, even resorting to tactics that pushed beyond the boundaries of the U.S. Constitution. In 1994, Police Commissioner William Bratton launched CompStat, regular meetings at One Police Plaza at which precinct commanders had their feet held to the fire and were held personally responsible for increased crime in their precincts. The process produced more-competent men at the command level and the implementation of a massive stop-and-frisk program that, in 2011, resulted in the stop and search of 685,000 young, mostly black and Hispanic men a year citywide. The highest concentration of stops was in Brownsville. Cops stopped people for "quality-of-life violations," code words for a program aimed at searching for guns. Some young men were stopped several times a week for years.

Despite the highest crime rate in New York City and stories like the June 2014 *New York* magazine feature "Woo Cho Bang Bang" by Eric Konigsberg, with the subheading "Join a gang, shoot a classmate, go to jail for a few decades: business as usual for some kids in Brownsville, murder capital of New York City," this is no longer the free-fire zone it once was.

There are clear signs of economic growth here. The vacant lots behind Thomas Jefferson High School that Gary Lemite and his fellow cops called the "lawless area" is home to a small grid of private Nehemiah Houses, affordable homes built at this location in 1997 by the city and a consortium of Brooklyn churches. A one-family home on the other side of Brownsville on Saratoga Avenue, Sharron Corley's old block, is listed for sale at $349,000. In 1993, Pitkin Avenue, the economic spine of Brownsville, was a lineup of bodegas, barbershops, furniture-on-time outlets, and sneaker shops. Now there are national chains: a Subway sandwich shop, a Foot Locker, Cohen's Optical, and even a Planet Fitness under construction. The lavish Loew's Pitkin Theater, opened in 1929 and shut down in the late 1960s, has been renovated with a charter school on the top floor and retail stores on street level. The businesses now remain open after dark.

Gary Lemite and Sharron Corley are long gone from the Brownsville stage. After PSA 2, Gary was promoted to sergeant. He moved to the 81st Precinct, where he was in charge of making sure the detectives punched in and worked their caseloads. It wasn't exactly a desk job but close to it. Gary moved on to the 77th Precinct in Crown Heights and SNEU, the street-level narcotics team that monitors hand-to-hand drug sales. He was more at home there, roaming rooftops in plainclothes and monitoring the "sets" of players: lookouts, steerers, dealers, and customers. More important, he was teamed with a kindred spirit, commanding officer Captain Mike Marino, formerly of the 73rd Precinct in Brownsville.

Gary and Lisa divorced. In 2006, he remarried. The wedding was held on the island of Jamaica as Gary's new bride's two teenage children and his three kids looked on. Soon, Gary was once again sergeant in the detective squad, this time at the 88th Precinct in a gentrified neighborhood of Bedford-Stuyvesant.

In the end, it wasn't a bullet that ended Gary Lemite's career with the NYPD. It was a bicycle going fast the wrong way on the street outside the 88th Precinct. Gary was injured badly enough to require several operations on his shoulder. After years of rehabilitation and an assortment of medications, doctors told him that the pain, numbness, and weakness would be companions for life. It was not a deal that he would have chosen, but, in another sense, Gary had hit the NYPD jackpot: a disability pension that would allow him to stop worrying about doing overtime to pay his bills. Following the crash of the housing market in 2008, there were houses available at bargain prices, especially in Florida. Gary considered moving to Panama, priced homes in that country, and calculated the living expenses, then settled on a three-bedroom in a development of about a hundred newly built homes in a gated community two blocks from the ocean in central Florida. He can't swim, jog, or play golf. He spends his days lining up bank shots at the pool table in his den and cooking gourmet meals.

For several years in the 1990s, after the publication of *The Ville*, Sharron Corley was a working actor in Hollywood. His very first part was as star of what has become a cult classic, *New Jersey Drive*, about kids who steal cars in Newark. Then he co-starred with Tom Berenger in a high school thriller titled *The Substitute* and was a guest performer on the television series "New York Undercover." But the acting jobs dried up. He took a job as a chauffeur and in a few years was back in New York working for an agency that asked for fees from aspiring actors to get them started in the business. He wrote a screenplay, *Public Figure*, about an aspiring singer who gets caught up in neighborhood beefs, but there were no takers.

By 1999, Sharron was back in New York City but not in Brownsville. He married a woman who had borne him a child and he filled his Facebook page with photos of their good times together. He set up a business in Harlem cutting hair in his apartment and found religion.

In an Internet video he speaks with the same voice he used to lower so girls would have to lean closer to hear. In a white bandana and with his trademark scar evident, Sharron lets his followers know about his activities. "People want to know where I've been and what I have been doing for the past few years. I have been on a journey of self-discovery. I found that I can't do anything without the Lord." He tells his listeners that he has been producing youth-empowerment events and is part of a movement called "Fire Squad," also known as OFFG (On Fire for God). He seems to lean closer to the camera without actually moving as he asks, "Are you a fire starter?"

Carol Beck suffered a heart attack during the tumultuous school year of 1993 and retired the next year.

Thomas Jefferson High School was closed in 2006 because of low graduation rates. Now called the Thomas Jefferson Educational Campus, the building is home to four small high schools. Sharon King left teaching to try her luck as a professional actor. She appeared in a few Off-Off-Broadway productions but couldn't make a living on the stage or film. In 2014 she found a position as a counselor at Crossroads Juvenile Center, the sprawling youth-detention facility behind the 73rd Precinct in Brownsville. During her overnight shifts she counsels troubled young people.

Ronald Haynes, Born Son, died of an undisclosed illness in a federal prison facility.

Detective Bobby Schulman is one of the few PSA 2 officers still on the job. After a long career working major cases, he is now a driver for the NYPD chief of detectives.

Basheem Inman, Sharron's hulking classmate at Thomas Jefferson High School, is a self-described success story. After leaving Jefferson, he did prison time and now works as a New York City sanitation worker and runs a small business on the side.

But even this happy ending has a Brownsville twist. In a corridor behind his office at the 73rd Precinct, commanding officer Deputy Inspector Joe Gulotta has placed four cops who do nothing but monitor the activities of a handful of gangs or street crews that have been shooting each other. One of the pictures in the photo array on the wall is of Kemni Inman, Basheem's nephew. Basheem's son, who left New York to get away from the gang life, returned to New York in the summer of 2014 to settle a court case and was wounded in what police say was a gang-related shooting.

Despite the dreadful echo, there are several differences. The young men and women of the Hood Starz, the Wave Gang, and the Very Crispy Gangsters are at each other's throats not so much over drug territory as they were in 1992 as for notoriety and project-to-project bragging rights. The officers don't plunge into the projects in hot pursuit but instead sit at computers and track gang activities by monitoring Facebook, Twitter, and Instagram posts. The gang unit scans the incessant postings for threats, triumphant acknowledgments of wrongdoing, and incriminating photos; it presents social media evidence of violent activity to judges and gains warrants to individual social media accounts. Then the Brooklyn district attorney pursues convictions using gang members' own words and selfies.

Unlike those in Brownsville, the changes in the past twenty years in the neighborhoods of Bedford-Stuyvesant, Fort Greene, and, to a lesser extent, Bushwick are startling. The receding tide of crime revealed wide streets and classic brownstones. Where the sight of a white man in Bedford-Stuyvesant in the seventies and eighties meant there was a landlord, a social worker, or a plainclothes cop on the scene, now white couples push baby strollers. The displaced residents scattered throughout the city or, in a reverse migration, returned to the southern states where their grandparents were born.

The future of Brownsville very well might lie in the collision of two seemingly unstoppable forces. For the past fifty years, no one has been able to redirect the propulsive energy of some young men with very limited prospects away from internecine violence. School initiatives, law enforcement strategies, and economic programs have come and gone, leaving a neighborhood where, for a male, growing to middle age is a feat. But there is another force at work. Many have said that Brownsville, with its mountain range of project buildings, could never be gentrified. But housing expert Rosanne Haggerty calls the L line, the train that brought yuppies and hipsters to Williamsburg and Bushwick and that runs through the heart of Brownsville, the "gentrification train." The IRT 3 train stops twice in the neighborhood. Real estate observers report loft renovations on Montgomery Street and Utica Avenue, a dozen narrow blocks from Brownsville. There are still empty lots ripe for development in the neighborhood. The Marcus Garvey Houses and Noble Drew Ali Plaza are privately run developments that could be flipped.

Finally, the New York City Housing Authority is considering making use of the extensive "air rights" to the generous city housing-project tracts for moderate-income housing. The likelihood is that history will repeat itself, market forces will eventually prevail, and, by the time the problems of poverty and crime in Brownsville are solved, many current residents will be gone.